The Most Correct Book

ABOUT THE AUTHOR

John A. Tvedtnes was born in 1941. At an early age, he developed an interest in the Bible, which he read at the age of eight. By that time, his Roman Catholic family had moved to Salt Lake City where he was introduced to The Church of Jesus Christ of Lat-ter-day Saints by friends at school who invited him to Primary. He was taught by stake missionaries and baptized. New Year's Day 2000 will mark fifty years since he was confirmed a member of the Church.

His grandfather, though a devout Catholic, sent him a copy of the Book of Mormon left by missionaries. This led to a new world of scripture that John continues to explore today as Associate Director of Research at the Foundation for Ancient Research and Mormon Studies (FARMS) now a part of BYU.

After earning a BA in anthropology at the University of Utah in 1969, John received a Graduate Certificate in Middle East area studies and an MA in Linguistics, with a minor in Arabic. In 1971, he received a second MA in Middle East Studies (Hebrew), with a minor in anthropology. He has taken courses at the University of California (Berkeley) and the BYU Salt Lake Center, and did extensive graduate work at the Hebrew University in Jerusalem, studying Egyptian and Semitic languages.

John taught Hebrew and linguistics at the University of Utah for three years and Hebrew and anthropology at the BYU Salt Lake Center for five years. During more than eight years in Israel, he was with the BYU Jerusalem program, where he taught Hebrew, anthropology, ancient Near Eastern history and archaeology, and historical geography of Israel and the Near East. He has also taught special CES courses for Gospel Doctrine teachers.

Always a missionary, John has served a full-time, a stake and a district mission. He has been a counselor in the young men's presidency, an elders' quorum president, and a high priest group leader. For six years, he was first counselor in the Jerusalem Branch presidency. He especially loves teaching Gospel Doctrine classes.

He is married to Carol Steffensen, and has six children and three grandchildren.

The Most Correct Book

Insights from a Book of Mormon Scholar

John A. Tvedtnes

Cornerstone Publishing & Distribution, Inc.
Salt Lake City & Phoenix

© 1999 Cornerstone Publishing & Distribution, Inc.

All Rights Reserved

04 02 00   5 4 3 2 1

Printed in the United States of America

International Standard Book Number 1-929281-00-5

Jesus Teaching in the Western Hemisphere, by John Scott and
Joseph Receives the Gold Plates, by Kenneth Riley,
© by Intellectual Reserve, Inc.
Used by Permission

Cover design by Adam R. Hopkins

Contents

ORIGINS 29
THE GENTILES TODAY 32
THE GENTILES, EPHRAIMITES? 33
THE FULNESS OF THE GENTILES 34
CONCLUSION 36

Chapter 6: **CONTENTS OF THE 116 LOST PAGES AND THE LARGE PLATES** 37
THE BOOK OF LEHI 38
HINTS FROM THE BOOK OF MORMON 39
EARLY RELATIONS WITH THE LAMANITES 41
THE HILL NORTH OF SHILOM 44
THE CITY AND LAND OF NEPHI 45
THE EARLY NEPHITE KINGS 46
TEACHINGS AND REVELATIONS OF LEHI AND
  NEPHI 47
THE LAMANITE CURSE 48
THE PROMISE OF PROSPERITY 49
NEPHITE RULES OF BATTLE 50
OTHER POSSIBLE EXAMPLES 51
CONCLUSION 52

Chapter 7: **"THAT WHICH YOU HAVE RETAINED"** . . 53
CONCLUSION 55

Chapter 8: **THE PROPHETS OF THE EXHILE** 56
CONCLUSION 58

Chapter 9: **THE ELDERS AT JERUSALEM IN THE DAYS OF LEHI** 59
THE ELDERS OF ISRAEL 60
ELDERS AND KINGS 62
LABAN AND THE ELDERS 64
A CONSPIRACY OF THE PRINCES 66
POSSIBLE INVOLVEMENT OF THE AMMONITES . . . 71
THE SECRET COMBINATION AMONG THE
  NEPHITES 73
CONCLUSION 75

CONTENTS

ABOUT THE AUTHOR ii
FOREWORD xiv
INTRODUCTION xvi
Chapter 1: **"I MAKE THIS SMALL ABRIDGMENT"** 1
    ABRIDGMENT IN THE OLD TESTAMENT 2
    OLD TESTAMENT "ABRIDGERS" 3
    WHAT RECORDS WERE ABRIDGED 5
    CONCLUSION 6
Chapter 2: **MORMON AS AN ABRIDGER OF ANCIENT RECORDS** 8
    MORMON'S PROMISES 9
    BAPTISM, CHILDREN & THE HOLY GHOST 11
    THE FULFILLMENT OF PROPHECY 12
    CHANGE IN PERSON 13
    THE NEPHITE ANNALS 14
    THE THREE NEPHITES 15
    INTERNAL CONSISTENCY 17
    MORMON'S INTERRUPTIONS 19
    COLOPHONS 20
    CONCLUSION 21
Chapter 3: **REFORMED EGYPTIAN** 22
    OTHER CULTURES USED "REFORMED" EGYPTIAN 23
    HOW DID THE NEPHITES "REFORM" EGYPTIAN? . 23
    CONCLUSION 24
Chapter 4: **HIDDEN RECORDS** 25
    BURIED AND SEALED RECORDS 25
    METAL RECORDS 26
    USE OF STONE BOXES 27
    CONCLUSION 28
Chapter 5: **WHO ARE THE "GENTILES"?** 29

Contents

Chapter 10: WAS LEHI A CARAVANEER? 76
   THE EGYPTIAN LANGUAGE 79
   BEDOUIN LIFESTYLE 81
   MURMURING IN THE DESERT 88
   LEHI: FARMER OR MERCHANT? 91
   LEHI: METALWORKER? 94
   CONCLUSION 98

Chapter 11: JEREMIAH'S PROPHECIES OF JESUS CHRIST 99
   THE HEBREW VERSION OF JEREMIAH 99
   THE SEPTUAGINT VERSION OF JEREMIAH 100
   WRITINGS OF JEREMIAH THAT TESTIFY OF CHRIST 101
   CONCLUSION 103

Chapter 12: "HE SHALL PREPARE A WAY" 104
   OBTAINING THE PLATES 105
   A WAY IS PREPARED IN THE WILDERNESS 106
   BUILDING A SHIP 107
   GOD PREPARES A WAY FOR OTHERS 108
   THE WAY IS PREPARED AGAIN IN THE MIDDLE EAST 109
   CONCLUSION 109

Chapter 13: THE SLAYING OF LABAN 110
   CONCLUSION 112

Chapter 14: A NEW TESTAMENT PARALLEL TO LEHI'S TREE OF LIFE VISION 113
   CONCLUSION 115

Chapter 15: "BY SMALL MEANS" 116
   "SMALL" EXAMPLES 116
   CONCLUSIONS 119

Chapter 16: "THAT THEY MIGHT HAVE JOY" 120
   THE MISERY OF THE DEVIL 121
   CONCLUSION 123

Chapter 17: OPPOSITON IN ALL THINGS 124

Contents

OPPOSITION IN NON-CANONICAL BOOKS 125
THE FALL MADE CHOICES POSSIBLE 127
SATAN OBSCURES THE DIFFERENCES 128
CONCLUSION 128
Chapter 18: **CAPTIVITY OF THE DEVIL** 129
THE DEVIL'S SNARES 130
THE BINDING POWER OF SIN 133
THE PIT 134
FLEE FROM EVIL 135
CONCLUSION 136
Chapter 19: **LUCIFER, SON OF THE MORNING** 137
SATAN, KING OF BABYLON 140
BABYLON IN HISTORY 147
COMPARING THE ISAIAH ACCOUNT TO
  JEREMIAH AND EZEKIEL 149
COMPARISONS WITH THE BOOK OF MORMON . . 153
CONCLUSION 160
Chapter 20: **PROMISCUITY AND THE SEARCH FOR
  WEALTH** 161
THE THREE NETS OF BELIAL 162
POLUTING THE SANCTUARY THROUGH SIN 163
SINS LEADING TO IDOLATRY 164
CONCLUSION 166
Chapter 21: **"THE CHOIRS ABOVE"** 167
THE "CHOIR" IN MIDDLE EASTERN TEXTS 168
THE SINGING LEVITES 169
CONCLUSION 169
Chapter 22: **THE THOUGHTS AND INTENTS OF
  THE HEART** 170
GOD KNOWS THE THOUGHTS AND INTENTS OF
  OUR HEARTS 170
THE IMPORTANCE OF OUR THOUGHTS 171
CONCLUSION 172
Chapter 23: **"HOW BEAUTIFUL UPON THE**

Contents

MOUNTAINS" 173
   A BOOK OF MORMON EXPOSITION 173
   OTHER ANCIENT EXPOSITIONS 174
   CONCLUSION 175

Chapter 24: **THE NEPHITE PURIFICATION CEREMONY** 176
   RITUAL PURIFICATION IN THE BIBLE AND OTHER CULTURES 176
   TIMING OF THE NEPHITE PURIFICATION CEREMONY 183
   CONCLUSION 186

Chapter 25: **SOME ASPECTS OF NEPHITE KINGSHIP** 187
   MOSIAH BECOMES KING OF ZARAHEMLA 188
   THE SERVICE OF THE NEPHITE KINGS 190
   ABOLITION OF THE NEPHITE MONARCHY 191
   CONCLUSION 192

Chapter 26: **KINGS AND JUDGES IN THE BIBLE AND THE BOOK OF MORMON** 194
   JUDGES AMONGST THE ISRAELITES 194
   THE TRANSITION TO KINGS 195
   THE OFFICE OF "JUDGE" UNDER THE KINGS 195
   JUDGES AMONGST THE NEPHITES 196
   CONCLUSION 197

Chapter 27: **THE CAPTIVITY OF THE FATHERS** 198
   THE BONDAGE OF ALMA AND HIS PEOPLE 198
   DELIVERY FROM SPIRITUAL BONDAGE 200
   COMPARING PHYSICAL AND SPIRITUAL BONDAGE 201
   CONCLUSION 202

Chapter 28: **WATCH AND PRAY** 203
   CONCLUSION 205

Chapter 29: **THE EVIL SPIRIT** 206
   CONCLUSION 209

Contents

Chapter 30: THE TWO GREAT SINS 210
   THE PROBLEM OF RESTITUTION 210
   MEANING OF THE TWO COMMANDMENTS 211
   THE UNPARDONABLE SIN 212
   "FLEE FORNICATION" 213
   CONCLUSION 214

Chapter 31: RAISED BY A HANDCLASP 215
   SIMILARITY TO OTHER ANCIENT WRITINGS 215
   LOSS OF PHYSICAL STRENGTH 217
   CONCLUSION 218

Chapter 32: "THAT THEY MAY BE KEPT BRIGHT" .. 219
   CONCLUSION 221

Chapter 33: OATHS IN THE BOOK OF MORMON ... 222
   OATHS IN THE LAW OF MOSES 223
   RASH OATHS 224
   LAMANITE OATHS 225
   CONCLUSION 227

Chapter 34: IN THE STRENGTH OF THE LORD 228
   THE LORD STRENGTHENS THE NEPHITE ARMIES 228
   THE LORD STRENGTHENS INDIVIDUALS 231
   CONCLUSION 234

Chapter 35: "THAT WHICH IS TO COME" 235
   CONCLUSION 241

Chapter 36: ANGELS ANNOUNCE THE COMING OF CHRIST 242
   THE "GOSPEL" ANNOUNCED IN THE BOOK OF MORMON 242
   ANGELS WILL ANNOUNCE CHRIST'S SECOND COMING 245

Chapter 37: EVENTS SURROUNDING CHRIST'S DEATH AND RESURRECTION 246
   GREAT EARTHQUAKES 246
   THE LIGHT-GLORY OF HEAVENLY BEINGS 248
   TEACHINGS OF CHRIST 249

Contents

    CONCLUSION 250
Chapter 38: **THE TIMING OF CHRIST'S APPEARANCE TO THE NEPHITES** 251
    THE "ASCENSION" 253
    THE "ENDING" OF THE YEAR 255
    THE "SETTLED CONDITION" OF THE NEPHITES . 259
    EXTENT OF THE DESTRUCTION 259
    BURYING THE DEAD 262
    AVAILABILITY OF BREAD AND WINE 264
    APPEARANCE AFTER THE PEOPLE HAD FAITH .. 264
    GATHERING AT THE TEMPLE 266
    SAMUEL'S PROPHECY 267
    ARGUMENTS FOR AN EARLY APPEARANCE 268
    CONCLUSION 269
Chapter 39: **CHRIST'S VISIT TO THE NEPHITES AS A TYPE OF HIS SECOND COMING** 270
    SIGNS PRECEDING CHRIST'S VISIT TO THE NEPHITES 271
    SIGNS PRECEDING CHRIST'S SECOND COMING .. 272
    LESSONS TO BE LEARNED 273
    CONCLUSION 274
Chapter 40: **PERFORMANCES AND ORDINANCES OF THE LAW** 275
    CONCLUSION 277
Chapter 41: **BECOMING AS LITTLE CHILDREN** 278
    CONCLUSION 281
Chapter 42: **HUNGERING AND THIRSTING AFTER RIGHTEOUSNESS** 282
    CONCLUSION 284
Chapter 43: **THE JAREDITE OCEAN VOYAGE** 285
    A COMPARISON TO ACCOUNTS OF THE FLOOD . 286
    LIGHT FOR THE VOYAGE 287
    POSSIBLE ROUTES 289
    CONCLUSION 290

Contents

Chapter 44: THE ROLE OF THE BOOK OF MORMON IN THE RESTORATION OF THE CHURCH 291
   THE FULNESS OF THE GOSPEL 292
   THE BOOK OF MORMON AND JOESPH SMITH'S MISSION 293
   CHURCH PRACTICES DRAWN FROM THE BOOK OF MORMON 296
   PRIESTHOOD OFFICES 297
   BAPTISM 299
   YOUNG CHILDREN NOT TO BE BAPTIZED 301
   CHURCH MEMBERSHIP AND DISCIPLINE 302
   HOME TEACHING 303
   SACRAMENT OF THE LORD'S SUPPER 304
   PUBLIC AND PRIVATE PRAYER 306
   LAW OF CONSECRATION 306
   THE BOOK OF MORMON AS A SOURCE OF CHURCH DOCTRINE 308
      Unity of the Godhead 310
      Salvation & Judgment 310
      Preaching Repentance 310
      The New Jerusalem 311
      The Lord's Law of Warfare 311
      Religious Tolerance 312
   CONCLUSION 315

Chapter 45: UNANSWERED QUESTIONS IN THE BOOK OF MORMON 317
   DID LEHI'S FAMILY ENCOUNTER OTHER PEOPLE IN THE NEW WORLD BESIDES THE MULEKITES? 317
   HOW DID MOSIAH GET THE INTERPRETERS? ... 318
   WHERE DID ALMA GET HIS PRIESTHOOD AUTHORITY? 323
   WAS ABINADI ONE OF ZENIFF'S PRIESTS? 323
   WHO WERE THE AMALEKITES? 324
   JUST HOW DID NEHOR DIE? 325

CONTENTS

    HOW DID AN ISHMAELITE BECOME KING OF THE
        LAMANITES? 326
    CONCLUSION 326
Chapter 46: **THE MESSIAH, THE BOOK OF MORMON,**
    AND THE DEAD SEA SCROLLS 328
    SOME MESSIAH TEXTS FROM THE DEAD SEA
        SCROLLS 330
    LEHI'S ADMONITIONS 335
    NEPHI'S TEACHING 335
    JACOB'S TEACHINGS 337
    KING BENJAMIN'S DISCOURSE 338
    ABINADI'S MESSAGE 339
    THE TEACHINGS OF ALMA THE YOUNGER 340
    CONCLUSION 342
Chapter 47: **UNTRANSLATED WORDS IN THE**
    BOOK OF MORMON 344
    ZIFF 344
    SHEUM AND NEAS 346
    CURELOMS AND CUMOMS 346
    CONCLUSION 347
Appendix: **OTHER BOOK OF MORMON ARTICLES**
    BY THE AUTHOR 348
    BOOK OF MORMON LANGUAGE 348
    COMPOSITION AND AUTHORSHIP OF THE
        BOOK OF MORMON 349
    ANCIENT NEAR EAST TIES 350
    NEPHITE CULTURE 351
    DOCTRINAL AND HISTORICAL ESSAYS 351
    REVIEWS 353
Bibliography: **ANCIENT AND MEDIEVAL SOURCES** . 355

FOREWORD

As scriptural scholarship in the Church expands, we are bound to see advances in the analysis of the Book of Mormon that parallel the kinds of studies commonly used to explore the Bible and other ancient texts. This outstanding volume is just such an advance. It represents a new step in LDS textual criticism.

Textual criticism normally involves a tedious examination of numerous copies of an ancient book to determine, as closely as possible, how the original text may have read. Since we have only one text of the Book of Mormon, textual criticism in that sense is not possible. But the efforts of textual critics involves more than just comparing texts. They also examine surrounding literature of the era from which the text is thought to arise in order to find evidence of its authenticity.

That is what John Tvedtnes has done with the Book of Mormon for many years. This collection of profound insights, written with both the scholar and the average LDS reader in mind, is the result. In a simple and inspiring manner, John compares over 45 texts from the Book of Mormon to ancient texts gleaned from the Bible and other ancient writings of the Near and Middle East. From this comparison comes extraordinary vistas of understanding that will inspire and thrill the reader at every turn of the page.

The ancient writings John uses have great historical value and were highly regarded by the cultures from which they came. Many stem from the same era and locale as the Book of Mormon peoples. A bibliography of these texts is provided at the end of this book. Glancing through it during the course of reading will help the reader understand the significance of each enlightening discovery.

Because these texts were not available to Joseph Smith during the translation of the Book of Mormon, the similarities that

FOREWORD

John brings to light could not have been a conscious device on Joseph's part. Instead, they lend strong evidence to the historical veracity of his work.

The information and understanding gleaned from these insights goes a long way toward strengthening the LDS position that the Book of Mormon is "the most correct of any book on earth" (DHC 4:461). Cornerstone Publishing is proud to offer this volume to Latter-day Saint readers as its inaugural publication.

Richard R. Hopkins
Publisher

INTRODUCTION

This book is a product of more than a decade of writing and research. Each chapter comprises an independent essay that can stand on its own. Some are fairly long, others quite short, with many in between. Two things tie them together : 1) all of the essays deal with the Book of Mormon, and 2) they are generally arranged in the order in which the various topics are encountered as one reads the Book of Mormon.

Because my academic background is so varied, the essays, too, vary considerably in content and approach. Some deal with linguistic issues, others with historical information, still others with questions regarding the authorship and internal consistency of the Book of Mormon. Much of the information in support of the Nephite record is drawn from the Bible and other ancient Near Eastern texts.

The varied nature of this book's contents will, I believe, ensure that there is something for everyone. Whether you teach a Primary class, serve in a leadership position, or teach seminary classes, you will find herein material that will help you appreciate the Book of Mormon as an authentic ancient record.

I hasten to add, however, that no book can take the place of reading the scriptures and asking the Spirit to guide your study thereof. If you learn nothing more from my work than to appreciate the value of the Book of Mormon and other sacred texts, I will have been successful in my efforts.

John A. Tvedtnes

Chapter 1

"I MAKE THIS SMALL ABRIDGMENT"

Therefore I write a small abridgment, daring not to give a full account of the things which I have seen, because of the commandment which I have received, and also that ye might not have too great sorrow because of the wickedness of this people. (Mormon 5:9)

Some sixty-four percent of the Book of Mormon (Mosiah through Mormon 7) comprises Mormon's abridgment of the Nephite records. While there are other hints about his work, Mormon uses the words "abridgment" only twice within the record (Words of Mormon 1:3; Mormon 5:9), with a third mention of his "abridgment of the record of the people of Nephi" occurring in the title page. Moroni continued his father's work in Mormon 8-9 and began "abridging the account of the people of Jared" (Moroni 1:1), noting, "I give not the full account, but a part of the account I give" (Ether 1:5). This "abridgment taken from the Book of Ether" is also mentioned in the title page.

Mormon and Moroni were not the only Nephites to have abridged records. In the beginning, Nephi instituted record-keeping among his people, and wrote, "Behold, I make an abridgment of the record of my father, upon plates which I have made with mine own hands; wherefore, after I have abridged the record of my father then will I make an account of mine own life" (1 Nephi 1:17).[1]

---

[1] For a discussion of Lehi's "running log" record from which Nephi abridged his account, see S. Kent Brown, "Lehi's Personal Record: Quest for a Missing Source," *BYU Studies* 24/1 (winter 1984), 19-42, and the latest iteration as chapter 3, "Recovering the Missing Record of Lehi," in his *From Jerusalem to Zarahemla:*

"I MAKE THIS SMALL ABRIDGEMENT"

ABRIDGMENT IN THE OLD TESTAMENT

But neither Mormon nor Nephi invented the concept of abridging records. It was already a common phenomenon evidenced in the Bible. Specific phrases and anachronisms, as well as reference to earlier writings containing greater detail, provide evidence for the abridgment of earlier records to produce our current Bible.

One such phrase is "unto this day," which refers to an historical event marking the establishment of something that remained in place at the time of the individual who made the final record. We find the expression in works attributed to Moses (Genesis 19:37-38; 26:33; 32:32; 35:20; 47:26; 48:15; Deuteronomy 2:22; 3:14; 10:8; 11:4; 34:6) and to Joshua (Joshua 4:9; 5:9; 6:25; 7:26; 8:28-29; 9:27; 14:14; 15:63; 16:10), as well as various historical books (Judges 1:21, 26; 6:14; 10:4; 15:19; 18:12; 19:30; 1 Samuel 5:5; 6:18; 27:6; 30:25; 2 Samuel 18:18; 1 Kings 8:8; 9:13, 21; 10:12; 12:19; 2 Kings 2:22; 8:22; 10:27; 14:7; 16:6; 17:23; 1 Chronicles 4:41, 43; 5:26; 2 Chronicles 5:9; 10:19; 20:26; 21:10). It is even found in Matthew 27:8 in reference to the purchase of a field with the money Judas had returned to the chief priests in Jerusalem.

Often, this expression denotes an anachronism in the text. For example, in Deuteronomy 3:14, we read of an event that occurred in the days of Moses: "Jair the son of Manasseh took all the country of Argob unto the coasts of Geshuri and Maachathi; and called them after his own name, Bashan-havoth-jair, *unto this day*." It seems obvious that this expression would have been inappropriate in Moses' own day and that it must have been added at a later date. Many Bible scholars see this as evidence that Moses did not write the books of the Pentateuch, but this need not be so. The phenomenon can just as easily be attributed to later editors of

---

Literary and Historical Studies of the Book of Mormon (Provo: BYU Religious Studies Center, 1998).

works originally prepared by Moses.

OLD TESTAMENT "ABRIDGERS"

Evidence for abridgment or redaction of earlier documents is found throughout the historical books of the Bible (Judges through 2 Chronicles). The book of Judges covers such a long period of time that it must have been compiled from earlier records or oral traditions. That it was composed by a single historian is suggested by the fact that the book, as a whole, describes what the author saw as a cycle of sin, followed by captivity, then the cry of the people for assistance, and their delivery by a judge called by God. The perspective is clearly *ex post facto* rather than contemporary.

According to the Talmud, Samuel wrote the book of Judges (TB *Baba Bathra* 14b). But the notice that "in *those* days there was no king in Israel" (Judges 17:6; 18:1; 19:1; 21:25) suggests that the book was composed at a time when there *was* a king in Israel. Moreover, the use of the name "Israel" leads to three possible conclusions. Either the book was written during the time of the united monarchy (Saul, David, Solomon), or it was composed in the kingdom of Israel after its split with Judah following the death of Solomon, or it was composed after both kingdoms had ceased to exist and had become mere historical facts. In any event, the author would have had to have access to earlier records (whether written or oral) and may thus be termed an "abridger." One of the records used by this abridger is the book of Joshua. Thus, for example, the story in Judges 1:11-15 is also found in Joshua 15:15-19, while Judges 2:6-9 draws upon Joshua 24:28-31.

But we can narrow down the time period for the composition of Judges even more. In Judges 18:30, we read of the establishment of a shrine at the site of Dan, in northern Israel, where the family of one Jonathan "were priests to the tribe of Dan until the day of the captivity of the land." Since the ten tribes were taken captive by the Assyrians in 722 B.C., it is likely that the book of Judges was written after that time or that, at the very least, an editor added these comments at the later date.

The dating of the book of Joshua is more clear, for Joshua 11:21 speaks of Joshua cutting off the Anakims "from all the mountains of Judah, and from all the mountains of Israel." This statement could only have made sense after the split that resulted in the establishment of the kingdom of Israel in the north and the kingdom of Judah in the south, which took place in the days of Rehoboam, son of Solomon (1 Kings 12:16-21; 2 Chronicles 10:16-17; 11:1).

Similar phenomena are found in the book of Samuel, which was only later divided into 1-2 Samuel.[2] Samuel, of course, did not write the book. His death is recorded in 1 Samuel 25:1. Since this is before the end of the later subdivision of 1 Samuel, it is clear that he did not write that book in its present form either. This does not mean that Samuel wrote nothing, for we have a clear statement in 1 Samuel 10:25 that Samuel had written some things. Some of his material may have been used by a the later author who composed the book of Samuel. Indeed, because it covers such a long span of time, Samuel evidently is a combination of various works (see 1 Chronicles 29:29).

The time period in which the book of Samuel was written may be indicated by some of the anachronisms that appear in it. For example, in 1 Samuel 2:10, there is reference to "his king," in a period supposedly predating the choosing of Saul (1 Samuel 9) as Israel's king. In several passages, we find mention of Judah and

---

[2] Samuel, according to the fourth-century Christian writers Eusebius and Jerome, was a single book in Hebrew. The Greek Septuagint Bible divided it and Kings into the 1-4 "Book of the Kingdoms," adopted by the Vulgate. This division was introduced into a Hebrew manuscript of 1448 and into the Bomberg Bible of 1517. The unity of the "books" of Samuel is confirmed by the fact that, among the Dead Sea Scrolls, several documents had 1-2 Samuel together on the same roll (1Q7, 4Q51, 4Q52, 4Q53) as a single book.

Israel at a time when they were supposedly a united people under either Saul or David (1 Samuel 11:8; 17:52; 18:16; 2 Samuel 3:10; 5:5; 11:11; 12:8; 19:11, 40-43; 21:2; 24:1, 9; see 1 Chronicles 21:5).

In 1 Samuel 1:9, there is reference to a temple, at a time when, according to other statements found in the Bible, there was not yet a temple. This places the writing at least in the time of Solomon, who constructed the temple. But the reference to the kingdom of Judah in 1 Samuel 27:6 provides evidence that the book was written after the death of Solomon, for the kingdom was not split in two until the time of his son Rehoboam.

Such phenomena continue into the books of Kings. Thus, some passages speak of Judah and Israel at a time when all the tribes constituted a united kingdom under Solomon (1 Kings 1:35; 4:20-21). In 1 Kings 4:25 we read that "Judah and Israel dwelt safely, every man under his vine and under his fig tree, from Dan even to Beersheba, all the days of Solomon." The mention of Judah and Israel as separate entites again suggests that the text was written after the split in the kingdom. Indeed, the passage may be dependent on Jeremiah 23:6, where we read, "In his days Judah shall be saved, and Israel shall dwell safely: and this is his name whereby he shall be called, the Lord our righteousness." This supports the story in the Talmud (TB *Baba Bathra* 14a) that makes Jeremiah the author of Kings.

WHAT RECORDS WERE ABRIDGED?

Elsewhere, we find evidence that the books of Kings were compiled from earlier records. These annals were known as the "chronicles of the kings of Judah" (1 Kings 14:29; 15:7, 23; 22:45; 2 Kings 8:23; 12:19; 14:18; 15:6, 36; 16:19; 20:20; 21:17, 25; 23:28; 24:5) and the "chronicles of the kings of Israel" (1 Kings 14:19; 15:31; 16:5, 14, 20, 27; 22:39; 2 Kings 1:18; 10:34; 13:8, 12; 14:15, 28; 15:11, 15, 21, 26, 31). They should not be confused with the books of Chronicles in our current Bible, which are a reworking of the account in Kings. The Hebrew term, rendered "chronicles" in both the lists of annals and in the title of the books of Chronicles, is the same, *spr dbry h-ymym*—literally, "book of the things/words of the days." Another source for the account in Kings is the "book of the acts of Solomon" (1 Kings 11:41).

The Chroniclers, who lived after the period of Babylonian exile, long after Lehi left Jerusalem, drew upon the accounts found in the books of Samuel and Kings as confirmed in their own record (1 Chronicles 9:1; 2 Chronicles 16:11; 20:34; 24:27; 25:26; 27:7; 28:26; 32:32; 33:18; 35:27; 36:8). They also referred to other annals, such as the "chronicles of king David" (1 Chronicles 27:24; cf. Nehemiah 12:23). One passage refers to "the book of Samuel the seer . . . the book of Nathan the prophet, and . . . the book of Gad the seer" (1 Chronicles 29:29) as sources for the acts of David, while another notes that the acts of Solomon were recorded in "the book of Nathan the prophet . . . the prophecy of Ahijah the Shilonite, and in the visions of Iddo the seer" (2 Chronicles 9:29). Elsewhere, we read that the acts of Rehoboam were "written in the book of Shemaiah the prophet, and of Iddo the seer" (2 Chronicles 12:15; cf. 13:22). Another passage (2 Chronicles 20:34) notes that the acts of Jehoshaphat had been "written in the book of Jehu the son of Hanani, who is mentioned in the book of the kings of Israel" (see 1 Kings 16:1, 7; 2 Chronicles 16:7; 19:2).

CONCLUSION

From this, we can see that the concept of abridging the records of former generations is a long-standing one in ancient Israel. Nephi's acquaintance with the brass plates of Laban may have given him insights into the methodology used by his predecessors (1 Nephi 3:3-4; 4:16, 38; 5:10-19; 19:21-23; 22:1, 30; 2 Nephi 4:15; 5:12). Indeed, he learned from an angel that the record of the Jews, the Bible, would be "a record like unto the engravings which are upon the plates of brass, save there are not so

CONCLUSION

many" (1 Nephi 13:23). Among the writings found on the brass plates but missing from the Bible were the prophecies of Joseph (2 Nephi 4:1-2) and, evidently, the records of the prophets Zenos, Zenock, Neum, and Ezias (1 Nephi 19:10, 12; Jacob 5:1; 6:1; Alma 33:3, 13, 15; 34:7; Helaman 8:19-20; 15:11; 3 Nephi 10:16). Extracts from these writings were included in the Nephite abridgements. While there remains some question as to the identity of the Old Testament abridgers, we may be grateful for the knowledge of exactly who it was that abridged the record we have as the Book of Mormon.

Chapter 2

MORMON AS AN ABRIDGER OF ANCIENT RECORDS[1]

Having been commanded of the Lord that I should not suffer the records which had been handed down by our fathers, which were sacred, to fall into the hands of the Lamanites, (for the Lamanites would destroy them) therefore I made this record out of the plates of Nephi, and hid up in the hill Cumorah all the records which had been entrusted to me by the hand of the Lord, save it were these few plates which I gave unto my son Moroni. (Mormon 6:6)

The source of the Book of Mormon has been long disputed. Its defenders generally accept Joseph Smith's testimony that, "through the gift and power of God," he was enabled to translate an ancient document into English. There is, in fact, internal evidence that the prophet was working from an extant text. This evidence includes examples of dittography (for example, the repetition of "work" in Mosiah 10:5). Dittography is common in copying extant texts, but is not typical in speech. Nevertheless, dittographs in the Book of Mormon could conceivably be attributed to the necessity for Joseph Smith to repeat some portions of the text to a scribe (usually Oliver Cowdery) who has had difficulty keeping up with the dictation. Consequently, we simply note here the existence of dittographs without discussing examples in detail. Instead, we shall concentrate our efforts on an examination of more complex issues such as flash-backs and previews.

---

[1] Portions of this article have previously appeared elsewhere.

MORMON'S PROMISES[2]

Anyone can make a promise to return to a particular subject and give further details. But memory limitations make it much easier to fulfill such a promise in writing than in speech. As an abridger of the Nephite records, Mormon makes several important promises which are later fulfilled. Here are examples:

In Mosiah 21:35, Mormon, speaking of Limhi's people, promised that "an account of their baptism shall be given hereafter." He kept that promise in Mosiah 25:17-18.

In Mosiah 28:9, 19-20, Mormon promised to tell the story of the mission of the sons of Mosiah. It is not until Alma 17-25, however, that we find the account.

In Alma 35:13, Mormon promised to give an account of the Nephite-Lamanite war which began in the eighteenth year, but since he proposed to first copy Alma's admonitions to his sons (Alma 36-42), he deferred the story of the war until Alma 43:3, where he introduced the topic by the words "And now I return to an account of the wars."

In Mosiah 28:11-19, Mormon promised to tell the story of the Jaredites, whose record had been translated by King Mosiah. The press of war with the Lamanites made it impossible for him to complete the work, however, so Moroni, his son and scribal successor, was left to give us the account known as the Book of Ether.

In 3 Nephi 18:36-37, Mormon wrote how Jesus had given the twelve disciples "power to give the Holy Ghost. And I will show unto you hereafter that this record is true." In 3 Nephi 19:13, he told how the Holy Ghost fell on the twelve after their baptism, and in 4 Nephi 1:1, he wrote that those baptized by the twelve "did also receive the Holy Ghost." But it was Moroni who

---

[2] This subject was discussed in the author's article "Mormon's Editorial Promises," in John L. Sorenson and Melvin J. Thorne (eds.), *Rediscovering the Book of Mormon* (Salt Lake City: Deseret and FARMS, 1991).

quoted Christ's actual words to the twelve (left out by Mormon in 3 Nephi 18): "ye shall have power that to him upon whom ye shall lay your hands, ye shall give the Holy Ghost" (Moroni 2:2), then adding, "and on as many as they laid their hands, fell the Holy Ghost" (Moroni 2:3).

In Words of Mormon 1:2, Mormon expressed the hope that his son Moroni would write "concerning Christ." In compliance, Moroni interjected much about Christ into his account of the Jaredites in the Book of Ether (see especially Ether 3:17-20; 12:7, 16-22, 38-41) and included his testimony of Christ in other places as well (Mormon 9:1f; Moroni 2; 6:3-4; 7:16f; 10:30f).

In Helaman 2:12-14, Mormon promised to speak more of Gadianton and his band "hereafter." The problems caused by the "robbers" are detailed in Helaman 6; 3 Nephi 1:27-29; 2:11-18; 3:1-4:29; 4 Nephi 1:42-44; Mormon 1:18.

Mormon's comments in Helaman 2:12-14 are particularly interesting, for they show how the historian worked. In verse 13, he wrote, "And behold, in the end of this book ye shall see that this Gadianton did prove the overthrow, yea, almost the entire destruction of the people of Nephi." He clarified what he meant by adding, "Behold I do not mean the end of the book of Helaman, but I mean the end of the book of Nephi, from which I have taken all the account which I have written."

Mormon's meaning is uncertain. Perhaps he had reference to the large plates of Nephi, kept by Helaman and other Nephite scribes. However, at no other time are the large plates called the "book" of Nephi (see 4 Nephi 1:21).

In Helaman 2, we read of the "secret acts of murder and of robbery" (verse 4). If the history recorded in this chapter was really a "secret plan" (verse 8), how is it that it was so readily known that there even existed a secret society? That there were murderers could not be doubted, for the crimes had indeed been committed. But contemporary Nephites could have known nothing of the secret pacts until, at some future time, there should be a confession or other evidence. The discovery of the Gadianton band is related beginning in Helaman 6, where we read of the arrest of some of the robbers.

If Helaman 6 comprises part of the record made by Nephi, son of Helaman, then it could be from the book of this Nephi that Mormon took his information for the account of the "secret band" in Helaman 2. As an historian, he had access to documents postdating the events themselves, documents that could elucidate the hitherto unknown aspects of those historical events. No doubt Helaman's record made mention of the murders, but without knowing about the organization of the Gadianton band. This information, being supplied by documents written at a later time, was added in its proper historical sequence by Mormon, during the abridgement process. It may be, however, that Helaman 6 is part of the record kept not by Nephi, but by his brother Lehi, as suggested by Sidney Sperry. If so, then the "book of Nephi" to which Mormon referred is perhaps the one known to us as 3 Nephi, where we also read much about the secret band.

BAPTISM, CHILDREN & THE HOLY GHOST

Similar in nature to Mormon's promises is the follow-through on Jesus' promise to give the Holy Ghost. In 3 Nephi 11:35-38, the Savior instructed the people to "become as a little child, and be baptized," after which they would be baptized "with fire and with the Holy Ghost." When, at length, the twelve disciples were baptized, they were filled with the Holy Ghost and encircled about by fire, while angels descended to minister to them (3 Nephi 19:9-14). These same heavenly manifestations were present the previous day, when Jesus blessed the children, who were likewise encircled by fire as angels descended from heaven to minister to them (3 Nephi 17:21-24).

It seems likely that the events accompanying the blessing of the children were deliberately designed to impress upon the Nephites the importance of following Jesus' admonition to become as a child. Seeing that baptism of adults produced the same results, they could better understand his meaning. Despite the consistency behind these events, Mormon does not expressly bring our attention to them, as one might expect had the book been written to prove a point to its readers. Rather, he merely recorded the stories as he found them in the ancient records.

THE FULFILLMENT OF PROPHECY

Similar in nature to Mormon's promises are prophecies which are later fulfilled in the Book of Mormon. One of the more complex prophecies was that of Abinadi. Speaking out in the city of Lehi-Nephi, he told of how the Lamanites would bring the people into bondage, smiting them on the cheek, driving and slaying them (Mosiah 12:2). He noted that "the life of king Noah shall be valued even as a garment in a hot furnace" (Mosiah 12:3). The people would "have burdens lashed upon their backs; and they shall be driven before like a dumb ass" and be subject to pestilence and famine (Mosiah 12:4-7).

Appearing before king Noah and his priests, Abinadi told them, "what you do with me, after this, shall be as a type and a shadow of things which are to come" (Mosiah 13:10). He subsequently was more clear, telling them, "Behold, even as ye have done unto me . . . thy seed shall cause that many shall suffer the pains that I do suffer, even the pains of death by fire; and this because they believe in the salvation of their God" (Mosiah 17:15).

Further, the prophet stated, "ye shall be smitten on every hand, and shall be driven and scattered to and fro, even as a wild flock is driven by wild and ferocious beasts. And in that day ye shall be hunted, and ye shall be taken by the hand of your enemies, and then ye shall suffer, as I suffer, the pains of death by fire" (Mosiah 17:17-18).

Subsequent events vindicated Abinadi's words. The Lamanites attacked, slaying some and driving others before them into the wilderness (Mosiah 19:6-19). Some of the Nephites, angry at Noah, burned him to death, while his priests escaped by fleeing

(Mosiah 19:20-21). After another brief battle (Mosiah 20), the Lamanites began to persecute the Nephites by "smit[ing] them on their cheeks, and exercis[ing] authority over them . . . put[ting] heavy burdens upon their backs, and driv[ing] them as they would a dumb ass," thus fulfilling the word of the Lord (Mosiah 21:2-4; see also verses 13-15).

In a later era, after the priests of Noah (called Amulonites) had joined with the Lamanites, they burned to death many of the Lamanites who had been converted by the sons of Mosiah, "because of their belief" (Alma 25:5-7). Non-believing Lamanites, angered at such atrocious acts against their brethren, began hunting down the Amulonites, consigning them to the flames, all in fulfillment of the words of Abinadi (Alma 25:8-12).

It is difficult to imagine that Joseph Smith, were he the author of the Book of Mormon, could have kept all of the details of the prophecy in mind sufficiently to record the fulfillment of each of these details. The evidence, rather, points to the author's reliance on a written text for such information. We thus have evidence that Mormon referred to the record of Limhi's people for his information.

CHANGE IN PERSON

If we presume that Mormon had access to ancient records, it seems likely that he would sometimes selectively rewrite the stories in his possession, while, at other times, he would paraphrase or abridge them. In some cases, he might wish to quote extracts from the texts. In all but complete rewrites, evidence for Mormon's hand might be reflected in the switch between first- and third-person accounts.

An example of this phenomenon can be found in Alma 56:52. This passage mentions Helaman by name and speaks of him in third person, despite the fact that it is in the middle of a letter (Alma 56-58) written by Helaman in which all other references to him are in first person. It is likely that Mormon, when including the letter in his account, simply slipped into the role of historian and, in retrospection, employed third person this one time.

We find another example in Alma 9-15, which tells the story of the mission of Alma and Amulek to Ammonihah. The preface situated before chapter 9 was evidently written by Mormon to indicate from which part of the Book of Alma he was abridging. It notes that what follows comprises "the words of Alma and also the words of Amulek," and that it is "according to the record of Alma."

The first part of the account comprises a direct extract from Alma's record, for he writes in first person (Alma 9:1, 7, 31-33). It is difficult, however, to know at which point Mormon began abridging in his own words. For example, it is not clear whether "this book" in Alma 9:34 refers to Alma's original record or to Mormon's abridgement. In any event, Amulek's words are introduced by another preface (Alma 10:1) and his speech is contained in Alma 10:2-11, followed by an historical explanation of what ensued, including further dialogue between Amulek and Zeezrom.

It seems certain that Mormon's abridgment has already resumed sometime before Alma 10:31 (see also Alma 11:20; 12:1ff), where Alma is mentioned, but no longer in first person. This might indicate that Mormon's abridgment begins again with Alma 9:34 or 10:1. If so, the words "this book" in Alma 9:34 could refer to the abridgment (see Alma 11:46 and cf. 13:31).

THE NEPHITE ANNALS

Most of Mormon's abridgement (Mosiah through Mormon) gives precise years for the various events, even when they are "flashbacks." Such precision implies that the records which Mormon possessed were very precise on chronology. It is likely that the historical records he consulted were in the form of annals.

Sometimes, Mormon listed years without recording any events for them. Thus, in 4 Nephi 1:6, he wrote, "And thus did the thirty and eighth year pass away, and also the thirty and ninth, and forty and first, and the forty and second, yea, even until forty and nine years had passed away, and also the fifty and first, and the fifty and second; yea, and even until fifty and nine years had passed away." Note also 4 Nephi 1:14: "And it came to pass that the seventy and first year passed away, and also the seventy and second year, yea, and in fine, till the seventy and ninth year had passed away; yea, even an hundred years had passed away."

Such rambling seems to be a waste of precious space on the plates. Mormon's run-down of dates in these verses is probably intended to record the years of the annals he consulted, even though he did not feel to write the history of each.

THE THREE NEPHITES

One of the evidences for Mormon's reliance on extant annals is found in the story of the three Nephite disciples who had been promised by Christ that they would not die. In order to illustrate the effects of this translation, Mormon wrote:

> And they were cast into prison by them who did not belong to the church. And the prisons could not hold them, for they were rent in twain. And they were cast down into the earth; but they did smite the earth with the word of God, insomuch that by his power they were delivered out of the depths of the earth; and therefore they could not dig pits sufficient to hold them. And thrice they were cast into a furnace and received no harm. And twice they were cast into a den of wild beasts; and behold they did play with the beasts as a child with a suckling lamb, and received no harm. (3 Nephi 28:19-22)

In 4 Nephi, Mormon told a similar story. After recounting the success of the Church, he wrote of the beginning of apostasy, then of "another church which . . . did persecute the true church of Christ" (4 Nephi 1:23-29). Then follows a description of that false church's acts toward the three Nephites, which events are said to have occurred between 210 (verse 27) and 230 years (verse 35) after the birth of Christ:

> Therefore they did exercise power and authority over the disciples of Jesus who did tarry with them, and they did cast them into prison; but by the power of the word of God, which was in them, the prisons were rent in twain, and they went forth doing mighty miracles among them. And they did cast them into furnaces of fire, and they came forth receiving no harm. And they also cast them into dens of wild beasts, and they did play with the wild beasts even as a child with a lamb; and they did come forth from among them, receiving no harm" (4 Nephi 1:30-33)

To the casual reader, it may appear that these tortures were inflicted upon the three Nephites soon after Christ's appearance in 3 Nephi 27-28 and were repeated nearly two centuries later. But the similarity between the two passages is such that we may suggest that Mormon was referring to a single written source in both cases. It is likely that the persecutions suffered by the three disciples were inflicted by the false church of the third century A.D. How, then, do we explain the fact that they are listed in 3 Nephi 28?

We cannot know in what year the events recorded in 3 Nephi 27-28 took place. They occurred "as the disciples of Jesus were journeying and were preaching" (3 Nephi 27:1). It was evidently after this visit from Christ that the disciples were able to convert the people (3 Nephi 28:23) and establish the era of peace described in the first part of 4 Nephi.

It would appear that the recitation of the trials of the three disciples found in 3 Nephi 28 was included merely to illustrate the benefits of their translation. Thus, verses 19-22 are not presented in their proper chronological order. Why, then, did Mormon list them here and repeat them in 4 Nephi? The answer is found in 3 Nephi 28:24, where we read that Mormon intended to stop writing for a time. Indeed, the two chapters that immediately follow this statement comprise exhortations that appear to be closing remarks addressed to a later generation.

In fact, Mormon cut short his abridgement at 3 Nephi 26:12, turning to some matters he had "been commanded" to write, which comprise a synopsis of the preaching and miracles performed by Jesus' disciples, his visit and the promise to the three, followed by concluding exhortations. It was probably the press of time that prompted Mormon to add his comments on the power that preserved the three disciples from death.

When, at length, Mormon returned to the abridgement and wrote 4 Nephi, he cut the story short. Centuries became but a few lines of text. But this time, at least, he included the story of the afflictions of the three disciples in its proper historical context.

It is the historian's perspective and access to written records that made it possible for Mormon to refer to the same event in two different parts of his work. These same factors made it possible for him to provide a measure of consistency to the text of his abridgement.

INTERNAL CONSISTENCY

In recent years, LDS scholars have been struck by some aspects of internal consistency in the Book of Mormon. Lengthy phrases and lists found in early parts of the book are repeated verbatim or nearly verbatim in later sections. For Joseph Smith to have remembered these long after he first dictated them to his scribe is an unreasonable expectation. It would have been much easier for Mormon to have quoted from earlier, written texts in his possession. Consequently, such passages can be seen as evidence that Joseph, too, worked from an extant text.

Ross Christensen was the first person to point out (1975)

that the lineage groups descended from Lehi were named several times in the same order in the Book of Mormon: Nephites, Jacobites, Josephites, Zoramites, Lamanites, Lemuelites, Ishmaelites. The first such listing was made by Jacob on the small plates (Jacob 1:13). The others were made nearly 1,000 years later in Mormon's abridgement (4 Nephi 1:37-38; Mormon 1:8). (The lineages comprising the Lamanite confederacy are also listed separately in Alma 47:35 and Mormon 1:8.) Lehi addressed his descendants and those of Ishmael in the same order near the close of his life (2 Nephi 1-4).[3]

A FARMS Update from 1987[4] noted several further instances of textual consistency in the Book of Mormon:

- Some 21 consecutive words from the account of Lehi's dream (1 Nephi 1:8) quoted verbatim by Alma and attributed to Lehi (Alma 36:22).

- Samuel the Lamanite (Helaman 14:12) included, in his warning to the people of Zarahemla, some 20 consecutive words found in an earlier speech by King Benjamin (Mosiah 3:8).

- Precise details of destructions which would take place at the crucifixion of the Savior had been given by the ancient prophet Zenos (1 Nephi 19:11-12). Each of the cataclysmic events he listed was included in the account of these destructions given in 3 Nephi 8:6-23.

- A list of five prohibited crimes (murder, plunder, theft, adultery and "any manner of wickedness") was laid down

---

[3] The topic of the lineage groups was discussed in a 1987 FARMS Update republished as "Seven Tribes: An Aspect of Lehi's Legacy," in John W. Welch, ed., *Reexploring the Book of Mormon* (Salt Lake City: Deseret and FARMS, 1992).

[4] "Textual Consistency," FARMS Update, October 1987, reprinted in John W. Welch, ed., *Reexploring the Book of Mormon*.

by King Benjamin (Mosiah 2:13) and reappears in seven subsequent passages (Mosiah 29:36; Alma 23:3; 30:10; Helaman 3:13; 6:23; 7:21; Ether 8:16).

Another series of items often repeated in the Book of Mormon is introduced in 1 Nephi 2:4, where we read that Lehi left the land of his inheritance, his gold, his silver and his precious things. When his sons later returned to the land of their inheritance, they went to retrieve the gold, silver and "all manner of riches" to use in purchasing the brass plates from Laban (1 Ne. 3:16). The three items of wealth are found listed in the same order in several other passages, with the words "precious things" alternating with "riches" and "precious metals/ores" (1 Ne. 3:24; Mosiah 2:12; 19:5; Hel. 6:9). They are sometimes listed in combination with other material possessions, such as ziff, copper, brass, iron, steel, flocks, herds, fatlings, grains, wood, silk, scarlets, fine-twined linen and precious clothing (1 Ne. 13:7; 18:25; 2 Ne. 5:15; Jacob 2:12; Mosiah 11:3; Alma 1:29; Alma 4:6). Gold and silver are always listed together in that order and, in all but three instances, are followed by "precious things" or a variant thereof. Such consistency bespeaks formulaic lists and/or reliance on earlier written records.[5]

MORMON'S INTERRUPTIONS

At several points in the history, Mormon interrupted his account to give some background material which he evidently felt was necessary to enable his audience to understand the story. It seems reasonable to assume that the conditions he explained were no longer extant in his day, leading him to add details available to him from other records, if not by revelation.

For example, we can attribute to Mormon the interjection regarding the Nephite monetary system in Alma 11:1-19. It would

---

[5] See the discussion in John A. Tvedtnes, "Word Groups in the Book of Mormon," *Journal of Book of Mormon Studies* 6/2 (Fall 1997).

have made little sense for Alma to interrupt his story to talk about money. But to Mormon, who lived many hundreds of years later, it was perfectly logical to interject with an explanation of the amounts of money that would be mentioned in the story to follow. We must recall that Mormon lived after the era of peace and united order following the visit of Jesus, and that the monetary system (if any) used in his day would probably have differed from that of Alma's day, hence necessitating an explanation. The digression is immediately followed (in Alma 11:20) by a recapitulation of the information given in Alma 10:32, just before the interjected material.

Another interruption at Alma 22:27b-35 inserts a geographical note, made either by Alma or, more likely, Mormon. Note how the story begun in Alma 22:27a continues in Alma 23:1, the two verses giving the same information, in order to show a return to an interrupted subject. This appears to be a literary device used by Mormon in the same way we use footnotes or parenthesis.

COLOPHONS

Another common feature in Mormon's abridgement is the use of colophons. These include text titles, prefaces, summaries and conclusions. Except for Mosiah (a special case that cannot be discussed here), Mormon wrote a preface for each of the books he abridged. In addition, he wrote prefaces to extracted material incorporated into the text of his abridgement. The latter are particularly helpful in seeing how Mormon prepared his materials.[6]

---

[6] For brief discussions of the subject, see John A. Tvedtnes, "Colophons in the Book of Mormon," *Insights: An Ancient Window* (Provo: FARMS, 1990), No. 3, reprinted in John W. Welch, *Reexploring the Book of Mormon*. A more in-depth study is found in John A. Tvedtnes, "Colophons in the Book of Mormon," in John L. Sorenson and Melvin J. Thorne (eds.), *Rediscovering the Book of Mormon* (Salt Lake City: Deseret and FARMS, 1991).

CONCLUSION

Several factors lend support to the idea that an ancient editor, working with various historical and religious texts, produced an abridgement known as the Book of Mormon. All of these factors demonstrate a consistency that can best be explained by postulating that the author of the book had immediate access to earlier records to which he could refer. Because Joseph Smith had no access to such materials, this retrospective nature of the Book of Mormon is the best evidence that Mormon was its author.

Chapter 3

REFORMED EGYPTIAN

And now, behold, we have written this record according to our knowledge, in the characters which are called among us the reformed Egyptian, being handed down and altered by us, according to our manner of speech. (Mormon 9:32)

In 1829, as Joseph Smith was finishing his translation of the Book of Mormon, a French scholar named Jean-François Champollion was busy preparing the first dictionary and grammar of the Egyptian language, which were published after his death in 1832. Until Champollion, no one had been able to translate ancient Egyptian texts since they fell into disuse in the fourth century A.D. But the Book of Mormon, according to one of its writers, Moroni, was written using "reformed Egyptian" characters, though the Nephites also knew Hebrew (Mormon 9:32-34). Another of its writers, Nephi, said he employed the "language of the Egyptians" to make his record (1 Nephi 1:2).

Egyptian hieroglyphs (Greek meaning "sacred symbols") were designed to be carved into stone--a slow and tedious process that involved the use of more than 700 characters that were very accurate depictions of things found in real life, such as people, animals, geographical features, heavenly bodies, clothing, and everyday utensils. A cursive ("flowing") script called hieratic (Greek for "sacred" or "priestly") was devised to make it possible to write faster and became extensively used on papyrus. Then, around 900 B.C., the Egyptians developed an even more cursive script we call demotic (Greek for "popular"), which, while based on the hieratic, bore little resemblance to the hieroglyphs. So the Egyptians had already reformed their writing system twice before the earliest parts of the Book of Mormon were written around 600 B.C.

OTHER CULTURES USED "REFORMED" EGYPTIAN

It may seem strange that the ancient Israelites who wrote the Book of Mormon should use an Egyptian writing system. But there are precedents for this practice and we now know that several writing systems of the ancient Near East were borrowed from Egyptian. Perhaps the most notable is the adoption, by the second century B.C., of some Egyptian hieroglyphs to form the alphabetic system used for the Meroitic language spoken anciently in Nubia (now in Sudan). Meroitic also developed a cursive writing system that resembles Egyptian demotic. Modified Egyptian hieroglyphic characters comprised the syllabic system used in writings (some of them on bronze plates) found during archaeological excavations of the ancient Phoenician city of Byblos.

HOW DID THE NEPHITES "REFORM" EGYPTIAN?

When Moroni noted that he was writing his record in reformed Egyptian, he also indicated that his people still used the Hebrew language (Mormon 9:32-34). Similarly, his ancestor Nephi had made "a record in the language of my father, which consists of the learning of the Jews and the language of the Egyptians" (1 Nephi 1:2). This suggests that the Book of Mormon may have been written in Hebrew but using Egyptian script. Evidence for this kind of writing has been discovered in recent years.

For example, a number of northwest Semitic texts (related to Hebrew) are included in three Egyptian magical papyri from the fourteenth and thirteenth centuries B.C., the London Magical Papyrus, the Harris Magical Papyrus, and Papyrus Anastasi I. Another Egyptian document, Ostracon 25759, from the early eleventh century B.C., also has a Semitic text that reads like Hebrew but is written in Egyptian characters.

Papyrus Amherst 63, a document written in Egyptian demotic and dating to the second century B.C., was found in an earthen jar at Thebes, Egypt, during the second half of the nineteenth century. Though the script is Egyptian, the underlying language is Aramaic, which is closely related to Hebrew. Among the writings included in the religious text is a paganized version of Psalms 20:2-6. Here, then, we have a Bible passage, in its Aramaic translation, written in late Egyptian characters.

In 1967, Israeli archaeologists discovered at the ancient site of Arad an ostracon (pottery fragment) from shortly before 600 B.C., the time of Lehi. The text on the ostracon is written in a combination of Egyptian hieratic and Hebrew characters, but can be read entirely as Egyptian. Of the seventeen words in the text, ten are written in hieratic and seven in Hebrew. This discovery suggests that when Lehi's son Nephi spoke of writing in a language consisting of "the learning of the Jews and the language of the Egyptians," he may have used such a combination script. Two more examples of combination Egyptian-Hebrew scripts from the same time period were discovered in the northern Sinai peninsula during the late 1970s.

CONCLUSION

Though ridiculed for his claims about the nature of the original record from which he translated the Book of Mormon, Joseph Smith's story has found support during the last half of the twentieth century.[1] Ancient records were sometimes written on metallic plates, and some of the Hebrew and other Semitic texts were written using Egyptian characters, just like the Book of Mormon.

---

[1] For further information, including bibliography, see John A. Tvedtnes and Stephen D. Ricks, "Jewish and Other Semitic Texts Written in Egyptian Characters," *Journal of Book of Mormon Studies* 5/2, Fall 1996.

Chapter 4

HIDDEN RECORDS

THE BOOK OF MORMON AN ACCOUNT WRITTEN BY THE HAND OF MORMON UPON PLATES TAKEN FROM THE PLATES OF NEPHI Wherefore, it is an abridgment of the record of the people of Nephi, and also of the Lamanites--Written to the Lamanites, who are a remnant of the house of Israel; and also to Jew and Gentile--Written by way of commandment, and also by the spirit of prophecy and of revelation--Written and sealed up, and hid up unto the Lord, that they might not be destroyed--To come forth by the gift and power of God unto the interpretation thereof--Sealed by the hand of Moroni, and hid up unto the Lord, to come forth in due time by way of the Gentile. (Title Page of the Book of Mormon)

When the Book of Mormon was first published in 1830, it seemed rather an anomaly, despite its biblical tone. No one had ever heard of ancient books being written on metallic plates and hidden in stone boxes. But all that changed in the mid-twentieth century.

BURIED AND SEALED RECORDS

In 1945, several leather-bound volumes of Christian writings from the fifth century A.D. were found at Chenoboskion, Egypt, also known as Nag Hammadi. Their contents included books purportedly composed by some of the early apostles. Like the Book of Mormon, these books had been hidden away in the ground, buried in a large pottery jar.

Two years later, a larger set of documents was found

concealed in caves near the Dead Sea. Some of them had been placed inside fired clay pots. In all, fragments of approximately 800 separate scrolls were found. These Dead Sea Scrolls included multiple copies of all of the books of the Old Testament except Esther, along with many other ancient religious texts. The scrolls had been written 2000 years ago.

METAL RECORDS

One of the most important of the Dead Sea Scrolls is a document inscribed on a copper plate that had been rolled up and hidden away. But this is just one of many examples of ancient texts that, like the Book of Mormon, had been written on sheets of metal.

Since the 1930s, nearly a hundred ancient and medieval documents written on metal plates or leaves have been found in various parts of the world. The ones that interest us most are the metallic records from the ancient Near East, the original homeland of the Book of Mormon peoples.

Three copper tablets containing a temple inscription from ancient Adab and dating to the third millennium B.C., were found in Iraq. A copper plate with Sumerian writing from the same time period has also been found. A small gold plate with an Akkadian inscription from the twenty-fifth century B.C. was found at Djokha Umma, Iraq, and is housed in the Louvre in Paris, along with several other inscribed metal plates. A bronze tablet with a fourteenth-century B.C. Ugaritic inscription was found in Lower Galilee. Silver and lead plates with Hittite inscriptions were found in 1950 in the Beritz valley of Lebanon. Six bronze tablets written in pseudo-hieroglyphic and dating to 2000-1800 B.C. were found at the ancient Phoenician site of Byblos, in Lebanon.

Egyptian examples are also not lacking. the treaty between Ramses II, king of Egypt, and the Hittite king Hatusilis, drafted in 1287 B.C., was written on silver plates. A decree of king Ramses III (1198-1167 B.C.) was found written on silver and gold tablets.

Metal Records

Thin gold plates that appear to have remnants of hieroglyphic writing were found in Egypt in the tomb of king Menkhure, builder of the third pyramid at Giza (ca. 2800 B.C.). A gold leaf with hieroglyphic writing from 2000-1788 B.C. was found at Lisht. A set of thirteen metal plates from after the fourth century B.C. contain a chronicle written in Egyptian demotic script, a type of reformed Egyptian.

Some metallic records have also been discovered in Israel. A small silver scroll written in Greek and Coptic and dating to about A.D. 400 was discovered in Bethany in 1968. In 1980, archaeologists opened a seventh-century B.C. tomb adjacent to the Scottish Presbyterian church of St. Andrew in Jerusalem and discovered two small rolled-up strips of silver with a Hebrew inscription from the Bible (Numbers 6:24-26).

USE OF STONE BOXES

The ancient Assyrians wrote on metallic plates, often used as dedicatory plaques for temples and palaces. The Assyrian king Sargon II (722-705 B.C.) repeats throughout his annals that he kept records on plates of gold, silver, bronze, and lead. During excavations of his palace at Khorsabad, six small inscribed plates (gold, silver, bronze, tin, and lead, with one alabaster) were found in a stone box buried beneath the palace foundation. Two of the plates and the box were lost during the sinking of a ship on the Tigris River in Iraq on May 23, 1855. The four surviving plates, of gold, silver, bronze, and tin, were taken to France and are housed in the Louvre in Paris.

The storing of metallic records in stone boxes is also known from ancient Persia, where a number of examples have been found. In 1923 at Hamadan, Persia (now Iran), two small tablets, one silver and the other gold, were discovered. They bore inscriptions from king Darius I (521-485 B.C.) telling about the erection of palaces in the city. In 1938, two pairs of plates (one silver and one gold in each pair) were found in stone boxes placed in the foundation corners of Darius's palace at Persepolis.[1]

CONCLUSION

Although perceived as an anomaly and a fabrication by scholars of his day, recent discoveries have vindicated Joseph Smith's account of a record written on gold plates and buried in the earth in a stone box. Indeed, the practice now appears to have been common among the cultures from which the Book of Mormon peoples derived.

---

[1] For an in-depth discussion of this subject, see H. Curtis Wright, "Ancient Burials of Metal Documents in Stone Boxes," in John M. Lundquist and Stephen D. Ricks, editors, *By Study and Also by Faith* (Salt Lake: FARMS and Deseret, 1990), 273-334.

Chapter 5

WHO ARE THE "GENTILES"?

The Book of Mormon . . . an abridgment of the record of the people of Nephi, and also of the Lamanites—Written to the Lamanites, who are a remnant of the house of Israel; and also to Jew and Gentile. (Title Page of the Book of Mormon)

Most readers of the Bible and the Book of Mormon assume that the term "Gentiles" refers to non-Israelites. While this is sometimes so, the full truth is a bit more complex. A better understanding of how the word is used will enable us to better understand the scriptures, and will clarify the purpose of the Book of Mormon.

ORIGINS

The English word Gentile is related to or derived from the Latin *gens* (whence "genus") and the Greek *genos* (whence "genealogy," "genetic," etc.), both meaning "race, people." In this respect, it accurately reflects the biblical words which it translates, Old Testament Hebrew *góy* (plural *góyîm*) and New Testament Greek *ethnos* (whence "ethnic" and "ethnology"), both meaning "nation, race, people." It must be noted, however, that these words are not always translated as "Gentile" in the King James version (KJV) of the Bible; most often, they are, in fact, rendered "nation." Hence, in any discussion of the biblical term "Gentile," we must refer back to the original Hebrew or Greek text, even when it is rendered "nation."

It is often asserted that the "Gentiles" are descendants of

WHO ARE THE "GENTILES"?

Japheth, son of Noah.[1] It is true that the King James Bible employs the word "Gentiles" in describing Japheth's descendants in Genesis 10:5, where the Hebrew reads *gôyîm*. However, that same Hebrew word is translated as "nations" in the same chapter, when referring to the descendants of Ham (verse 20) and of Shem (verse 31) and of their father Noah (verse 32). It is also used in reference to the Egyptians (Genesis 15:13-14; Exodus 9:24), the Ishmaelites (Genesis 17:20; 22:13, 18), the people of Abimelech (Genesis 20:4), the Moabites (Deuteronomy 29:16, 18), the Amalekites (Numbers 24:20), and especially the Canaanites (Exodus 34:24; Leviticus 18:24, 28; 20:23; Deuteronomy 4:38; 7:1, 17, 22; 8:20; 9:1, 4, 5; 11:23; 12:2, 29, 30; 17:14; 18:9, 14; 19:1; 20:15; 31:3).

Clearly, the word *gôyîm* has wide application, referring to various peoples of the world. In later Judaism, it came to denote non-Jews and, because of this, "Gentiles" has come to be used in Latter-day Saint culture to refer to non-Israelites. However, it never had such a connotation originally, as we shall see. In fact, the term may be applied equally well to Israel, and is often so used in the Bible.

Abraham received the promise that he would become a "great nation (*gôy*)" (Genesis 12:2) and a "father of many nations (*gôyîm*)" (Genesis 17:4-6). Of his wife Sarah, it is written she "shall become nations" (*gôyîm*)" (Genesis 17:16; KJV adds "be *a mother* of nations," but this is not in the Hebrew original.) It is also written that all nations (*gôyîm*) were to be blessed through (or "in"—same word in Hebrew) Abraham's seed (Genesis 18:18; 22:18; 26:4). In one sense, this was fulfilled in the salvation brought through Jesus, himself of the seed of Abraham (see Galatians 3:14-16). However, one must consider that Abraham's seed has mixed with the nations of the world (see Abraham 2:9-11), to be a blessing for them, as we shall discuss below.

---

[1] See, for example, Edward J. Brandt, "Early Families of the Earth," *Ensign*, March, 1973, 17.

Origins

Isaac, Abraham's son, was also promised that all nations (*gôyîm*) of the earth would be blessed in his seed (Genesis 26:4). When his wife Rebekah was pregnant, it was said that there were two nations (*gôyîm*) in her womb (Genesis 25:23). These were Esau, father of the Edomites, and his twin brother Jacob, who is Israel.

Jacob was also promised that he would become a great nation (*gôy*) (Genesis 46:3), and this promise was repeated to his descendants, the Israelites (Numbers 14:12; Deuteronomy 9:14; 26:5), who were told to be a "holy nation (*gôy qādôš*)" (Exodus 19:6). Though it is said that Israel is not to be "reckoned among the nations (*gôyîm*)" (Numbers 23:9), nevertheless, Israel is called a nation (*gôy*) in Exodus 33:13 and Deuteronomy 28:36. Moreover, it is said that Israel was to be a greater nation (*gôy*) than the other nations (*gôyîm*) (Deuteronomy 4:6-8).

Jacob was told that a "nation (*gôy*)" and a "company of nations (*qᵉhal gôyîm*)" would come out of him (Genesis 35:11). This has reference to the nation of Judah and the confederacy of the "ten tribes" of Israel which broke away under Jeroboam after the death of Solomon. The ten tribes lived to the north of the land, and a portion of their territory in the extreme north, bordering on Phoenicia and Syria, was called Galilee. In Isaiah 9:1, it is termed "Galilee of the nations (*Galîl ha-gôyîm*)," in reference to the ten "nations" or tribes that lived in the region. This passage is cited in Matthew 4:15 as Greek *Galilaia tôn ethnôn*, which KJV renders "Galilee of the Gentiles."

The immediate fate of the ten tribes is well known. They were taken captive in 722 B.C. by the Assyrians, who deported large numbers of the Israelites to other parts of their empire. Many years later, the Jews (those of the kingdom of Judah) were exiled to Babylonia, where many remained even after some returned in the days of Ezra. (There were more Jews in Babylonia in Jesus' day then in Palestine.) Further dispersion of Jews took place following the two wars with Rome, ending in A.D. 70 and 135, when Jews were forbidden to enter Jerusalem.

Thus, Israel was dispersed to the four corners of the world, mingling with the "nations" of the earth. This, indeed, had been foreseen, and it is interesting to note that the Hebrew word *gôyim*, used in reference to the nations where Israel would be dispersed, is translated "heathen" in the KJV in some of the prophecies concerning the dispersion (see, for example, Leviticus 26:33, 38, 45; Deuteronomy 4:27). Elsewhere, in similar prophecies, the same word is translated "nations" (for example, Deuteronomy 28:65; 30:1). Ezekiel wrote that, in the last days, the two kingdoms of Israel and Judah would be joined and become "one nation" (*gôy*) in the land of Israel (Ezekiel 37:22).

THE GENTILES TODAY

Brigham Young taught that "Israel is dispersed among all the nations of the earth; the blood of Ephraim is mixed with the blood of all the earth. Abraham's seed is mingled with the rebellious seed through the whole world of mankind" (*Journal of Discourses* 16:75). He also declared that "the Elders who have arisen in this Church and Kingdom are actually of Israel" (*Journal of Discourses* 2:268). On another occasion, he indicated that "Joseph Smith was a pure Ephraimite" (*Journal of Discourses* 2:268).

Patriarchal blessings given today indicate clearly that many members of the restored Church are literal descendants of certain of the tribes of Israel, and particularly of Ephraim and Manasseh, sons of Joseph. This has made the "Mormons" a defined unit of Israel in these last days, as the Jews have been a defined unit because they have held so closely to their culture over the past two millennia.

For Jews, it seems presumptuous for "Mormons" to call themselves "Israelites" for, to the Jew, they are just more "Gentiles." But we have already established the fact that, often, the "Gentiles" are, in the Bible, Israelites. Moreover, there seems to be abundant evidence (see especially Isaiah 2:2-3; 5:26-30; 11:1-12; 66:19-21; Jeremiah 3:7-10; Micah 4:1-2; Zechariah 2:7-12) that the "Gentiles" of prophecy are merely Israelites who have lost their identity during their long dispersion among the nations we have commonly termed the "Gentiles." After all, the Lord made a distinction between those Israelites who would be gathered by fishers (as in a net, meaning as a group, such as the Jews) and those who would be gathered by hunters (in this case through the Church's proselyting program), in Jeremiah 16:13-16.

In his dedicatory prayer for the Kirtland Temple, D&C 109 (which was given by revelation), Joseph Smith referred to the Latter-day Saints as the "sons of Jacob" in verse 58. Then, in verse 60, he spoke of "us who are identified with the Gentiles." He prayed for the return of the Jews to their beloved Jerusalem (verses 61-64), then spoke of the Lamanites, also a remnant of Israel (verses 65-66). Finally, he spoke of "all the scattered remnants of Israel" (verse 67), which either sums up the preceding list or is meant to include those not already specifically mentioned, possibly referring to Nephite peoples of the Pacific or the "ten lost tribes."

THE GENTILES, EPHRAIMITES?

The Preface or Title Page of the Book of Mormon states that the record was "written to the Lamanites, who are a remnant of the house of Israel; and also to Jew and Gentile . . . Which is to show unto the remnant of the house of Israel what great things the Lord hath done for their fathers . . . And also to the convincing of the Jew and Gentile that Jesus is the Christ." Here we have the same tripartite listing we noted in D&C 109: (1) the Lamanites or "remnant of the house of Israel," (2) the Jews, and (3) the "Gentiles." Since the Book of Mormon is the record of descendants of Joseph, delivered to other descendants of Joseph in the last days, one might well wonder why its preface does not mention that tribe, when the Jews are singled out. The answer appears to be that the "Gentiles" mentioned in the Title Page are, in fact, descendants of Joseph.

Who Are the "Gentiles"?

The Book of Mormon is God's "word to the Gentile, that soon it may go to the Jew, of whom the Lamanites are a remnant" (D&C 19:20-27; see also 20:8-9). The fulness of the Gospel came to Joseph Smith, a "Gentile" who was nevertheless an Ephraimite, and it is to go "from the Gentiles unto the house of Israel" (D&C 14:10; see 86:11). In D&C 42:39, the Lord declared, "I will consecrate the riches of those who embrace my gospel among the Gentiles unto the poor of my people who are of the house of Israel."

THE FULNESS OF THE GENTILES

One might argue, on the basis of Zenos' allegory of the tame and wild olive trees (Jacob 5-6; see also 1 Nephi 10), that the "Gentiles" who join the Church are "grafted in" to the tree of Israel and become Israelites by adoption. While this is certainly true to some extent, it seems that many become Israelites because their ancestors intermarried with Israelites, just as Ephraim has been termed a "Gentile" because of intermarriage with other peoples.

In explaining the olive tree allegory, Nephi spoke of the "fulness of the Gentiles" (1 Nephi 15:13; see also 3 Nephi 16:4). This seems to relate to the "times of the Gentiles" encountered elsewhere in prophecies concerning the last days and mentioned below. To understand the term, we return to Genesis 48:19, where Jacob blessed Joseph's son Ephraim to become a "multitude of nations." The Hebrew text reads *mᵉlô' ha-gôyîm*, which literally means "fulness of the nations." This is an exact equivalent to the Book of Mormon term "fulness of the Gentiles." It has specific reference to Ephraim and his special blessing in preparing the restoration of the kingdom of Israel.

In D&C 45, Jesus, referring to statements he had made 1800 years previous to his Jewish disciples, spoke of "the restoration of the scattered Israel" who "shall be gathered again; but they shall remain until the times of the Gentiles be fulfilled" (see also D&C:9, 17, 24-25, 28-30). The "times of the Gentiles" refers to that time during which the gospel is to be preached to the "Gentiles" or non-Jewish Israel (that is, those Israelites whose ancestry must be determined by patriarchal blessings), specifically Ephraim. This is to be followed by the preaching of the Gospel to Judah or the Jews (D&C 18:6, 26-27; 88:84; 90:9; 107:6, 33-35, 97).

In another revelation, the Lord addressed the "people of my church," commanding them, "Send forth the elders of my church unto the nations which are afar off; unto the islands of the sea; send forth unto foreign lands; call upon all nations, first upon the Gentiles, and then upon the Jews . . . Let them, therefore, which are among the Gentiles flee unto Zion. And let them who be of Judah flee unto Jerusalem" (D&C 133:1, 8, 12-13).

Jesus made it clear that he was sent only to "the lost sheep of the house of Israel" (Matthew 15:24). In 3 Nephi 15-16, he indicated that this meant (1) the Jews, (2) the descendants of Joseph (the Nephites and Lamanites) and (3) the other tribes of Israel. In addition, he appeared to Joseph Smith in these last days, showing again that the latter was an Israelite (to whom also the keys of the "gathering of Israel" were committed - D&C 110:11). When Jesus first commissioned his disciples, he sent them also to the "lost sheep of the house of Israel," and forbade them to visit the "Gentiles" and the Samaritans (Matthew 28:19), though the latter group were partly Israelite, being a mixture of peoples, as the "Gentiles" were also a mixture. On the day of ascension, however, Jesus told his disciples to go into all the world and to make disciples of "every nation" (Matthew 28:19), here using the same word translated "Gentiles" in Matthew 10:5.

Whereas in our day the Gospel is first for the Gentiles, then for the Jews, following Jesus' instructions, the opposite was true in the days of the early apostles (Romans 2:9-14). Paul followed this practice, going first to the Jewish synagogues wherever he traveled and turning to the Gentiles only after being rejected by the Jews (see Acts 13:14-16, 42, 46-50; 18:4-8;[2]

---

[2] Acts 18:4 uses "Greeks" rather than "nations" in the original.

28:23-29). Paul noted that he was sent to the "Gentiles" (Acts 9:15; Romans 11:13; 1 Timothy 2:7), but this may merely mean the "nations" in general.

We know that it was prophesied that the Gospel would be taken from the Jews and given to another "nation" (Matthew 21:42-43; Romans 9:30-33). Some have maintained that this meant it would go to the non-Israelites of Christ's time. But it may mean the Ephraimites, through Joseph Smith. As long as the Church still existed and was recognized by the Lord in the early days after Christ's ministry, it was directed through Jewish apostles, never the Greek proselytes. It was not until Joseph Smith's time (he being ordained to the priesthood by three Jewish apostles, Peter, James, and John) that the Church was "given to another nation."

CONCLUSION

The view that the Gospel cannot be taught to the Jews until it has been presented to all the other peoples of the earth may be incorrect, since the "Gentiles" to whom the Gospel is to go are those of Israel, particularly of Ephraim, the "fulness of the Gentiles." The specific responsibility given to the twelve apostles of our day is to seek out those of Israel (D&C 18:26-27; 107:33-35).

The order in which the Gospel is to be preached is given in D&C 90:9-10 as "unto the Gentiles first, and then, behold, and lo, they shall turn unto the Jews. And then cometh the day when the arm of the Lord shall be revealed in power in convincing the nations, the heathen nations, the house of Joseph, of the gospel of their salvation." It would appear that the teaching of the Gospel in these last days would then be (1) to the descendants of Ephraim (the "Gentiles"), (2) to the Jews, and (3) to the heathens, including the "house of Joseph," perhaps meaning the Lamanites. Again, these are the same groupings named in the Title Page of the Book of Mormon.

Chapter 6

CONTENTS OF THE 116 LOST PAGES AND THE LARGE PLATES

Now, behold, I say unto you, that because you delivered up those writings which you had power given unto you to translate by the means of the Urim and Thummim, into the hands of a wicked man, you have lost them. (D&C 10:1)

Latter-day Saints are generally aware of the loss of the first 116 pages translated from Mormon's abridgement. Martin Harris, under pressure from his wife to demonstrate that he was not wasting his time and money helping Joseph Smith, begged the prophet to loan him the sheets on which the English translation had been written. Martin lost the sheets and the Lord withdrew from Joseph the plates for a time. When, at length, the angel Moroni returned them, the Lord instructed that the portion already translated should not be redone, for those who had taken the handwritten sheets planned to alter their content in an attempt to discredit the work.

In place of the lost material, Joseph was to translate from another set of plates—often called the "small plates"—that had been prepared by Nephi and passed down to the time of King Benjamin. This translation comprises the earliest portion of our present Book of Mormon, from 1 Nephi through Words of Mormon. The story of the loss of the 116 pages is found in sections 3 and 10 of the Doctrine and Covenants.

Nephi explained that he had prepared two sets of plates. The larger set contained "a full account of the history of my people," including "an account of the reign of the kings, and the wars and contentions of my people." The smaller set of plates comprised "an account engraven of the ministry of my people" (1 Nephi 9:2-4; see also 1 Nephi 19:1-6; 2 Nephi 5:30-33).

The small plates were passed to Nephi's brother Jacob, with a charge that he and his descendants write on them only sacred things. Like Nephi, Jacob and his descendant Jarom noted the difference in content of the small and large plates of Nephi (Jacob 1:2-4; 7:26; Jarom 1:14).

In translating the Book of Mormon, Joseph Smith never worked with the large plates of Nephi. Rather, he received from Moroni the abridgment of that earlier record prepared by Moroni's father, Mormon, along with the small plates, which Mormon had found and which he included with his abridgment (Words of Mormon 1:1-9).

THE BOOK OF LEHI

Joseph Smith included, in the first (1830) edition of the Book of Mormon, a preface in which he wrote about the loss of the 116 pages:

> I translated, by the gift and power of God, and caused to be written, one hundred and sixteen pages, the which I took from the Book of Lehi, which was an account abridged from the plates of Lehi, by the hand of Mormon; which said account, some persons or persons have stolen and kept from me, notwithstanding my utmost exertions to recover it again.

The Book of Lehi probably comprised only part—though perhaps the largest portion—of the contents of the lost pages, for the account in the book of Mosiah begins near the end of the reign of King Benjamin, about four and a half centuries after Lehi left Jerusalem. Mormon must have abridged other records that had been written during that interval.

HINTS FROM THE BOOK OF MORMON

Despite the loss of the 116 pages, our current Book of Mormon contains hints as to its contents. Brigham Young University professor S. Kent Brown has noted, for example, items in the writings of Nephi (1-2 Nephi) that seem to be abridged from the record of Lehi.[1]

Later portions of the Book of Mormon provide information that is not in the extant writings of Nephi. For example, Alma described to his son Helaman the device the Lord provided to guide Lehi's family during their travels through the wilderness and across the ocean:

> And now, my son, I have somewhat to say concerning the thing which our fathers call a ball, or director—or our fathers called it Liahona, which is, being interpreted, a compass; and the Lord prepared it. And behold, there cannot any man work after the manner of so curious a workmanship. And behold, it was prepared to show unto our fathers the course which they should travel in the wilderness. And it did work for them according to their faith in God; therefore, if they had faith to believe that God could cause that those spindles should point the way they should go, behold, it was done; therefore they had this miracle, and also many other miracles wrought by the power of God, day by

---

[1] See chapter 3, "Recovering the Missing Record of Lehi," in S. Kent Brown, *From Jerusalem to Zarahemla: Literary and Historical Studies of the Book of Mormon* (BYU Religious Studies Center, 1998). The chapter is a revised version of his "Lehi's Personal Record: Quest for a Missing Source," *BYU Studies* 24/1 (winter 1984): 9-42.

day. Nevertheless, because those miracles were
worked by small means it did show unto them
marvelous works. They were slothful, and forgot
to exercise their faith and diligence and then those
marvelous works ceased, and they did not progress
in their journey; Therefore, they tarried in the
wilderness, or did not travel a direct course, and
were afflicted with hunger and thirst, because of
their transgressions. (Alma 37:38-42)

Alma's explanation includes information not found in the record kept on the small plates, suggesting that he drew it from the large plates of Nephi, which may therefore have been in the 116 lost pages. For example, while Nephi refers to the device as a "ball" (1 Nephi 16:10, 16, 26-28, 30; 2 Nephi 5:12) or a "compass" (2 Nephi 5:12; 18:12, 21), the term "Liahona" is unique to Alma's account.

Another unique element in Alma's record is the idea that because Lehi's family "forgot to exercise their faith and diligence . . . they did not progress in their journey; therefore they tarried in the wilderness, or did not travel a direct course, and were afflicted with hunger and thirst" (Alma 37:41-42). Nephi indeed stresses that "the pointers which were in the ball . . . did work according to the faith and diligence and heed which we did give unto them" (1 Nephi 16:28). He further noted that "the ball . . . led us in the more fertile parts of the wilderness" (1 Nephi 16:16). But he never suggests, as does Alma, that their progress in traveling through the wilderness had been impeded or that it was their lack faith in the ball that led to hunger and thirst.[2] Alma probably drew this

---

[2] Nephi does note that he was able to "slay wild beasts" for food after his father had consulted the ball, but he never says, in the account on the small plates, that their hunger had resulted from not paying attention to the directions given by the ball. And while it is true Nephi noted that their progress across the ocean was impeded until he was able to consult "the compass" (1 Nephi 18:12-13, 21), Alma's wording suggests that "they did not progress in their journey . . . in the wilderness"

additional information from the large plates, and it may have been part of Mormon's abridgement of that record, the translation of which Martin Harris lost.

King Benjamin also seems to have relied on the large plates of Nephi for his account of the "ball or director," for he notes that Lehi's family "did not prosper nor progress in their journey, but were driven back, and incurred the displeasure of God upon them; and therefore they were smitten with famine and sore afflictions" (Mosiah 1:16-17).[3] The fact that both Benjamin and Alma used the same words--"progress in their journey"--to describe what happened to Lehi's group, and that these words are not found in Nephi's account on the small plates suggests that they were derived from a common source, the large plates, the source of the abridgement from which the 116 pages were later translated.

EARLY RELATIONS WITH THE LAMANITES

Following the death of Lehi in the New World, Nephi's brothers sought to kill him. To avoid that danger, Nephi took those who would follow him and "did journey in the wilderness for the space of many days," settling in a place they called Nephi (2 Nephi 5:1-8).

(Alma 37:41-42), thus referring to an earlier time when the family traveled in the desert. Alma does refer to the ocean crossing in Alma 37:44.

[3] Nephi refers to being "driven back" during the ocean crossing while he had been bound by his brothers and was unable to consult the compass (1 Nephi 18:13). While it is conceivable that King Benjamin was referring to this event, Nephi never mentions "famine" (the word used by Benjamin) in connection with that event. One could suggest that the "sore afflictions" and famine in Benjamin's version of the story refers to 1 Nephi 18:19, in which we read that "Jacob and Joseph also, being young, having need of much nourishment, were grieved because of the afflictions of their mother." But this may not have been a general lack of food for the group, only that Sariah's younger sons were not being properly nourished because of their mother's illness (1 Nephi 18:18), perhaps from seasickness due to the storm (1 Nephi 18:15). This may even suggest that one or both of them were still being nursed.

CONTENTS OF THE 116 LOST PAGES AND THE LARGE PLATES

Despite this geographical separation, the two peoples seem to have maintained some level of contact. By the fortieth year after the group's departure from Jerusalem, they were already engaged in armed conflict (2 Nephi 5:34). But the contacts seem to have gone beyond that level, for Jacob, Nephi's brother, was aware of both the Lamanite sub-tribes (Jacob 1:13-14) and suggested that the Nephites had "done greater iniquities than the Lamanites," whom he called "our brethren" (Jacob 2:35). He especially noted that the Lamanites were monogamous, whereas some Nephites had begun taking wives and concubines, and that the Lamanite "husbands love their wives, and their wives love their husbands; and their husbands and their wives love their children" (Jacob 3:3-7).

Jacob also noted "that many means were devised to reclaim and restore the Lamanites to the knowledge of the truth; but it all was vain, for they delighted in wars and bloodshed, and they had an eternal hatred against us, their brethren. And they sought by the power of their arms to destroy us continually" (Jacob 7:24; see also verse 26).

Jacob's son Enos prayed for the Lamanites (Enos 1:11) and also noted:

> The people of Nephi did seek diligently to restore the Lamanites unto the true faith in God. But our labors were vain; their hatred was fixed, and they were led by their evil nature that they became wild, and ferocious, and a blood-thirsty people, full of idolatry and filthiness; feeding upon beasts of prey; dwelling in tents, and wandering about in the wilderness with a short skin girdle about their loins and their heads shaven; and their skill was in the bow, and in the cimeter, and the ax. And many of them did eat nothing save it was raw meat; and they were continually seeking to destroy us . . . And I saw wars between the Nephites and Lamanites in the course of my days.

Early Relations with the Lamanites

(Enos 1:20, 24)

Enos's son Jarom also recorded details about the Lamanites:

> And they were scattered upon much of the face of the land, and the Lamanites also. And they were exceedingly more numerous than were they of the Nephites; and they loved murder and would drink the blood of beasts. And it came to pass that they came many times against us, the Nephites, to battle. But our kings and our leaders were mighty men in the faith of the Lord; and they taught the people the ways of the Lord; wherefore, we withstood the Lamanites and swept them away out of our lands, and began to fortify our cities, or whatsoever place of our inheritance . . . And thus being prepared to meet the Lamanites, they did not prosper against us. (Jarom 1:6-7, 9; see also verse 13)

Omni, another of Jacob's descendants, also wrote of the wars with the Lamanites, adding that during an especially "serious war . . . king Benjamin did drive them out of the land of Zarahemla" (Omni 1:2, 10, 23-24).

Statements such as these suggest that the earliest generations of Nephites were well acquainted with Lamanite culture and that they continued to have contact with them, both in missionary efforts and in acts of warfare initiated by the Lamanites. It is reasonable to assume that the 116 pages included even more detail about these matters than the small plates, particularly in view of the fact that Nephi himself intended that the large plates contain information about "the wars and contentions of my people" (1 Nephi 9:4; 19:4; Jacob 3:13), some of which he had foreseen in vision (1 Nephi 12:3; 2 Nephi 26:2).

The account contained in the 116 pages may also have

contained information that would clarify the question of whether Lehi's family encountered other people upon their arrival in the New World and whether the Lamanites may have merged with such people.[4]

THE HILL NORTH OF SHILOM

Mosiah 11:13, describing the construction efforts of King Noah in the land of Nephi, has passing reference to "the hill north of the land Shilom, which had been a resort for the children of Nephi at the time they fled out of the land." This undoubtedly relates to the flight of the first Mosiah and his people from the land of Nephi, described in Omni 1:12:

> Behold, I will speak unto you somewhat concerning Mosiah, who was made king over the land of Zarahemla; for behold, he being warned of the Lord that he should flee out of the land of Nephi, and as many as would hearken unto the voice of the Lord should also depart out of the land with him, into the wilderness--And it came to pass that he did according as the Lord had commanded him. And they departed out of the land into the wilderness, as many as would hearken unto the voice of the Lord; and they were led by many preachings and prophesyings. And they were admonished continually by the word of God; and they were led by the power of his arm, through the wilderness until they came down into the land which is called the land of Zarahemla.

The importance of this geographical note is stressed by the fact that a group of Nephites led by Zeniff later returned to the

---

[4] For a discussion, see John L. Sorenson, "When Lehi's Party Arrived in the Land, Did They Find Others There?" *Journal of Book of Mormon Studies* 1/1 (1992).

land of Lehi and settled there under Lamanite suzerainty, but, after suffering much oppression, they fled once again. We read that they traveled "around the land of Shilom," then "bent their course towards the land of Zarahemla, being led by Ammon and his brethren" (Mosiah 22:8, 11). Clearly, Shilom was on a direct line between Nephi and Zarahemla, and was the course taken by the earlier group led by Mosiah.

Not wanting the Lamanites to see their departure, the group led by Ammon did not take the direct route, but "did depart by night into the wilderness with their flocks and their herds, and they went round about the land of Shilom in the wilderness," then corrected their course after they were at a safe distance from the Lamanite city of Shemlon, which was near Shilom (Mosiah 11:12; 24:1; Alma 23:12).

One wonders how the hill north of Shilom served as "a resort" to Mosiah's group when they fled from the land of Nephi. It is likely that the answer would have been found in the 116 lost pages.

THE CITY AND LAND OF NEPHI

We have already noted that the city of Nephi was built in the time of the original Nephi and named after him (2 Nephi 5:8). We have also noted Mosiah's flight from the land of Nephi to the land of Zarahemla, where they merged with the people of Zarahemla (Omni 1:12-19). Two generations later, a group of Nephites led by one Zeniff decided to return to Nephi.

While the records of this time period always denominated it "the land of Nephi" (Omni 1:27; Mosiah 9:1, 14-15; 19:15, 19, 22, 24; 20:7; 21:21, 26; 23:35-38; 27:16), the city is sometimes called Nephi (Mosiah 20:3; 21:1, 12) and sometimes Lehi-Nephi (Mosiah 7:1-3, 21; 9:6, 8). It is possible that the Lamanites who had moved into the city following Mosiah's departure changed the name to Lehi, not wanting to commemorate the name of the hated Nephi. But the Nephites continued to call it Nephi, though they often merged the Lamanite and Nephite names in the form Lehi-Nephi.[5] The 116 pages may have described the Lamanite takeover of the city and the name change.

Zeniff readily convinced the Lamanite king to move his people out of the cities of Lehi-Nephi and to allow the newly-arrived Nephites to settle in their place (Mosiah 9:6-7). One might wonder why the Lamanites would so readily desert their houses and lands. The answer probably lies in the fact that they were still principally a nomadic people (Enos 1:20; Alma 22:28). They had evidently not kept the former Nephite cities in repair, for Zeniff's people were obligated "to build buildings, and to repair the walls of the city, yea, even the walls of the city of Lehi-Nephi, and the city of Shilom" (Mosiah 9:8).

THE EARLY NEPHITE KINGS

Nephi noted that, "Upon the other [large] plates should be engraven an account of the reign of the *kings*, and the wars and contentions of my people" (1 Nephi 9:4, emphasis added). Consequently, the writers of the small plates said very little about their kings, referring their readers to "the larger plates" which spoke of "the reigns of their kings" (Jacob 3:13). Jacob noted in passing the appointment of Nephi's successor, without naming him (Jacob 1:9, 15). He informs us that, in memory of Nephi, their first king (2 Nephi 5:18; 6:2), the people conferred the name Nephi on each of their kings (Jacob 1:10-11).

This practice was discontinued some time before the ascension of the first Mosiah to the throne (Omni 1:12). He and his son and grandson (Benjamin and Mosiah) were the last of the Nephite kings and all were known by their given names rather than the throne-name Nephi.

---

[5] After the arrival of the sons of Mosiah II to teach the Lamanites, the Nephite record never again uses the compound name Lehi-Nephi, but refers to the then-Lamanite capital by its original name, Nephi.

We do not know when the practice ceased, but there may be a clue in the wording of Mosiah 18:4, in which we read of the mission of Alma the elder:

> And it came to pass that as many as did believe him did go forth to a place which was called Mormon, having received its name from the king, being in the borders of the land having been infested, by times or at seasons, by wild beasts.

On the surface, one might suspect that it was King Noah, who reigned in Nephi in Alma's time, who had given the name Mormon to the site. But there is another possibility. In an unpublished paper, Charles Eads has suggested that the king from whom the place received its name was a man named Mormon and that he was one of the Nephite kings who reigned in the land of Nephi before the departure of Mosiah. Eads draws attention to the Nephite practice described in Alma 8:7:

> Now it was the custom of the people of Nephi to call their lands, and their cities, and their villages, yea, even all their small villages, after the name of him who first possessed them; and thus it was with the land of Ammonihah.

If Mormon was, indeed, the name of an early Nephite king, he would surely have been mentioned in the 116 lost pages.

TEACHINGS AND REVELATIONS OF LEHI AND NEPHI

Some of the teachings of Lehi and Nephi were recorded on the large plates. Nephi wrote:

> For I, Nephi, was constrained to speak unto them, according to his word; for I had spoken many things unto them, and also my father, before his death; many of which sayings are written upon

> mine other plates; for a more history part are
> written upon mine other plates. (2 Nephi 4:14)

S. Kent Brown has noted that one of the teachings of Lehi that is not mentioned until after that prophet's death was that his family should not engage in plural marriage (Jacob 3:5).[6] The precise words delivered to Lehi (see Jacob 2:34) are evidently the ones cited by Jacob in Jacob 2:23-33. Presumably, they were recorded on the large plates of Nephi and may have been included in Mormon's abridgement thereof and, consequently, in the 116 lost pages.

THE LAMANITE CURSE

In his account written on the small plates, Nephi recorded the curse that had come upon the Lamanites:

> And he had caused the cursing to come upon
> them, yea, even a sore cursing, because of their
> iniquity. For behold, they had hardened their
> hearts against him, that they had become like unto
> a flint; wherefore, as they were white, and
> exceedingly fair and delightsome, that they might
> not be enticing unto my people the Lord God did
> cause a skin of blackness to come upon them. And
> thus saith the Lord God: I will cause that they
> shall be loathsome unto thy people, save they shall
> repent of their iniquities. And cursed shall be the
> seed of him that mixeth with their seed; for they
> shall be cursed even with the same cursing. And
> the Lord spake it, and it was done. (2 Nephi 5:21-
> 23)

---

[6] S. Kent Brown, *From Jerusalem to Zarahemla: Literary and Historical Studies of the Book of Mormon*, 43-44.

THE LAMANITE CURSE

Centuries later, Alma discussed this curse (Alma 3:6-17), but includes verbiage not found in Nephi's account:

> Thus the word of God is fulfilled, for these are the words which he said to Nephi: Behold, the Lamanites have I cursed, and I will set a mark on them that they and their seed may be separated from thee and thy seed, from this time henceforth and forever, except they repent of their wickedness and turn to me that I may have mercy upon them. And again: I will set a mark upon him that mingleth his seed with thy brethren, that they may be cursed also. And again: I will set a mark upon him that fighteth against thee and thy seed. And again, I say he that departeth from thee shall no more be called thy seed; and I will bless thee, and whomsoever shall be called thy seed, henceforth and forever; and these were the promises of the Lord unto Nephi and to his seed. (Alma 3:14-17)

Because Alma cites precise words of the Lord to Nephi that are not found in the account on the small plates, it seems evident that he must be reporting what was found on the large plates. Again, assuming that Mormon included some of those words in his abridgement, they may have been lost with the 116 pages.

THE PROMISE OF PROSPERITY

The Lord promised Lehi and Nephi that their descendants would prosper in the land if they kept his commandments, but that they would be cut off if they disobeyed him (1 Nephi 2:20; 4:14; 2 Nephi 1:9, 20; 4:4). Subsequent generations frequently cited this promise (Jarom 1:9; Omni 1:6; Mosiah 1:7; 2:22, 31; Alma 9:13; 36:30; 37:13; 38:1; 48:25). The Lord's precise words are recited twice on the small plates: "Inasmuch as ye shall keep my commandments ye shall prosper in the land; but inasmuch as ye will not keep my commandments ye shall be cut off from my presence" (2 Nephi 1:20; 2 Nephi 4:4).[7]

But the words of the promise "which he [God] spake unto Lehi" (Alma 50:19) are recorded differently in Alma 50:20: "Blessed art thou and thy children; and they shall be blessed, inasmuch as they shall keep my commandments they shall prosper in the land. But remember, inasmuch as they will not keep my commandments they shall be cut off from the presence of the Lord." Presumably, this verbiage was drawn from the large plates, and hence may have appeared in the lost 116 pages.

NEPHITE RULES OF BATTLE

In the time of Alma and Moroni, the Lamanites attacked the Nephites, who fought hard "for their homes and their liberties, their wives and their children, and their all, yea, for their rites of worship and their church" (Alma 43:45).

> And they were doing that which they felt was the duty which they owed to their God; for the Lord had said unto them, and also unto their fathers, that: Inasmuch as ye are not guilty of the first offense, neither the second, ye shall not suffer yourselves to be slain by the hands of your enemies. And again, the Lord has said that: Ye shall defend your families even unto bloodshed. Therefore for this cause were the Nephites contending with the Lamanites, to defend themselves, and their families, and their lands,

---

[7] The two passages are identical except that 2 Nephi 4:4 uses "and" where 2 Nephi 1:20 employs "but." The original Nephite record would not have reflected this difference, however, since the Hebrew conjunction *w-* can be translated either way (as in the King James Bible). In this case, the contrastive "but" is appropriate, though "and" is more literal.

their country, and their rights, and their religion. (Alma 43:46-47)

From D&C 98:32-44, we learn that this commandment had been given to "Nephi, and thy fathers, Joseph, and Jacob, and Isaac, and Abraham, and all mine ancient prophets and apostles . . . that they should not go out unto battle" unless commanded, and that they should thrice "lift up a standard of peace" to aggressors before they would be justified in taking action (see also verses 23-31). This would explain the reference to the first and second offenses in Alma 43:46.

Though the Lord told Joseph Smith that Nephi had received this commandment, it is nowhere recorded in 1-2 Nephi. The account of the Lord's words in Alma must therefore have been drawn from the large plates of Nephi translated as part of the 116 pages lost.

OTHER POSSIBLE EXAMPLES

Near the end of his ministry, Alma blessed his son Helaman and pronounced a curse on the land.

> And he said: Thus saith the Lord God—Cursed shall be the land, yea, this land, unto every nation, kindred, tongue, and people, unto destruction, which do wickedly, when they are fully ripe; and as I have said so shall it be; for this is the cursing and the blessing of God upon the land, for the Lord cannot look upon sin with the least degree of allowance. (Alma 45:16)

While it is possible that Alma was reporting the Lord's words to him, it is also possible that he was citing an earlier divine declaration. Certainly the concept was known to both Lehi and Nephi. While blessing his children, Lehi declared,

> Wherefore, this land is consecrated unto him

> whom he shall bring. And if it so be that they shall serve him according to the commandments which he hath given, it shall be a land of liberty unto them; wherefore, they shall never be brought down into captivity; if so, it shall be because of iniquity; for if iniquity shall abound cursed shall be the land for their sakes, but unto the righteous it shall be blessed forever. (2 Nephi 1:7)

Two of Lehi's sons, Nephi (1 Nephi 17:38) and Jacob (Jacob 2:29; 3:3) expressed the same thought, and the Lord said something similar to Jacob's son Enos (Enos 1:10). None of these is worded the same as Alma's quote of the Lord. If Alma was citing an earlier revelation, he may have read it on the large plates of Nephi. During an earlier discourse, Alma cited another revelation that may have come from the same source:

> For behold, the Lord hath said: I will not succor my people in the day of their transgression; but I will hedge up their ways that they prosper not; and their doings shall be as a stumbling block before them. (Mosiah 7:29)

CONCLUSION

From various passages found throughout later Book of Mormon accounts, especially concerning the life of Lehi and his immediate family, we can glean a few insights into the contents of the large plates of Nephi. Some, if not all, of these elements, likely made it into Mormon's abridgement of the large plates and were part of Joseph Smith's translation of the 116 pages lost when he loaned them to Martin Harris.

Chapter 7

"THAT WHICH YOU HAVE RETAINED"

And now, because the account which is engraven upon the plates of Nephi is more particular concerning the things which, in my wisdom, I would bring to the knowledge of the people in this account—Therefore, you shall translate the engravings which are on the plates of Nephi, down even till you come to the reign of king Benjamin, or until you come to that which you have translated, which you have retained. (D&C 10:40-41)

In the revelation known as D&C 10, received after Martin Harris lost the 116 pages of the Book of Mormon translation, the Lord distinguished between "the words which you have caused to be written, or which you have translated which have gone out of your hands" (D&C 10:10) and "that which you have translated, which you have retained" (D&C 10:41). Presumably, Joseph Smith kept some of the translation back and did not give it to Martin Harris. This would have included at least the first part of our current book of Mosiah.[1]

The same revelation may contain an important clue about how much of the dictated manuscript Joseph retained. In D&C 10:4, the Lord instructs him, "Do not run faster or labor more

---

[1] For a brief discussion, see John A. Tvedtnes, Review of Jerald and Sandra Tanner, *Covering Up the Black Hole in the Book of Mormon*, in Daniel C. Peterson (ed.), *Review of Books on The Book of Mormon* 3 (1991); Royal Skousen, "Critical Methodology and the Text of the Book of Mormon," *Review of Books on the Book of Mormon* 6/1 (1994), 139.

than you have strength and means provided to enable you to translate; but be diligent unto the end." This seems to be based on Mosiah 4:27, where we read, "And see that all these things are done in wisdom and order; for it is not requisite that a man should run faster than he has strength. And again, it is expedient that he should be diligent, that thereby he might win the prize; therefore, all things must be done in order."

The expression "run faster" is found in no other passages of scripture. This fact, coupled with the words "than you/he have/has strength" and "be diligent" suggest that the passage in Mosiah 4:17 is the source of the words in D&C 10:4. One could, of course, argue that the Lord was certainly able to reveal to Joseph Smith parts of the Book of Mormon that he had not yet seen. But it seems much more reasonable that he would refer to a passage with which the prophet was already familiar—a pattern found throughout the Doctrine & Covenants, which contains a wide variety of quotes from the Old and New Testaments and the Book of Mormon.[2]

D&C 10 cannot be read in isolation from D&C 3. While the latter notes Joseph's loss of the plates and the power to translate, the former speaks of the restoration of these privileges. Because both were received at a time of heavy involvement with the Book of Mormon translation, we should not be surprised to find that D&C 3:2 also quotes from the Nephite record: "For God doth not walk in crooked paths, neither doth he turn to the right hand nor to the left, neither doth he vary from that which he hath said, therefore his paths are straight, and his course is one eternal round."

Compare this passage with Alma 7:20:

> I perceive that it has been made known

---

[2] Revelations in the Doctrine and Covenants frequently quote from the Book of Mormon or the Bible, just as the New Testament often quotes Old Testament passages and the Book of Mormon cites the Bible.

"THAT WHICH YOU HAVE RETAINED"

unto you, by the testimony of his word, that he
cannot walk in crooked paths; neither doth he
vary from that which he hath said; neither hath he
a shadow of turning from the right to the left, or
from that which is right to that which is wrong;
therefore, his course is one eternal round.

Turning to the right hand or the left is an expression found in the Bible and would be insignificant by itself. But the expression "crooked paths" is unique to these two passages, which also share the phrase, "his course is one eternal round."[3]

This suggests that the portion of the manuscript that Joseph had retained may have gone as far as Alma 7 or Alma 8. Further support for this idea comes from the fact that there are other expressions found in D&C 3 and 10 that first appear in the book of Mosiah or the early part of Alma. These include "boast(s) in his/their own strength" (D&C 3:4; Mosiah 11:19) and "Satan has great hold upon their hearts" (D&C 10:20; Alma 8:9).[4] Neither expression is biblical.

CONCLUSION

We cannot know for sure how many pages Joseph held back, but the suggestion that he may have retained more than a handful is intriguing and merits consideration.

---

[3] The latter is also found in 1 Nephi 10:19, while in Alma 37:12 it is combined with the words "his paths are straight."

[4] To be sure, some of these expressions are also found in later passages of the Book of Mormon, but in this case they may have been borrowings from the Mosiah passages or at least have become idiomatic in the Nephite language.

Chapter 8

THE PROPHETS OF THE EXILE[1]

In the commencement of the first year of the reign of Zedekiah, king of Judah, (my father, Lehi, having dwelt at Jerusalem in all his days); and in that same year there came many prophets, prophesying unto the people that they must repent, or the great city Jerusalem must be destroyed. (1 Nephi 1:4)

Who are the prophets of the time of Lehi? Some of them are known to us from the Bible, and all of them follow in the footsteps of Isaiah, who prophesied a century earlier that the kingdom of Judah would be conquered by the Babylonians and many of its people deported to Babylon.

The most notable prophet of Zedekiah's time was Jeremiah, whose ministry began in 628 B.C., in the time of Josiah and lasted until 587 B.C., when the Babylonians laid waste to Jerusalem (Jeremiah 1:2-3). He is mentioned twice by Nephi (1 Nephi 5:13; 7:14). Among Jeremiah's early contemporaries were the prophets Zephaniah and Obadiah, whose books are also found in the Bible. In 605 B.C., when Jehoiakim was king of Judah, the Babylonian king Nebuchadrezzar (sometimes called Nebuchadnezzar) attacked the kingdom of Judah and took members of the royal family captive to Babylon, among them a young man named Daniel who later became a prophet and left us the book that bears his name (Daniel 1:1-6).

---

[1] This article was originally published in the *Orem Daily Journal*, November 29, 1998.

The Prophets of the Exile

Urijah, who also prophesied that the Babylonians would destroy Jerusalem. When king Jehoiakim sought to kill him, he fled into Egypt, but was brought back by the king's men and put to death (Jeremiah 26:20-23).

In 598 B.C. Nebuchadrezzer sent an army of foreigners to Jerusalem to slay Jehoiakim, who was succeeded by his son Jehoiachin, also called Jeconiah or Coniah (2 Kings 24:1-6). After a short time, the Babylonians came and took the new king and other members of the royal family and government officials captive to Babylon and appointed Zedekiah king of Judah (2 Kings 24:10-17; Jeremiah 24:1; 27:20).

Among the captives was a young priest named Ezekiel. Five years later, at the age of thirty, following requirements of the law of Moses (Numbers 4:34, 47), he entered into his priestly service and received a vision from God (Ezekiel 1:1-3). Another prophet who began his ministry around this time was Habakkuk, whose book is also known from the Bible.

In the days of Zedekiah, "the Lord God of their fathers sent to them by his messengers . . . but they mocked the messengers of God, and despised his words, and misused his prophets" (2 Chronicles 36:15-16). One of these prophets was Lehi, who went forth to warn the people that Jerusalem would be destroyed because of wickedness. But "they were angry with him . . . and they also sought his life, that they might take it away" (1 Nephi 1:18-20). As a result, the Lord told Lehi to leave his homeland and brought him to the New World.

Meanwhile, Jeremiah remained in Jerusalem and suffered great persecution. He wrote a letter to those who had been taken captive to Babylon (Jeremiah 29:1-2), instructing them to build houses, plant gardens, and live normal lives (Jeremiah 29:4-7). He also promised that after seventy years of captivity, God would restore them to their land (Jeremiah 29:10). In the letter, he warned the people of false prophets who had risen up in Babylon and condemned them by name. Significantly, he did not name Ezekiel who, though living in Babylonia, was also speaking out against the wickedness of the people in Jerusalem.

Ezekiel lived in the town of Tel-Abib, after which the modern Israeli city of Tel-Aviv is named (Ezekiel 3:15). Some scholars believe the name reflects Babylonian Tel-Abubi, "mound of the deluge," situated near Nippur, south of Babylon. Nippur is where the Jewish Murashu family lived. For some 150 years, the Murashus operated their banking/insurance/legal firm. The official records of "Murashu and Sons" were discovered during archaeological excavations on the site. Included were a large number of deeds, found in clay jars sealed with asphalt, in the pattern described in Jeremiah 32:8-14. Thus, archaeology has confirmed that the Jews in Babylonian exile followed Jeremiah's advice about carrying on normal lives.

Back in Jerusalem, things grew worse. In 587 B.C., the Babylonians destroyed Jerusalem and its temple and took most of its inhabitants captive (2 Kings 25:8-21). A Jewish official named Gedaliah became governor of the new Babylonian province, but he was soon assassinated by a man named Ishmael, a member of the Jewish royal family (Jeremiah 41). Fearing Babylonian reprisals for the death of Gedaliah, many of the Jews decided to flee to Egypt. Jeremiah tried to dissuade them, but they forced him and others to go with them (Jeremiah 41-43). Some of Jeremiah's last prophecies were recorded in the Egyptian city of Tahpenhes (Jeremiah 43:8; 44:1).

CONCLUSION

In the end, none of the prophets of the exile remained in Jerusalem. Urijah had been brought back from Egypt and slain. Ezekiel and Daniel were in Babylon. Jeremiah lived out his life in Egypt. Lehi brought his family and a few others to the New World. Jerusalem, whose inhabitants had rejected the prophets, lay desolate for the next few generations.

Chapter 9

THE ELDERS AT JERUSALEM IN THE DAYS OF LEHI

And he spake unto me concerning the elders of the Jews, he knowing that his master, Laban, had been out by night among them. (1 Nephi 4:22)

The Book of Mormon owes its existence to a chain of historical events that began when the prophet Lehi was compelled to leave Jerusalem in the early part of the sixth century B.C. and establish a colony in the New World. Lehi's life was sought by "those at Jerusalem" (1 Nephi 1:19-20; 17:44). Only one of these Jerusalemites, a man named Laban, is named in the Nephite record. He possessed a set of brass plates containing the scriptures and genealogical records that the Lord wanted Lehi to bring with him on his journey. Lehi sent his sons back to Jerusalem to retrieve the records (1 Nephi 3:1-9).

Laban was not just unwilling to part with the plates; he actively sought to slay Lehi's sons and stole the precious metals with which they hoped to purchase the plates (1 Nephi 3:10-14, 22-26). The young men fled and sought refuge in a cave (1 Nephi 3:27), where they discussed their options. Nephi, leader of the expedition, determined that the Lord would help them (1 Nephi 4:1-4). Leaving his brothers outside the walls of the city, he "crept towards the house of Laban" (1 Nephi 4:5-6). As he approached, he found Laban fallen to the ground and, following the direction of the Spirit, slew him with his own sword, then donned his armor (1 Nephi 4:7-19). He then went to retrieve the plates and encountered Laban's servant, who, in the dark, took him for his master (1 Nephi 4:20-21).

And he spake unto me concerning the elders of the

THE ELDERS AT JERUSALEM IN THE DAYS OF LEHI

Jews, he knowing that his master, Laban, had been out by night among them. And I spake unto him as if it had been Laban. And I also spake unto him that I should carry the engravings, which were upon the plates of brass, to my elder brethren, who were without the walls. And I also bade him that he should follow me. And he, supposing that I spake of the brethren of the church, and that I was truly that Laban whom I had slain, wherefore he did follow me. And he spake unto me many times concerning the elders of the Jews, as I went forth unto my brethren, who were without the walls. (1 Nephi 4:22-27)

From this account, it seems that Laban was one of "the elders of the Jews," who seem to be the same as "the brethren of the church." The English word "church" means "assembly" or "congregation." Psalm 107:32 speaks of the "assembly of the elders," paralleled in the same passage by the term "congregation of the people." Other Old Testament passages speak of "the elders of the congregation" (Leviticus 4:15; Judges 21:16) and the duty of the elders to address the assembly of the people (Jeremiah 26:17; Joel 1:14; 2:16).[1] In order to understand the role the elders played in Lehi's day, we must investigate the institution of the office of elder.

THE ELDERS OF ISRAEL

The Hebrew term rendered "elder" in English is *zāqēn*, deriving from the word for "beard" (*zāqān*), suggesting that one could not attain that rank until able to grow a beard. The first use of the term "elders" for Israelite officers appears in the days of

---

[1] Different Hebrew words are used in these passages, but all of them mean "assembly" or "congregation." For modern assemblies of elders, see D&C 108:4.

The Elders of Israel

Moses. Sent back by God to lead his people out of Egypt, Moses went first to the elders and thereafter worked closely with them (Exodus 3:16-18; 4:29; 12:21; 17:5-6; 19:7; Numbers 16:25; Deuteronomy 27:1).

Through Moses, the Lord established the duties of the elders, some of them ritual in nature. The elders, along with the priests, were to bring animals for sacrifices (Exodus 18:12; Leviticus 9:1-6). When the people sinned through ignorance, it was ordained that the elders should lay their hands on the bullock to be sacrificed as a sin offering (Leviticus 4:13-15). When the Lord placed the Israelites under covenant, he commanded that "your captains of your tribes, your elders, and your officers" assemble with the rest of the people (Deuteronomy 29:10; 31:28). The elders joined Moses in commanding the people to keep the law God had given them. Later, Moses delivered the law "unto the priests the sons of Levi . . . and unto all the elders of Israel," and commanded them that they should assemble the people once in seven years at the feast of tabernacles to rehearse to them the law (Deuteronomy 31:9-12).

The Lord commanded Moses to select from the body of elders seventy who were already known "to be the elders of the people, and officers over them," to assist him in the government of the people (Numbers 11:16-17). The Lord gave his Spirit to these men (Numbers 11:24-30) and they were allowed to accompany Moses and the priests to meet with the Lord atop the mountain where the law had been given (Exodus 24:1, 9-11).

Moses' successor, Joshua, also worked through the elders to govern the people (Joshua 7:6; 8:10). Following instructions from Moses (Deuteronomy 11:29; 27:1-26), Joshua assembled "all Israel, and their elders, and officers, and their judges" and placed them under covenant to obey the law of the Lord (Joshua 8:33). Near the end of his life, he twice "called for the elders of Israel, and for their heads, and for their judges, and for their officers" and gave them instructions to observe the law of God (Joshua 24:1; see also Joshua 23:2). Thereafter, it was "the elders that outlived Joshua" who governed the people (Joshua 24:31; Judges 2:7). It was these elders who selected military leaders in time of war (Judges 11:5-6, 11; 1 Samuel 4:3) and who made other decisions for the people (Judges 21:16).

While the elders occasionally assembled to determine matters of national concern, their normal activities took place within their own cities. Indeed, throughout Israelite history, it was the elders who governed the cities (1 Samuel 11:3; 16:4; Ezra 10:14).

The elders typically performed their duties at the city gate (Proverbs 31:23; Lamentations 5:14),[2] where they passed judgment on sinners (Deuteronomy 21:19-21; 22:13-21), judged various legal matters (Deuteronomy 25:7-9), and witnessed contracts (Ruth 4:1-11). When a murderer could not be identified, the elders of the city closest to the site of the crime were to take an oath and to perform a ceremony that absolved their people of responsibility (Deuteronomy 21:2-9).

The elders living in one of the six designated "cities of refuge" had additional responsibilities. They had to sit in the gate and pass judgment on refugees accused of killing another person. If the killing was accidental, they gave asylum (Joshua 20:4-5), but they delivered murderers up for punishment (Deuteronomy 19:11-12).

ELDERS AND KINGS

At the end of the second millennium B.C., the elders of Israel came to the prophet Samuel to ask that he select a king to rule the people (1 Samuel 8:4). Samuel reluctantly agreed and, guided by the Lord, anointed Saul (1 Samuel 9). The new king knew that he owed his position to the elders and, when confronted

---

[2] The earliest Biblical references to legal discussions in the gate, albeit referring to Canaanite cities, appear in Genesis 23:10, 18; 34:20, 24.

by Samuel with wrongdoing, asked that the prophet not dishonor him before the elders of the people (1 Samuel 15:30-31).

David, anointed by Samuel as Saul's successor (1 Samuel 16), curried favor with "the elders of Judah" by sending them spoil taken in battle (1 Samuel 30:26). Following the death of Saul, David was accepted by the "men of Judah" (probably the elders) as king (2 Samuel 2:4). Seven years later, Saul's uncle, Abner, persuaded the elders of Israel to make David king over the northern tribes as well (2 Samuel 3:17). "So all the elders of Israel came to the king to Hebron; and king David made a league with them in Hebron before the Lord: and they anointed David king over Israel" (2 Samuel 5:3; see also 1 Chronicles 11:3).

Royal dependence on the elders is suggested by the fact that Absalom, when he revolted against his father David, sought the support of the elders (2 Samuel 17:4). After a fierce civil war in which Absalom was killed, David was restored to kingship, but was disappointed that the elders of his own tribe were the last to accept him (2 Samuel 19:11-12).

Subsequent kings are also known to have worked through the city elders (1 Kings 21:8, 11; 2 Kings 10:1, 5), even consulting the elders about foreign affairs (1 Kings 20:7-8). The elders joined with the king in religious festivals and prayers, including covenant ceremonies (1 Kings 8:1-3; 2 Kings 23:1; 1 Chronicles 15:25; 2 Chronicles 5:4; Joel 1:14; 2:16). When troubles befell the people, the elders dressed in sackcloth and joined the king in mourning (1 Chronicles 21:16; Isaiah 37:2; Lamentations 2:10).

During the monarchy, the elders continued to address assemblies of the people (Jeremiah 16:17). When the first group of Jews was taken captive to Babylon, the prophet Jeremiah addressed a letter to its elders, priest, and prophets (Jeremiah 29:1). Upon returning from captivity, the elders became heavily involved in rebuilding the temple in Jerusalem (Ezra 5:5, 9; 6:7-8, 14; 10:8).

THE ELDERS AT JERUSALEM IN THE DAYS OF LEHI

LABAN AND THE ELDERS

Jerusalem was a royal city and, consequently, its elders were public officials in the service of the king. The fact that Laban had been meeting with the "elders of the Jews" on the night Nephi found him drunk in the street (1 Nephi 4:22) suggests that he was a member of the ruling body at Jerusalem, one of its chief elders. Hugh Nibley[3] has noted evidence that Laban was, in fact, a military leader as well. Nephi found him dressed in his military armor, with a beautiful sheathed sword on his person (1 Nephi 4:8-9, 19-21). He evidently commanded a group of fifty men—perhaps a personal guard—plus tens of thousands of others (1 Nephi 3:31-4:1).

Some Bible passages connect the elders with the "princes" (Judges 8:14; Lamentations 5:12; Ezra 10:8). The Hebrew term behind "princes" is *śārîm*, which refers to government officials, whether of royal ancestry or not (usually not). Though usually translated *prince(s)* in the King James Bible,[4] it is sometimes rendered *officer(s)* (1 Kings 9:23), *chief(s)*,[5] *governor(s)*,[6] *captain(s)*,[7]

---

[3] Hugh Nibley, *Lehi in the Desert, The World of the Jaredites, There Were Jaredites* (Salt Lake City: Deseret and FARMS, 1988), 97-98.

[4] 1 Samuel 18:30; 29:3-4, 9; 2 Samuel 3:38; 10:3; 1 Kings 20:14-15, 17, 19; 1 Chronicles 19:3; 23:2; 27:22; 2 Chronicles 12:6; 21:9; 22:8; 24:17, 23; 32:3, 31; Ezra 7:28; 8:20; Nehemiah 9:34; Psalms 105:22; 119:23, 161; 148:11; Proverbs 8:16; 28:2; Isaiah 1:23; 3:4; 9:6; 10:8; 19:11, 13; 23:8; 30:4; 31:9; 43:28; 49:7; Jeremiah 2:26; 8:1; 24:1, 8; 25:18-19; 26:10-12, 16, 21; 29:2; 32:32; 34:19, 21; 36:21; 37:15; 38:4, 17-18, 22; 39:3, 13; 50:35; 51:57, 59; 52:10; Lamentations 1:6; 5:12; Ezekiel 11:1; 17:12; 22:27; Daniel 1:7, 9-11, 18; 8:11, 25; 9:6; 10:20-21; 11:5; Hosea 3:4; 5:10; 7:3, 5, 16; 8:10; 9:15; Amos 2:3; Zephaniah 3:3.

[5] 1 Kings 14:27; 1 Chronicles 15:22; 35:9; 36:14; Ezra 8:29; 10:5; "chief... officers" in 2 Chronicles 8:10 and "principal" in Jeremiah 52:25.

[6] 1Kings 22:26; 2 Kings 23:8; 1 Chronicles 24:5; 2 Chronicles 18:25; 34:8.

[7] 1 Samuel 12:9; 14:50; 17:55; 18:13; 22:7; 26:5; 2 Samuel 2:8; 4:2; 10:16, 18; 18:1; 19:13; 24:2, 4; 1 Kings 1:19; 2:5, 32; 11:15, 21, 24; 15:20; 16:9, 16; 22:31-33; 2 Kings 1:9-11, 13-14; 4:13; 5:1; 8:21; 9:5; 11:4, 9, 15, 19; 25:18, 20,

or *ruler(s)*.⁸ Thus, when we read in Ezra 10:14 of the "rulers of all the congregation . . . and with them the elders of every city, and the judges thereof," we are to understand the elders to be rulers of the various cities, while the "rulers" or *śārîm* are general officers over the nation. The "rulers" (*śārîm*) are also listed with the elders in 2 Kings 10:1. Another passage (1 Chronicles 15:25) mentions "the elders of Israel, and the captains (*śārîm*) over thousands," suggesting that some of the *śārîm* were military leaders.

Hugh Nibley identified the "elders" with whom Laban met with the *śārîm* of the Bible who opposed the work of the prophet Jeremiah, Lehi's contemporary.⁹ Laban's unwillingness to let Lehi's sons have the records on the brass plates (1 Nephi 3:3:11-13, 22-25) reminds one of the "princes" of Judah who wanted to keep Jeremiah's writings from the people (Jeremiah 36:21-23). When Nephi, dressed in Laban's armor and speaking in his voice (perhaps easier to imitate because Laban had been drunk), met Zoram, the steward of Laban's treasury, he readily convinced him to bring the precious plates to his "elder brethren, who were without the walls" (1 Nephi 4:24). This meant going to one of the city gates, which is where the elders typically met, and explains why Zoram did not question the decision to go there.

23; 1 Chronicles 19:16, 18; 27:3, 5; 2 Chronicles 16:4; 17:14; 18:30-32; 23:1, 14, 20; 32:6; 33:11, 14; Nehemiah 2:9; Isaiah 3:3; Jeremiah 40:7, 13; 41:11, 13, 16; 42:1, 8; 43:4-5.

⁸ 2 Kings 10:11; Chronicles 21:2; 27:31; 2 Chronicles 29:20; Nehemiah 3:9, 12, 14-19; 7:2; 11:1; 12:32-32). In 1 Chronicles 28:1, the same Hebrew word, is translated "princes," "captains," and "stewards," with a different Hebrew word being rendered "officers." In 1 Chronicles 29:6, it is variously rendered "chief(s)," "princes," "captains," and "rulers."

⁹ Hugh Nibley, *Lehi in the Desert, The World of the Jaredites, There Were Jaredites*, 7-9, 98-99; *An Approach to the Book of Mormon* (3rd ed., Salt Lake City: Deseret and FARMS, 1988), 112-13.

THE ELDERS AT JERUSALEM IN THE DAYS OF LEHI

A CONSPIRACY OF THE PRINCES

The fact that Laban was meeting with the elders by night, in full dress armor (1 Nephi 4:19-22, 27) suggested to Nibley that this group may have been involved in a conspiracy of some sort.[10] Such a conspiracy may have been like the "secret combinations" among the Nephites, whose purpose was to "get gain" and political power by means of murder (Helaman 7:4; Mormon 8:40-41; Ether 8:13-23; 11:15; cf. Moses 5:31).

Thirty years before the birth of Christ, the Nephite secret society was responsible for the attempted assassination of one chief judge (Helaman 2:7-8) and the murder of two chief judges in succession (Helaman 6:16-24). Three decades later, the society, now called the "Gadianton robbers," tried to convince the people that the time had passed for the fulfillment of the prophecies concerning Christ (3 Nephi 1:5-7). Even after the signs of his birth were given, these robbers "did commit many murders" (3 Nephi 1:27). Though defeated for a time (3 Nephi 1:4), they managed to murder the chief judge (3 Nephi 7:1) and appoint their own king (3 Nephi 7:9). They murdered the prophets (3 Nephi 7:6) and "entered into a covenant to destroy the government" (3 Nephi 7:11). From Moroni's words in Ether 8:22-24, it seems that secret societies typically destroy governments. Among the Nephites, they twice took political control (Helaman 6:38-39; 3 Nephi 7:5).

If a similar secret society existed in Jerusalem in the time of Lehi, we can logically expect that it, too, would have engaged in some of these same activities.[11] It would have sought to place its

---

[10] Hugh Nibley, *Lehi in the Desert, The World of the Jaredites, There Were Jaredites*, 98.

[11] A letter purportedly written by Joseph Smith's mother, Lucy Mack Smith, to her sister in 1829 indicates that Jerusalem of Lehi's time was destroyed because of the work of a "secret society," which made its way to the New World and was had among the Nephites. The letter, however, was one of Mark Hoffman's forgeries.

own men in charge and would have resorted to murder if necessary. From Alma 37:30, we learn that it is typical of secret combinations to slay prophets.[12] Is it possible that the attempts to slay the prophets Jeremiah (Jeremiah 18:23) and Lehi (1 Nephi 1:18-2:1) resulted from such a conspiracy, designed to silence those who warned that Jerusalem would fall captive to Babylon?

There is, in fact, evidence from the Bible that there was such a secret combination in Jerusalem in Lehi's time. Ezekiel, a contemporary of Lehi, writing in the year 593 B.C.,[13] saw in vision a group of seventy elders in the temple, doing things "in the dark . . . for they say, The Lord seeth us not" (Ezekiel 8:11-12).[14] He was then shown in vision a group of 25 men living at Jerusalem. They were worshiping the sun, with their backs toward the temple (Ezekiel 8:16). When next he saw the group of 25, he was told that these "princes of the people" were the men responsible for the impending fall of Jerusalem (Ezekiel 11:1-13). Of particular note are the facts that (1) these men evidently thought their actions to be secret (Ezekiel 11:5), and (2) they had slain many people (Ezekiel 11:6; cf. Jeremiah 5:26-28; Ezekiel 7:23).

One of the men mentioned by Ezekiel was Jaazaniah, son of Azur (Ezekiel 11:1). The name of Jaazaniah, son of a Maachathite, is also known to us from a list of army captains (*sārîm*) who came to the Gedaliah at Mizpeh after the destruction of Jerusalem (2 Kings 25:23; Jeremiah 40:7-8). A clay seal dating from about the time of the Babylonian captivity and found during excavations at Mizpeh (Tel en-Nasbeh), about eight miles north of

---

[12] Since the devil was considered to be the founder of these conspiracies, this is not surprising (2 Nephi 9:9; 26:22).

[13] This was the sixth year of the captivity of Jehoiachin (Ezekiel 8:1).

[14] Ezekiel was then living in Babylonia, having been one of those carried away captive in 598/7 B.C.

Jerusalem, bears the inscription "Jaazaniah, servant of the king." All of these may refer to the same man.

Gedaliah is known from examples of his seal of office (reading "Gedaliah, who is over the House"), found in archaeological excavations at Mizpeh and Lachish (Tell ed-Duweir, about 28 miles southwest of Jerusalem). He was a Jew appointed by the Babylonians to govern Judah after the destruction of Jerusalem in 586 B.C.[15] Of the four captains (*śārîm*) who came to him at Mizpeh, one, Johanan son of Kareah (see also Jeremiah 43:2, 4-5), offered to slay one of the others, Ishmael son of Nethaniah, who had been commissioned by the Ammonite king to murder Gedaliah (Jeremiah 40:13-15). It is likely that Ishmael—himself "of the seed royal" (Jeremiah 41:1)—was seen as a claimant to the throne and hence a threat to the governor's position.

Gedaliah, however, believing the rumor to be untrue, did not order the death of Ishmael. Not long afterward, Ishmael and ten of "the princes of the king" slew the governor and a large number of others at Mizpeh. The murder was kept secret for a short while but, ultimately, Ishmael had to flee to Ammon (Jeremiah 41; 2 Kings 23:25). The parallel with the Book of Mormon account of the murder of three Nephite chief judges is striking (Helaman 6:17-19; 3 Nephi 7).

The men involved in the murder of Gedaliah were quite possibly the same ones called "princes," who, according to Ezekiel and Jeremiah, persecuted the Lord's prophets and even had one of

---

[15] Gedaliah, though one of the princes, was evidently a member of the pro-Babylonian party. It was his father, Ahikam, who had prevented Jeremiah's death at the hands of the other princes (Jeremiah 26:24). For the genealogy of Gedaliah's family, who served the kings of Judah before the arrival of the Babylonians, see Nili Fox, "Royal Officials and Court Families: A New Look at the ילדים (*yĕdādîm*) in 1 Kings 12," *Biblical Archaeologist* 54/4 (December 1996): 225-232.

them brought back from Egypt to be killed (Jeremiah 26:20-24).[16] Both Ezekiel (Ezekiel 34) and Jeremiah (Jeremiah 12:10-11, 21-22; 23:1-2; 25:34-36) referred to the leaders of Israel as wicked pastors or shepherds, who scattered or killed the sheep.

Ezekiel condemned the inhabitants of Jerusalem for shedding blood (Ezekiel 22:1-2, 9, 12-13). He was particularly harsh in his assessment of the princes: "Behold, the princes of Israel, every one were in thee to their power to shed blood" (Ezekiel 22:6). He wrote of the conspiracy of the prophets and priests (Ezekiel 22:25-26), then added, "Her princes in the midst thereof are like wolves ravening the prey, to shed blood, and to destroy souls, to get dishonest gain" (Ezekiel 22:27). The parallel with the description of the "secret combinations" in the Book of Mormon, organized to get gain by means of murder, is remarkable (Helaman 6:17-19; 7:4-5).

Jeremiah likewise spoke out against the princes and other leaders, saying that they were deceiving the people and Jerusalem by saying that there would be peace (Jeremiah 4:9-10). Like Ezekiel, he spoke of the murders committed in Jerusalem (Jeremiah 4:31) and of those who sought to take the life of Jerusalem (Jeremiah 4:30). The princes retaliated by accusing the prophet of "weakening the hands" of the people (Jeremiah 38:4). Interestingly, one of the Hebrew letters found at Lachish and written about 588 B.C., during the siege of Jerusalem (that is, during the time of Jeremiah and only a few short years after Lehi's departure) mentions a letter from "the princes" (*śārîm*) saying that the words of someone (perhaps a prophet) "weaken the hands."[17]

---

[16] See Lachish letter 3, written in Jeremiah's day, in which it is Coniah, son of Elnathan, commander (*śar*) of the army, rather than Elnathan, son of Achbor, who went into Egypt. An English translation of the text appears in James B. Pritchard, *Ancient Near Eastern Texts Relating to the Old Testament* (3rd ed., Princeton University Press, 1969), 322.

[17] Lachish letter 6. For an English translation of the text, see *ibid*.

The Elders at Jerusalem in the Days of Lehi

It would be an understatement to say that Jeremiah was not on good terms with the leaders of Judah. They conspired against him, saying, "Come, and let us devise devices against Jeremiah" (Jeremiah 18:18). At one point, the priests, prophets, and people wished to slay him and complained of the prophet before the assembly of princes, who, however, declared that he was not worthy of death (Jeremiah 26:7-16). Ironically, it was the princes who later imprisoned Jeremiah in the house of Jonathan the scribe (Jeremiah 37:15). The prophet expressed to King Zedekiah his fear that he would be left to perish there, so the king had him transferred to the palace prison (Jeremiah 37:20-21). But the princes besought the king to execute Jeremiah (Jeremiah 38:4).

The power of these *śārîm* is reflected in Zedekiah's admission that he could do nothing to stop them from taking the prophet, whom they then removed from the palace and placed in a pit full of mire (Jeremiah 38:5-6). The king subsequently allowed some of his loyal servants to deliver the prophet from the mire before he died (Jeremiah 38:7-13) and promised that he would not again turn him over to those who wished to kill him (Jeremiah 38:16). But he still feared the princes and requested that Jeremiah keep the content of their conversation secret from them (Jeremiah 38:24-27).

Jeremiah's major complaint against the princes was that they were leading the people astray in the matter of foreign policy. It was the Lord's intention to allow the Babylonians domination over the world. But the princes of Judah still clung to their old alliance with Egypt (Jeremiah 2:13-18, 36; 37:5-10; 42:7-19; 43:2; 44:12-14). Their belief that the Babylonian king, Nebuchadrezzar II, could not take their land was bolstered by a number of false prophets. Ezekiel spoke out against these false prophets (Ezekiel 13, especially verse 16) in terms very reminiscent of those of his contemporary, Jeremiah (Jeremiah 5:31; 6:13-14; 8:9-11; 14:14-15; 23:11-17, 21, 25-38; 27:1-18). One of Jeremiah's harshest critics was the false prophet Hananiah, son of Azur—perhaps the same Azur listed in Ezekiel 11:1 as father of the conspirator Jaazaniah (Jeremiah 28).

Nibley suggests that the power of the elders began in the time of Hezekiah (ca. 726-697 B.C.), a century earlier, when the king's attempts at reform "had been systematically frustrated by the *sarim*."[18] While this was undoubtedly the time when the princes rose to great political power in the kingdom of Judah, it is possible that the secret plots were going on long before that time.

POSSIBLE INVOLVEMENT OF THE AMMONITES

In the history of conspiracies against Israel, it is interesting to note the role played by the Ammonites and related peoples. For example, it was the Ammonite king who sent Ishmael to slay Gedaliah (Jeremiah 40:11, 14) and, after the deed had been accomplished, Ishmael fled to Ammon (Jeremiah 41:10, 15).[19]

It may be that the Ammonites had long been involved in secret plots formulated against Judah. They and their neighbors, the Moabites,[20] were the ones who hired Balaam to prophecy against Israel in the wilderness, and who would not allow Moses and his people to pass through their lands without a fight (Numbers 22-25).

At one point, we read that the Ammonites allied with the king of Maacah against Israel (2 Samuel 10:6-8; 2 Chronicles 18:6-7), reminding us that one of the princes who came

---

[18] Hugh Nibley, *An Approach to the Book of Mormon*, 97.

[19] The attack on Judah and the land of Ammon by Nebuchadnezzar's army seems to have been for a single cause. On his way south, the Babylonian king resorted to divination to decide whether to attack the Ammonite capital of Rabbath or the Judaean capital of Jerusalem (Ezekiel 21:20-22; Ezekiel's polemic against Ammon begins in verse 28).

[20] The Moabites and Ammonites were descendants of Lot, Abraham's nephew, (Genesis 19:36-38) and were excluded from the congregation of the Lord (Deuteronomy 23:3).

to Gedaliah at Mizpeh was Jaazaniah, son of a Maachathite (2 Kings 25:23; Jeremiah 40:8). The Maachathites and Geshurites were transjordanian neighbors of the Ammonites, with whom they are sometimes listed in Bible passages (Joshua 12:5-6; 13:10-13; Deuteronomy 3:13-16).

When Joash, king of Judah, was slain by a conspiracy of his own servants, the culprits were Zabad, son of an Ammonitess, and Jehoazabad, son of a Moabitess (2 Chronicles 24:25-27). Absalom, who revolted against his father David after slaying his half-brother Amnon, was the son of Maacah, daughter of Talmai, king of Geshur (2 Samuel 3:3; 1 Chronicles 3:2). He fled to his maternal grandfather after slaying Amnon (2 Samuel 13:37-38) and subsequently plotted the overthrow of his own father, after building up popular support by means of rhetoric and bribes (2 Samuel 15-18).

Rehoboam, son and successor of Solomon, was the son of an Ammonitess woman (1 Kings 14:21, 31; 2 Chronicles 12:13). It was he who, despising the counsel of older men (the elders who had served his father), followed the advice of his younger companions to reject some of the demands of the northern tribes. This led to the dissolution of the kingdom (1 Kings 12). Interestingly, he married one Maacah, daughter of his uncle Absalom, and their son Abijah reigned after him (2 Chronicles 11:20; 1 Kings 15:1-2, 13). The Ammonites thus had influence both in the palace and on the throne of Judah at various times.

Absalom's revolt against his father David is termed a "conspiracy" in 2 Samuel 15:12, 31. The Hebrew word is *qešer*, which derives from a root meaning "to encircle, to bind," and hence has reference to a group of plotters tied together by a common cause or perhaps even by oaths and penalties. Two of Judah's kings, Joash (2 Kings 12:20) and his son Amaziah (2 Kings 14:18-19; 2 Chronicles 25:27) were slain by such "conspiracies," the first of these led, as we have noted above, by an Ammonite. During that same time period, we read of "conspiracy" in the northern kingdom of Israel (2 Kings 15:15, 30), where a number of kings succeeded to the throne by murdering their predecessors.[21] This is reminiscent of the actions of the Jaredite secret combinations, as recorded in the Book of Mormon (Ether, especially chapters 8-9).

That there was a conspiracy in Jerusalem in the days of Lehi is confirmed by Jeremiah 9:2-8, where we read of the "secret lying conspiracy" (the term is also used in Jeremiah 11:9; see 12:6). The Lord told Jeremiah that "a conspiracy is found among the men of Judah, and among the inhabitants of Jerusalem" (Jeremiah 11:9). Ezekiel spoke of the same in these terms: "There is a conspiracy of [Jerusalem's false] prophets in the midst thereof . . . they have taken the treasure and precious things" (Ezekiel 22:25). Again, we are reminded that the goal of the conspirators among the Nephites was to murder and "get gain." The existence of a conspiracy is also suggested by the fact that Jeremiah's enemies said, "Come, and let us devise devices against Jeremiah" (Jeremiah 18:18).

Like Jeremiah and Ezekiel, Lehi and Nephi may have learned by revelation of the intrigues going on in Jerusalem in their day. Lehi spoke of the "abominations" in Jerusalem and prophesied its destruction (1 Nephi 1:13, 18-19). Nephi, noting that he had "dwelt at Jerusalem" also wrote of the "works of darkness" and "doings of abominations" he had observed there (2 Nephi 25:2, 6, 9-10). In connection with the wickedness at Jerusalem, he noted the rejection of the prophets, the imprisonment of Jeremiah, and the attempt to slay his own father, Lehi (1 Nephi 7:14).

THE SECRET COMBINATION AMONG THE NEPHITES

One is intrigued by the possibility that the secret

---

[21] For the conspiratorial actions of the princes of the kingdom of Israel, see Hosea 7:1-5; 9:15.

combination among the Nephites had its origin in Jerusalem.[22] Who, then, brought the organization to the New World? One possible answer is Laman and Lemuel or the sons of Ishmael, whose rebelliousness and attempts to slay Lehi and Nephi betray their true allegiance (1 Nephi 7:16-19; 16:37; 17:44; 2 Nephi 1:24; 5:3). Hugh Nibley hinted that Laman and Lemuel may have had such ties.[23] Nephi noted that they did not believe their father's prophecy of the destruction of Jerusalem "and they were like unto the Jews who were at Jerusalem, who sought to take away the life of my father" (1 Nephi 2:11-13; see also 1:20; 2:1; 7:14). He also recorded their declaration "that the people who were in the land of Jerusalem were a righteous people" (1 Nephi 17:22). This declaration is reminiscent of the words of Giddianhi, leader of the Gadianton band nearly six centuries later, who wrote that his "society and the works thereof I know to be good" (3 Nephi 3:9).

But the first appearance of the secret combination was among the Nephites, not the Lamanites (Helaman 1:9-12; 2:3-12). Since Nephi and those who followed him were righteous, if the introduction of the combination came from the Old World, it would more likely have been introduced by the Mulekites, who left Jerusalem not long after Lehi. At the time of Mosiah, descendants of the Mulekite colony merged with the Nephites (Omni 1:12-19). Nibley notes that the rebels in the Nephite nation often appear to be Mulekites, bearing Jaredite names.[24] They are apparently the "king-men" of the Book of Mormon, who sought to change the

---

[22] While it is true that the Jaredites had such a conspiratorial group, the knowledge of its exact nature, including its oaths, was kept from the Nephites even after the Jaredite record was translated by king Mosiah$_2$ (Alma 37:29).

[23] See his discussion of the Laban incident in Hugh Nibley, *Lehi in the Desert, The World of the Jaredites, There Were Jaredites*, 91-99.

[24] Ibid., 5:242-246. It was the Mulekites who made contact with the last of the Jaredites (Omni 1:20-22).

Nephite form of government (Alma 51, 60, 62).[25] This would be natural for a people who came to the New World in company with the last surviving son of king Zedekiah of Judah, named Mulek. The Hebrew word *melek* means "king" and the title "king-men" and "Mulekite" may be identical. In any event, the Book of Mormon record makes it clear that it was because of their "high birth" that they felt they should possess political power (Alma 51:8).

The king-men were evidently the same people who had supported Amalickiah in his bid to become king. From Alma 46:4, we learn that "they were the greater part of them the lower judges of the land, and they were seeking for power." In ancient Israel, these judges were, as we have noted earlier, the elders. Thus the predecessors to the king-men were probably the "princes" in Jerusalem who convinced king Zedekiah to ignore the words of the prophets, thus contributing to the destruction of the kingdom, just as the Gadianton band nearly led to the destruction of the Nephite nation (Helaman 2:13; 6:38-40; 3 Nephi 9:9).

CONCLUSION

We cannot be certain of the origin of the secret combinations among the Nephites and related groups. But there is clear evidence in the Bible that there was a similar secret conspiracy in Jerusalem in Lehi's day, whose influence may have spread to the New World. In both cases, the conspirators were nobles, elders who sought to increase their power among the people, and who rejected the message of the prophets. Thus, a system of leadership established for Israel in the days of Moses as an aid to government had become corrupted by the time of Lehi, with the elders or princes forcing their will on king and people alike.

---

[25] See the discussion in John A. Tvedtnes, "Book of Mormon Tribal Affiliation and Military Caste," in Stephen D. Ricks & William J. Hamblin (eds.), *Warfare in the Book of Mormon* (Salt Lake City: Deseret Book & FARMS, 1990), 296-326.

Chapter 10

WAS LEHI A CAVAVANEER?[1]

And it came to pass that the Lord commanded my father, even in a dream, that he should take his family and depart into the wilderness. And it came to pass that he was obedient unto the word of the Lord, wherefore he did as the Lord commanded him. And it came to pass that he departed into the wilderness. And he left his house, and the land of his inheritance, and his gold, and his silver, and his precious things, and took nothing with him, save it were his family, and provisions, and tents, and departed into the wilderness.
(1 Nephi 2:2-4)

Hugh Nibley has contributed perhaps more than any other single scholar to our understanding of the historical and cultural background of the Book of Mormon, especially in its Old World origins.[2] With regard to Lehi, whose departure from Jerusalem led to the colonization of the New World by Israelites, Nibley has shown a large number of cultural ties to the Near East of circa 600 BC.

---

[1] This article was issued as a FARMS preliminary report in 1984. It is published here for the first time.

[2] Of particular note are three of his books, *Lehi in the Desert* (originally published by Bookcraft in 1952), *An Approach to the Book of Mormon* (originally published by the LDS Church in 1957, with the second edition published by Deseret in 1964), and *Since Cumorah* (originally published by Deseret in1967). All of these have since been reissued in new editions: *An Approach to the Book of Mormon* (Salt Lake City: FARMS and Deseret, 1988); *Lehi in the Desert, The World of the Jaredites, There Were Jaredites* (Salt Lake City: FARMS and Deseret, 1988); *Since Cumorah* (Salt Lake City: FARMS and Deseret, 1988).

Was Lehi a Caravaneer?

The question of Lehi's profession before he left Jerusalem, however, is one subject Nibley explores that may, in fact, profit from some reexamination in light of more recent research. His thoughts on Lehi's profession are found in two of his books and read as follows:

> There is ample evidence in the Book of Mormon that Lehi was an expert on caravan travel, as one might expect. Consider a few general points. Upon receiving a warning dream, he is ready apparently at a moment's notice to take his whole 'family, and provisions, and tents' out into the wilderness. While he took absolutely nothing but the most necessary provisions with him (1 Nephi 2:4), he knew exactly what those provisions should be, and when he had to send back to the city to supply unanticipated wants, it was for records that he sent and not for any necessaries for the journey. This argues a high degree of preparation and knowledge in the man, as does the masterly way in which he established a base camp.[3]

Other facts cited as evidence that Lehi was a caravaneer will be noted below. We will examine all this evidence and explore some other possible explanations, then propose alternative professions in which Lehi might have worked that now appear more consistent with the record we have. At the outset, let us begin with the Book of Mormon passage cited by Nibley above, 1 Nephi 2:4:

> And it came to pass that he [Lehi] departed into the wilderness. And he left his house, and the

---

[3] Nibley, *An Approach to the Book of Mormon*, 77; *Lehi in the Desert, The World of the Jaredites, There Were Jaredites*, 36.

land of his inheritance, and his gold, and his silver, and his precious things, and took nothing with him, save it were his family, and provisions, and tents, and departed into the wilderness.

There are indications in this passage that Lehi was not prepared for a sudden journey into the wilderness. While most things are labeled (in true Hebraic style) "his . . . and his . . . ," ("his gold, and his silver, and his precious things") the pronoun's absence is striking when it comes to "provisions and tents," which are the very things one would expect a caravaneer to have on hand. Because the rest of the verse is so consistent in using the possessive pronoun, its absence here may mean that Lehi had to procure provisions and tents for the trip. If so, this would imply that he was not involved in the caravan trade.

If Lehi recorded all of the details of his trip into the desert, they do not appear to be included in the record on the small plates of Nephi from which Joseph Smith translated the account in 1 Nephi. For example, Nibley points out that Lehi probably had camels as pack animals, though these are not mentioned in the text.[4] If this detail is omitted, it is possible that others, such as the purchase of tents and supplies, are also missing from the record we now have.[5]

---

[4] Nibley, *Lehi in the Desert* 54-58.

[5] In a private communication on March 22, 1984, Lisa Hawkins commented as follows on an early draft of this chapter: "Wouldn't Lehi's purchase of those kinds of tents etc. have called attention to his plans to escape? Could that be a problem—would someone have tried to prevent them?" This would perhaps be true had Lehi tried to make such a purchase in Jerusalem. But it seems unlikely that Judah's capital city had a local tent shop. It is more plausible to suggest that tents would have to be purchased from those who manufactured and used them, such as a nomadic family living out in the steppe. Such people, assuming them to be like the Bedouin of today, would have taken very little interest in the political machinations of their sedentary neighbors (and perhaps a high interest in whatever Lehi might pay them). Consequently, the possibility of his plans being disclosed by those who sold him the tents is remote.

WAS LEHI A CARAVANEER?

The apparent swiftness with which Lehi left Jerusalem is cited as one of the strongest reasons for the idea that he was a caravaneer.[6] But the Book of Mormon does not specify how long it took him to prepare for his journey. Since the record is an abridgment, one cannot assume that Lehi left Jerusalem on a moment's notice simply because the passage omits details about his preparations.

THE EGYPTIAN LANGUAGE

The fact that Lehi is said to have known the Egyptian "language" (Mosiah 1:4) has been used to bolster the possibility that Lehi was a traveling merchant.[7] Nibley even suggests that the Book of Mormon plates were written in the Egyptian language,[8] but recent evidence suggests that the language of the Nephites was Hebrew, which they symbolized in writing by making use of Egyptian signs.[9] This was also the view of Sidney B. Sperry.[10]

---

[6] Besides Nibley, see S. Kent Brown, *From Jerusalem to Zarahemla: Literary and Historical Studies of the Book of Mormon* (Provo: BYU Religious Studies Center, 1998), 69, note 16.

[7] Nibley, *Lehi in the Desert*, 11-12; *Approach to the Book of Mormon*, 47.

[8] Nibley, *Lehi in the Desert*, 13-19.

[9] There are several different views found among Book of Mormon scholars concerning the nature of the Nephite language, both spoken and written. As indicated in Chapter 2, I have opted for the proposition that the Nephites spoke Hebrew and wrote Hebrew using a writing system partially derived from the Egyptian written language. For further study of this view, see John A. Tvedtnes "Linguistic Implications of the Tel Arad Ostraca," *Newsletter & Proceedings of the Society for Early Historic Archaeology* No. 127 (October 1971); John A. Tvedtnes, "The Hebrew Background of the Book of Mormon," in John L. Sorenson and Melvin J. Thorne (eds.), *Rediscovering the Book of Mormon* (Salt Lake City: Deseret & FARMS, 1991).

[10] Sidney B. Sperry, *Our Book of Mormon* (Salt Lake City: Bookcraft, 1950), Chapter 3.

Was Lehi a Caravaneer?

The use of Egyptian symbols to transliterate Hebrew words and vice versa, is known from sixth century B.C. texts discovered at Arad and Kadesh-Barnea.[11] The fact that these texts were used by local people shows that one did not have to be a traveling merchant in order to have some background in the Egyptian writing system and to use it as Lehi did. Indeed, the fact that Egyptian symbols are used as the sole representation of numerals in ninth- through sixth-century B.C. Hebrew texts from various locations is an indication of the fact that even non-travelers picked up information from the caravaneers and used it locally.[12]

Nibley suggested, "Lehi's main business was with Egypt, carried on both by land and sea.."[13] If this were so, however, Nephi, following Near Eastern custom, should have been engaged in the same profession as his father, and hence should have been acquainted with ships. So unacquainted was he, however, that his brothers mocked not only his project to construct a seagoing vessel, but his ability to sail it (1 Nephi 17:17).

A millennium before Lehi, the text of Ipuwer states that all foreigners knew the language of Egypt.[14] But this was not because all foreigners traveled to Egypt as merchants, but, more likely, because Egyptian merchants traveled far and wide. Thus, in Lehi's day, nearly a thousand years later, it was most likely that he picked up a knowledge of Egyptian without ever leaving home.

Another point mentioned by Nibley to show that Lehi was involved in foreign trade is that the name of the Phoenician

---

[11] For a discussion and bibliography, see John A. Tvedtnes and Stephen D. Ricks, "Jewish and Other Semitic Texts Written in Egyptian Characters," *Journal of Book of Mormon Studies* 5/2, Fall 1996.

[12] These weight numerals used in ancient Israel have been demonstrated to be of Egyptian origin. See the bibliography in my "Linguistic Implications of the Arad Ostraca."

[13] Nibley, *Approach to the Book of Mormon*, 87.

[14] Ibid., 86; *Lehi in the Desert*, 13.

port-city of Sidon appears in the Book of Mormon in both its Egyptian and Hebrew forms.[15] While the fact itself may be significant, we must not omit the possibility that it was the Mulekites and not the Nephites who brought the name to the New World.[16] Indeed, some LDS scholars have theorized that the Mulek colony came across the ocean in Phoenician ships.[17]

BEDOUIN LIFESTYLE

Many aspects of Lehi's sojourn in the wilderness are noted as possible evidence of his caravaneer experience. But the facts that have been cited are not necessarily evidence that Lehi was used to a nomadic lifestyle. Rather, they may simply be examples of his trust in the Lord.[18]

---

[15] The name of the river Sidon does not appear in the Book of Mormon until after the Nephites and Mulekites merged under the first Mosiah. The river was situated in former Mulekite territory, not in the lands first settled by the Nephites or Lamanites.

[16] The name of the river Sidon does not appear in the Book of Mormon until after the Nephites and Mulekites merged under the first Mosiah. The river was situated in former Mulekite territory, not in the lands first settled by the Nephites or Lamanites.

[17] See, for example, Ross T. Christensen, "The Phoenicians and the Ancient Civilizations of America," *Newsletter & Proceedings of the Society for Early Historic Archaeology*, No. 111 (January 13, 1969); Ross T. Christensen, "Did the Phoenicians Cross the Atlantic?" *Newsletter & Proceedings of the Society for Early Historic Archaeology*, No. 118 (January 12, 1970); Ross T. & Ruth R. Christensen, "Perspective on the Route of Mulek's Colony," *Newsletter & Proceedings of the Society for Early Historic Archaeology*, No. 131 (September 1972); Bernhart Johnson, "Israelite-Phoenician Commercial Relations & the Voyage of Mulek to the New World," *Newsletter & Proceedings of the Society for Early Historic Archaeology*, No. 140 (March 1977).

[18] Nibley is correct in saying that the word "wilderness" in 1 Nephi 8:4, 7 is desert and not jungle (*Lehi in the Desert*, 50). But it is not certain that the word "wilderness" in the Book of Mormon means "desert most of the time" (*Approach to the Book of Mormon*, 135-7). In 1 Nephi 18:26 (and apparently in Alma 58:13-14,

WAS LEHI A CARAVANEER?

For example, Nibley suggests that the Israelites typically maintained ties to the desert—and specifically to a nomadic way of life. But further study has indicated that this cannot be fully substantiated. Idioms such as "to your tents, O Israel" (2 Samuel 20:1; 1 Kings 12:16; 2 Chronicles 10:16) may be nothing more than that—just idiomatic, based on a reality that no longer existed in the Iron Age.

One item of evidence used to tie Israelites to the nomadic life is the example of Jonadab ben Rekhab, mistakenly said by Nibley to have been a contemporary of Lehi. His family left Jerusalem to take up a nomadic lifestyle.[19] But this man is named in 2 Kings 10:15 and lived in the ninth century BC, more than two centuries before Lehi's time.[20] There is no indication that Jonadab previously lived in Jerusalem. Indeed, Jeremiah 35 indicates that it was in Lehi's day that the Rechabites, Jonadab's descendants, first came to Jerusalem, probably because of the press of the Babylonian army then invading the land.[21]

In reference to 1 Nephi 2:15, Nibley wrote, "To an Arab, 'my father dwelt in a tent' says everything."[22] But to have said, "we

---

19-20), the word obviously refers to "forest." This may have been a transference of meaning based on the fact that both the forest encountered in the New World and the desert in the Old were relatively uninhabited. (Along similar lines, we find that the word meaning "horse" in some of the Yuman Indian languages is the native word for "deer," which was applied to the animal later introduced into the area.) Thus, most serious Book of Mormon scholars believe that the word "wilderness," as applied by the Book of Mormon to regions in the New World, refers to forest land.

[19] Nibley, *Approach to the Book of Mormon*, 68.

[20] This is based on a rather detailed book-length study on the Kenites, of whom the Rechabites are a part. As yet unpublished, it is entitled: John A. Tvedtnes, "The House of Jethro: A History of the Kenites."

[21] The Rechabites, descendants of Jethro via Rechab, Jonadab's ancestor, became priests in the temple in Jerusalem.

[22] Nibley, *Lehi in the Desert*, 51.

had camels for pack animals" would have said the same thing, yet Nephi never mentions this fact, as Nibley points out. Why, then, did Nephi mention the tents?

There are a number of references to the tents of Lehi and his party (1 Nephi 2:15; 3:1; 4:38; 5:7; 7:5, 21-22; 15:1; 16:32.). After recounting his explanation of the tree of life vision to his brethren, Nephi wrote, "Now, all these things were said and done as my father dwelt in a tent in the valley which he called Lemuel" (1 Nephi 16:6). This statement may imply the extraordinary circumstances under which Lehi and his family were living. In fact, "My father dwelt in a tent" may have been an indication that this was not normal! It could have been a striking and an unusual fact, a new life style for a man whose background was sedentary, perhaps even urban.

As further proof that Lehi was at home in the desert, Nibley pointed to the absence of any references to camels in the 1 Nephi account. This may be because, as he explains, "in the East the common words for travel are camel-words."[23] While this is true for medieval and modern Arabic, we cannot know if it is true for the Arabic of Lehi's time, of which there are no existing records.[24] Most scholars today see these "camel-words" as a secondary development in Arabic, which is notable for making verbs of nouns in a deliberate attempt to make the language more complex and hence a more useful tool for the composition of a special type of poetry.

Though Lehi's establishment of a "base camp" (1 Nephi 2:5) was described by Nibley as "masterly," the Book of Mormon text doesn't really have enough information in it to justify the adjective. In fact, very little is said about Lehi's camp aside from

---

[23] *Ibid.*, 56.

[24] There are numerous inscriptions in Epigraphic South Arabic from the Iron II period (tenth to sixth centuries B.C.), but this language, while related to Arabic, is a different branch of the Semitic language family, more closely related to Ethiopic.

locating it in a valley beside water and noting that Lehi lived in a tent. Moreover, the "base camp" was but a temporary location and the bulk of Lehi's time before departing for the New World (eight years) appears to have been spent in the wilderness after leaving the Valley of Lemuel.

After their arrival in the New World, Nephi's departure from Laman and Lemuel using tents is also cited as evidence of the nomadic pattern of his family (2 Nephi 5:5-7). It is noted further that the Lamanites continued to live in tents (Enos 20).[25] But this pattern may have been due to their eight years of living in tents on the Arabian peninsula. Indeed, shortly after Nephi's group separated from that of his elder brethren, the Nephites began planting crops, raising herds and constructing buildings, including a temple (2 Nephi 5:11-17)—hardly typical of a nomadic lifestyle.

Later, the Nephite pattern of settlement was to establish city-states, wherein cities would control the land surrounding them. This gave rise to the Book of Mormon practice of calling the city and the land surrounding it by the same name.[26] This was typical of Judah in the time of Lehi,[27] but not of nomadic peoples or of caravaneers. The people's wish to make Nephi their king (2 Nephi 5:18) is also typical of sedentary populations, not of nomads.[28]

As for the fact that the Lamanites continued to live in tents, we must remember what Nephi wrote of them. They "did

---

[25] Nibley, *Approach to the Book of Mormon*, 141-42.

[26] See John A. Tvedtnes, "Cities and Lands in the Book of Mormon," *Journal of Book of Mormon Studies* 4/2, Fall 1995.

[27] Nibley himself demonstrated this in *Approach to the Book of Mormon*, 100-102 and *Lehi in the Desert*, 6-7.

[28] Nomadic peoples, because they generally travel in small groups (due to the scarcity of water and pasturage), tend not to have kings. Indeed, the chroniclers of ancient Assyria took note of the rather peculiar fact that the first seventeen Assyrian kings had lived in tents. See James B. Pritchard, *The Ancient Near East in Texts, Relating to the Old Testament* (Princeton Univ., 1969), 564.

become an idle people, full of mischief and subtlety, and did seek in the wilderness for beasts of prey" (2 Nephi 5:24).[29] This laziness is reflected in the story of the building of the ship, in which Laman and Lemuel complained against Nephi "and were desirous that they might not labor" (1 Nephi 17:18). Had they been industrious like Nephi and his group, they, too, would probably have built more permanent homes and settled down.

A number of the things done by Lehi and his party while traveling through the wilderness are, as Nibley has shown, typical of Middle Eastern nomadic peoples. But some of these "Bedouin traits" turn out to be poor evidence of Lehi's traveling skills. For example, though it may be typically Bedouin to travel in the "more fertile parts of the wilderness" (1 Nephi 16:14), as Lehi did,[30] we read that it was the Lord who led them into these areas by means of the mysterious "ball" or Liahona (1 Nephi 16:16). If Lehi were an experienced desert caravaneer, why would he need divine assistance to locate these fertile areas?

Lehi's restricted use of fire in the wilderness is cited as another trait of desert Arabs, whose campfires might alert nearby enemies to their presence.[31] As a consequence of this, we read that they had to eat "raw meat in the wilderness" (1 Nephi 17:2). Again, however, it was the Lord who commanded them not to build fires (1 Nephi 17:12). Would this have been necessary if Lehi were already experienced in desert travel?

Some of the wording of Nephi's hymn of praise in 2 Nephi 4 is marked as evidence that his family had desert connections. In

---

[29] That Laman and Lemuel did not suddenly "become" lazy in the New World is evidenced in earlier statements by Nephi concerning their laziness. John W. Welch, in a private communication, has suggested that the words "did become an idle people" may have reference to the establishment of a cultural pattern rather than to any personal characteristics of the Lamanites.

[30] Nibley, *Lehi in the Desert*, 58-59.

[31] *Ibid.*, 63-64.

verse 32, Nephi prays "that I may walk in the path of the low valley, that I may be strict in the plain road"— thoughts expressed (as are those in verse 33) in Arabic greetings and blessings.[32] But these expressions could have resulted from the fact that Nephi spent eight years in the Arabian desert. They need not imply that he or his family had been there before. Moreover, the Bible is replete with examples of "desert speech" which became idiomatic after the Israelites settled in the land of Canaan.[33] Some of these idioms undoubtedly remained in the Hebrew of Lehi's day. Idioms are expressions whose original meaning is often forgotten. Thus, we could also conclude that Americans have close ties to the Arabian desert, for we not only employ a large number of Arabic words in our language (including sugar, cotton, hazard, albatross, and the like), but we also say "So long" as an idiomatic equivalent of "goodbye" (itself idiomatic, from "God abide with you"). "So long" is a corruption of the Arabic greeting salâm, picked up by our Crusader ancestors.

Attributing an Arabic origin to 2 Nephi 4:32, fails to note that the prayer cited above is immediately preceded by the words, "O Lord, wilt thou not shut the gates of thy righteousness before me." Gates, of course, are common to cities but not to deserts. So this verse provides just as much evidence for Nephi's urban origins as it does for a desert habitat.

In 2 Nephi 4:33, Nephi continues his hymn by saying, "O Lord, wilt thou encircle me around in the robe of thy righteousness!" Nibley suggests that this may be tied to the throwing of the desert sheikh's robe around those seeking protection.[34] Again, however, the expression may simply have been

---

[32] Nibley, *Approach to the Book of Mormon* 74-75; *Since Cumorah*, 157.

[33] For a study of this topic, with many examples from the Bible, see Morris S. Seale, *The Desert Bible: Nomadic Tribal Culture and Old Testament Interpretation* (London: Weidenfeld & Nicolson, 1974).

[34] Nibley, *Approach to the Book of Mormon*, 75; *Since Cumorah*, 157.

idiomatic to Lehi or its desert origins may have been obscured. In 1 Kings 19:19, we read that Elijah cast his mantle around Elisha who was, according to that text, a farmer. But the Bible stories of Elijah show that the prophet felt at home in the towns and villages of Israel.

In further support of the thesis that Lehi had ties with the desert, the names Ishmael, Lehi, Lemuel, Alma and Sam are said to be Arabic in origin.[35] However, in attempting to tie Lehi to Egypt, Nibley also says the name Sam is Egyptian.[36] Rather than tie the name Lehi to the Biblical site known as Ramat-Lehi (Judges 15:17), he has been connected with the well (Hebrew *be'ēr*) of Lehai-Ro'i.[37] That well plays an important role in the story of Sarah's Egyptian handmaiden, Hagar, mother of Ishmael, whose descendants settled the Hijazi region of western Arabia (Genesis 16:14). But Ishmael is also the name of a member of the royal family of Judah from the time of Lehi (Jeremiah 40). The name Alma is probably more correctly to be associated with the Aramaic name Alma found in Nahal Hever, as Nibley notes.[38] Hence, these names give but little support to the idea that Lehi and his family had ties to Arabia prior to his flight from Jerusalem. Furthermore, Lehi gave the names Jacob and Joseph to the two sons born to him in Arabia, and these are typical Hebrew names.[39]

With regard to the fact that Lehi named some of the sites he visited during his desert travels (see, for example, 1 Nephi 2:8; 9:1; 16:13), Nibley is certainly correct in noting that the naming of

---

[35] Nibley, *Approach to the Book of Mormon*, 75-76; *Lehi in the Desert*, 41-42.

[36] Nibley, *Approach to the Book of Mormon*, 286.

[37] *Ibid.*, 75, 290, 499 (note 25).

[38] Hugh Nibley, Review of Yigael Yadin, *Bar Kochba* in *BYU Studies* 14 (Autumn 1973), 120-121.

[39] While it is true that both names can be found among Arabs, they are borrowing from the Bible, not using native Arabic names.

places in the desert is an Arabic feature.[40] However, we find it in the Bible in reference to more sedentary peoples as well.[41] It is therefore not evidence of Lehi's prior ties with Arabia.[42]

MURMURING IN THE DESERT

The complaints and disputes that characterized life during Lehi's travels through the wilderness of Arabia (1 Nephi 2:11-13; 3:5, 28, 31; 5:2-3; 7:6-8, 16-19; 16:20-22, 35-38; 17:17-22) are cited as typical of Bedouin life, where the children frequently quarrel with their parents, including the sheikh.[43] However, it would be atypical of the Bedouin to go so far as to seek the life of the father and brother, as did Laman and Lemuel (1 Nephi 16:37).

Concerning the nature of these quarrels, Nibley wrote that Lehi's family complain "like all Arabs, against the terrible and dangerous deserts through which they pass, but they do not include ignorance of the desert among their hazards, though that would be their first and last objection to his wild project were Lehi nothing

---

[40] Nibley, *Approach to the Book of Mormon*, 81-82; *Lehi in the Desert*, 74-79.

[41] See, for example, Judges 1:26; 2:5; 6:24; 15:17, 19; 18:12, 29; 1 Samuel 23:28; 2 Samuel 5:9, 20; 6:2; 18:18; 1 Kings 9:13; 2 Kings 14:7; 1 Chronicles 11:7; 14:11.

[42] Philby's story (recounted in *Lehi in the Desert*, 75-76) of the Arab who gave the same name to three different hills (because that was the way it was done) is not a good example of the Arabic custom of naming desert sites. When an Arab does not have an answer to a question, he tends to give a stock one or to invent something This is because he cannot, in his culture, disappoint someone who wants an answer, so he must supply one, even if it is not true. This is a typical Arab trait. See John A. Tvedtnes, "Arab Logic" in *Languages & Linguistics Symposium, 1977* (Provo: Deseret Language & Linguistics Society and the BYU College of Humanities, in conjunction with the Language and Intercultural Research Center, 1977). Others who have discussed this trait are John Laffin, *The Arab Mind* (London: Cassell, 1975), 23, 81, 91-92, 146, 149; and Raphael Patai, *The Arab Mind* (New York: Charles Scribner's Sons, 1973), 49-59.

[43] Nibley, *Lehi in the Desert*, 68-70.

but a city Jew unacquainted with the wild and dangerous world of the waste places."[44]

> Lehi's family charged him with irresponsibility and lack of candor in leading them out into the wastes, and in view of what they had to suffer and what they left behind they were, from the common sense point of view, quite right. The decision to depart into the wilderness came suddenly to Lehi, by a dream. (1 Nephi 2:2.) In the same way ". . . the Lord commanded that I, Nephi, should return unto the land of Jerusalem, and bring down Ishmael and his family into the wilderness." (1 Nephi 7:2)[45]

It is true that Laman and Lemuel, along with the sons of Ishmael murmured "because of their sufferings and afflictions in the wilderness," but so, too, did Lehi (1 Nephi 16:20). And we discover in another passage that Laman and Lemuel objected to the long return trip to Jerusalem to obtain the brass plates because it was "a hard thing...required of them" (1 Nephi 3:5).[46] But this does not appear to be their principal complaint against their father.

Laman and Lemuel murmured because their father "was a visionary man" who made them leave "their precious things . . . because of the foolish imaginations of his heart . . . because they knew not the dealings of that God . . . neither did they believe that Jerusalem, that great city, could be destroyed" (1 Nephi 2:11-13). This complaint was even echoed at one point by their mother Sariah (1 Nephi 5:2). The elder sons believed that Lehi had led them away from Jerusalem "by the foolish imaginations of his

---

[44] *Ibid.*, 36; *Approach to the Book of Mormon*, 78.

[45] Nibley, *Approach to the Book of Mormon*, 72.

[46] They may have referred to their encounter with Laban rather than to the actual journey.

heart" (1 Nephi 17:20).

Nephi, on the other hand, "did not rebel" like his brothers because the Lord confirmed to him by means of visions and revelations the truth of his father's words. Furthermore, Sam believed Nephi (1 Nephi 2:16-17). For this reason, Laman and Lemuel sought to slay both Lehi and Nephi, saying, "Now, he says that the Lord has talked with him" (1 Nephi 16:37-38). To Nephi, his brethren were not rebelling against their father, but "against the Lord their God," who had commanded Lehi to leave his homeland (1 Nephi 16:22). Clearly, the real problem with Laman and Lemuel was their lack of faith in the principle of revelation, coupled with the fact that they regretted living in the wilderness, where they could no longer enjoy their possessions in the land of their inheritance (1 Nephi 17:21).[47]

The fact that Lehi's elder sons complained about his prophetic calling rather than about his ignorance of the desert does not mean that Lehi was acquainted with desert travel. If he was unacquainted with the desert and went only because the Lord sent him there, the only way they could get him to return home was to prove that the Lord did not send him. Therefore, Laman and Lemuel's best course of attack was to convince Lehi that the Lord did not speak to him.[48] If Lehi did not know desert life but was convinced that the Lord had sent him, he would not change his mind because of lack of expertise, so such arguments would not have had much effect.

More importantly, we must note that if Lehi was a caravaneer, then it was to be expected that his elder sons were already involved in their father's business. They would have been used to traveling. But they seemed to care nothing at all for such

---

[47] They also complained that Nephi, their younger brother, wanted to rule over them (see 1 Nephi 2:22; 16:38).

[48] They were not even impressed by the fact that an angel had appeared to them, as noted in 1 Nephi 7:10; 17:45.

ventures. In fact, it is clear they preferred to have remained at home.

Another objection to the theory that Lehi was involved in caravan trade lies in the evidence for the time of his departure from Jerusalem. Since there was water in the Wadi Laman at which he stopped, he must have left his home during the winter. One would expect that, since caravans in the Middle East do not travel during the rainy winter season, when muddy ground and flash floods present dangers and discomfort, Laman and Lemuel, had they been from a caravaneering family, would have objected to travel in the off-season. But they did not do so, indicating that such travel was not part of their lifestyle.

LEHI: FARMER OR MERCHANT?

Lehi's wealth (1 Nephi 3:16; 2:4) is cited as evidence that he must have been involved in caravan trade.[49] "One did not acquire 'exceeding great riches' by running a shop in Jerusalem or a farm in the suburbs," Nibley explains.[50]

It is certainly true that a farmer or a shopkeeper could not be expected to have been a wealthy man. Ironically, however, there is a lot of evidence that Lehi was, indeed, a farmer. Nibley notes that "from his sons Nephi and Jacob one gathers that Lehi must have been something of an expert in vine, olive and fig and honey culture."[51] But the parables told by these men (for example, Jacob 5) do not constitute the totality of our evidence for Lehi's agricultural expertise.

In describing the party's departure from their original campsite beside the River Laman, Nephi wrote, "And we did take seed of every kind that we might carry into the wilderness" (1

---

[49] Nibley, *Approach to the Book of Mormon*, 47.

[50] *Ibid.*, 59.

[51] *Ibid.*, 47.

Nephi 16:11). That the seed was not intended for food is noted by Nibley.[52] Indeed, it was loaded onto the ship and carried to the New World. In recounting this fact, Nephi tells us that they loaded "meat from the wilderness, and honey in abundance, and provisions according to that which the Lord had commanded us . . . and our seeds, and whatsoever thing we had brought with us" (1 Nephi 18:6). From whence were the seeds brought? In a later passage, describing the arrival in the New World, he tells us that they had been "brought from the land of Jerusalem" (1 Nephi 18:24).

The origin of the seeds is unclear. We do not read about them being taken from Jerusalem, only that they were carried through the wilderness and loaded onto the ship, then planted in the New World. At what point did Lehi bring the seeds from Jerusalem? Nephi and his three elder brethren departed from Jerusalem three times (once with Lehi, once with Zoram and the plates of Laban, and once with Ishmael and his family). There is evidence to indicate that they brought the seeds with them on the third trip.

Immediately after recounting the return of Lehi's sons from Jerusalem with the family of Ishmael, Nephi recorded, "And it came to pass that we had gathered together all manner of seeds of every kind, both of grain of every kind, and also of the seeds of fruit of every kind" (1 Nephi 8:1). The implication is that these were gathered at the time they returned to fetch Ishmael. Certainly, if the seeds were "from the land of Jerusalem," Nephi could not have meant that they gathered them in the wilderness of northern Arabia.

This is not consistent with the idea that Lehi knew exactly what provisions should be taken when he left, or the claim that he did not have to send back to Jerusalem "for any necessaries for the journey." It is also inconsistent with Nibley's statement that "this argues a high degree of preparation and knowledge in the man"

---

[52] Nibley, *Lehi in the Desert*, 61.

LEHI: FARMER OR MERCHANT?

regarding travel. Thus it further brings into doubt the conclusion that Lehi was a caravaneer.

The use of the seeds at the group's final destination provides further evidence that Lehi was from a sedentary culture. The description of their arrival in the New World is not that of a nomadic group, with the exception of the mention of "tents." Rather, it describes a group of people well-acquainted with agricultural pursuits:

> We did arrive at the promised land; and we went forth upon the land, and did pitch our tents; and we did call it the promised land. And it came to pass that we did begin to till the earth, and we began to plant seeds; yea, we did put all our seeds into the earth, which we had brought from the land of Jerusalem. And it came to pass that they did grow exceedingly; wherefore, we were blessed in abundance. And it came to pass that we did find upon the land of promise, as we journeyed in the wilderness, that there were beasts in the forests of every kind, both the cow and the ox, and the ass and the horse, and the goat and the wild goat, and all manner of wild animals, which were for the use of men. And we did find all manner of ore, both of gold, and of silver, and of copper. (1 Nephi 18:23-25; see also 2 Nephi 5:11)

It is true that Lehi was a wealthy man living in the "land of Jerusalem," but not in the city by that name.[53] Wherever Lehi lived

---

[53] *Ibid.*, 6-7; *Approach to the Book of Mormon*, 100-102. It was Nibley who first pointed out that one of the Amarna letters, dating from the fourteenth century B.C., mentioned the "land of Jerusalem," thus justifying the Book of Mormon's statement that Jesus would be born "at Jerusalem which is the land of our forefathers" (Alma 7:10), for Bethlehem would have been included in the land governed by the city of Jerusalem.

it appears that he had sufficient land to grow crops and plant trees of various sorts.

LEHI: METALWORKER?

But we must still deal with the question of how Lehi acquired his wealth. As noted above from Nibley's study, it is not reasonable to believe that Lehi could have accumulated wealth from agricultural pursuits. Caravaneering is Nibley's recourse as the only reasonable means by which the prophet could have become rich. But another possibility suggests itself. There is evidence to show that Lehi and his family were craftsmen and artisans—probably metalworkers.[54]

For example, we have Nephi's keen interest in the sword of Laban when he encounters him drunk on the streets (1 Nephi 4:9). Nephi's steel bow (1 Nephi 16:18) might also be an indication of his occupation. (His inability to repair the bow in the desert could be explained by either the lack of iron ore in the region or by the fact that the Lord had forbidden them to make fires, as noted in 1 Nephi 17:12.) And if Laban was somehow related to Lehi, as Nibley first suggested,[55] then this might be further evidence that the family was involved in metal-working, for Laban was the custodian of the brass plates containing the scriptures.

When the Lord told Nephi, in the land of Bountiful, to build a ship, he had to give detailed instructions on how to do it (1 Nephi 17:8; 18;1-4). But there is no record that Nephi had to ask how to prepare the metal tools with which he built the ship. Rather, he simply asked the Lord where he could find the "ore to

---

[54] In the Near East, sons typically enter into the same occupation as their fathers. Hence, the occupation pursued by Nephi can be reasonably expected to be that of his father as well.

[55] Nibley, *Lehi in the Desert*, 97. If Lehi and Laban are not related, then one is left to wonder why Lehi's genealogy was on the plates in Laban's posession. See 1 Nephi 5:14-16, where we also note that both were descendants of Joseph.

LEHI: METALWORKER?

molten, that I may make tools to construct the ship." He then constructed a bellows, lit a fire and fabricated the tools (1 Nephi 17:8-11, 16). Nephi stressed that he built the ship according to the way shown him by the Lord, but makes no similar statement regarding the smelting of ore and the making of the bellows and tools for building the ship (1 Nephi 18:1-2). Furthermore, while his brothers mocked his efforts to build a ship, they said not a (recorded) word about his abilities as a smith (1 Nephi 17:17).

Further evidence for Nephi's metal-working skills came after the group's arrival in the New World. He reported that they found "all manner of ore, both of gold, and of silver, and of copper" (1 Nephi 18:25). Nephi prepared the plates of ore from which the Book of Mormon ultimately developed, smelting the ore and forming the plates themselves.[56] He also manufactured "many swords" based on the pattern of the weapon he had taken from Laban in Jerusalem (2 Nephi 5:14), though we cannot be sure that these were metal swords. The full range of his talents is explained in the verses that follow this entry:

> And I did teach my people to build buildings, and to work in all manner of wood, and of iron, and of copper, and of brass, and of steel, and of gold, and of silver, and of precious ores, which were in great abundance. And I, Nephi, did build a temple . . . I, Nephi, did cause my people to be industrious, and to labor with their hands. (2 Nephi 5:15-17)

The descendants of Lehi's colony found "all manner of gold . . . and of silver, and of precious ore of every kind; and there were also curious workmen, who did work all kinds of ore and did refine it; and thus they did become rich" (Helaman 6:11; see Jacob 1:16; 2:12). One of Nephi's descendants, Moroni, complained that

---

[56] 1 Nephi 19:1-5; 2 Nephi 5:30-31. In 1 Nephi 1:17, he wrote of the "plates which I have made with mine own hands."

he was running out of "room upon the plates," and lamented, "and ore I have none" (Mormon 8:5). This implies that he knew what to do with the ore.

John W. Welch has suggested in private conversations with the author that the skepticism of Laman and Lemuel upon the discovery of the Liahona or compass outside Lehi's tent one morning (1 Nephi 16:10) may be yet another indication of Nephi's metalworking skills. Lehi's elder sons seem not to be impressed by this marvelous instrument. Welch has proposed that this may be because they thought the brass ball-like device had been manufactured by their brother in an attempt to convince them that they were doing the right thing by following their father into the wilderness. He notes that 1 Nephi 16:38 refers to Nephi's using "cunning crafts." If this suggestion is correct, it would explain why Alma was so insistent in his declaration that no human hand could have fabricated the Liahona (Alma 37:38-39).

If Lehi and his family were metalworkers (living on a plot of land sufficiently large to grow crops as well),[57] then the source of their wealth is readily explained. From Biblical passages (2 Kings 24:11-15; Jeremiah 24:1; 29:2), as well as the Assyrian and Babylonian documents of that era,[58] we have learned that craftsmen and smiths were considered in Lehi's day to belong to the upper class.

S. Kent Brown has suggested that Lehi's family were bondservants to one or more Arabian clans during their sojourn in

---

[57] While it is true that there are and have been nomadic smiths in the Near East, yet the evidence of some Biblical passages is that there were urbanized artisans of various types in the time of Lehi.

[58] For examples of texts showing the importance of smiths in ancient times, see James B. Pritchard, *The Ancient Near East in Texts, Relating to the Old Testament*, pp. 269, 292, 556. He cites two further texts in which smiths are listed with royalty (ibid., 293). Other artisans were likewise important. For example, the Babylonian texts that list the food allocations given to the captive king of Judah also list the food given to foreign carpenters who had been taken to Babylon (ibid., 308).

the desert.[59] But it seems unlikely that a group of caravaneers could have been of much use in Arabia unless they actually traveled elsewhere with the caravans—travel that is never suggested by the Book of Mormon. Moreover, any Arabians already involved in the caravan trade would likely have been much more skilled at it than Lehi. On the other hand, desert nomads could clearly have made use of the skills of metalworkers. Indeed, itinerant metalworkers have long been known in the Middle East.[60]

CONCLUSION

Having presented all the evidence then available to him, Nibley wrote, "Put all these things together, and you have a perfectly consistent and convincing picture of Lehi the merchant."[61] As noted above, however, the picture is not entirely consistent or convincing today. Of course, there is no question as to the importance of trade in Lehi's day, nor the relevance of comparing Bedouin lifestyle with accounts found in the Bible and the Book of Mormon. Indeed, these are important topics, and Hugh Nibley has not only led the discussion of Lehi's Old World ties, but has far outdistanced other scholars in the field. But even the inestimable value of his contributions to Book of Mormon studies cannot close the door on further research, as he himself has often said.

That research suggests that Lehi was, in fact, a sedentary resident of the land of Jerusalem, living on a plot of land large

---

[59] S. Kent Brown, "A Case for Lehi's Bondage in Arabia," *Journal of Book of Mormon Studies* 6/2 (fall 1997): 206-17. See also chapter 4, "Sojourn, Dwell, and Stay: Terms of Servitude," in his *From Jerusalem to Zarahemla: Literary and Historical Studies of the Book of Mormon*.

[60] See, for example, the discussion in William Foxwell Albright, *Archaeology & the Religion of Israel*, 96, 121, 197 (note 4), 198 (notes 5 and 7). This issue will be dealt with in greater detail in the author's forthcoming book, "The House of Jethro: A History of the Kenites."

[61] Nibley, *Approach to the Book of Mormon*, 47.

enough to enable him to grow food for his family, but also trained in metallurgy. It would have been from the latter that he made his living. His elder sons, Laman and Lemuel, were content to have the fine lifestyle afforded by their family's chosen profession, but they were not interested in working, nor did they believe in their father's prophetic calling. Nephi, on the other hand, followed in his father's footsteps both in terms of his occupational skills and his deep and abiding faith.

Chapter 11

JEREMIAH'S PROPHECIES OF JESUS CHRIST[1]

And now I would that ye should know, that even since the days of Abraham there have been many prophets that have testified these things; yea, behold, the prophet Zenos did testify boldly; for the which he was slain. And behold, also Zenock, and also Ezias, and also Isaiah, and Jeremiah, (Jeremiah being that same prophet who testified of the destruction of Jerusalem) and now we know that Jerusalem was destroyed according to the words of Jeremiah. O then why not the Son of God come, according to his prophecy? (Helaman 8:19-20)

The declaration in Helaman 8:19-20 suggests that several ancient prophets, including Jeremiah, had prophesied of the coming of Christ. But there are no specific prophecies of Christ in the biblical book of Jeremiah. To be sure, Jeremiah 31:31-34 speaks of a new covenant to be established, but it does not mention Christ, who brought that new covenant. How, then, do we explain Nephi's statement to the people in the city of Zarahemla that Jeremiah had prophesied of Christ.

THE HEBREW VERSION OF JEREMIAH

The Old Testament book of Jeremiah may seem rather straightforward at first, but it is an extremely complex work.

---

[1] Portions of this article were previously published in the *Orem Daily Journal*, November 22, 1998, under the title, "Jeremiah's Nonbiblical Writings."

Though many of the prophecies bear dates (expressed in terms of the year of the reigning monarch), they do not appear in chronological order in the book. Jeremiah is, after all, not an historical book, but a collection of prophecies with an interspersing of personal recollections by the prophet.

The earliest portions of Jeremiah are actually chapters 26 and 27, which were written in the beginning of the reign of king Jehoiakim, and chapter 35, written while he was yet king. Chapter 25 is next, being dated to the first year of the Babylonian king Nebuchadnezzar, and is closely followed by chapters 36, 45, and 46. And on it goes.

The lack of chronological order of the various revelations suggests that the book of Jeremiah is a later collection of separate documents, to which a preface was added (Jeremiah 1:1-3). Because it was not written as a single book, it is possible that some of Jeremiah's writings never made it into the collection.

THE SEPTUAGINT VERSION OF JEREMIAH

In the second or third century B.C., the books of the Old Testament were translated into Greek for the convenience of the Jewish community living in Alexandria, Egypt. This translation is known as the Septuagint. Its version of Jeremiah has the chapters in a different order than that found in the Hebrew text. Ironically, the Greek Jeremiah is an eighth shorter than the Hebrew, lacking a translation of some 2700 Hebrew words. Our modern English Bibles, being translated from the Hebrew, have the longer version and retain the chapter order found in the Hebrew text.

The Septuagint version of Jeremiah makes up for the missing portions by including two items not found in the Hebrew or English text. These are the writings of Baruch, Jeremiah's scribe (see Jeremiah 36:4) and a letter attributed to Jeremiah. Later versions of the Septuagint and the Latin Vulgate Bibles separated these portions off and they became part of the Apocrypha, books whose canonicity had been questioned. They were part of earlier editions of the King James Bible and are still included in Catholic Bibles.

WRITINGS OF JEREMIAH THAT TESTIFY OF CHRIST

Six copies of the book of Jeremiah were found among the Dead Sea Scrolls, along with a copy of the epistle of Jeremiah in Greek. One of the Jeremiah scrolls has a Hebrew version that follows the shorter Septuagint text. The Dead Sea Scrolls also include fragments of two texts about Jeremiah that are not in the Bible.

The idea that Jeremiah wrote more than is in the biblical book that bears his name is supported by early Christian tradition as well. We have, for example, the testimony of two second-century Church Fathers, Justin Martyr and Irenaeus. Writing of Christ's preaching to the dead while his body lay in the tomb, each of them attributed to Jeremiah a prophecy not found in the biblical account, in which the prophet wrote that the Lord would descend to preach salvation to the dead. Justin Martyr wrote:

> And again, from the sayings of the same Jeremiah these have been cut out [by the Jews]: "The Lord God remembered His dead people of Israel who lay in the graves; and He descended to preach to them His own salvation." (*Dialogue with Trypho* 72)[2]

Irenaeus cites the same passage in *Against Heresies* 4:22.[3]

The *Book of the Bee*, written in the Syriac language in the thirteenth century by the Nestorian bishop Solomon, has preserved

---

[2] Alexander Roberts and James Donaldson, eds., *Ante-Nicene Fathers* (orig. 1885; reprint Peabody, MA: Hendrickson, 1994), 1:235.

[3] *Ibid.*, 1:493-94. Irenaeus also cites the passage in *Against Heresies* 3:20.4, where he mistakenly attributes it to Isaiah. *Ibid.*, 1:451.

an earlier tradition of another non-biblical prophecy of Jeremiah, declaring that,

> This (prophet) during his life said to the Egyptians, "a child shall be born—that is the Messiah—of a virgin, and He shall be laid in a crib, and He will shake and cast down the idols." From that time and until Christ was born, the Egyptians used to set a virgin and a baby in a crib, and to worship him, because of what Jeremiah said to them, that He should be born in a crib. (*Book of the Bee* 32)[4]

The story is drawn from *The Lives of the Prophets* 2:8-10, a text that a number of scholars have suggested was originally written in Hebrew by Egyptian Jews during the lifetime of Jesus himself.[5]

Another Christian document known from medieval manuscripts in various languages is *4 Baruch*, which is subtitled "The Things Omitted from Jeremiah the Prophet." The Ethiopic version attributes the book to Jeremiah's scribe Baruch, but the Greek says it was written by Jeremiah. Chapter 9 has Jeremiah prophesying of the coming of Jesus Christ, the Son of God, of his selection of twelve apostles, of his death and resurrection after three days, and of his return in glory to the mount of Olives. According to the account, Jeremiah was stoned for this declaration.[6]

---

[4] Ernest A. Wallis Budge, *The Book of the Bee* (Oxford: Clarendon, 1886), 72.

[5] For an English translation of the Jeremiah passage, see James H. Charlesworth, *The Old Testament Pseudepigrapha* (Garden City: Doubleday, 1985), 2:387-88. Both *The Lives of the Prophets* and *Book of the Bee* include prophets of Christ attributed to other Old Testament prophets but not found in the Bible version of their books.

[6] *Ibid.*, 1:424-25.

CONCLUSION

The Book of Mormon confirms these earlier traditions about Jeremiah's prophecies of Christ, none of which were known in Joseph Smith's day. Nephi, the son of Helaman, spoke of "Jeremiah, (Jeremiah being that same prophet who testified of the destruction of Jerusalem) and now we know that Jerusalem was destroyed according to the words of Jeremiah. O then why not the Son of God come, according to his prophecy?" (Helaman 8:20).

According to 1 Nephi 5:13, the brass plates of Laban that Lehi's family brought from Jerusalem to the New World contained "many prophecies which have been spoken by the mouth of Jeremiah." Some of these prophecies may be represented in the various non-biblical texts we have discussed here.

Chapter 12

"HE SHALL PREPARE A WAY"

I will go and do the things which the Lord hath commanded, for I know that the Lord giveth no commandments unto the children of men, save he shall prepare a way for them that they may accomplish the thing which he commandeth them. (1 Nephi 3:7)

In 1 Nephi 3:7, Nephi expressed his unqualified trust in the Lord to help his servants accomplish his will. The Lord instructed Nephi's father, Lehi, to send his sons back to Jerusalem to procure the brass plates from Laban. It was not an easy task, but Nephi had faith that the Lord would prepare the way for them. He recorded, "When my father heard these words he was exceedingly glad, for he knew that I had been blessed of the Lord" (1 Nephi 3:8).

Lehi's sons were unsuccessful in their first attempt to obtain the plates. When Laman, Nephi's brother, was driven from Laban's house, the young men began contemplating a return trip to their father's camp in the wilderness (1 Nephi 3:11-14). But Nephi persuaded them to continue with their mission:

> I said unto them that: As the Lord liveth, and as we live, we will not go down unto our father in the wilderness until we have accomplished the thing which the Lord hath commanded us. Wherefore, let us be faithful in keeping the commandments of the Lord. (1 Nephi 3:15-16)

These words reflect those he uttered in the presence of his father before leaving for Jerusalem. Nephi proposed to his brothers that they should go to their father's house to gather up their wealth to purchase the plates from Laban. This would prove that they were not the thieves he accused them of being (1 Nephi 3:13).

Ironically, this gesture resulted in Laban's theft of Lehi's possessions and the sons were again driven away and hid out in a cave. Laman and Lemuel were angry at Nephi and Sam and beat them until an angel stopped them (1 Nephi 3:16-27).

OBTAINING THE PLATES

When the angel departed, Nephi reiterated his belief that the Lord would help them get the plates from Laban. "Let us go up again unto Jerusalem," he said, "and let us be faithful in keeping the commandments of the Lord; for behold he is mightier than Laban and his fifty, yea, or even than his tens of thousands" (1 Nephi 4:1). As proof of his words, he reminded his brothers that the Lord had saved the Israelites from the Egyptians by parting the Red Sea for them (1 Nephi 4:2-3).

The brothers returned to Jerusalem and Nephi crept inside the city wall by night. He noted, "And I was led by the Spirit, not knowing beforehand the things which I should do" (1 Nephi 4:6). Having demonstrated his faith in the Lord by his works, Nephi now received divine guidance. He found Laban drunken and unconscious on the ground and was constrained by the Spirit to slay him (1 Nephi 4:5-18). Dressing in Laban's clothing, he was then able to procure the plates and return to his brethren outside the city (1 Nephi 4:19-14).

When the brothers returned to their father's tent in the wilderness, their mother Sariah declared,

> Now I know of a surety that the Lord hath commanded my husband to flee into the wilderness; yea, and I also know of a surety that the Lord hath protected my sons, and delivered them out of the hands of Laban, and given them power whereby they could accomplish the thing which the Lord hath commanded them. (1 Nephi 5:8)

Sariah had learned the lesson that Nephi already knew—the Lord does not give commandments his children cannot obey.

"He Shall Prepare a Way"

A WAY IS PREPARED IN THE WILDERNESS

Nephi had another opportunity to demonstrate his faith in the Lord after he and his brothers had made a second trip to Jerusalem to bring Ishmael's family into the wilderness with them (1 Nephi 7:2-5). One night, the Lord commanded Lehi that the group should leave their camp and move on. In order that Lehi might accomplish this, the Lord provided him a ball or director (called the Liahona in Alma 37:38), which Lehi discovered outside his tent the following morning (1 Nephi 16:9-10). This device, working according to the group's faith, showed the direction they should travel and gave additional instructions as necessary.

When Nephi broke his steel bow, the family despaired of having sufficient food to eat (1 Nephi 16:18). Not only did Laman, Lemuel and the sons of Ishmael complain in their usual fashion, but, Nephi added, "my father began to murmur against the Lord his God" (1 Nephi 16:20). Nephi's reaction was quite different. Believing that God would not have sent them into the wilderness without making provision for their survival, he chastised the others (1 Nephi 16:22). As before, he demonstrated his faith by works, manufacturing a bow and arrow and preparing a sling and stones. He then asked his father where he should go to obtain food (1 Nephi 16:23). Ashamed, the other members of the family humbled themselves, and Lehi enquired of the Lord by means of the Liahona. Nephi followed the divine instructions and returned to camp with food (1 Nephi 16:24-32). He explained,

> And thus we see that the commandments of God must be fulfilled. And if it so be that the children of men keep the commandments of God he doth nourish them, and strengthen them, and provide means whereby they can accomplish the thing which he has commanded them; wherefore, he did provide means for us while we did sojourn in the wilderness. (1 Nephi 17:3)

BUILDING A SHIP

When the group arrived at the sea, the Lord commanded Nephi to build a ship. Nephi had no skills in shipbuilding, but he did not hesitate to obey the Lord's instructions. He had faith that the Lord would provide the means to accomplish his commandments. Nephi asked only that the Lord show him where to find ore with which to make tools. Again he demonstrated his faith by works, constructing a bellows to begin making the tools. He explained, "Wherefore, I, Nephi, did strive to keep the commandments of the Lord, and I did exhort my brethren to faithfulness and diligence. And it came to pass that I did make tools of the ore which I did molten out of the rock" (1 Nephi 17:15-16).

Making tools was one thing,[1] but Nephi's brothers mocked his plans to construct a ship (1 Nephi 17:17-22). In reply, he again used the example of the deliverance of Egypt under Moses at the Red Sea and other miracles in the wilderness (1 Nephi 17:23-32). He also reminded his brethren that the last time he had told them this they had been chastised by an angel for their disobedience (1 Nephi 17:45). He added,

> If God had commanded me to do all things I could do them. If he should command me that I should say unto this water, be thou earth, it should be earth; and if I should say it, it would be done. And now, if the Lord has such great power, and has wrought so many miracles among the children of men, how is it that he cannot instruct me, that I should build a ship? (1 Nephi 17:50-51)[2]

---

[1] Nephi may have been a smith by profession. See Chapter 10, "Was Lehi a Caravaneer?" in this volume.

[2] Compare the stories of Enoch (Moses 6:34; 7:13-14) and Nephi the son of Helaman (Helaman 10:5-10; 11:4-6), who were told to call upon the powers of nature to affect the earth.

"He Shall Prepare a Way"

GOD PREPARES A WAY FOR OTHERS

There is no indication in the scriptures that Noah, described as "a just man and perfect in his generations," hesitated to construct the ark when the Lord commanded him. There have been a few prophets who hesitated because they lacked faith in their own abilities, but the Lord was able to overcome their objections.[3] Jonah didn't want to preach to the people of Nineveh, so he tried to run away from his prophetic responsibilities. In the end, the Ninevites repented as the Lord expected.

The sons of Mosiah were in a situation like that of Jonah. They proposed a mission to convert the Lamanites, noted for their hatred and harsh treatment of Nephites (Alma 17:14; 26:9). Their father, perhaps with some anxiety, asked the Lord's counsel and was assured that the Lord would be with and protect his sons (Mosiah 28:1-8).[4] Demonstrating their faith by their deeds, they managed to convert many thousands of Lamanites to the Nephite religion (Alma 26:4, 13, 22).[5]

Alma the younger faced a similar situation when he went to teach the people in the city of Ammonihah. Driven from the city, he decided to go to the town of Aaron. But the Lord sent an angel to stop him and instruct him to return to Ammonihah. Meanwhile, the angel prepared the way for him by telling one of the city's inhabitants, a man named Amulek, to expect a prophet of God as a visitor (Alma 8:13-22; 10:7-10).

---

[3] Note, for example, the stories of Enoch (Moses 6:31-34), Moses (Exodus 3:11-15; 4:1-16), and Jeremiah (Jeremiah 1:6-9).

[4] Mosiah's grandfather, for whom he was named, had demonstrated such faith that, when the Lord told him to leave the city of Nephi, he gathered together the faithful and departed into the wilderness (Omni 1:12-14).

[5] For a discussion of the mission of the sons of Mosiah, see John A. Tvedtnes, "The Sons of Mosiah: Emissaries of Peace," in Stephen D. Ricks and William J. Hamblin (eds.), *Warfare in the Book of Mormon* (Salt Lake City: Deseret & FARMS, 1990).

THE WAY IS PREPARED AGAIN IN THE MIDDLE EAST

Two nearly identical incidents have occurred in the Middle East. In each, the Lord prepared both the missionary and the individual he would convert by revealing his will to both. One is recorded in Acts 10. A Roman army officer named Cornelius, living at Caesarea, was told by an angel that he should seek knowledge from Simon Peter. While Cornelius' servants made their way to the port city of Joppa, where Peter was staying, the apostle experienced a unique dream in which he learned that he could now take the gospel to non-Jews. After seeing the Holy Ghost fall on Cornelius and his family, he baptized them. They were the first non-Jewish members of Christ's church in the meridian of time.

A similar event happened nearly two millennia later. In 1886, Jacob Spori, a missionary for the LDS Church in the Middle East, on board a ship bound for the Palestinian port-city of Haifa, had a dream in which he learned that he should walk down a certain street. In his dream, he saw a blacksmith with a short coal-black beard, whom he was told would be prepared to receive the message of the restored gospel. Spori reported that, while walking down the street in Haifi (during his first visit to that city), he was met by the blacksmith, Georg Johann Grau. Grau came running out to see him and informed him that he had seen Spori in a dream and had been told that the stranger would have a divine message for him. On August 29, 1886, Georg and Magdalena Grau were the first persons baptized by priesthood authority in modern times in the land of Jesus, only a few miles from Caesarea, where Peter had baptized Cornelius and his family.

CONCLUSION

The message of Nephi remains as valid today as it was nearly 2,600 years ago. When the Lord commands us to do anything, he prepares the way for us to accomplish his will.

Chapter 13

THE SLAYING OF LABAN

And it came to pass that I was constrained by the Spirit that I should kill Laban; but I said in my heart: Never at any time have I shed the blood of man. And I shrunk and would that I might not slay him. (1 Nephi 4:10)

Critics point to Nephi's slaying of Laban in 1 Nephi 4 as evidence that the Book of Mormon is false. They contend that God would never have approved such an act. God's commandment to expel and destroy the wicked inhabitants of the land of Canaan (Deuteronomy 7:1-2) puts the lie to this kind of reasoning. More important are the legal issues behind Nephi's actions, discussed at length by John W. Welch.[1] Among the evidences for justifying Nephi's actions, Welch refers to the precedent of Moses' slaying of the Egyptian in Exodus 2.

An ancient rabbinic source sheds further light on Moses' actions. According to *Abot de Rabbi Nathan* 20, Moses summoned a court of ministering angels and asked them if he should kill the Egyptian, to which the angels responded "Kill him."[2] The same

---

[1] John W. Welch, "Legal Perspectives on the Slaying of Laban," *Journal of Book of Mormon Studies* 1/1 (Fall 1992), 119-141.

[2] The text goes on to specify that it was not with a sword that Moses slew the Egyptian, but with "the word." This was intended to explain why the Hebrew text of Exodus 2:14 adds *'ōmēr* (here understood to mean "word") before "as thou killedst the Egyptian." The extra word may be a dittograph from the preceding line, but the interpretation in *Abot de Rabbi Nathan* is interesting in light of other passages that compare the word of God to a rod or sword. See John A. Tvedtnes,

story is told in *Midrash Rabbah* Exodus 1:29, which adds that, before calling on the angels for counsel, Moses perceived that no righteous persons would descend from the Egyptian man. A similar tale is told of David in the *Tosefta Targum* on 1 Samuel 17:43, where we read that, before killing Goliath, David looked up to heaven and saw the angels deliberating the fate of the giant. The Lord then expresses his will to David by telling him which stone to put in the sling.[3]

The Aramaic translation of Exodus 2:12 found in the second-century A.D. *Targum Pseudo-Jonathan* notes that Moses knew that no proselyte would come from the Egyptian's posterity. The medieval *Zohar* Exodus 12b records the story as follows: "He looked 'here' to see whether there were any good works wrought by the man, and 'there' to see whether a good son would issue from him. 'And he saw that there was no man'; he saw through the holy spirit that no such good son would ever descend from him, for he was aware, as R[abbi] Abba has said, that there are many wicked parents who beget more good sons than righteous parents, and that a good son born of wicked parents is of special excellence, being pure out of impure, light out of darkness, wisdom out of folly. The word 'saw' here indicates discernment through the holy spirit, and therefore he did not shrink from killing the Egyptian."[4]

"Rod and Sword as the Word of God," *Journal of Book of Mormon Studies* 5/2 (1996), 148-155.

[3] The story of David has other parallels with that of Nephi: 1) Goliath and Laban were dressed in armor (1 Samuel 17:4-6; 1 Nephi 4:1); 2) David and Nephi cut off their adversaries heads with the man's own sword (1 Samuel 17:51; 1 Nephi 4:18); 3) both David and Nephi took the dead man's armor (1 Samuel 17:54; 1 Nephi 4:1); and 4) David and Nephi each took the dead man's sword, which became a national treasure (1 Samuel 21:9; 22:10; 1 Nephi 4:21; 2 Nephi 4:14; Jacob 1:10; Words of Mormon 1:13; Mosiah 1:17; D&C 17:1).

[4] Harry Sperling, Maurice Simon, and Paul P. Levertoff, *The Zohar* (New York: The Rebecca Bennet Publications, 1958), 3:39.

The idea that no righteous person would descend from the wicked man the Lord has commanded to be slain may be reflected in the words of the Spirit to Nephi: "Behold the Lord slayeth the wicked to bring forth his righteous purposes. It is better that one man should perish than that a nation should dwindle and perish in unbelief" (1 Nephi 4:13).

CONCLUSION

The fact that the rabbis attributed Moses' actions to a heavenly commandment, just as Nephi attributed his actions to the voice of the Spirit (1 Nephi 4:10-13), lends further support to Welch's study and to the Book of Mormon account.

Chapter 14

A NEW TESTAMENT PARALLEL TO LEHI'S TREE OF LIFE VISION

And it came to pass that while my father tarried in the wilderness he spake unto us, saying: Behold, I have dreamed a dream; or, in other words, I have seen a vision. And behold, because of the thing which I have seen, I have reason to rejoice in the Lord. (1 Nephi 8:2-3)

During his sojourn in the wilderness, the prophet Lehi reported a dream or vision in which he had seen the tree of life. A strait and narrow path led to the tree, alongside which was a rod of iron (1 Nephi 8:19-20). Many people pressed forward to obtain the path (1 Nephi 8:21), but not all were successful.

A river separated the tree of life from a large a spacious building (1 Nephi 8:26). Multitudes of people felt their way toward the building, where they were attired in fine clothing. Though a great number of them entered the building, many were drowned in the river or wandered away (1 Nephi 8:31-33).

Others managed to find the path leading to the tree but became lost when a mist of darkness arose and they wandered away (1 Nephi 8:22-23). Still others managed to stay on the path by catching hold of the rod. Arriving at the tree, they were able to partake of its fruit. But some of them became ashamed when people in the large building began mocking them, and they wandered off (1 Nephi 8:24-28). Many, however, were fortunate enough to remain on the path and to find happiness in the fruit of the tree (1 Nephi 8:30).

After hearing his father's account, Nephi sought to

A New Testament Parallel to Lehi's Tree of Life Vision

experience the same vision and to gain a personal testimony of the truths found therein (1 Nephi 10:17; 11:1-3). He learned that the rod of iron represented the word of God, which can bring us to eternal life (1 Nephi 11:25; 15:23-24). The large building symbolized humanity's vain imaginations and pride (1 Nephi 11:36; 12:18), while the deep river which separated it from the tree was hell (1 Nephi 12:16; 15:26-30).

The mists of darkness, Nephi learned, were the temptations of the devil, designed to thwart man's quest to find God (1 Nephi 12:17). But by holding to the rod, he declared, one could not be tempted or blinded by "the fiery darts of the adversary" (1 Nephi 15:24).

From the Book of Mormon account, we learn, then, of four things that can happen to human beings during their earthly sojourn:

1. Unwilling to seek the kingdom of God, some are deceived into thinking that worldly pleasure is the reason for their existence. Some succeed in attaining the riches represented by the large building, while others lose their way and some fall into the gulf.

2. Some start on the path to eternal life but fall prey to temptation and lose their way.

3. Others follow the path and partake of God's blessings, but become ashamed during times of persecution and fall away.

4. The truly valiant, who "hold fast" to the word of the Lord (1 Nephi 15:24), are able to withstand temptation and deceit and are blessed to attain the celestial kingdom.

The same message is found in the parable of the sower, recorded in the New Testament (Matthew 13:3-8; Mark 4:3-8; Luke 8:5-8). (Jesus' explanation of the parable is found in Matthew 13:18-23; Mark 4:14-20; Luke 8:11-15.) Some of the seed fell by the wayside and was eaten by birds. Jesus explained that this represented those who did not understand God's word and who were taken away by the devil. They are the ones Lehi saw go into the large building.

The seed that fell among thorns began to grow but was choked by the thorns. Jesus told his disciples that these were people deceived by riches, pleasures and lusts. To Lehi, they are the ones whose way was lost when the mist of darkness arose.

The seed that fell on stony ground began to sprout, but had no root whereby it could store up nourishment and water, so it withered in the sun. Jesus noted that such people had received the word of God with joy, but that they were offended and fell during time of persecution. They are clearly the ones seen by Lehi to partake of the fruit of the tree, then wander away when the mockery of the world shamed them.

Finally, we have the seed that fell into good ground and that produced well. These, Jesus said, were those who kept the word. In Lehi's vision, they held fast to the iron rod, the word of God, and were rewarded accordingly.

CONCLUSION

The same message was given in two different forms to different people living in different time periods. But whether delivered in parable form, in symbolic vision, or in straightforward discourse by modern prophets, its meaning is clear: We must hold to the word of God, resisting all temptation and enduring whatever persecution may come our way.

Chapter 15

"BY SMALL MEANS"

And thus we see that by small means the Lord can bring about great things. (1 Nephi 16:29)

With these words, Nephi described the working of the Liahona, the ball or director that led Lehi's family during their travels in the wilderness. The theme was taken up several centuries later when Alma explained the workings of the Liahona to his son Helaman. "And it did work for them according to their faith in God," he said, "Nevertheless, because those miracles were worked by small means it did show unto them marvelous works [and] they were slothful, and forgot to exercise their faith and diligence and then those marvelous works ceased" (Alma 37:40-41). Alma also told Helaman that

> By small and simple things are great things brought to pass; and small means in many instances doth confound the wise. And the Lord God doth work by means to bring about his great and eternal purposes; and by very small means the Lord doth confound the wise and bringeth about the salvation of many souls. (Alma 37:6-7)

The Lord expressed the same idea in a revelation to the prophet Joseph Smith: "Be not weary in well-doing, for ye are laying the foundation of a great work. And out of small things proceedeth that which is great" (D&C 64:33).

"SMALL" EXAMPLES

When the great Syrian general Naaman sought a miraculous cure for his leprosy, he came to the Israelite prophet

"Small" Examples

Elisha. He expected that the prophet would make some dramatic gestures and call on God to heal him. Instead, Elisha instructed him to dip himself seven times in the muddy Jordan river. Naaman was greatly disappointed and prepared to return home to Damascus, where there were much cleaner rivers in which to bathe. But the words of a servant girl changed his plans. She asked, "if the prophet had bid thee do some great thing, wouldst thou not have done it? how much rather, then, when he saith to thee, Wash and be clean?" (2 Kings 5:13).

It is said that J. Golden Kimball, a president of the Seventy, once asked a Latter-day Saint congregation how many would be willing to die for the Church. All hands were raised. He then asked how many would be willing to donate fifty cents. It seems that we are all willing to perform great works for the Lord's work, but we often ignore the small tasks, such as daily prayer and scripture reading, family home evening, and home teaching.

We mortals sometimes belittle our callings in life—including church callings—because they seem too insignificant to make an impact in the "grand scheme of things." Paul saw this problem among the early saints at Corinth, and told them that, like a body whose various parts must all perform their role in order to maintain health and be effective, each office in the church was important to the Lord's work (1 Corinthians 12:12-31).

We can take a lesson from the biblical Joseph. As a son, he did not hesitate to do his father's bidding (Genesis 37:13). Sold into slavery in Egypt, he was determined to remain faithful to God and to his mortal master even in the face of unjust accusations and punishment (Genesis 37:1-19). Falsely accused and imprisoned, he became the most reliable prisoner by retaining his dignity and convictions (Genesis 39:21-23; 40). When released and promoted to the second-highest office in the kingdom of Egypt, he served his king and his people to the very best of his ability (Genesis 45). In other words, Joseph was determined to do the very best job regardless of his position in life. The result was that his actions blessed the nations of Egypt and Israel.

"BY SMALL MEANS"

The role that can be played by seemingly insignificant things was stressed by James when he wrote, "Behold also the ships, which though they be so great, and are driven of fierce winds, yet are they turned about with a very small helm" (James 3:4). The prophet Joseph Smith drew upon this imagery in a letter written to early church leaders: "You know, brethren, that a very large ship is benefited very much by a very small helm in the time of a storm, by being kept workways with the wind and the waves" (D&C 123:16).

Consider some of the great advances to the Lord's work that have resulted from small, seemingly insignificant acts of devotion to duty. Jesus placed mud on the blind man's eyes and told him to wash it off in the pool of Siloam, whereupon the man recovered his sight (John 9:1-7). David, too young to serve in the army with his elder brethren, pitted his simple sling against the most advanced weaponry in the ancient Near East to defeat the Philistine Goliath (1 Samuel 17).[1] Joseph Smith, with the simplest possible kind of faith, went into the grove of trees near his father's home and saw the heavens opened for the first time in nearly two millennia. Simple acts of faith, relying on the Lord to do the rest, have resulted in miracles whose stories will live through all eternity.

Nephi's experience with the Liahona led him to reflect on earlier events in the history of Israel in which faith was the only requirement for the performance of a miracle. One short chapter after describing the operation of the Liahona, he wrote of the brass serpent constructed by Moses to heal Israelites who had been bitten by poisonous serpents in the wilderness (see Numbers 21:6-9). Nephi noted that "the labor which they had to perform was to look; and because of the simpleness of the way, or the easiness of it, there were many who perished" (1 Nephi 17:41).

Nephi had carefully chosen his words, noting that the

---

[1] In David's time, the Philistines held a monopoly on iron (see 1 Samuel 13:19-22).

Israelites had only "to look." He undoubtedly had in mind the words of the Lord to his father Lehi, "Look upon the ball, and behold the things which are written" (1 Nephi 16:26). This brings us back to Alma's admonitions to Helaman regarding the Liahona:

> O my son, do not let us be slothful because of the easiness of the way; for so was it with our fathers; for so was it prepared for them, that if they would look they might live; even so it is with us. The way is prepared, and if we will look we may live forever. (Alma 37:46)

The essential element in performing these simple acts is faith in the word of God. Jesus stressed the importance of even a small amount of faith in accomplishing great works: "If ye have faith as a grain of mustard seed, ye shall say unto this mountain, Remove hence to yonder place; and it shall remove; and nothing shall be impossible unto you" (Matthew 17:20).[2]

CONCLUSION

The exercise of faith does not require that we perform great deeds. Rather, it requires that we call upon God to accept our small deeds and our faith and to use us as instruments in performing his great work. It was, after all, not Moses who parted the Red Sea and performed other miracles in Egypt. He merely held up his rod and repeated what the Lord had told him. In like manner, our small but righteous acts can lead to great and marvelous results.

---

[2] The Book of Mormon notes that the brother of Jared once used his faith to move a mountain (Ether 12:30). Enoch and his people moved mountains and changed the courses of rivers by means of faith (Moses 7:13-14). See also Mormon 8:24.

Chapter 16

"THAT THEY MIGHT HAVE JOY"

Adam fell that men might be; and men are, that they might have joy. (2 Nephi 2:25)

In his admonition to his son Jacob, Lehi spoke of the fall of Adam and contrasted Satan's plans with those of the Lord. Satan fell from heaven "and because he had fallen from heaven and had become miserable forever, he sought also the misery of all mankind" and set about tempting Eve to bring about the fall of mankind as well (2 Nephi 2:17-18). Had they not succumbed to Satan's will, Adam and Eve "would have remained in a state of innocence, having no joy, for they knew no misery; doing no good, for they knew no sin. But behold all things have been done in the wisdom of him who knoweth all things. Adam fell that men might be; and men are, that they might have joy" (2 Nephi 2:22-25).

From this, we learn that God's intent is that we have joy, while Satan wants us to become miserable like himself, this being part of the "opposition in all things" that resulted from the fall (2 Nephi 2:10-16; see also Moses 6:48). Lehi noted, for example, that Satan drags people "down to the eternal gulf of misery and woe" (2 Nephi 1:13; see also Helaman 5:12), represented by the filthy river in Lehi's tree of life vision (1 Nephi 8:26, 32; 15:27-30). But the atonement of Christ frees mankind from the fall (2 Nephi 2:26) and "they are free to choose liberty and eternal life through the great Mediator of all men, or to choose captivity and death according to the captivity of the devil; for he seeketh that all men might be miserable like unto himself" (2 Nephi 2:27).

This theme is frequently repeated in the Book of Mormon. Lehi's son Nephi alluded to it in 2 Nephi 28:19-23. Not surprisingly, it is not exclusive to the Book of Mormon. According to the pseudepigraphic *Life of Adam and Eve* 12:1; 16:3, Satan brought about the fall so that men would be like him.[1]

THE MISERY OF THE DEVIL

Jacob, recalling his father Lehi's words,[2] spoke of the "misery" of the devil (2 Nephi 9:46) and taught that the righteous "shall inherit the kingdom of God, which was prepared for them from the foundation of the world, and their joy shall be full forever" because they have been rescued from the devil "and that lake of fire and brimstone, which is endless torment" (2 Nephi 9:18-19; cf. verses 26-27, 43).

King Benjamin repeated Lehi's teachings when he assembled the people at the temple in Zarahemla:

> I would desire that ye should consider on the blessed and happy state of those that keep the commandments of God. For behold, they are blessed in all things, both temporal and spiritual; and if they hold out faithful to the end they are received into heaven, that thereby they may dwell with God in a state of never-ending happiness. (Mosiah 2:41)

On the other hand, he noted, the wicked "shrink from the presence of the Lord into a state of misery and endless torment, whence they can no more return . . . and their torment is as a lake of fire and brimstone, whose flames are unquenchable, and whose

---

[1] Compare this with D&C 29:36-41, where we read that the devil, having fallen from heaven, became the cause of Adam's fall and expulsion from the garden of Eden.

[2] Jacob's discourses and writings frequently reflected his father's admonitions. See John A. Tvedtnes, "The Influence of Lehi's Admonitions on the Teachings of his son Jacob," in *Journal of Book of Mormon Studies* 3/2 (Fall 1994).

smoke ascendeth up forever and ever." (Mosiah 3:25, 27)

From these statements, it is clear that happiness results from obedience to God's commandments, while misery is a result of a guilty conscience. Alma explained the principle to his son Corianton, noting that the period between death and resurrection is one of separation into a "state of happiness" for the righteous and a "state of misery" for the wicked. Paradise, he said, was the "state of happiness," while those who had been led captive by the devil were in "a state of awful fearful looking for the fiery indignation of the wrath of God upon them" (Alma 40:12-15; cf. 42:1; see Mormon 9:4). The resurrection, he taught, brought about a restoration. But, he cautioned,

> Do not suppose, because it has been spoken concerning restoration, that ye shall be restored from sin to happiness. Behold, I say unto you, wickedness never was happiness . . . All men that are in a state of nature, or I would say, in a carnal state, are in the gall of bitterness and in the bonds of iniquity; they are without God in the world, and they have gone contrary to the nature of God; therefore they are in a state contrary to the nature of happiness. (Alma 41:10-11; see Mormon 2:13)

Samuel the Lamanite used similar terminology when he told the Nephites in the city of Zarahemla, "Ye have sought for happiness in doing iniquity, which thing is contrary to the nature of that righteousness which is in our great and Eternal Head" (Helaman 13:38).

Alma knew firsthand the terrible pains of hell and the exquisite joy that comes from having one's guilt removed through Christ (Alma 36:12-21). He taught that it is God who rescues us from the "state of endless misery and woe" (Alma 9:11). Elsewhere, we read that it is the strait and narrow path seen in Lehi's vision (1 Nephi 8:20-24) that leads us "across that everlasting gulf of misery, which is prepared to engulf the wicked"

(Helaman 3:29). In other passages, we find that it is the atonement of Christ that brings joy (Mosiah 3:3; 4:20; Alma 4:14; 19:6, 14; 22:15; 33:23. Cf. D&C 42:61; 51:19; 52:43; 93:33; 101:36; 138:11-17). This joy comes from obedience to God's will and by good works. Moroni wrote, "Greater is the value of an endless happiness than that misery which never dies" (Mormon 8:38).

CONCLUSION

The unrepentant will be cast out at the last day and "consigned to a state of endless misery" (Helaman 12:25-26; cf. Moses 7:37, 41; D&C 19:15-17, 33). Even though they "have joy in their works for a season," in the end "they are hewn down and cast into the fire, from whence there is no return" (3 Nephi 27:11). The end of all mankind is "to reap eternal happiness or eternal misery, according to the spirit which they listed to obey, whether it be a good spirit or a bad one" (Alma 3:26).

Joseph Smith summed up the Book of Mormon's teachings on this subject as follows:

> Happiness is the object and design of our existence; and will be the end thereof; if we pursue the path that leads to it; and this path is virtue, uprightness, faithfulness, holiness, and keeping all the commandments of God.[3]

---

[3] Joseph Fielding Smith, *Teachings of the Prophet Joseph Smith* (Salt Lake City: Deseret, 1979), 255-256.

Chapter 17

OPPOSITION IN ALL THINGS

For it must needs be, that there is an opposition in all things. If not so, my first-born in the wilderness, righteousness could not be brought to pass, neither wickedness, neither holiness nor misery, neither good nor bad. Wherefore, all things must needs be a compound in one; wherefore, if it should be one body it must needs remain as dead, having no life neither death, nor corruption nor incorruption, happiness nor misery, neither sense nor insensibility. (2 Nephi 2:11)

The concept of the two choices offered mankind is familiar to readers of the Book of Mormon. "Opposition in all things" forms the basis of Lehi's teachings about the atonement in 2 Nephi 2:11-29.[1] Lehi contrasted wickedness and holiness, good and bad, life and death, corruption and incorruption, happiness and misery, sense and insensibility (2 Nephi 2:11-13).

Man's ability to choose between good and evil, life and death, joy or misery, is also discussed in Alma 13:3-4, 10; 29:4-5; 41:4-7, 10-11; 42:16-18. Omni 1:25 declares, "There is nothing which is good save it comes from the Lord: and that which is evil cometh from the devil." The same idea is reflected in Alma 5:39-42 and *Testimony of Naphtali* 3:1 from *Testaments of the Twelve Patriarchs*, an Old Testament apocryphal work.

The importance of the principle of opposition in allowing humans to choose between good and evil is also explained in Moses 5:11. Isaiah 5:20 (cited in 2 Nephi 15:20) contains a list of oppo-

---

[1] Compare Moroni 7:11-19, which contrasts the devil and his works (associated with night) with God and his works (associated with day), each enticing man to do either evil or good.

sites that includes good and evil, light and darkness, sweet and bitter, and notes, like *Ben-Sirach* 11:31 in the Apocrypha, that the wicked garble the two. *Ben-Sirach* 11:14-17 has a similar list (prosperity and adversity, life and death, poverty and riches) and notes that while wisdom, knowledge, and love are from God, sinners are noted for error and darkness. In words that parallel those of Lehi, he declared, "All things are double one against another; and he hath made nothing imperfect. One thing establisheth the good of another" (*Ben-Sirach* 42:24-25, King James translation).

OPPOSITION IN NON-CANONICAL BOOKS

A number of noncanonical books discuss the concept of opposition in ways that are reminiscent of Lehi's teachings. This is particularly true of the *Testaments of the Twelve Patriarchs*. Note the following list of opposites from *Testament of Asher* 5:1-3:

> Children, you see how in everything there are two factors, one against the other, one concealed by the other: In possessions is greed, in merriment is drunkeness, in laughter is lamentation, in marriage is dissoluteness. Death is successor to life, dishonor to glory, night to day, darkness to light, but all these things lead ultimately to day: righteous actions to life, unjust actions to death, since eternal life wards off death. One cannot say truth is a lie, nor a righteous act is unjust, because all truth is subject ultimately to the light, just as all things are subject ultimately to God.

Another list of opposites is found in *Testament of Benjamin* 6:5-6:

> The good set of mind does not talk from both sides of its mouth: praises and curses, abuse and honor, calm and strife, hypocrisy and truth, poverty and wealth, but it has one disposition,

uncontaminated and pure, toward all men. There is no duplicity in its perception or its hearing.

According to *Testament of Gad* 5:1, hatred turns good things into their bad counterparts; among the contrasts listed are small and big, light and darkness, sweet and bitter. *Testament of Naphtali* 2:6-7 contrasts the laws of God and of Beliar [the devil], saying that "there is a distinction between light and darkness."

Testament of Judah 20:1-3 speaks of the two opposing ways thus:

> So understand, my children, that two spirits await an opportunity with humanity: the spirit of truth and the spirit of error. In between is the conscience of the mind which inclines as it will. The things of truth and the things of error are written in the affections of man, each one of whom the Lord knows.

Asher admonished his children to "not be two-faced," following both good and evil, but "rather, cling only to goodness" (*Testament of Asher* 3:1-2; see also 6:1-5 and *Testament of Benjamin* 6:5-7). His words remind us of Jesus' teaching that one "cannot serve two masters" (Matthew 6:24; 3 Nephi 13:24). Mormon wrote that one cannot serve both Christ and the devil, for "the devil is an enemy unto God, and fighteth against him continually" (Moroni 7:11-12). He further warned against confusing evil with good and the devil with God (Moroni 7:14), for "the devil . . . persuadeth no man to do good" (Moroni 7:17). *Testament of Asher* 6:3 also warns against seeing evil as good.

James 1:18 declares that "a double minded man is unstable in all his ways." According to the Book of Mormon, the carnal or natural man, who follows Satan, becomes, like his master, "an enemy to God" (Mosiah 2:37-38; 3:19; 16:5). Having chosen works of darkness rather than light, he yields himself to the devil and becomes subject to destruction and goes down to hell (2 Nephi

26:10).

THE FALL MADE CHOICES POSSIBLE

Lehi taught that it was because of the devil and the fall that mankind was exposed to the opposites of good and evil and became capable of choosing between sweet and bitter (2 Nephi 2:15-16; see Alma 12:31-32; 36:19-21). The same topic is discussed in D&C 29:39-40, where we read "it must needs be that the devil should tempt the children of men, or they could not be agents unto themselves; for if they never should have bitter they could not know the sweet" (D&C 29:39). It is ironic that the fall made it possible for mortals to "taste the bitter, that they may know to prize the good. And it is given unto them to know good from evil; wherefore they are agents unto themselves" (Moses 6:55-56).

After learning of the redemption of Christ that would rescue them from the fall, Eve declared, "Were it not for our transgression we never should have had seed, and never should have known good and evil, and the joy of our redemption, and the eternal life which God giveth unto all the obedient" (Moses 5:11).

A similar statement is found in the medieval Jewish document, the *Zohar* Exodus 187a. Commenting on Daniel 2:22, it states that "were it not for darkness we would not know what light is."[2]

It is interesting to note that the contrast between good and evil is often defined as the difference between sweet and bitter, as in D&C 29:39, cited above. In describing the two trees in the garden of Eden as opposite choices for Adam and Eve, Lehi said, "it must needs be that there was an opposition; even the forbidden fruit in opposition to the tree of life; the one being sweet and the other

---

[2] Maurice Simon, and Paul P. Levertoff, *The Zohar* (New York: Rebecca Bennet Publications, 1958), 4:130.

bitter" (2 Nephi 2:15).³

In an early Coptic document, the serpent says to Eve, "Ye shall not surely die, but ye shall be like unto these gods, ye shall know the good and the evil, and ye shall [be able] to separate the sweet from the bitter."⁴ Alma experienced these opposites firsthand, noting the bitterness of the pains caused by his sins compared with the sweetness of the joy he received when he repented and called on Christ (Alma 36:21).

SATAN OBSCURES THE DIFFERENCES

Satan, in his efforts to get mankind to follow him, tries to minimize the differences between his way and God's way, uses various deceitful tactics, such as telling us that there is no devil (2 Nephi 28:22) and that there is no harm in committing a "little" sin. Moses 4:3-4 informs us that Satan "sought to destroy the agency of man, which I, the Lord God, had given him."

CONCLUSION

The prophet Isaiah condemned "them that call evil good, and good evil; that put darkness for light, and light for darkness; that put bitter for sweet, and sweet for bitter!" (Isaiah 5:20, cited in 2 Nephi 15:20). The Apocryphal *Ben-Sirach* 11:31 also notes that the wicked confuse good and evil. Such actions are contrary to the Lord's plan in making us agents and in enabling us to distinguish between good and evil.

---

³ The *Zohar* frequently speaks of the left and right sides, sometimes comparing them with the two trees in the garden of Eden.

⁴ *Discourse on Abbaton by Timothy Archbishop of Alexandria* folio 16b, in Ernest A. Wallis Budge, *Coptic Martyrdoms in the Dialect of Upper Egypt* (London: Oxford University, 1914), 485.

Chapter 18

CAPTIVITY OF THE DEVIL

Wherefore, men are free according to the flesh; and all things are given them which are expedient unto man. And they are free to choose liberty and eternal life, through the great Mediator of all men, or to choose captivity and death, according to the captivity and power of the devil; for he seeketh that all men might be miserable like unto himself. And now, my sons, I would that ye should look to the great Mediator, and hearken unto his great commandments; and be faithful unto his words, and choose eternal life, according to the will of his Holy Spirit; And not choose eternal death, according to the will of the flesh and the evil which is therein, which giveth the spirit of the devil power to captivate, to bring you down to hell, that he may reign over you in his own kingdom. (2 Nephi 2:27-29)

The captivity of the devil is a major topic in the Book of Mormon (1 Nephi 14:7; Alma 9:28; 34:35) and is mentioned in Moses 4:4. It results from men choosing "evil works rather than good" (Alma 40:13; see also Alma 34:33-35). The Book of Mormon warns of "the grasp of this awful monster; yea, that monster, death and hell" (2 Nephi 9:10) and speaks of how one can be delivered (2 Nephi 9:19, 26; Jacob 3:11).

Similarly, one version of the Armenian text *Concerning Adam, Eve and the Incarnation* 64-65 notes that the risen Christ "released us from the captivity of Satan."[1] The collection of ancient

---

[1] Michael E. Stone, *Armenian Apocrypha Relating to Adam and Eve* (Leiden: Brill, 1996), 79, 266.

texts known as the *Testaments of the Twelve Patriarchs* speaks of being "enslaved" to the devil by choosing evil (*Testament of Judah* 18:6; *Testament of Dan* 2:4; *Testament of Asher* 3:1-2).[2] *Testament of Dan* 5:11 speaks of "captives" taken by the devil, in terminology reminiscent of Isaiah 14:17; 24:22; 42:7; 49:9; 61:1 (cited by Jacob in Jacob 2:19 and Jesus in Luke 4:18).[3] Asher teaches that the two-faced, who perform both good and evil deeds, "are enslaved to their evil desires" (*Testament of Asher* 3:2) and that the mind of the wicked man "is overmastered by Belial" (*Testament of Asher* 1:8).[4] Similarly, Nephi wrote that Satan has "power over the hearts of the children of men" (2 Nephi 30:18) and Alma noted that the devil's plan is to "ensnare the hearts of men" (Alma 28:13).

THE DEVIL'S SNARES

Such passages remind us of the "snares" or "nets" of the devil, by which he brings people into captivity (Alma 28:13-14; Helaman 3:29; 1 Timothy 3:7 [cf. 6:9]; 2 Timothy 2:26; *Testament of Dan* 2:4-5; *1 Enoch* 103:2; Ignatius, *Epistle to the Philadelphians* 6:2; *Pistis Sophia* 67). The Falasha *Book of the Angels*, referring to the devil as Mastima and "the Angel of Darkness," speaks of "the serpent and its snares."[5]

The snares of the devil are the sins committed by men. *Jubilees* 1:20-21 says that Beliar ensnares people through their sins.

---

[2] The brief quotes from the *Testaments of the Twelve Patriarchs* are drawn from the English translation by Howard Clark Kee in James H. Charlesworth, *The Old Testament Pseudepigrapha* (Garden City: Doubleday, 1983), 775-828.

[3] See also the comments on captivity in *Testament of Joseph* 1:4-2:4; 10:3; 18:2.

[4] The Hebrew term Belial also appears under the Greek form Beliar and is sometimes used as the name of the devil.

[5] Wolf Leslau, *Falasha Anthology* (New Haven: Yale, 1951), 55-56. The Falasha are the "black Jews" of Ethiopia.

The Devil's Snares

The *Damascus (Zadokite) Document* speaks of the "three nets of Belial," the sins of sexual promiscuity, riches, and pollution of the sanctuary or temple (CD 4.15). Similarly, Revelation 2:14 speaks of the "snares" (the King James Bible has "stumblingblock") of fornication and eating polluted sacrifices.

Sin is termed a "snare" in Mosiah 23:9, while lies and slander are considered to be a snare in the Apocryphal *Ben Sirach* 51:2. *Testament of Dan* 2:4-5 speaks of the snare of "the spirit of anger." "High-mindedness and pride," we are informed in D&C 90:17, "bringeth a snare upon your souls." The first-century A.D. Jewish philosopher Philo wrote that riches and glory are a snare to weak minds (*De Iosepho* 254). In one of the Dead Sea Scrolls, we read that Moses, in preparation for his farewell address to the Israelites, told them that idolatry would be "a snare and a pitfall."[6]

The Apocrypha, *Tobit* 14:10-11, contrasting light and darkness, speaks of the "snares of death." The same expression is found in Proverbs 13:14; 14:27 and 2 Samuel 22:6 (same as Psalm 18:5; cf. 116:3). In the latter, these snares are paralleled by the "sorrows of hell." D&C 10:26 tells us that the devil flatters men "and leadeth them along until he draggeth their souls down to hell . . . in their own snare" (cf. D&C 10:40).[7] We can compare these passages with the "nets of deceit" in *Testament of Dan* 2:4.[8]

In Alma 10:17-18, "foundations of the devil" parallels "traps and snares." Alma 12:6, speaks of "a snare of the adversary,

---

[6] 1Q22, in Geza Vermes, *The Dead Sea Scrolls in English* (3rd ed., London: Penguin, 1990), 264.

[7] For Joseph Smith's discussions on the devil's use of snares, see *History of the Church* 1.468; 3.351, 394, 396.

[8] In a Coptic gospel fragment recapped by James, the devil appears with his demons in the form of a fisherman, carrying nets and hooks to catch human beings. See Montague Rhodes James, *The Apocryphal New Testament* (Oxford: Clarendon Press, 1955), 149.

which he has laid to catch this people, that he might bring you into subjection unto him, that he might encircle you about with his chains, that he might chain you down to everlasting destruction, according to the power of his captivity" (cf. 1 Nephi 15:24; Alma 10:11; 30:60; Helaman 6:28). Alma admitted that, while a priest of wicked king Noah, he was "caught in a snare" (Mosiah 23:9; compare *Ben-Sirach* 27:29) and declared that the people under king Noah had been "bound with the bands/bonds of iniquity," from which they had been "delivered by the power of God" (Mosiah 23:12-13). His son, Alma the younger, also spoke of darkness and the bonds of iniquity that came from choosing evil (Alma 41:4-7, 10-11).

The scriptures also teach that the devil binds men with strong cords (2 Nephi 26:22) and "grasps [the wicked] with his awful chains" (2 Nephi 28:18-23; see also 2 Nephi 1:13; 9:45-47; Alma 12:17; 13:30; 36:17-18; D&C 138:23; Moses 7:26). Lehi warned his family about the "captivity of the devil" (2 Nephi 1:18) and admonished them to "awake from a deep sleep, yea, even from the sleep of hell, and shake off the awful chains by which ye are bound, which are the chains which bind the children of men, that they are carried away captive down to the eternal gulf of misery and woe" (2 Nephi 1:13; see also verse 23).

Ammon spoke to his brethren about how "the Lamanites, were in darkness, yea, even in the darkest abyss, but behold, how many of them are brought to behold the marvelous light of God!" (Alma 26:3). God had loosed these converts "from the pains of hell" (Alma 26:13), "from the chains of death" (Alma 26:14). "Yea, they were encircled about with everlasting darkness and destruction; but behold, he has brought them into his everlasting light, yea, into everlasting salvation" (Alma 26:15). Similarly, *Odes of Solomon* 22:1-8 speaks of deliverance from chains, the dragon, evil, poison, and the grave.

One pseudepigraphic text describes how Enoch, during his heavenly vision, saw angels of plague preparing chains for Satan and the wicked, then saw the wicked bound by chains (*1 Enoch*

53:3-5; 54:1-6; 62:1-11; 69:27-29; 88:1-3). He describes the nets of iron and bronze that would be used to bind the wicked Israelites (*1 Enoch* 56:1-4). The chains that bind the wicked are also mentioned in Moses 7:57 and *Qur'an* 76:5; according to *Qur'an* 36:9, they are customs and habits.

THE BINDING POWER OF SIN

The scriptures frequently mention "the bands of death, and the chains of hell" (Alma 5:7, 9-10; 12:11; 13:30; 26:13-14; cf. 2 Peter 2:4; Mormon 9:13; D&C 123:8; 138:23), which are the same as the "pains of hell" of Alma 14:6. Alma 7:15 notes that sin binds one down to destruction. Thus, the Israelite king Manasseh, according to the Apocrypha, confessed his sins, saying, "I am bowed down with many iron bands" (Prayer of Manasseh 1:10, King James translation). According to Alma 7:15, sins "bind you down to destruction."

D&C 84:49 speaks of the "bondage of sin," which is similar to the "captivity to the law of sin" (Romans 7:23) or the captivity of hell (2 Nephi 9:12), from which one can be freed (Romans 6:18; 8:2). Related terms are the "bonds of iniquity," which are linked with the "darkest abyss," from which one can be delivered by coming to the "light of God" (Mosiah 27:29; see Acts 8:23; Mosiah 23:13; 26:3, 15; Alma 41:11; Mormon 8:31). Deliverance from the snare is also mentioned in Psalms 91:3; 124:7.

A small scroll fragment found among the Dead Sea Scrolls (4Q171) speaks of the repentant being delivered from the snares of Satan. Another of the Dead Sea Scrolls, *Damascus (Zadokite) Document* 16.12 says that righteousness saves a man from the pit, while a third, the *Thanksgiving Psalms*, indicates that it is the Lord who saves from the pit or Abaddon (1QH 3.19).

But Peter warned that the "servants of corruption," who were "in bondage" and then freed through Christ, could again fall (2 Peter 2:19-20; note the "mist of darkness" with which the wicked are punished in verse 17). Compare the pit of darkness in 4Q186 1.2.

THE PIT

The Book of Mormon speaks of sinners being in an abyss (Mosiah 27:29; Alma 26:3). *Testament of Reuben* 2:8 says that fornication "leads the young person like a blind man into a ditch." Jesus declared, "If the blind lead the blind, both shall fall into the ditch" (Matthew 15:14; Luke 6:39; see *Ben-Sirach* 27:26). The Greek word rendered "ditch" in the King James Bible means "cistern" or "pit." Psalm 7:15 speaks of the wicked falling "into the ditch which he made."

Nephi evidently had this passage in mind when he wrote of the wicked nations that "shall fall into the pit which they digged to ensnare the people of the Lord." He goes on to speak of "that great whore . . . that great and abominable church" and of Satan (1 Nephi 22:14-15). Elsewhere, Satan is called the "founder" of the wicked church (1 Nephi 13:6; 14:9, 17; cf. 2 Nephi 26:22). In another passage, Nephi wrote of the captivity of the devil and of the pit that he has dug (1 Nephi 14:3-4).

In Revelation 9:11, the devil is called "the angel of the bottomless pit, whose name in the Hebrew tongue is Abaddon ["loss, perdition"], but in the Greek tongue hath his name Apollyon."[9] In hymn 5 of the *Thanksgiving Psalms* Dead Sea Scroll,

---

[9] D&C 76:26 calls Satan "Perdition." Because he followed Satan, Cain was given two of the devil's titles, "father of his lies," and "Perdition" (Moses 5:24); significantly, in *2 Adam & Eve* 20:35, the abode of Cain's descendants is called "the abode of perdition and of sin." The term "son of perdition," used in the New Testament in reference to Judah, who betrayed Christ (John 17:12), refers to those who remain with Satan in the day of salvation (D&C 76:32, 43; 3 Nephi 27:32; 29:7; see 2 Thessalonians 2:3; 1 Timothy 6:9; 2 Timothy 3:7; 2 Peter 3:7; Revelation 17:8, 11). In *Martyrdom and Ascension of Isaiah* 10:8, Perdition is the name of the place where the devil dwells and rules over the spirits of dead sinners. The Hebrew word *'abbadôn*, rendered "destruction" is found in a number of Bible

THE PIT

the term "pit" also parallels Abaddon (1QH 3.19). The pit and perdition are likewise found together in Revelation 17:8. The term "angel of the pit" is also used of the devil (called Belial) in one of the Dead Sea Scrolls (4Q286), which also mentions the darkness with which he is associated.[10] The *Damascus (Zadokite) Document* calls the wicked "sons of the pit" (CD 6.12). The devil is associated with the bottomless pit in *Gospel of Bartholomew* 4:40-41 and is called both Beliar and the "dragon of the pit" in *Gospel of Bartholomew* 4:46. The pit, as the punishment for sinners, is known from *Ben Sirach* 21:10; *4 Ezra* 7:36; and *Pirqe Abot* 5:22 (citing Psalm 55:24).

FLEE FROM EVIL

Because evil and the devil imprison the soul, the *Testaments of the Twelve Patriarchs* advise fleeing from both. Asher taught, "cling only to goodness . . . Flee from the evil tendency, destroying the devil by your good works" (*Testament of Asher* 3:1-2). *Testament of Benjamin* 8:1 admonishes, "run from evil, corruption, and hatred of brothers." Simeon promised his family, "If anyone flees to the Lord for refuge, the evil spirit will quickly depart from him, and his mind will be eased" (*Testament of Simeon* 3:5).

In the Armenian version of *Testament of Benjamin* 7:1, the patriarch advises, "Flee, my children, malice [and fornication]," while the Greek and Slavonic versions read, "flee from the evil of Beliar." In *Testament of Reuben* 5:5, the patriarch instructs his children to "flee from sexual promiscuity." The words remind us of Paul's admonition to the Corinthians to "flee fornication" (1

---

passages, where it appears with "hell" or sheol (Job 26:6; Proverbs 15:11), and "death" (Job 28:22; Psalms 88:11 [verse 12 in the Hebrew text]).

[10] Other Dead Sea Scrolls that speak of the pit include 4Q186 and the scroll of *Thanksgiving Hymns* (1QH, hymns 4, 5, and 8). The pit is associated with Mastemah, another of the devil's titles in 4Q525.

Christian Father, wrote, "Flee therefore the wicked devices and snares of the prince of this world" (Ignatius, *Epistle to the Philadelphians* 6).[11]

But the concept of fleeing from evil goes back to the Old Testament, where we find it in Psalms 34:14; 37:27; Proverbs 3:7; 13:14, 19; 14:27; 15:24; 16:6, 17; Isaiah 52:11 (cited in 3 Nephi 20:41); and Lamentations 4:15. Joseph is perhaps the greatest example of fleeing from evil, when he ran from the Egyptian woman who tried to seduce him (Genesis 39:7-13).

CONCLUSION

A major theme in the teachings of Lehi, Nephi, Jacob, and Alma is that the devil has the power to captivate men when they succumb to temptation and commit sin.[12] To illustrate the seriousness of the subject, they describe this captivity in terms of nets, snares, bonds, and chains, all of which represent sinful acts. Many other ancient texts use the same imagery to describe the consequences of sin, suggesting that the Book of Mormon writers were drawing on something very old for their analogies.

---

[11] Alexander Roberts and James Donaldson, *Ante-Nicene Fathers* (orig. 1885; reprint Peabody, MA: Hendrickson, 1994), 1:83.

[12] See also the discussion in Chapter 29, The Evil Spirit, included in this volume.

Chapter 19

LUCIFER, SON OF THE MORNING

How art thou fallen from heaven, O Lucifer, son of the morning! how art thou cut down to the ground, which didst weaken the nations! (Isaiah 14:12=2 Nephi 24:12)

Lehi, the first prophet in the Book of Mormon, knew of the devil from records in his possession (2 Nephi 2:17). In this study, we will examine the concept of the devil as taught by Lehi and his sons, Nephi and Jacob, and compare it with what Isaiah 14 says about him to determine if Isaiah's writings may have influenced the thinking of the early Book of Mormon writers.

The principal passages dealing with Satan are found in the second and ninth chapters of 1-2 Nephi, in admonitions by Lehi and his son Jacob.[1] In these and other chapters of 2 Nephi, we learn that Satan was an angel of God who fell from heaven and became a devil because he had "sought that which was evil before God" (2 Nephi 2:17-18; 9:8). Wanting to make men miserable like himself (2 Nephi 2:18, 27; 9:9; cf. 9:46), he has become the enemy of man's soul (2 Nephi 4:27-29, 33). He not only brought about the fall of Adam and Eve by tempting Eve to take the forbidden fruit (2 Nephi 2:18; 9:9), but he continues to blind men's eyes and harden their hearts by tempting them (1 Nephi 12:17) and is the "father of lies," who is able to transform "himself nigh into an angel of light" (2 Nephi 9:9). But while he has power over sinners (1 Nephi 13:29), he has no power over the righteous

---

[1] The similarities between these two discourses is discussed in the author's article, "The Influence of Lehi's Admonitions on the Teachings of His Son Jacob," *Journal of Book of Mormon Studies* 3/2:34-48.

(1 Nephi 22:26). Indeed, the day will come when his power over the hearts of men will be taken from him (1 Nephi 22:15; 30:18).

To Lehi and his sons, the devil is an "evil one" (2 Nephi 4:27; 32:8), a "cunning one" (2 Nephi 9:39), who has a "cunning plan" (2 Nephi 9:28) by which he tempts men to commit evil deeds (1 Nephi 12:19; 2 Nephi 9:9), enabling him to grasp them with chains and bring them into captivity down to hell (1 Nephi 12:16-17; 14:4, 7, 13; 15:29, 35; 2 Nephi 1:13, 18; 2:27, 29; 9:12, 34, 36; 26:10; 28:15, 18-19, 21-22). Consequently, he is a monster associated with death and hell from which God must deliver the righteous (2 Nephi 1:15; 9:10, 19, 26; 10:23-25; 33:6; cf. 4:31-32; 28:23). The Lord provides the resurrection, without which our spirits would be subject to the devil, becoming "angels to a devil" and being "shut out from the presence of our God" (2 Nephi 9:8-9). But "the devil and his angels . . . shall go away into everlasting fire . . . and their torment is as a lake of fire and brimstone" (2 Nephi 9:16; cf. 9:19, 26; 28:23).

Though Satan reigns over the wicked in hell (2 Nephi 9:29; cf. 26:10), he also has a kingdom established on the earth (1 Nephi 22:22-23), identified in 2 Nephi 28:18-19 as the "great and abominable church" of which the devil is the founder and by means of which he dug the pit known as hell (1 Nephi 13:6; 14:3, 9-10, 17). The devil is also seen as the founder of "secret combinations of murder" (2 Nephi 9:9; 26:22) and especially delights in those who worship idols (2 Nephi 9:37).

The earliest biblical reference[2] to Satan's fall is in Isaiah 14, which Lehi's son Nephi quotes *in extenso* in 2 Nephi 24. In this passage, we read of "Lucifer, son of the morning," who had "fallen from heaven" (Isaiah 14:12). The Hebrew behind "Lucifer" is *hêlel*, which means "shining one," rendered by the Greek Septuagint as *heôsforos*. The term *Lucifer*, meaning "light-bearer," is the Latin name for the planet Venus, which, because it shines brightly on the

---

[2] There are, of course, earlier Bible references to Satan, but not to his fall. This fall is mentioned in Moses 4:1-4, but is missing from the account in Genesis.

horizon just before the dawn during half the year, has long been known as the "morning star." *Lucifer* was first used in Isaiah 14:12 by Saint Jerome in his Bible translation, the Latin Vulgate, in the late fourth century A.D. By then, the passage had been tied to Jesus' declaration in Luke 10:18, "I beheld Satan as lightning fall from heaven,"[3] and Christians came to accept Lucifer as the devil's name. The term has become common in Bibles such as the King James Version, which borrowed it from the Vulgate. Indeed, the devil is called "Lucifer, a son of the morning" in Doctrine and Covenants 76:25–27, which speaks of his pre-earth fall from heaven.[4]

Satan's fall[5] is probably intended in Revelation 8:10, where

---

[3] The lightning reflects Satan's role as a light-bearer. The context of Jesus' statement is instructive. The seventy had just returned, rejoicing that evil spirits were subject to them (Luke 10:17). In the preceding verses, Jesus had spoken of the wickedness of Tyre and Sidon, cities where Baal or Melqart was worshipped. He compared their wickedness with that of several Galilean cities, including Capernaum, saying, "for if the mighty works had been done in Tyre and Sidon, which have been done in you, they had a great while ago repented" (10:13), and "thou, Capernaum, which are exalted to heaven, shalt be thrust down to hell" (10:15). These words seem to be based on Isaiah's words about Lucifer (Isaiah 14:13–15).

[4] Isaiah's "Lucifer" was identified as a fallen angel in early Jewish and Christian lore. In *2 Enoch* 29:4–5, 23, one of the archangels wanted to place his throne higher than the clouds and to be equal to God in power, but was cast out with his angels and made to fly over the abyss. The story clearly parallels Isaiah 14:12–15, even in using the term "most High" (discussed further in note 17) for God. Similarly, in *Life of Adam and Eve* 15:15–16, we read that the devil was cast out of heaven because he sought to place his throne above the stars of heaven and become like the most High. For stars falling from heaven being the fallen angels, see 1 Enoch 86. In an Ethiopic document, the star that falls in Revelation 8:10 is said to be Satan, referred to in Isaiah 14:12, while the wormwood of Revelation 3:11 is also Satan. Sir E. A. Wallis Budge, *The Book of the Mysteries of the Heavens and the Earth and Other Works of Bakhayla Mika'el (Zosimas)* (Oxford, 1935), p.104.

[5] Satan's fall from heaven in the premortal life will be paralleled by his final fall. This chapter does not attempt to assign passages such as the ones cited here to one or the other.

John writes that "there fell a great star from heaven, burning as it were a lamp, and it fell upon the third part of the rivers, and upon the fountains of waters."[6] John further writes, "I saw a star fall from heaven unto the earth: and to him was given the key of the bottomless pit" (Revelation 9:1).[7] The devil is often associated with a pit[8] and, in fact, Lucifer is cast into a pit in Isaiah 14:15.

SATAN, KING OF BABYLON

The identification of Lucifer with Satan in Isaiah 13–14 is complicated by the fact that those chapters claim to discuss not the devil, but "the burden of Babylon, which Isaiah the son of Amoz did see" (Isaiah 13:1). Lucifer is mentioned in Isaiah 14:12, in the middle of a section that begins, "Thou shalt take up this proverb against the king of Babylon" (Isaiah 14:4). While some have sought to reconcile this inconsistency by attributing dual meaning to Isaiah's words, there is a simpler answer to this seeming dilemma: Satan was, in fact, the god Marduk, who was the real king of Babylon. That is, Isaiah was identifying Satan with the pagan god Marduk.

While some may be astounded at the assertion that Satan was the real power in Babylon, there is nevertheless evidence for it. In Ezekiel 28, we read of both "the prince of Tyrus" and "the king of Tyrus," Tyrus being the Latin name used in the King James

---

[6] We can perhaps compare the third part of the waters to the third of the host of heaven that followed Satan in his rebellion (Revelation 12:3–9; D&C 29:36).

[7] In Revelation 20:1–11, it is an angel who comes down with "the key of the bottomless pit and a great chain in his hand" to lay hold on the dragon, who is then brought to judgment before God and cast into the lake of fire and brimstone. The same story is depicted in *1 Enoch* 86:1–6; 88:1; 90:20–27; cf.10:4.

[8] Revelation 9:11; 17:8; 20:1–3; 1 Nephi 14:3–4; *Gospel of Bartholomew* 4:40–41, 46; *Apocalypse of Elijah* 5:35. Among the Dead Sea Scrolls, see *1QH* 3.19; *4Q286*; *4Q525* 5.1–6; *CD* 6.12. See also Chapter 15 above.

Satan, King of Babylon

Version for the city of Tyre. The prince, though a mortal, compares himself to El, the chief god of the Canaanites, whose very name means "God," as it is rendered in the King James translation. Ezekiel points out the folly of the Tyrian ruler's claims. When he turns to address the king of Tyre, he terms him "the anointed cherub" and notes that he has dwelt in Eden, the garden of God or El.[9] Evidently, the "prince of Tyre" refers to the city's earthly ruler, while the "king of Tyre" is its spiritual ruler. We know from other sources that the god of Tyre was Baal, who is often termed Melqart, meaning "king of the city."[10]

Babylon, too, had its spiritual king, who similarly goes by two different names. He is often called Bel, "lord," which corresponds to the Canaanite Baal, but his proper name is Marduk.[11] Marduk was considered to be the real king of Babylon.[12] It was he who chose a mortal king to represent him. In one inscription, we read that Marduk gives the sceptre to the king who reveres him.[13]

Nebuchadrezzar II, after writing of "Marduk, my king,"

---

[9] The description of Eden in Ezekiel 28:13 fits the Ugaritic description of the island on which El dwells, where the plants are made of precious stones.

[10] The title is a compound, *mlk qrt*. The treaty between Baal, (mortal) king of Tyre, and Esarhaddon, king of Assyria, lists Melqart among the gods of the land; see *Ancient Near Eastern Texts Relating to the Old Testament* (hereinafter *ANET*), ed. James B. Pritchard, 3rd ed. (Princeton: Princeton University Press, 1969), 534. A stela dedicated to Melqart by Bar-Hadad (biblical Ben-Hadad), king of Aram, was found at Damascus (*ANET*, 655).

[11] Bel and Marduk are identified in *ANET*, 332.

[12] Babylon is called Marduk's city in a clay-barrel inscription from the time of Cyrus (*ANET*, 315). According to the Code of Hammurabi, Babylon was created for Marduk, who was made its king (*ANET*, 164). In a psalm to Marduk, found at Babylon, he is termed "Lord of Babylon" (*ANET*, 390).

[13] *ANET*, 332.

\indicates that he owes his kingship to Marduk.[14] The Code of Hammurabi says that Hammurabi was appointed king of Babylon by Marduk.[15] In another text, we read that Marduk chose the Persian king Cyrus to be king of Babylon, ordered him to march against "his [Marduk's] city," and allowed him to enter the city. This god also made the inhabitants of Babylon accept Cyrus and then gave commandments to Cyrus.[16]

In order to become earthly king of Babylon, one had to go into the temple of Marduk and grasp the hands of his statue. (Evidently, it was believed that Marduk would slay a pretender he was not willing to accept.) Even foreign conquerors, such as the kings of Assyria, followed this practice.[17] Each year, at the *essesu* festival, the king would surrender his royal accouterments to the god at the temple of Marduk, only to receive them again after a prescribed ceremony.[18]

The identification of Satan with pagan gods is not unknown.[19] The Ugaritic term Baal Zebul (generally rendered

---

[14] Wadi Brisa Inscription, *ANET*, 307.

[15] *ANET*, 165, 177.

[16] *Ibid.*, 316.

[17] For some examples, see Georges Roux, *Ancient Iraq* (Harmondsworth, England: Penguin, 1969), 280, 285, 370.

[18] For a description of the rite, see *ANET*, 334. The ruler chosen by Marduk is also expected to take the god's statue out for an annual procession (*ANET*, 315).

[19] It may not be coincidental that in medieval Christianity Satan was considered to have horns. The ancient Ugaritic/Canaanite gods such as El and Baal had horns or wore headgear with horns. Indeed, El's full title in the Ugaritic texts is "Father Bull El," probably reflecting the use of the horns. According to Sanchuniathon (cited in Eusebius, *Praeparatio Evangelii* 1.10), the goddess Astarte wore a bull's head as an ensign of royalty. For depictions of ancient Near Eastern gods with horns or horned caps, see James B. Pritchard, *The Ancient Near East in Pictures* (hereinafter *ANEP*) (Princeton: Princeton University Press, 1969), illustration numbers 425,

"prince Baal") shows up in the form Baal-zebub or Beelzebub ("lord of the flies") at the Philistine city of Ekron (2 Kings 1:1–2) and is applied in the New Testament to Satan (Matthew 12:22–32; Luke 11:14–23).[20]

A clay tablet written during the Seleucid era helps establish that the Lucifer of Isaiah 14 is Marduk. It calls Babylon's deity "bright light, god Marduk,"[21] reflecting the meaning of the word rendered "Lucifer"("light-bearer") in Isaiah 14:12.

When Isaiah prophesies the fall of Babylon in Isaiah 21:9, he declares, "Babylon is fallen, is fallen; and all the graven images of her gods he hath broken unto the ground." The Lord tells Jeremiah that he will "do judgment upon the graven images of Babylon" (Jeremiah 51:47). This emphasis on the destruction of the idols of Babylon is reiterated in another of Jeremiah's

---

487, 489, 490 (Baal), 491, 493 (probably El), 498, 516, 525–7, 532, 537–40, 544, 555, 601, 644, 654, 655, and 826 (probably El). Even Greek gods sometimes had horns. The "Hymn to Apollo" (one of the Orphic Hymns) calls him "the two-horned god." Bacchus is sometimes depicted wearing horns and is called "bull-horned." Significantly, Venus, with which the Vulgate identifies the devil in the title Lucifer (Isaiah 14:12), is a horned planet because, like the moon, it goes through phases and appears in its crescent form to be horned. In connection with Satan as a king, we should note that the king's crown consists of a number of projecting horns, whence its name, *corona*, evidently related to Hebrew *qrn*, "horn." For depictions of Marduk's emblem as god of war (the spear-point) with a horned dragon (the emblem of Satan in Revelation 12 and elsewhere) lying beside it, see *ANEP* illustrations 454, 519–521, and 523.

[20] Another Ugaritic divine title is *'lyn*, an epithet of Baal. It is found in Isaiah 14:14, where the King James Version (hereinafter KJV) renders it "the most High," as elsewhere in the Bible (e.g., Genesis 14:19, where we have *El Elyon* translated as "most high God"). According to Philo of Byblos (first century A.D.) Alyan was the grandfather of El, the chief Canaanite deity. A treaty from ca. 750 B.C. includes both Elyon and Marduk among the gods of Mesopotamia (*ANET*, 659). One of El's sons, in the Ugaritic texts, is Shahar, the name rendered "morning" in Isaiah 14:12, while another of his sons is Helel, which gives us "Lucifer" in the same passage.

[21] *ANET*, 332.

prophecies against the city:

> The word that the Lord spake against Babylon and against the land of the Chaldeans by Jeremiah the prophet. Declare ye among the nations, and publish, and set up a standard; publish, and conceal not: say, Babylon is taken, Bel is confounded, Merodach is broken in pieces; her idols are confounded, her images are broken in pieces. (Jeremiah 50:1–2)

It is interesting that the fall of Babylon should be tied so strongly to the confounding of Bel and the destruction of the statue of Merodach (the Hebrew rendering of Marduk). Jeremiah employs similar language in the next chapter, where he quotes the Lord as saying, "I will punish Bel in Babylon" (Jeremiah 51:44)[22] and "I will do judgment upon the graven images of Babylon" (Jeremiah 51:47). In 2 Nephi 9:37, Nephi implies that all idol worship is of Satan, which would make God's judgment of the idols part of his war against the devil.

The Babylonian myth of Marduk provides further evidence that the god and king of Babylon was Satan. The creation epic known as the Enuma Elish[23] describes how Apsu and Tiamat engendered all of the gods. When Apsu threatened to destroy his children, he was slain by one of them, the god Ea. Subsequently, when Tiamat made Kingu, her firstborn, chief of the gods, Marduk, son of Ea and Damkina, led a revolt against his divine

---

[22] Aside from these passages, the name Bel appears in the Bible only in Isaiah 46:1, while Merodach is found only in the name of the Babylonian king Merodach-baladan.

[23] For the text of the Enuma Elish, see *ANET,* 62–72.

progenitors and became king of the gods.[24] He then cut up the body of Tiamat and created from it the earth, while using the blood of Kingu to mold the first men. This rebellion against the gods reminds one of the premortal war waged by Satan against God (Moses 4:1–4; Abraham 3:22–28; D&C 29:36–41; D&C 76:25–29; see also Revelation 12:3–4, 7–9). In the version told at Babylon, however, it was the rebel, Marduk, who won.

The role of Marduk as a rebel ties him to Nimrod,[25] who founded Babel, which came to be called Babylon in Greek. According to rabbinic sources, the name Nimrod derives from the Semitic root *mrd*, "to rebel."[26] The same consonants appear at the beginning of the name Marduk, though the origin of the name is generally considered to be from Sumerian *MAR.UTU*.

According to Jewish tradition, Nimrod's rebellion consisted in the building of the city and tower of Babel.[27] Genesis 11:1–9 says that the tower was designed to reach unto heaven. This

---

[24] The title "king of the gods" is applied to Marduk in several ancient texts; see *ANET,* 309–311, 315, 332, 503.

[25] See the discussion in Bruce W. Warren and John A. Tvedtnes, "In Search of the Historic Nimrod," *Newsletter and Proceedings of the S.E.H.A.* 155 (November 1983): 1–6. According to Epiphanius (*Against Heresies* 1.1), after the flood, when the first city and tower were built, Nimrod was the first to gather the people together and rule over them.

[26] Babylonian Talmud (TB): *Pesahim* 94b, *Hagigah* 13a; *Midrash Bereshit Rabbah* 42.5; *Targum Jerushalmi* B on Genesis 10:9.

[27] TB: *Abodah Zarah* 50b, *Hullin* 99b; *Pirqe de Rabbi Eliezer* 24; Josephus, *Antiquities of the Jews* I.iv.2–3; *Book of Jasher* 9:20–27; *Chronicles of Jerahmeel* 31:20. The *Jasher* account indicates that there were three basic groups of people. One wanted to ascend to heaven and attack God. The second group wanted to place their own gods in heaven. The third wanted to kill God. Those in the first group were changed into apes and elephants, those in the second were slain, and those in the third were scattered in the earth. The scattering of a third of humanity may reflect the exile of the third of the host of heaven who followed Satan (Revelation 12:3–9; D&C 29:36).

may explain the name by which the city was known to its local inhabitants, *Bab-ilû*, generally understood to mean "gate of the gods." That Nimrod built Babel is confirmed in Genesis 10:9–10, though the Bible never ties him to the tower itself.[28]

According to *Chronicles of Jerahmeel* 31:20, Nimrod forced the people to acknowledge him as a god and counseled them to erect the city and tower of Babel to rebel against God. Thereafter, everyone who rebelled against the Lord was compared to Nimrod.[29] *Chronicles of Jerahmeel* 30:6 indicates that those who built the tower of Babel did so to reach and break open the firmament of heaven, preempting another flood from God.[30] They sought to "wage war with those in heaven and establish themselves as gods." This was also Satan's intention.[31] The thought of ascending to heaven attributed to Lucifer in Isaiah 14:13 is the same one that brought about the fall of the tower of Babel (the origin of Babylon) in Genesis 11:1–9. Indeed, according to Helaman 6:28, it was Satan who inspired the building of the tower.

If the early Jewish traditions have a basis in fact, then Nimrod seems to have been inspired by Satan to build the city and tower of Babel, in direct disobedience to the Lord's instructions

---

[28] According to *Book of Jasher* 12:45; 27:2, Nimrod was king of Babel.

[29] The *Chronicles of Jerahmeel* is a "collection of apocryphal and pseudo-epigraphical books dealing with the history of the world from the creation to the death of Judas Maccabeus." The edition used here is the translation by M. Gaster published by Ktav Publishing House, New York, 1971.

[30] See Stephen Ricks's discussion of the Near Eastern worldview in his FARMS preliminary report, "Heavenly Visions of Isaiah—and the Revelation of John."

[31] Some critics of LDS doctrine point to Satan's effort as an indication that the idea of becoming like God is Satanic. Note, however, that the context of Satan's effort, as identified in these passages, is rebellion against God, not cooperation with His plan to make men His heirs (Romans 8:16-17).

that the people should disperse and fill the earth (Genesis 9:1).[32] It is significant that some early stories indicate that Nimrod named his son Bel, which is a title of Marduk, and that Bel's son Ninus is said to have erected an idol of his father (*Chronicles of Jerahmeel* 32:2–5).[33] The story is evidently intended to explain how the worship of Bel or Marduk began in Babylon. In *Book of Jasher* 7:47–48 and 11:7, Nimrod's son is Mardon, a name that derives from the same root as Nimrod and means "rebel."[34]

BABYLON IN HISTORY

By the time John composed the book of Revelation, Babylon had become a generalized term for the wickedness of the world, whose destruction was foreseen by John (Revelation 17–18; see especially 17:5). He borrowed from Isaiah and other Old Testament prophets in referring to the wickedness of the last days. Thus, Revelation 18:2 is based on Isaiah 21:9, though it connects Babylon with devils and foul spirits rather than graven images. In Revelation 14:8 and 16:19, fallen Babylon is compared to a harlot, whose tie to drunkenness and wine is based on Jeremiah 51:6–9

---

[32] Though we generally emphasize the tower, we often overlook the fact that the people at Babel wanted to build a city to avoid being scattered throughout the earth (Genesis 11:4).

[33] Belus is the first in the list of Assyrian kings in Eusebius' *Chronicon*. While Genesis 10:11 has Asshur (or Nimrod, according to the reading of many scholars) leaving the area of Babel to found cities in the north (Assyria, known as Asshur in Hebrew), in *Jasher* 10:35 it is Bela who founds those cities.

[34] Note also the name of the Kassite god Murudash, who was identified with the Sumerian Ninurta, whose deeds are often attributed to Marduk in parallel Babylonian texts. Like Marduk, the Hittite god Kumarbi rebelled against the seventy gods of heaven. His intention was to launch an attack from atop the head of a stone giant. The stories are noted in Robert Graves and Raphael Patai, *Hebrew Myths: The Book of Genesis* (New York: McGraw-Hill, 1963), 127–28.

(see also D&C 35:11; 86:3).³⁵

Nephi, who saw the same woman as John in his vision (1 Nephi 14:10–27), evidently connects her with the "great and abominable church" of which the devil is said to be the founder (1 Nephi 13:6; 14:3, 9–10, 17; see also 2 Nephi 26:22). The "kingdom of the devil" is referred to in 2 Nephi 28:19 and 2:29 and in Alma 5:25 and 41:4. In 1 Nephi 22:22–23 and Doctrine and Covenants 10:56, it is mentioned in connection with false churches.

This association of the devil with controlling political and religious organizations is further reflected in the Book of Mormon, where he is the founder of the secret combinations that seek power and authority (2 Nephi 26:22; 3 Nephi 6:15–18, 28; Ether 8:16; Moses 6:15; 7:24; see also Moses 5:29–30, 49, 52). In Ether 8:25, we read that his purpose in establishing secret combinations is to overthrow the nations of the world.

Modern revelation, too, identifies Babylon with the wickedness of the world (D&C 35:11; 64:24). The Lord has commanded his people to flee from spiritual Babylon, meaning the wickedness of the world in the latter days (D&C 133:5, 7, 14; see also 64:24). The idea comes from Old Testament passages that relate to the original Babylon (Isaiah 48:20; Jeremiah 50:8; 51:6, 45). Doctrine and Covenants 86:3 ties spiritual Babylon to Satan, while Doctrine and Covenants 1:16 indicates that the latter-day Babylon has its own idols. In all this, we are reminded that Paul calls Satan "the god of this world" (2 Corinthians 4:4).³⁶

---

[35] For a description of the harlotry of Babylon, see Herodotus, *The Histories* 1.181, 197, 199.

[36] The same title is applied to Satan in *Martyrdom and Ascension of Isaiah* 9:14 (cf. 2:4, where he is called the angel who rules the world). In the New Testament, Satan is termed "the prince of the devils" (Matthew 9:34; 12:24; Mark 3:22), "the prince of this world" (John 12:31; 14:30 [cited in D&C 127:11]; 16:11), and "the prince of the power of the air" (Ephesians 2:2). The devil is given the title "prince" or "king" in the *Testaments of the Twelve Patriarchs* (*Testament of Simeon* 2:7;

Isaiah's description of Babylon was taken up by two of his successors, Jeremiah and Ezekiel, who lived to see the Jews taken captive by the Babylonians in fulfillment of Isaiah's prophecies. The prophecies of the fall of Babylon in Jeremiah 50–51 are particularly revealing.[37] It is here that we find mention of the judgment of Bel or Merodach noted earlier (Jeremiah 50:2; 51:44) and the commandment to flee from Babylon (Jeremiah 50:8; 51:6, 45). It is from Jeremiah 51:7 that Revelation 14:8 and 16:19 borrows the idea of the nations' being drunk with the wine of Babylon. While Isaiah 14:4 calls Babylon "the golden city," in Jeremiah 51:7 it is "a golden cup."

In Jeremiah's prophecy, Babylon, like Satan and Nimrod, is said to have "striven against the Lord" (Jeremiah 50:24). Like Lucifer (Isaiah 14:12), Babylon will fall (Jeremiah 51:8, 44). Lucifer desired to "ascend into heaven," to "exalt [his] throne above the stars" and the clouds, but would "be brought down to hell" (Isaiah 14:13–14). Jeremiah declared that "though Babylon should mount up to heaven, and though she should fortify the height of her strength" (Jeremiah 51:53), only the city's "judgment reacheth unto heaven, and is lifted up even to the skies" (Jeremiah 51:9).

COMPARING THE ISAIAH ACCOUNT TO JEREMIAH AND EZEKIEL

In Isaiah's account, Lucifer sought to "sit upon the mount of the congregation" (Isaiah 14:13). Jeremiah called Babylon a

---

Testament of Judah 19:4; *Testament of Dan* 5:6); in *Book of the Rolls* (f.90b, f.91a, f.112b); in one of the Dead Sea Scrolls (*1QM* 17.5f); in *Martyrdom and Ascension of Isaiah* 4:2; and in *Jubilees* 11:5, 11; 17:16; 18:9, 12; 48:2, 9, 12, 15. *Epistle of Barnabas* 2:1 notes that "the adversary" (the meaning of the title Satan) rules this world.

[37] These prophecies are undated. If they were written before Lehi's departure from Jerusalem, they may have been on the brass plates of Laban.

"destroying mountain" that the Lord would roll down and make a "burnt mountain" (Jeremiah 51:25). The "astonishment among the nations" that Babylon should be destroyed (Jeremiah 51:41) is reflected in the words of those who would see Lucifer in the pit in Isaiah 14:16–17.

Jeremiah even uses some of the same expressions employed by Isaiah in his Lucifer prophecy. For example the Hebrew *kol ha-'areṣ*, "the whole earth/land" or "all the earth/land," used in Isaiah 14:7, is also found in Jeremiah 50:23 and 51:7, 25, and 41 and with the variant pronominal suffix in Jeremiah 51:47. The expression of astonishment, beginning with "how," in Isaiah 14:12,[38] is also used in Jeremiah 50:23 and 51:41.[39] Jeremiah 50:46 says that "the earth is moved," using the same Hebrew root (*r'š*) as Isaiah 14:16 when speaking about the shaking of the kingdoms.[40] Both Isaiah 14:17 and Jeremiah 51:43 speak of a desolation that makes the world a wilderness (*midbar*), while Isaiah 14:20 and Jeremiah 51:25 speak of destruction of the land, using the Hebrew root *šḥt*.[41]

Ezekiel, too, uses Isaiah's motifs in writing about the kingdoms of Tyre and Egypt. We have already noted that he seems to refer to Satan when addressing the king of Tyre in Ezekiel 28. On closer examination, we find a number of parallels between the prophecy in Ezekiel 28:1–19 and the one in Isaiah 14:4–20. While Isaiah's Lucifer seeks to set his throne on high and become like

---

[38] Though KJV has "how" twice in this verse, only the first reflects the Hebrew word.

[39] While KJV has "how" three times in this verse, the second is nonexistent in the Hebrew.

[40] Isaiah also wrote about hell being moved (Isaiah 14:9) and the trembling of the earth (Isaiah 14:16), but in both cases, a different Hebrew verb (*rgz*) is used.

[41] The Hebrew behind "desolation" in Jeremiah 50:22 and 51:43 is a different root, as is the Hebrew behind "destroyed" in Isaiah 14:17.

God (Isaiah 14:13–14), Ezekiel has the prince of Tyre declaring, "I am a God, I sit in the seat of God" (Ezekiel 28:2) and setting his "heart as the heart of God" (Ezekiel 28:6; see also verse 9). Lucifer's desire to "sit also upon the mount of the congregation" (Isaiah 14:13) is paralleled by Ezekiel's declaration that the king of Tyre was an "anointed cherub . . . upon the holy mountain of God" (Ezekiel 28:14; see also verse 16) "in Eden the garden of God" (Ezekiel 28:13).[42] As in Isaiah 14:9, 12, and 15, the usurper is "cast . . . as profane out of the mountain of God" and "cast . . . to the ground" (Ezekiel 28:16–17). A few verses earlier, the prince of Tyre, like the king of Babylon (Isaiah 14:15), is told he will be brought "down to the pit" (Ezekiel 28:8).

The fall of the king of Tyre is to cause astonishment among the people (Ezekiel 28:19), like that accompanying the fall of Babylon in Jeremiah's prophecy (Jeremiah 51:41). This astonishment is reflected in Isaiah 14:15–17, where people look upon the fallen king of Babylon lying in the pit of hell. Similarly, the Lord, through Ezekiel, tells the king of Tyre, "I will cast thee to the ground, I will lay thee before kings, that they may behold thee" (Ezekiel 28:17). The "kings of the nations" are also mentioned in Isaiah 14:18 in connection with the casting down of Lucifer.

Of particular interest is the fact that Ezekiel wrote of the "brightness" of both the prince and the king of Tyre (Ezekiel 28:7, 17), reminding us that the Hebrew word rendered "Lucifer" in Isaiah 14:12 means "shining."[43] Satan sometimes appears as an

---

[42] Early traditions place the garden of Eden atop a mountain (see particularly the pseudepigraphal work known as *2 Adam and Eve,* or *Conflict of Adam and Eve with Satan*). The "stones of fire" mentioned in Ezekiel 28:14, 16 reflect the descriptions of God's dwelling as a place of fire. See the discussion in the author's chapter on "The Heavens" in the forthcoming FARMS book on the *Testaments of the Twelve Patriarchs.*

[43] In Ezekiel 26:17, Tyre is called "the renowned city." The word rendered "renowned" derives from the same root as the one from which we have "Lucifer" in Isaiah 14:12. A different Hebrew word is rendered "brightness" in Ezekiel 28:7, 17.

"angel of light" (2 Corinthians 11:14; 2 Nephi 9:9; Alma 30:53; D&C 128:20 and 129:8; *Life of Adam and Eve* 9:1; *The Conflict of Adam and Eve with Satan* I: 27; 33[44]), though he really represents forces of darkness.[45]

In his parable about the king of Assyria addressed to the king of Egypt (Ezekiel 31), Ezekiel employs some of the same imagery. He speaks again of "Eden" and "the garden of God" (Ezekiel 31:8-9, 16, 18). He has the Lord mentioning the "fall" of the king of Assyria, "when I cast him down to hell with them that descend into the pit" (Ezekiel 31:16; cf. verse 17), evidently borrowing terminology from Isaiah 14:9, 15. Isaiah mentions the "kings of the nations" who "lie in glory," while Lucifer is compared to "those that are slain, thrust through with a sword" (Isaiah 14:18-19). Ezekiel appears to have borrowed these ideas when he speaks of the king of Assyria's "glory . . . among the trees of Eden, of his being "brought down" to the "nether parts of the earth," to "lie . . . with them that be slain by the sword" (Ezekiel 31:16, 18).

In Isaiah 14:16, Lucifer's fall prompts others to ask, "Is this the man that made the earth to tremble, that did shake kingdoms?" In Ezekiel, the Lord says, "I made the nations to shake at the sound of his fall, when I cast him down to hell." The mention of the branches and trees in Ezekiel 31:8-9, 16, 18 may derive from Isaiah 14:8, 19. In both of his prophecies, Ezekiel refers to the use of swords (Ezekiel 28:7 and 31:18), reminding us that Isaiah also uses this theme in his Lucifer prophecy (Isaiah

---

[44] This work, originally composed in Arabic, probably in the eleventh century A.D., was translated and published by S. C. Malan in 1882. Two of its four books were reprinted in *The Forgotten Books of Eden,* ed. Rutherford H. Platt, Jr. (Cleveland: World Publishing; copyrighted 1927 by Alpha House), as *1* and *2 Adam and Eve.*

[45] This subject and some of the others mentioned here are discussed in detail in the author's chapter on "The Devil" in the forthcoming FARMS book on the *Testaments of the Twelve Patriarchs.* See also the chapter, "The Sons of God" in the same volume.

14:19). Isaiah, Jeremiah, and Ezekiel all include mention of "the nations" in the prophecies in question (Isaiah 14:18; Jeremiah 50:2, 23, 46 and 51:7; Ezekiel 28:7).

COMPARISONS WITH THE BOOK OF MORMON

While Jeremiah and Ezekiel seem to be imitating Isaiah in their prophetic utterances against Babylon and other wicked kingdoms of the sixth century B.C., Book of Mormon prophets use some of the same terminology in their discussions of the devil. There is some evidence that Isaiah's Lucifer prophecy may have influenced Lehi and his sons, Nephi and Jacob, all of whom discuss Satan in some detail. Significantly, all of these discussions postdate the acquisition of the brass plates of Laban, which contained the writings of Isaiah.

We have already noted that Lehi speaks of the devil as "an angel of God . . . [who] had fallen from heaven . . . [and] became a devil, having sought that which was evil before God" (2 Nephi 2:17). He declares that he had learned this from "the things which I have read . . . according to that which is written." He then cites Satan's words to Eve in the garden of Eden (2 Nephi 2:18; see also Genesis 3:4–5). But since the story of the fall of man as given in Genesis 3 does not include the fall of Lucifer, Lehi must have learned of it from another source, possibly Isaiah 14.[46]

Satan's fall in 2 Nephi 2:17–18 clearly parallels that of Lucifer in Isaiah 14:12–14. In the Isaiah account, the fall was the consequence of his attempt to exalt himself above God. Lehi merely

---

[46] Some might argue that Lehi had read the account now known to us as Moses 1:12–22; 4:1–4 (the latter immediately preceding the temptation of Eve). However, the information in these passages, though revealed to Moses, may never have been part of the book of Genesis. (Moses 1:23 need not mean that Moses "bore record" in that book.) Words like those found in Moses 4:1 ("I, the Lord God, spake unto Moses") are more likely to have been revealed to Joseph Smith than written by Moses himself, while those in Moses 1:42 clearly show that the revelation as we have it was addressed to Joseph Smith.

states that he had "sought that which was evil before God." In Isaiah 14:9, 15, Lucifer is brought down to hell. The Hebrew word rendered "hell" is sometimes translated "grave"; it refers to the place where one goes at death, and hence seems to be the spirit world, part of which, known as a "prison," is Satan's domain. Lehi warns that the devil will bring the wicked "down to hell, that he may reign over [them] in his own kingdom" (2 Nephi 2:29). This he terms the "captivity and power of the devil" (2 Nephi 2:27–28).

In Isaiah 14:17, Lucifer is described as he who "opened not the house of his prisoners." The rescue of the prisoners by Christ is described in 1 Peter 3:18–20. When called upon to read in the synagogue in Nazareth, Jesus read Isaiah 61:1–3 and declared that it was fulfilled in him (Luke 4:18–21). The passage, considered even in Jesus' time to refer to the Messiah, speaks of the opening of the prison.[47]

After speaking of Satan's fall from heaven, Lehi notes that Satan "sought also the misery of all mankind," for which reason he tempted Eve with the same idea that, according to Isaiah 14:13–14, had gotten him into trouble, namely, becoming like God (2 Nephi 2:17–19; see also Genesis 3:1–14; D&C 29:36–41).[48] The result was the same: Adam and Eve, like Satan before them, were cast out of God's presence into a world of misery. Lehi stresses that Satan still seeks to captivate the children of Adam and Eve and bring them into misery (2 Nephi 2:27–29; see also his words in 2 Nephi 1:13, 15, 18).[49]

---

[47] For similar passages, see Psalms 146:7–9; Isaiah 24:22; 42:6–7; 49:8–9.

[48] LDS doctrine certainly includes the concept that any attempt to become like God, other than through the means He provides, will result in misery.

[49] That Adam and Eve became miserable at the time of the fall is confirmed in 2 Nephi 2:5 (cf. 2:23) and in Alma 12:26 and 42:11. Jacob noted that, without the Atonement, we would all be in misery with the devil (2 Nephi 9:9). One of the most frequent themes of the Book of Mormon is that those who follow Satan will be miserable (2 Nephi 1:13; 9:46; Mosiah 3:25; Alma 3:26; 9:11; 26:20; 40:15, 17,

Comparisons With the Book of Mormon

Some of Lehi's information about the devil evidently came from his vision of the tree of life. Nephi declines to write the entire account of his father's vision (1 Nephi 8:29); instead, he leaves a more detailed account of the same vision given to him in response to his prayer (1 Nephi 10:17; 11:1). In this account (1 Nephi 10–14), he speaks of the devil, hell, captivity, and the devil's church several times (1 Nephi 12:16–19; 13:6, 29; 14:3–4, 7–10, 17). Of interest is his mention of the destruction of men as part of the devil's plan (1 Nephi 14:3, 7)—an idea that he may have borrowed from such passages as Isaiah 14:6, 17, 19–20. When explaining the vision to his brothers, Nephi again mentions the devil and hell and notes that while the righteous will "dwell in the kingdom of God," the wicked will be "cast out" (1 Nephi 15:29, 35). This, of course, is what happens to Lucifer in Isaiah 14:12–15.

Nephi subsequently elaborates on the subject, noting that Satan would lose his power on earth but would retain a kingdom to which the wicked would be consigned (1 Nephi 22:15, 22–23, 26). The wicked, he wrote, "must be brought low in the dust," which is the same fate that befalls Lucifer when he is cast into the pit like a carcass (or "carcase") in Isaiah 14:9, 15, 19.

Nephi's brother, Jacob, influenced by their father, Lehi,[50] speaks at length of the devil in a two-part sermon recorded by Nephi (2 Nephi 9:7–19, 26, 34–37, 45–46; 10:23–24). Among the themes possibly drawn from Isaiah's Lucifer prophecy are Jacob's declaration that Satan was an "angel who fell from before the presence of the Eternal God, and became the devil" (2 Nephi 9:8). Having thus become miserable, he sought the misery of mankind and "beguiled our first parents," being able to transform "himself nigh unto an angel of light." Those whom he is able to

---

21; 41:9–11; 42:1, 26; Helaman 3:29; 5:12; 7:9; 12:26; Mormon 8:38).

[50] For more information, see "The Influence of Lehi's Admonitions on the Teachings of His Son Jacob," by the author, in *Journal of Book of Mormon Studies* 3.2 (Fall 1994), 34–48.

deceive become, like him, "devils, angels to a devil, to be shut out from the presence of our God" (2 Nephi 9:9; see also 2 Nephi 2:17; Jacob 3:11). Like Lehi, Jacob speaks of the "captivity of the devil," whom he calls an "awful monster" who seeks to bring men down to hell (2 Nephi 9:10, 12, 19, 26, 34, 36, 45, 46).

Some of these ideas may come from Isaiah 5, cited by Nephi in 2 Nephi 15.[51] After speaking of the "captivity" of Israel because of wickedness (Isaiah 5:13; 2 Nephi 15:13), the prophet declares that "hell hath enlarged herself, and opened her mouth without measure; and their glory, and their multitude, and their pomp, and he that rejoiceth, shall descend into it" (Isaiah 5:14; 2 Nephi 15:14). This verse may have given birth to the idea of the devil as a monster.[52] In the same chapter, Isaiah declares that the wicked will be destroyed "as the fire devoureth the stubble . . . and their blossom shall go up as dust" (Isaiah 5:24; 2 Nephi 15:24). In his discussion of those who follow Satan, Nephi speaks of the wicked being burned "as stubble" and "brought low in the dust . . . according to the words of the prophet" (1 Nephi 22:23; see also 1 Nephi 22:15). Jacob speaks of the wicked being cast "into everlasting fire . . . a lake of fire and brimstone" (2 Nephi 9:16, 19, 26).

Following his record of Jacob's speech in 2 Nephi 6–10 (in which Jacob quotes Isaiah 50:1–52:2), Nephi copies Isaiah 2–14

---

[51] Note Isaiah 5:12-14 (same as 2 Nephi 15:12-14), where we have mention of the tabret and pipe, as in Ezekiel's "king of Tyrus" prophecy (Ezekiel 28:13), along with mention of "captivity" and "glory," terms associated with the Lucifer prophecies we have already examined.

[52] Satan is identified with a dragon or serpent in Revelation 12:7–9; 20:2 (cf. 13:1–2, 11); and *Gospel of Bartholomew* 4:46. He spoke to Eve through the serpent (Genesis 3:1–15; Moses 4:1–21; 2 Nephi 2:17–18; D&C 29:36–40). He is tied to vipers (cf. Job 20:16) in several of the Dead Sea Scrolls, such as *Testament of Amram* (*4QAmram* Ms. B), *4Q525* 5.4. Cf. *Testament of Asher* 7:3, where the Lord incarnate comes "crushing the dragon's head in the water," in terms similar to those found in Psalms 74:13–14.

onto the small plates (2 Nephi 12–24). This is followed by his own prophecy, in which he draws upon some of Isaiah's themes for commentary (2 Nephi 25–31). In this prophecy, he devotes a number of verses to a discussion of the devil and hell (2 Nephi 26:10, 22; 28:15–23; 30:15–18). Among the themes he repeats are those of the devil's church (2 Nephi 28:18), the captivity of the devil (2 Nephi 26:22; 28:19, 21–23), death and hell (2 Nephi 28:23), and the power and kingdom of Satan (2 Nephi 28:19; 30:18).

To this he adds that the devil is the founder of secret combinations (2 Nephi 26:22)—a theme repeated by subsequent Book of Mormon authors.[53] It may be significant that, among the Isaiah passages found in this speech, is one in which the prophet speaks again of "Eden . . . the garden of the Lord" (Isaiah 51:3=2 Nephi 8:3) and describes the ancient struggle between the Lord and the sea-monster Rahab, also called a "dragon" in KJV (Isaiah 51:9-10, same as 2 Nephi 8:10; cf. Psalms 89:9-10). In Psalms 87:4, "Rahab and Babylon" are listed together, again suggesting the identification of this monster of the deep with the king of Babylon.

Some of Nephi's comments may derive from Isaiah's Lucifer prophecy. We have, for example, the idea of the wicked being thrust down to hell (2 Nephi 26:10; 28:15; see also Isaiah 14:9, 15 and compare the fall of the devil's church in 2 Nephi 28:18), the destruction of the inhabitants of the earth (2 Nephi 28:17; see also Isaiah 14:6, 8, 16–17, 20), and the shaking of the devil's kingdom (2 Nephi 28:19; see also Isaiah 14:16).

According to Isaiah 14:12–14, Lucifer's rebellion consisted in wanting to become like God, to "sit also upon the mount of the congregation, in the sides of the north." The term rendered "north" in this passage is the Hebrew *Saphon*, the name of the mountain on the Syrian coast, north of Ugarit, on which, according to the

---

[53] Helaman 6:26–30; 3 Nephi 6:28–29; Ether 8:15, 25; 10:33.

Ugaritic texts, Baal's palace was built. The word Ṣ*aphon*, meaning "high place,"[54] came to mean "north" because of the mountain's location.[55]

In Israel, the temple mount in Jerusalem was seen as the dwelling-place of Jehovah on the earth, perhaps in view of the rival Baal cult. Consequently, we read of "mount Zion, on the sides of the north, the city of the great king" in Psalm 48:2.[56] The "great king," of course, is Jehovah, just as in Tyre the "king of the city" (Melqart) was Baal. The Lord uses the expression "my holy mountain" in reference to Jerusalem and its temple in Isaiah 11:9, 56:7, 57:13, 65:11, 65:25, and 66:20; Joel 2:1 and 3:17; Obadiah 1:16; and Zephaniah 3:11.[57]

The passage in Isaiah 11:9 is particularly instructive. It reads, "They shall not hurt nor destroy in all my holy mountain: for the earth shall be full of the knowledge of the Lord, as the waters cover the sea." Nephi includes the prophecy in his lengthy recitation of Isaiah passages (2 Nephi 21:9); and in the prophetic commentary that follows, he cites it in reference to the millennial era, when "Satan shall have power over the hearts of the children of

---

[54] This is not the word usually rendered "high place" by the King James translators, but refers to a mountain from which one has a view of the surrounding territory.

[55] The site was called Mount Cassius in the Greco-Roman era (from Hazi, the Assyrian name of the mountain) and is today known by the Arabic name Jebel Aqra. Compare the place-name Baal-Zaphon in Exodus 14:2, 9.

[56] Note that Joshua was buried on the north side of the hill (Joshua 24:30; Judges 2:9).

[57] In *1 Enoch* 25:3, we read that there is a mountain that serves as God's throne when he comes to visit the earth and that "the Holy and Great Lord of Glory" sits on this throne. According to *Ezekiel the Tragedian* 68–76, Moses saw the throne of God on mount Sinai and was invited to sit with the Lord. In Doctrine and Covenants 76:66–68, the celestial kingdom is compared to "Mount Zion . . . the city of the living God, the heavenly place, the holiest of all."

men no more" (2 Nephi 30:15).

In Isaiah 14:13, Lucifer desires to sit on the "mount of the congregation," Hebrew *hr m'd*. The second element is found in the Ugaritic expression *phr m'd*, referring to the assembly of the gods, and in the biblical Hebrew *'hl m'd*, generally rendered "tent of the congregation" in the King James Bible, in reference to the tabernacle of Moses. The heavenly council is described in Psalm 82:1, which Julian Morgenstern saw as a New Year's Day judgment scene with God sitting on his throne. He further believed that the fall of "one of the princes" in verses 6–7 was a reference to Satan's being cast out of heaven.[58]

While the devil is expelled from the mountain of God in Isaiah 14:13 and Ezekiel 28:14 and 16, in Ezekiel 28:13 he is said to have been in Eden, the garden of God. In early Jewish tradition, the garden was situated atop a mountain. Some early traditions indicate that the tower of Babel (built by Nimrod, inspired by Satan, in an attempt to ascend to heaven) was an imitation of the holy mountain of Eden.[59]

---

[58] Julian Morgenstern, "The Mythological Background of Psalm 82," *Hebrew Union College Annual* 14 (1939): 29–126. Thanks to Brian J. Thomas of Denver, Colorado, for bringing this article to the author's attention. Morgenstern notes that Hupfeld has already indicated, in his commentary on Psalm 82, that the Lord, in that passage, was angry with angels who had rebelled against his authority (115 n. 159). He further notes that *Midrash Tehillim* interprets the word "princes" in Psalms 82:7 as referring to the highest rank of angels (117 n. 164). Morgenstern also compares the assembly in Psalms 82 with the assembly of the "sons of God" in Job 1:6–12; 2:1–7, where Satan comes to accuse Job (Job 40–59).

[59] The concept of Eden being atop a mountain is particularly strong throughout *The Conflict of Adam and Eve with Satan*. See particularly the following passages: in Book II: 5:5; 9:5; 10:6–7; 11:1–3, 10–11; 12:10, 16; 15:2; 16:5–7; 17:16–17; 19:8–9; 20:11, 15–21, 29–30, 33, 36–37; 21:5–7; and 22:6, 10. In Book III: 2:3; 3:8; 4:2; 5:12, 14, 21; 6:7; 7:2,5,10,12; 9:9, 14; 13:2; and 13:13, 20. See also Targum Yonathan on Genesis 3.

CONCLUSION

Lucifer's attempt to sit on the holy mountain reflects his desire to become part of the heavenly council. Indeed, in the premortal world, he challenged Christ's support for the Father's plan of salvation and asked to be sent in his place.[60] He went so far as to tell Moses that he was the Only Begotten (Moses 1:12–22) and "a son of God" (Moses 5:13). It is likely that the title rendered Lucifer ("shining one"), son of the morning, reflects this claim, for in the New Testament we read that it is Jesus who is truly "the bright and morning star" (Revelation 22:16; see also Revelation 2:28; 2 Peter 1:18–19).

According to Doctrine and Covenants 76:28, Satan "rebelled against God, and sought to take the kingdom of our God and his Christ." In Doctrine and Covenants 88:115, he is called "him who seeketh the throne of him who sitteth upon the throne, even the Lamb." The irony is that, because of his rebellion, he will be called to account before that throne. "Death, and hell, and the devil, and all that have been seized therewith must stand before the throne of God, and be judged according to their works, from whence they must go into the place prepared for them, even a lake of fire and brimstone, which is endless torment" (2 Nephi 28:23).

---

[60] Moses 4:1; Abraham 3:27. According to Moses 4:1–3, Satan sought God's own power.

Chapter 20

PROMISCUITY AND THE SEARCH FOR WEALTH

And now I make an end of speaking unto you concerning this pride. And were it not that I must speak unto you concerning a grosser crime, my heart would rejoice exceedingly because of you. But the word of God burdens me because of your grosser crimes. For behold, thus saith the Lord: This people begin to wax in iniquity; they understand not the scriptures, for they seek to excuse themselves in committing whoredoms, because of the things which were written concerning David, and Solomon his son. (Jacob 2:22-23)

In one of his speeches to the Nephites, Jacob condemned sexual promiscuity ("whoredoms") and the love of riches and its resulting pride (Jacob 1:15-17; 2:12-35).[1] Jacob's brother, Nephi, likewise spoke against pride, wickedness, abominations and whoredoms (2 Nephi 28:13-15). A few centuries later, the Nephite prophet Abinadi accused the priests of Noah of whoredom and seeking for riches (Mosiah 12:29). Significantly, Alma's discussion of fornication (Alma 39:5-9, 11) is immediately followed by his condemnation of riches (Alma 39:14). The sins of sexual promiscuity and love of riches are similarly condemned in the

---

[1] The pride that comes from excessive wealth (including fine clothing) is frequently denounced elsewhere in the Book of Mormon (Helaman 13:22, 33; 3 Nephi 6:10-15; 4 Nephi 1:24-26, 43; Mormon 8:36-37) and in the Apocrypha (*Wisdom of Solomon* 5:8; *Ben-Sirach* 5:1-2; 11:4-5). The pseudepigraphic *1 Enoch* 94:7-8 condemns those who seek wealth instead of God. Nevertheless, both Jacob 2:18-19 and *Ben-Sirach* 13:24; 31:8 indicate that wealth is permissible if its pursuit is for the intent to accomplish righteous deeds.

centuries-old *Testament of Judah* 17:1-2; 18:2-3, where they are listed among the blinding tools of Satan.

THE THREE NETS OF BELIAL

One might well wonder why sexual sins and the love of wealth are mentioned together in these passages. The answer can be found in a number of early sources. One of the Dead Sea scrolls, the *Damascus (Zadokite) Document*, a copy of which was also found in 1898 in the old Cairo genizah, speaks of the "three nets of Belial,"[2] which it lists as sexual promiscuity, riches, and pollution of the sanctuary (CD 4.15), generally through idolatry.[3] The same three sins (sexual promiscuity, stealing from the temple, and polluting the temple) are listed in the same order in the pseudepigraphic *Psalms of Solomon* 8:9-12.

Testament of Levi 17:11 lists "money lovers" right after "adulterers" and "idolators" and elaborates by including the "arrogant, lawless, voluptuaries, pederasts, those who practice beastiality." *Testament of Judah* 18:2-5 mentions "sexual promiscuity and love of money, [which] blind the direction of the soul" and "impede the sacrifices to God."

The three sins or nets of the devil are mentioned in several pseudepigraphic sources as well. In *Jubilees* 7:20-21, we read that Noah instructed his grandsons to keep themselves from fornication, pollution, and injustice, and that it was these three sins that brought the flood. *Jubilees* 20:3-6 notes that Abraham, when

---

[2] These may be the same as "the nets of deceit" by which men are ensnared, mentioned in *Testament of Dan* 2:4.

[3] The passage is commenting on Isaiah 24:17-18, which speaks of those who escape fear being taken in the pit, while those who escape the pit are taken in the snare. For a discussion of this topic, see the appendix "The 'Three Nets of Belial' in the Zadokite Document and 'balla/BELA' in the Temple Scroll," in Robert Eisenmann, *James the Just in the Habakkuk Pesher* (Rome: Tipographia Gregoriana, 1985; reprinted Leiden: E. J. Brill, 1986), 87-94.

blessing his sons and grandsons, warned them against fornication, impurity, and pollution; verse 5 specifically states that the giants and Sodomites had been destroyed because of fornication, impurity, and corruption.

In another passage, we read that the sins for which the flood was sent were fornication, pollution of the earth, and injustice (*Jubilees* 7:20-21), especially fornication (verses 22-25). The sins for which the people of Sodom and the cities of the plain were destroyed were fornication, pollution of themselves, and pollution of the earth (Jubilees 16:5-6). In the last days, the evil generation will likewise be destroyed because of fornication, contamination, and abomination (*Jubilees* 23:14-18).

The book of Mormon similarly condems the same sins. All three of the nets of Belial are mentioned in Mosiah 11:6, which condemns laziness (i.e., the desire to get gain without labor), idolatry, and whoredom. Alma 1:32 lists a number of sins, of which some (idolatry, sorcery, wearing of costly apparel, pride, and whoredom) are clearly tied to the nets of Belial.

POLLUTING THE SANCTUARY THROUGH SIN

In this context, we must note that Jacob's condemnation of sexual sins and the search for riches, discussed above, was part of a sermon he delivered in the temple located in the city of Nephi (Jacob 1:17; 2:2, 11). Revelation 2:14 speaks of the "snares" ("stumblingblock" in the King James Bible) of fornication and eating polluted sacrifices (by which is meant sacrifices made to idols rather than sacrifices to the Lord). *Testament of Levi* 9:9 notes that promiscuity defiles the sanctuary, while *Testament of Levi* 14:6-15:1 lists the same "nets," condemning priests who steal, have illicit sexual relations, and pollute the sanctuary. *Testament of Levi* 17:11 prophesies of wicked priests who would be "idolators, adulterers, money lovers, arrogant, lawless, voluptuaries, pederasts, those who practice bestiality." The profanation of the sanctuary by the priests is also noted in Ezekiel 44:7-8 and Zephaniah 3:4. Ezekiel wrote of the three sins of whoredom, idolatry, and the search for wealth (Ezekiel 22:4, 9-12, 26-29; see Ezekiel 20:30-32, 39, where he speaks of idolatry and whoredom). In Ezekiel 17:6-8, 11-13, 15-17, he lists the sins as idolatry, women, and usery.

The concept of the wicked priests whose covetousness caused them to steal, to commit adultery, and to pollute the Lord's sanctuary seems to derive from the story of the sons of the high priest Eli, who served Israel when the prophet Samuel was a boy. We read that ""the sons of Eli were sons of Belial" (1 Samuel 2:12), that they stole from worshipers both the meat that the people were to eat, as well as the fat that was to be offered on the altar to the Lord (1 Samuel 2:13-17). They also "lay with the women that assembled at the door of the tabernacle of the congregation" (1 Samuel 2:22).

SINS LEADING TO IDOLATRY

A number of ancient texts see the sins of sexual promiscuity and covetousness leading to idolatry, which is the same as pollution of the sanctuary. Thus, the apostle Paul listed "fornication, and all uncleanness, or covetousness" together (Ephesians 5:3), then denounced the "whoremonger," the "unclean person," and the "covetous man, who is an idolator" (Ephesians 5:5). In the Book of Mormon, we read that the Lamanites "delighted in murdering the Nephites, and robbing and plundering them; and their hearts were set upon riches, or upon gold and silver, and precious stones; yet they sought to obtain these things by murdering and plundering . . . Thus they became a very indolent people, many of whom did worship idols" (Alma 17:14-15).

Habbakuk Commentary 8-10, 12-13 (one of the Dead Sea Scrolls) also groups together sins related to the search for riches (robbing the poor, gathering riches, profiteering from the wealth of others) and pollution of the sanctuary. Another of the scrolls, the *Temple Scroll* (11QT 2) mentions the search for wealth and idolatry together. According to *Testament of Judah* 19:1, the love of money

Sins Leading to Idolatry

leads to idolatry.[4] The same concept is taught in the Book of Mormon (Alma 7:6). Similarly, Colossians 3:5 equates covetousness to idolatry. Paul clearly ties the love of money to the devil[5] in 1 Timothy 6:4-11, where he speaks of "temptation and snare . . . destruction and perdition." *Ben-Sirach* 31:1-11 denounces corruption and the love of gold, indicating (verse 7) that it is a stumblingblock to those who sacrifice to it.

In *Testament of Reuben* 4:6, it is promiscuity that leads to idolatry. This concept is also found in the medieval *Chronicles of Jerahmeel* 55:10-11, referring to the story in Numbers 25, where we read that fornication with the Moabites led Israelites to worship the Moabites' false gods. Solomon, out of his desire for many wives, was led to introduce idolatry into Israel by constructing temples to their pagan gods (1 Kings 11:1-10). *Qur'an* 24:3 ties adultery to idolatry and the Old Testament prophet Hosea based his entire book on a comparison of adultery to idolatry (see especially Hosea 4:11-17). *Wisdom of Solomon* 14:12 declares that "the devising of idols was the beginning of [spiritual] fornication," while verses 22-30 list idolatry with various sexual sins. The Babylonian Talmud (*Ketubot* 11b) indicates that "most idolators are adulterers." *Testament of Judah* 23:1 lists "licentiousness and witchcraft and idolatry" together, while *Testament of Benjamin* 10:10 has fornication and idolatry together. *Testament of Naphtali* 3:3-5 similarly ties sexual promiscuity to idolatry.

---

[4] Among the Gadianton robbers, the desire for gain led to murder, plunder, theft, false witness, and "all manner of iniquity" (Helaman 7:21-26). The love of wealth is also condemned in Ecclesiastes 5:9-14. *Testament of Issachar* 4:2 notes that a good man does not desire gold, defraud his neighbor, or want fancy foods and fine clothes.

[5] The second-century Church Father Irenaeus tied idolatry to Satan, noting that the devil is worshiped through idols (*Against Heresies* 25:1).

CONCLUSION

The Book of Mormon's contention that sexual promiscuity and the unrighteous search for wealth are major sins is supported by a large number of other early Jewish and Christian texts. Many of these teach that these two sins, because they have such a strong influence on man, can lead us away from God. The message is just as important in our day, when promiscuity and materialism occupy so much of people's minds and time.

Chapter 21

"THE CHOIRS ABOVE"

I say unto you that I have caused that ye should assemble yourselves together that I might rid my garments of your blood, at this period of time when I am about to go down to my grave, that I might go down in peace, and my immortal spirit may join the choirs above in singing the praises of a just God. (Mosiah 2:28)

During his address to the Nephites assembled at the temple in Zarahemla, King Benjamin expressed the hope that he might "join the choirs above." The heavenly choir is noted in two other places in the Book of Mormon. Lehi declared that he "saw the heavens open, and he thought he saw God sitting upon his throne, surrounded with numberless concourses of angels in the attitude of singing and praising their God" (1 Nephi 1:8). Alma the Younger told his sons, "Yea, methought I saw, even as our father Lehi saw, God sitting upon his throne, surrounded with numberless concourses of angels, in the attitude of singing and praising their God; yea, and my soul did long to be there" (Alma 36:22). Mormon declared that the heirs of the celestial kingdom will "dwell in the presence of God in his kingdom, to sing ceaseless praises with the choirs above" (Mormon 7:7).

In his prayer dedicating the Kirtland Temple, Joseph Smith expressed a desire similar to that of King Benjamin: "And help us by the power of thy Spirit, that we may mingle our voices with those bright, shining seraphs around thy throne, with acclamations of praise, singing Hosanna to God and the Lamb!" (D&C 109:79).

"The Choirs Above"

THE "CHOIR" IN MIDDLE EASTERN TEXTS

The heavenly choir of angels is noted in the Bible (Job 38:7; Luke 2:13-14) and throughout the pseudepigraphic literature. According to *4 Maccabees* 18:23, the righteous dead join the (heavenly) choir of the fathers. Ezra saw the innumerable company of righteous souls in the last days praising the Lord with songs (*4 Ezra* 2:42). According to *3 Baruch* 10:5, the souls of the righteous in the third heaven are organized into choirs. One of the Dead Sea Scrolls, the *Thanksgiving Hymns*, likewise declares that humans will sing in the angelic chorus (1QH 3.22-24).

Especially relevant to King Benjamin's wish are those stories that have a mortal being taken to heaven and singing with the host of angels. Thus, in *Apocalypse of Abraham* 17:4-18:1, we read that Abraham, during his heavenly vision, sang a song of praise to God, taught him by angels. Similarly, *Testament of Isaac* 6:6 informs us that Abraham's son Isaac was taken to heaven, where he worshiped before the divine throne with a host of saints.

The prophet Zephaniah is said to have been taken to the fifth heaven, where he joined the thousands of angels praising and praying (*Apocalypse of Zephaniah* [Akhmimic] 8:2-3). Similarly, Isaiah is said to have joined with the heavenly throng in the sixth heaven to sing praises to God (*Martyrdom and Ascension of Isaiah* 8:16-17), then joined with his righteous ancestors in the seventh heaven in singing praises to God (*Martyrdom and Ascension of Isaiah* 9:29-32). Rabbi Ishmael the high priest also reported being taken to heaven, where he sang praises with the heavenly creatures below the throne of God (*3 Enoch* 1:10-12).

A medieval Jewish text, *Zohar* Exodus 19a, has Rabbi Judah saying, "Why are the singers here below called Levites? Because they are joined closely to (*lava* = to be joined to) and united with (the singers) above in absolute unison."[1]

---

[1] Harry Sperling, Maurice Simon, and Paul P. Levertoff, *The Zohar* (New York: The Rebecca Bennet Publications, 1958), 3:60.

THE SINGING LEVITES

When King Benjamin expressed the desire to "join the choirs above, he may have been playing on the Hebrew word "join" that lies behind the name Levi, ancestor of the Israelite tribe that performed priesthood functions in Old Testament times. Of his birth, we read, "And she [Leah] conceived again, and bare a son; and said, Now this time will my husband be *joined* unto me, because I have born him three sons: therefore was his name called Levi" (Genesis 29:34, emphasis added).

One of the functions of the Levites was to sing in the tabernacle and later the temple in Jerusalem (1 Chronicles 6:33; 9:33; 15:27; 2 Chronicles 5:12-13; 29:30; 35:15; Ezra 2:40-41; Nehemiah 7:1, 73; 10:28, 39; 11:22). Chief among the singing Levites in David's day were Heman, Asaph, and Ethan (1 Chronicles 15:16-19), who wrote some of the psalms found in the Bible (see Psalms 50, 73-83, 88-89).

CONCLUSION

Significantly, King Benjamin was at the temple at the time he spoke of the heavenly choir (Mosiah 2:1). It is likely that his discourse and the designation of his son Mosiah as the new king occurred at the Israelite feast of tabernacles, when a choir of Levites sang in imitation of the choir of angels.[2]

---

[2] See John A. Tvedtnes, "King Benjamin and the Feast of Tabernacles," in volume 2 of John M. Lundquist & Stephen D. Ricks (eds.), *By Study and Also By Faith: Essays in Honor of Hugh Nibley* (Salt Lake City: Deseret and FARMS, 1990); Terrence L. Szink and John W. Welch, "King Benjamin's Speech in the Context of Ancient Israelite Festivals," in John W. Welch and Stephen D. Ricks (eds.), *King Benjamin's Speech* (Provo: FARMS, 1998).

Chapter 22

THE THOUGHTS AND INTENTS OF THE HEART

But this much I can tell you, that if ye do not watch yourselves, and your thoughts, and your words, and your deeds, and observe the commandments of God, and continue in the faith of what ye have heard concerning the coming of our Lord, even unto the end of your lives, ye must perish. And now, O man, remember, and perish not. (Mosiah 4:30)

From this passage, we learn that we will be judged not only on the basis of our actions, but also according to our speech and even our thoughts. The same idea is expressed in Alma 12:14: "For our words will condemn us, yea, all our works will condemn us." Since all deeds and words are governed by our inward desires, it seems obvious that, in order to control our outward actions, we must begin by directing our thoughts aright.

GOD KNOWS THE THOUGHTS AND INTENTS OF OUR HEARTS

Because he alone knows our thoughts, only the Lord is capable of passing judgment on mankind. Both the Bible and the Book of Mormon teach that God knows our thoughts. Ammon taught that "he knows all the thoughts and intents of the heart; for by his hand were they all created from the beginning" (Alma 18:32).

Indeed, the flood came in punishment because "God saw that the wickedness of man was great in the earth, and that every imagination of the thoughts of his heart was only evil continually" (Genesis 6:5). Had the intent of their hearts been better, perhaps the generation living at the time of the flood would have been given more time to bring their actions in conformity with their thoughts.

In a letter to his son Moroni, the Nephite prophet Mormon demonstrated the seriousness of correct thoughts, when he wrote, "Behold I say unto you, that he that supposeth that little children need baptism is in the gall of bitterness and in the bonds of iniquity, for he hath neither faith, hope, nor charity; wherefore, should he be cut off while in the thought, he must go down to hell" (Moroni 8:14). In this example, there is no hint of sinful acts, only of sinful thoughts condemning a man.

THE IMPORTANCE OF OUR THOUGHTS

Mormon stressed the importance of righteous thinking during his discourse on the subject of faith, hope, and charity:

> For I remember the word of God, which saith by their works ye shall know them; for if their works be good, then they are good also. For behold, God hath said a man being evil cannot do that which is good; for if he offereth a gift, or prayeth unto God, except he shall do it with real intent it profiteth him nothing. For behold, it is not counted unto him for righteous-ness. For behold, if a man being evil giveth a gift, he doeth it grudgingly; wherefore it is counted unto him the same as if he had retained the gift; wherefore he is counted evil before God. And likewise also is it counted evil unto a man, if he shall pray and not with real intent of heart; yea, and it profiteth him nothing, for God receiveth none such. Wherefore, a man being evil cannot do that which is good; neither will he give a good gift. (Moroni 7:5-10)

The stress Mormon placed on praying "with real intent of heart" was probably what influenced his son Moroni to admonish that future readers of the Book of Mormon pray about the truthfulness of the book "with a sincere heart, with real intent, having faith in Christ" (Moroni 10:4). But the idea began a millennium earlier with Nephi, who admonished, "follow the Son, with full purpose of heart, acting no hypocrisy and no deception before God, but with real intent, repenting of your sins" (2 Nephi 31:13).

Alma gave similar counsel regarding prayer: "Yea, and cry unto God for all thy support; yea, let all thy doings be unto the Lord, and whithersoever thou goest let it be in the Lord; yea, let all thy thoughts be directed unto the Lord; yea, let the affections of thy heart be placed upon the Lord forever" (Alma 37:36).

CONCLUSION

The message is clear: While men observe only their actions and speech, God knows the thoughts and intents of their hearts. It is impossible to deceive him, and it is impossible to be truly righteous unless all three of these expressions of our character are in harmony with God's will.

Chapter 23

"HOW BEAUTIFUL UPON THE MOUNTAINS"[1]

How beautiful upon the mountains are the feet of him that bringeth good tidings, that publisheth peace; that bringeth good tidings of good, that publisheth salvation; that saith unto Zion, Thy God reigneth! (Isaiah 52:7 = Mosiah 12:21)

Nearly 300 verses from the biblical book of Isaiah are cited in the Book of Mormon. Of these, the first portion of chapter 52 is the most frequently quoted. Thus, 1 Nephi 52:7 cites verse 7; 1 Nephi 22:10-11 cites verse 10; 2 Nephi 8:24-25 and Moroni 10:31 cite verses 1-2; Mosiah 12:21-25 cites verses 7-10; Mosiah 15:14-18, and 29-31 cite verses 7-10; 3 Nephi 16:18-10 and 20:32-35 cite verses 8-10; 3 Nephi 20:36-42, and 45 cite verses 1-3, 6-7, 11-12, 15; 3 Nephi 21:8 cites verse 15; and 3 Nephi 21:29 cites verses 11-12.

A BOOK OF MORMON EXPOSITION

During their interrogation of the prophet Abinadi, the priests of wicked king Noah asked him the meaning of the passage found in Isaiah 52:7-10 (Mosiah 12:20-25). Wanting to explain the importance of prophets and of the law of Moses, Abinadi delayed responding (Mosiah 13:3). When, at length, he gave his answer, he began by citing the great prophecy of the coming Savior from Isaiah 53 (Mosiah 14), then began to expound both that chapter and the passage from the preceding chapter about which

---

[1] This article was originally published in the *Provo Sun*, October 25, 1998.

the priests had asked their question.

Of particular interest is the fact that Abinadi's interpretation of Isaiah 52:7 corresponds to that found in other ancient documents (including the Dead Sea Scrolls) that were unknown in Joseph Smith's day. That passage, cited by Abinadi in Mosiah 12:21, reads, "How beautiful upon the mountains are the feet of him that bringeth good tidings, that publisheth peace; that bringeth good tidings of good, that publisheth salvation."

Abinadi's explanation of this verse is found in Mosiah 15:13-18, where he notes that the passage refers to both the prophets who have foreseen the coming of Christ and also "the founder of peace, yea, even the Lord, who has redeemed his people; yea, him who has granted salvation unto his people."

OTHER ANCIENT EXPOSITIONS

This interpretation is strikingly similar to the one found in one of the DeadSea Scrolls, 11QMelchizedek (11Q13), column II, lines 15-19:

> This is the day of [peace about which God] spoke [of old through the words of Isa]iah the prophet, who said: 'How beautiful upon the mountains are the feet of the messenger who announces peace, of the mess[enger of good who announces salvation,] saying to Zion: "your God [reigns."] Its interpretation: The mountains are the pro[phets . . .] And the messenger is [the ano]inted of the spirit about whom Dan[iel] spoke [. . . and the messenger of] good who announces salv[ation is the one about whom it is written that [he will send him] "to comfo[rt the afflicted, to watch over the afflicted ones of

OTHER ANCIENT EXPOSITIONS

Zion."][2]

The latter portion of the text is actually from Isaiah 61:2-3, and is the one that speaks about being anointed of the spirit (rather than Daniel, who wrote only about the Messiah or "anointed one" in Daniel 9:24-26). This is the passage that Jesus cited in reference to his messianic calling (Luke 4:18-19, see verses 17-21). The interpretation of the Isaiah passage in the Qumran scroll accords with Abinadi's teachings. It also supports Jesus' statement in 3 Nephi 20:39-40, in which he indicates that the prophecy in Isaiah 52:7 refers to him.

The concept of the prophets being represented by the mountains is paralleled by the rabbinic interpretation, found in several sources, of the expression "top of the hill" in Exodus 17:9, where "top" is said to refer to the patriarchs and "hill" to the matriarchs. Early Jewish Aramaic translations of the Bible reflect this idea. Thus, in *Targum Neofiti* and *Targum Pseudo-Jonathan* to Numbers 23:9 and Deuteronomy 33:15, the patriarchs (Abraham, Isaac, and Jacob) are compared to the mountains, while their wives (Sarah, Rebekah, and Leah) are compared to the hills. In medieval Jewish texts such as *Zohar* Exodus 58b and *Pesikta Rabbati* 33:4 Abraham, Isaac, and Jacob are termed "the three mountains of the world."

CONCLUSION

From this, we can see that the traditional Jewish interpretation of Isaiah 52:7, going back at least to the time of Christ when the Dead Sea Scrolls were written, agrees with the one given in the Book of Mormon by the prophet Abinadi.

---

[2] Florentino García Martínez, *The Dead Sea Scrolls Translated* (2nd ed., Leiden: Brill, 1996), 140.

Chapter 24

THE NEPHITE PURIFICATION CEREMONY[1]

And the people told the men of Gideon that they had slain the king, and his priests had fled from them farther into the wilderness. And it came to pass that after they had ended the ceremony, that they returned to the land of Nephi, rejoicing, because their wives and their children were not slain; and they told Gideon what they had done to the king. (Mosiah 19:23-24)

In Mosiah 19:23-24, we read that, after the Nephite soldiers slew king Noah they "ended the ceremony" before returning to their homes. What ceremony? Its nature is not described in the text. Is this an inadvertent error in Joseph Smith's writing, or is it further evidence of the authenticity of his translation? Examination of other ancient Near Eastern sources—including the Bible—not only provide evidence for the latter, they allow us to make a guess at what this ceremony was.

RITUAL PURIFICATION IN THE BIBLE AND OTHER CULTURES

Ritual purification of the manslayer is common to many societies throughout the world. In ancient Greece, the individual would flee to a king for pardon and would be assigned certain tasks

---

[1] This article, though written in the 1970s, was presented as a paper at the sixth annual Spend a Day with the Book of Mormon symposium, October 6, 1990, sponsored by the Foundation for Research in Ancient America. It is published here for the first time.

to complete in order to be purified, as in the story of Hercules. The law of Moses, while not allowing the murderer to live, required that the accidental killer remain in one of the cities of refuge until the death of the current high priest, whereupon he was free to continue his normal life (Numbers 35:9-28).

The very act of touching a dead body brought ritual impurity in ancient Israel, calling for ablution (Numbers 19; 31:19). As a consequence, one would expect that soldiers returning from battle would undergo the purification rite, making them ritually clean.

In the Book of Mormon, Jacob performed a rite that may, in fact, be related to the ritual purification in Mosiah 19. "I take off my garments, and I shake them before you," he said, "I shook your iniquities from my soul . . . and am rid of your blood" (2 Nephi 9:44). This act may have been performed at the temple, where Jacob sometimes resorted to address the people (Jacob 1:17; 2:2, 11).

In the fourteenth-century B.C. texts found at Ugarit in northwestern Syria, we find Anat, goddess of war, bespattered by blood and gore as she slays men on the earth. She casts her filth into the sea and receives rain from her husband, the sky-god Baal, to wash her clean.[2] The annual rains were seen by the Canaanites and related peoples to be Baal's means of cleansing the blood of the slain from the body of his wife, who was the earth.[3]

There are several places in the scriptures where purification of the land is evidently related to the concept of Anat, the earth-goddess, being cleansed after the summer battles, when the

---

[2] See the text and translation in Umberto Cassuto, *The Goddess Anath* (trans. Israel Abrahams) (Jerusalem: The Magnes Press, The Hebrew University, 1971), 88-89.

[3] The idea of washing away "filthiness" is found in Proverbs 30:12 and Isaiah 4:4 (where the word parallels "blood"). In both passages, the Hebrew word for "filth" is cognate to the Ugaritic word used in the story of Anat.

fall rains come. A prime example is found in Moses 7:48, where the earth is said to cry, "Wo, wo is me, the mother of men; I am pained, I am weary, because of the wickedness of my children. When shall I rest, and be cleansed from the filthiness which is gone forth out of me? When will my Creator sanctify me, that I may rest, and righteousness for a season abide upon my face?"

The passage would fit very well in the Ugaritic context, where the earth-goddess Anat, called the "mother of men," is cleansed from her filthiness by Baal, here paralleled by the "Creator." When the Lord found the earth corrupt, he decided to cleanse it by means of water, resulting in the flood of Noah (Genesis 6:11-17). In the last days, the earth, because of the blood which pollutes it, is to be cleansed by fire (2 Nephi 26:3-6).

After the earth received Abel's blood, it ceased producing crops for Cain, who was a farmer (Genesis 4:9-12). This leads one to wonder if the purification ceremony did not go hand-in-hand with the prayers for rain. It would appear that, in order for the earth to produce crops beginning in the spring, it had to be cleansed by ceremony and by rains during the winter. Interestingly, it is the blood of sacrificial animals which, in part, purifies the earth of the blood of men shed during war.

In the Bible, the cleansing of the earth[4] comes both by means of water and by means of fire, perhaps referring to lightning or "fire from heaven" (see 2 Kings 1:10), which the Canaanites believed to be Baal's spear. Ezekiel 21-24 is a good example. The prophecy is addressed against Jerusalem and the "land of Israel" (Ezekiel 21:2). The wicked are to be slain by the sword (Ezekiel 21:3-5; 9-19, 28-31), and there is blood in the land (Ezekiel 21:32) and bloodshed in Jerusalem (Ezekiel 22:2-4). "In thee have they humbled her that was set apart for pollution" (Ezekiel 22:10; see also verses 6, 9, 12-13, 27).

---

[4] The Hebrew word is rendered both "earth" and "land" in the King James Bible.

Ritual Purification in the Bible and Other Cultures

The Lord will punish Jerusalem and Israel by fire (Ezekiel 22:18-22, 31) and will consume the filthiness in the land (Ezekiel 22:15). Then follows the key passage: "Thou art the land that is not cleansed, nor rained upon in the day of indignation" (Ezekiel 22:24). Because of the pollutant blood, the wicked of Jerusalem are to be destroyed by sword and by fire, in order that evil might be removed from the land (Ezekiel 23:46-48; 24:6-13).

In Ezekiel 36, we find that the water which comes down to bring cleansing also brings crops, clearly indicating that rain is meant.

> Then will I sprinkle clean water upon you, and ye shall be clean: from all your filthiness, and from all your idols, will I cleanse you . . . I will also save you from all your uncleanness; and I will call for the corn, and will increase it, and lay no famine upon you. And I will multiply the fruit of the tree, and the increase of the field, that ye shall receive no more reproach of famine among the heathen. (Ezekiel 36:25, 29-30)

This clearly reflects the ideas found in the law of Moses concerning rain and crops being the result of obedience to the Lord's commandments.[5] Isaiah, too, discusses the same subject, writing, "Your hands are full of blood. Wash you, make you clean; put away the evil of your doings from before mine eyes." Sins, though scarlet, will be as white as snow and though red like crimson will become like wool (Isaiah 1:15-18). The tie between blood and sin is clear.

Isaiah further wrote that if the people would obey, they would eat the good of the land (Isaiah 1:20), which, of course,

---

[5] Note especially Leviticus 25 & 26; Deuteronomy 11; even Jeremiah, in Chapter 14, notes that the Lord punishes the wrongs of his people by withholding rain.

comes from abundant rains. On the other hand, if they rebelled, they would be devoured with the sword (Isaiah 1:20) and burned (Isaiah 1:31). In Isaiah 4:4, we read of the time "when the Lord shall have washed away the filth of the daughters of Zion, and shall have purged the blood of Jerusalem from the midst thereof by the spirit of judgment, and by the spirit of burning."

The tie between the baptism of the earth at the flood and the "burning" of the last days (especially in connection with Elijah's coming, predicted in Malachi 3-4) is of prime importance, particularly when one notes the symbolic ties to the baptisms of water and fire required of each of us in order to become "clean from the blood of this generation" (D&C 88:85; see also verses 74-75, 86, 138, and 109:42).

Of interest in this connection is Psalm 24, known to have been borrowed from Canaanite literature, with a change in the divine name. "The earth is the Lord's" (Psalm 24:1) reminds us that Baal (who is the Canaanite parallel to Jehovah or "the Lord") was the husband of Anat, the earth, just as Jehovah is the husband of Israel (who, in the passages quoted above, is filthy with blood and must be washed clean). "Who shall ascend into the hill of the Lord? or who shall stand in his holy place? He that hath clean hands, and a pure heart" (Psalm 24:3).

In the Ugaritic texts, Anat, after battle and prior to going into the palace of her father, El, was cleansed of the blood which had pollutted her. Several scholars have compared her victory march (after slaying Yamm) with the passage in Psalm 24:7-10, declaring Jehovah's victory in battle. While marching through the fields, Anat was cleansed by water sent by her consort, Baal, the sky-god.

Wars in the ancient Near East took place during the summer, when the land was not muddy and the rivers were not overflowing and thus difficult to traverse. The Assyrian and Egyptian records make it clear that it was typical to mount military campaigns into the Syro-Palestine region during this time. The same is true of the Israelites and of their predecessors, the

RITUAL PURIFICATION IN THE BIBLE AND OTHER CULTURES

Canaanites.

The Israelites, when they first entered into the "rest of the Lord," crossed over the Jordan, significantly at the same spot which later became the site of Jesus' baptism by John (Beth Abarah, meaning "house of the crossing"). The crossing into the land of Canaan probably took place shortly before Passover, for we read that they encamped at Gilgal and there were circumcised and celebrated the Passover (Joshua 5). It is significant that they did not go to war until after the Passover had been observed—again indicating that wars typically took place during the summer interval separating Passover and Yom Kippur (or even Rosh ha-Shanah).

The rains in the Holy Land come in the fall, after the Jewish festivals of the month of Tishre: Rosh ha-Shanah (new year), Yom Kippur (day of atonement) and Sukkot (feast of tabernacles). Indeed, the prayers for rain are offered at the feast of Sukkot. It is possible that the coming of the rains was seen as a purification of the earth after it had been defiled by the blood and sins of mankind. Human beings became ritually pure on Yom Kippur (Day of Atonement), just four days prior to the onset of Sukkot. In preparation for the purification, Jews still go to running water, such as the sea or a stream, and empty their pocket lint (symbolic of sins) into the water.

The casting out of the pocket lint during the month of Tishre, paralleled by Anat's casting of her filth into the sea, is reminiscent of 1 Nephi 15:33-34, where we read that those who remain filthy must be cast out of the kingdom of God. The kingdom, from the evidence of Zechariah 14, is to be established during the feast of Tabernacles.

The necessity for cleansing the earth by rain at the time of the fall festivals reflects the fact that war was conducted during the long dry season between rains (that is, between the Jewish festivals of Passover and Tabernacles).

The casting of Lamanites slain in battle into the River Sidon by the Nephites in Alma 3:3; 44:22 appears to be related to the ritual purification of the land after the summer season of war.[6] This may be compared with Elijah's casting of the corpses of the slain prophets of Baal into the River Kishon, whence they would have washed into the nearby Mediterranean Sea (1 Kings 18:40).[7]

Significantly, Elijah's contest appears to have taken place around the time of the first rains when, according to Canaanite belief, Baal resurrected for the winter-time and returned to the sky, whence he could send down rains to cleanse his wife, the earth-goddess Anat. Mt. Carmel, beside which the Kishon River runs, is the ideal representation of Anat, for it is a prominent piece of the goddess' body, the region that receives the greatest amount of rain and lighting (ostensibly from Baal), and the spot where the earth (Anat), represented by the mountain, juts out into the sea (Yamm), symbolic of the battle between Anat and Yamm.

Elijah's prayer for rain while the false prophets were being slain might imply that it was, in fact, the feast of Tabernacles.[8] The enthronement of Jehovah as king took place immediately thereafter, as Elijah, his earthly representative, ran the foot-race to Jezreel, thus making Jehovah the winner of both the spear or lightning throw and the foot-race contests required of the king as successor to Baal, according to the Ugaritic texts. Ahab, even in his chariot, lost that race, indicating his rejection as king.[9] When, at length,

---

[6] Here, we refer to the seasonal pattern in the Near East, which need not parallel that of Mesoamerica.

[7] For a detailed explanation of how Elijah deliberately flaunted the Canaanite religion before the people during the contest atop Mount Carmel, see the author's article, "Elijah: Champion of Israel's God," *Ensign*, July 1990.

[8] Praying for rain while putting prisoners to death is a feature found in Mesoamerica. The Aztecs, in order to supplicate the storm-god Tlaloc for rain, would tie children to stakes and shoot them with arrows. The tears of the children acted like sympathetic magic, while their blood fertilized the ground.

[9] It was Elijah who was commissioned to anoint Jehu as king to overthrow the house of Ahab (1 Kings 19:16).

Ahab died, it was in a battle which may have been at the end of the dry season.[10]

Final retribution against Ahab's family came when Jehu, then in battle at Ramoth-Gilead (where Ahab had been wounded), was proclaimed king, and returned to Jezreel to destroy the kings of Israel and Judah, along with Jezebel (2 Kings 9).[11] Then, in celebration—again, perhaps at the feast of Tabernacles—he slew both the sons of Ahab and the priests of Baal (2 Kings 10).[12] The priests may have gathered together to celebrate the fall festival, when Baal arose from the dead, for the assembly took place in the temple of Baal and Jehu pretended that he would offer sacrifice to the weather-god.

TIMING OF THE NEPHITE PURIFICATION CEREMONY

On the surface, one might simply conclude that the "ceremony" mentioned in Mosiah 19:24, while probably purificatory, has no relationship to any of the Old Testament festivals. However, there is additional evidence that the event, in fact, took place during the seventh month (Tishre). Note, for example, that the Lamanite attack which had precipitated the entire incident was discovered by king Noah as he fought Gideon atop the "tower" near the temple in the city of Nephi (Mosiah 19:4-5f). The tower may have been constructed, as previously suggested in

---

[10] After the battle, the Israelite soldiers all returned home (see 1 Kings 22:36-37).

[11] The ceremony marking Jehu's selection as king had elements from the feast of tabernacles, when kings were often anointed, as pointed out in the author's "King Benjamin and the Feast of Tabernacles," in John M. Lundquist and Stephen D. Ricks (eds.), *By Study and Also by Faith (Essays in Honor of Hugh Nibley)*, Volume 2 (Salt Lake City: Deseret and FARMS, 1990).

[12] Meanwhile, in Judah, the royal seed were also killed off by Athaliah, the sister or daughter of Ahab (2 Kings 11).

regard to the speech of King Benjamin, for the feast of tabernacles.

Soon after the battle, Noah's priests came to capture Lamanite girls whom they saw dancing (Mosiah 20:1-5). The incident is so similar to the story in Judges 20:19-23 as to suggest that, in fact, the dance was at a sacred place and was part of the celebration of the feast of tabernacles.[13]

The Lamanites, unhappy at the capture of the girls and suspecting the inhabitants of the city of Nephi of the deed, began assembling their warriors for an attack. It was at this moment that Limhi, who had replaced his father as king, spied their preparations from atop the tower (Mosiah 20:8).

The choice of Limhi as the new king of the Nephites in the land of Nephi is another minor bit of evidence for placing this incident at the feast of tabernacles (Mosiah 19:26). To be sure, Limhi's appointment would have been necessary because his father was dead. But one wonders at the timing of Gideon's attempt to overthrow King Noah in the first place. Was the feast of tabernacles chosen for the revolt, in order to enthrone a righteous man as the Lord's representative on earth?[14] We are reminded of Hugh Nibley's study of the slaying of the Egyptian king at the $ḥb\ sd$ festival.[15] Though Gideon was unsuccessful in his attempt, it was to this noted warrior that the slayers of King Noah reported their own success.

---

[13] Here, too, we find the Benjaminite men stealing dancing girls as wives after a great battle has been waged. In the case of the Bible story, we are specifically told that it took place in Shiloh (where the Tabernacle was located) at feast-time. The name Shiloh bears a superficial resemblance to Shemlon, the place where the Lamanite women were captured.

[14] The text, even before mentioning Limhi's appointment as king, takes pains to mention Limhi's awareness of his father's iniquity and the fact that he deserved to die—though Limhi wanted to save him.

[15] Hugh Nibley, "A New Look at the Pearl of Great Price", *Improvement Era*, June-August 1969.

TIMING OF THE NEPHITE PURIFICATION CEREMONY

As an afterthought, it would be well to note a possible reason for which Israelite girls used to dance before the tabernacle in ancient times. In Canaan, the coming of the rains in the fall symbolized the marriage union between the sky-god Baal and his earth-goddess wife Anat. Impregnated by these rains, she produced vegetation in the early spring. Hence, the fall was a time of the *hieros gamos* or sacred marriage.[16] The feast of tabernacles would have been an ideal time for marriage for the Israelites as well, both from a symbolic and a practical point-of-view. With the young men out to war during the dry summer months, this was the first opportunity to marry.

Sexual abstinence during wartime is a common practice in many societies throughout the world. Typically, while warriors or hunters are away from the village on an expedition, neither they nor their kinsfolk at home engage in sexual relations.[17]

---

[16] I.e., during the summer months, when Baal was not sexually active, men were at war and away from their wives. Rape of captive women would not have had the same meaning in the ancient Near East as intercourse with one's own wife.

[17] The Toaripi or Motumotu tribe of southeastern New Guinea not only enjoins men to abstain from sex from the night before a hunting, fishing or war expedition, but also requires that all who remain behind in the village must so abstain while the men are away. A Toaripi man who has slain another, whether in battle or in anger, is considered impure and must live apart from his wife until the following new moon. The Creek and related Amerind tribes required warriors to refrain from sex for three days and nights before and after a military expedition. The Melanesians of New Britain believe that if a man has sex in wartime he will be killed or wounded. The Kiwi Papuans of British New Guinea also believe that sex prior to battle will cause a man's death. Men preparing for war avoid speaking to women; they sit together in the men's house and refuse to eat food prepared by married women. The Ba-Pedi and the Ba-Thonga tribes of South Africa believe that if men at war or even those who stay behind engage in sex, thorns will grow on the ground traversed by the warriors. In a number of societies, sexual continence is required of returning warriors if they have slain an enemy. The period of abstinence ranges from several days for some Dyak tribes (when enemy heads were taken), to a week for the inhabitants of Logea Island on the southeastern end of New Guinea (where the warriors were shut up), to ten days for warriors living in the Washington group of

This situation is reflected in the Biblical story of King David. "At the time when kings go forth to battle," [18] David remained behind at Jerusalem, and got into trouble by committing adultery with the wife of one of his officers. Trying to cover up her illegitimate pregnancy, David called for Uriah to return home and then invited him to spend the night with his wife Bath-Sheba. Uriah refused, on the grounds that his comrades were engaged in battle in the field (2 Samuel 11).

CONCLUSION

In summary, then, it is suggested that the "ceremony" of Mosiah 19:23-24 is one of purification associated with the onset of the fall festivals of the month of Tishre, at which time citizen-soldiers in the ancient Near East returned home to engage in the fall harvest. Seen in this light, it is further evidence that the Nephites and Lamanites continued to observe Old World traditions which are reflected in the law of Moses.

---

the Marquesas Islands (who were considered taboo during that period). This may be the idea behind the Old Testament law which exempts a newly-married man from military service for a full year (Deuteronomy 24:5).

[18] Identified in 2 Samuel 11:1 as "after the year was expired," hence after the beginning of the year which, under the law of Moses, took place in the month of Abib or Nisan (March/April).

Chapter 25

SOME ASPECTS OF NEPHITE KINGSHIP

Behold, it is not expedient that we should have a king; for thus saith the Lord: Ye shall not esteem one flesh above another, or one man shall not think himself above another; therefore I say unto you it is not expedient that ye should have a king. Nevertheless, if it were possible that ye could always have just men to be your kings it would be well for you to have a king. (Mosiah 23:7-8)

From the beginning, righteous Nephite leaders refused kingship when offered by the people. Nephi wrote of those who followed him into the wilderness to escape persecution by his brothers Laman and Lemuel, "And it came to pass that they would that I should be their king. But I, Nephi, was desirous that they should have no king; nevertheless, I did for them according to that which was in my power" (2 Nephi 5:18).[1]

Though Nephi declined the royal title, his brother Jacob later spoke to the people of "my brother Nephi, unto whom ye look as a king or a protector" (2 Nephi 6:2). Ultimately, the people had their way and got a king. Jacob noted, "Now Nephi began to be old, and he saw that he must soon die; wherefore, he anointed a man to be a king and a ruler over his people now, according to the reigns of the kings" (Jacob 1:9).

Things did not always go well in the land of Nephi. There were frequent attacks by the Lamanites, and the Nephite kings were obliged to lead their people in battle (Jacob 7:24; Enos 1:24;

---

[1] Ironically, Laman and Lemuel accused Nephi of wanting to "make himself a king and a ruler over us" (1 Nephi 16:38).

Jarom 1:7, 9; Omni 1:2, 10). In these difficult circumstances, King Mosiah (the first of that name) led a group of his people out of the land and came to the land of Zarahemla, where he was made king (Omni 1:12-13).

MOSIAH BECOMES KING IN ZARAHEMLA

The circumstances surrounding Mosiah's ascension to the throne of Zarahemla are unusual. The land of Zarahemla was already inhabited by a people whom we know as the Mulekites, who already had a leader named Zarahemla (Omni 1:14-18), who was a descendant of Mulek, son of Zedekiah, the last king of Judah (Mosiah 25:2; Helaman 6:10; 8:21). Despite his royal heritage, "the people of Zarahemla, and of Mosiah, did unite together; and Mosiah was appointed to be their king" (Omni 1:19).

What prompted Zarahemla to yield his claim to kingship to Mosiah? We cannot be certain, but there are several possibilities.

While Zarahemla's people evidently had no written records, Mosiah possessed records that had been handed down from the time of Nephi, who had lived in Jerusalem during the reign of Zarahemla's ancestor Zedekiah. Indeed, "Zarahemla did rejoice exceedingly, because the Lord had sent the people of Mosiah with the plates of brass which contained the record of the Jews" (Omni 1:14). Possession of the records may have given Mosiah a claim to leadership.

Mosiah, like his grandson of the same name, had the ability to translate ancient records and was able to read the account of the Jaredites found inscribed on a large stone (Omni 1:20-22). He may have possessed the interpreters later held by the second Mosiah, which made him a seer (Mosiah 8:13-18). This may have strengthened his leadership position.

Mosiah evidently possessed the sword of Laban, which was passed down in the Nephite royal family (2 Nephi 5:14; Jacob

1:10; Words of Mormon 1:13; Mosiah 1:16).[2] The possession of this artifact, brought to the New World from the ancient Israelite capital of Jerusalem, may well have suggested to Zarahemla that Mosiah should rule the people.

Another possible factor in Zarahemla's acceptance of Mosiah as king may lie in the fact that Mosiah's ancestor, Lehi, had been brought to the New World by the Lord and given a "land of promise" (1 Nephi 5:4). The major territory settled by Lehi's family comprised the lands of Nephi (which the Lamanites took from the Nephites) and Zarahemla, which were in what came to be known as the "land southward." In Helaman 6:10, we read:

> Now the land south was called Lehi and the land north was called Mulek, which was after the son of Zedekiah; for the Lord did bring Mulek into the land north, and Lehi into the land south.

The northern territories had previously been occupied by the Jaredites, and it "was discovered by the people of Zarahemla, it being the place of their first landing. And they came from there up into the south wilderness" (Alma 22:30-31). From this, it seems that the Mulekites were brought into the land northward but that at least a part of them, under the leadership of Zarahemla, moved southward and settled in territory the Lord had allotted to Lehi's posterity. This may have been another factor in Zarahemla's decision to accept Mosiah as king over their two peoples.

---

[2] That the sword of Laban was a symbol of royalty among the Nephites has been discussed by several scholars. See Todd R. Kerr, "Ancient Aspects of Nephite Kingship in the Book of Mormon," *Journal of Book of Mormon Studies* 1/1 (Fall 1992):85-118; Brett L. Holbrook, "The Sword of Laban as a Symbol of Divine Authority and Kingship," *Journal of Book of Mormon Studies* 2/1 (Spring 1993): 39–72; Daniel N. Rolph, "Prophets, Kings, and Swords: The Sword of Laban and Its Possible Pre-Laban Origin," *Journal of Book of Mormon Studies* 2/1 (Spring 1993): 73–79.

Some Aspects of Nephite Kingship

THE SERVICE OF NEPHITE KINGS

In ancient monarchies the king had absolute power. His word was the word of the gods and he held the power of life and death over his subjects. Such was not the case among the Nephites. The pattern had been begun by Nephi who, when pressed to become king, observed that he "did for them according to that which was in my power" (2 Nephi 5:18).

Nephi's descendants followed the pattern of service to the people, both in leading the people in battle, as we have noted earlier, and in assisting them in the construction of temples and other public buildings. Three Nephite kings reigned in the city of Zarahemla, passing the office from father to son. These were Mosiah, Benjamin, and another Mosiah.

Mormon wrote that "king Benjamin was a holy man, and he did reign over his people in righteousness" (Words of Mormon 1:17). Nearing the end of his days, Benjamin assembled his people to announce his retirement and to appoint his son Mosiah as king. The marvelous discourse he delivered to his people reflects the nature of Nephite kingship:

> I have not commanded you to come up hither that ye should fear me, or that ye should think that I of myself am more than a mortal man. But I am like as yourselves, subject to all manner of infirmities in body and mind; yet I have been chosen by this people, and consecrated by my father, and was suffered by the hand of the Lord that I should be a ruler and a king over this people . . . to serve you with all the might, mind and strength which the Lord hath granted unto me. I say unto you that as I have been suffered to spend my days in your service, even up to this time, and have not sought gold nor silver nor any manner of riches of you . . . And even I, myself, have labored with mine own hands that I might serve you, and

that ye should not be laden with taxes, and that there should nothing come upon you which was grievous to be borne. (Mosiah 2:10-12, 14)

He went on to stress that he considered that his service to the people had also been service to God, "your heavenly King" (Mosiah 2:16-19).

ABOLITION OF THE NEPHITE MONARCHY

Nephite kingship came to an end in the days of Benjamin's son Mosiah. His four sons had gone up to the land of Nephi to preach to the Lamanites, so he could not appoint one of them as his successor (Mosiah 29:1-9). He proposed to "newly arrange the affairs of this people" by allowing the people to appoint judges to govern them (Mosiah 29:10-12, 25-26).

But there were two other factors behind Mosiah's decision to abolish the monarchy, and both were related to the recent arrival in Zarahemla of the Nephites who had been living in the land of Nephi (Mosiah 22:13-14; 24:25). Their last king, Noah, was a very wicked man who imposed heavy taxes on the people in order to support his opulent lifestyle (Mosiah 11:3-11). Mosiah told the people,

> Therefore, if it were possible that you could have just men to be your kings, who would establish the laws of God, and judge this people according to his commandments, yea, if ye could have men for your kings who would do even as my father Benjamin did for this people—I say unto you, if this could always be the case then it would be expedient that ye should always have kings to rule over you. And even I myself have labored with all the power and faculties which I have possessed, to teach you the commandments of God, and to establish peace throughout the

land. (Mosiah 29:13-14)

But he noted "how much iniquity doth one wicked king cause to be committed, yea, and what great destruction," and admonished the people to "remember king Noah, his wickedness and his abominations" and the bondage that resulted therefrom (Mosiah 29:17-18; see also verses 21-24).

In addition, Mosiah evidently had in mind the wickedness of the Jaredite kings. He had recently translated that record (Mosiah 28:11-18). Indeed, he had entrusted it, along with all the Nephite records, to the keeping of the younger Alma—who became the first chief judge under the new system—just prior to announcing that he would allow the people to elect their own leaders (Mosiah 28:20).

That Mosiah had the wicked Jaredite kings in mind is evidenced in Mosiah 29:7, where he says, "And who knoweth but what my son, to whom the kingdom doth belong, should turn to be angry and draw away a part of this people after him, which would cause wars and contentions among you." Aside from the Book of Ether, which recounts the history of the Jaredites, this is the only place in the Book of Mormon where the idiom "draw away . . . people" is used. Throughout Ether, we read of usurpers to the throne who "drew away" people in a revolt against the current monarch (Ether 7:4, 15; 9:11; 10:32). Though Mosiah mentioned wicked king Noah by name, he never gave explicit examples from Jaredite history. But his use of this idiom suggests that it was in his mind as he proposed the abolition of the Nephite monarchy.

CONCLUSION

The establishment of kingship began and ended with a protest from the Nephite leader. Nephi declined the title "king" and Mosiah, the last of the royal line, announced that it would henceforth be abolished. With the sole exception of Noah, all of the Nephite kings named in the Book of Mormon served their people

CONCLUSION

well and were righteous men. The example of service set by such men as Nephi, Benjamin, and the two Mosiahs, can guide us in our own callings in life.

Chapter 26

KINGS AND JUDGES IN THE BIBLE AND THE BOOK OF MORMON[1]

Let us appoint judges, to judge this people according to our law; and we will newly arrange the affairs of this people, for we will appoint wise men to be judges, that will judge this people according to the commandments of God. (Mosiah 29:11)

Both the Bible and the Book of Mormon mention rule by kings and judges. The office of judge existed in the time of Moses, who had commanded "the judges of Israel" to slay a group of sinners (Numbers 25:5). The mosaic law provided for judges to "hear the causes between your brethren," making "diligent inquisition" of witnesses, and settling every "controversy between men" (Deuteronomy 1:5; 16:18; 19:17-19; 21:1-2; 25:1-2). Judges in the time of Joshua are listed with the elders and officers (Joshua 8:33; 23:2; 24:1).

JUDGES AMONGST THE ISRAELITES

After Joshua's death, "the Lord raised up judges, which delivered them . . . out of the hand of their enemies all the days of the judge" (Judges 2:16-19). "The Lord raised up a deliverer to the children of Israel, who delivered them . . . and he judged Israel, and went out to war" (Judges 3:9-10). From this, it appears that the principal role of these judges was to deliver Israel from their enemies (Judges 3:15, 31; 6:14; 10:1; 11:1; 13:5).

But the judges also performed other functions. Deborah,

---

[1] Originally published in the *Provo Sun*, June 28, 1998.

for example, was a prophetess as well as a liberator (Judges 4:4, 6), and "the children of Israel came up to her for judgment" (Judges 4:5). That the judges did not function only in wartime is suggested by the length of their tenure, ranging from six to 23 years (Judges 10:2-3; 12:7, 9, 11, 13; 15:20, 31).

THE TRANSITION TO KINGS

The transition from judges to kings began in the time of Gideon, also called Jerubbaal. After he had successfully freed Israel from its enemies, "the men of Israel said unto Gideon, Rule thou over us, both thou, and thy son, and thy son's son also," but Gideon declined (Judges 8:22-23). Later, his son Abimelech convinced the people of Shechem to make him king (Judges 9:1-6, 18), and he "reigned three years over Israel" until he was slain (Judges 9:22).

Some years later, the last of the judges, the prophet Samuel, acceded to the wishes of the people and anointed Saul to be their "captain" (Hebrew *nagid*, "commander"). Like the judges before him, he was to lead Israel's army (1 Samuel 9:16; 10:1). Saul was subsequently replaced by David, who was also anointed to be "captain" (1 Samuel 13:14; 2 Samuel 5:2; 11:2).

THE OFFICE OF "JUDGE" UNDER THE KINGS

The office of judge did not disappear with the monarchy, however. Judges are noted from the time of the Judean kings David (1 Chronicles 23:4; 26:29), Solomon (2 Chronicles 1:2), and Jehoshaphat (2 Chronicles 19:5-6). The close tie between kings, judges, and other officers is evident from the fact that the title "judges" sometimes parallels "kings" and "princes" (Psalms 2:10; 148:11; Isaiah 40:23; Hosea 7:7; 13:10-11; Zephaniah 3:3).

After the Babylonian captivity, Jews returning to Jerusalem re-established the office of judge (Ezra 10:14), in accord with the promise made through Isaiah, "And I will restore thy judges as at the first, and thy counselors as at the beginning" (Isaiah 1:26).

KINGS AND JUDGES IN THE BIBLE AND THE BOOK OF MORMON

JUDGES AMONGST THE NEPHITES

The last Nephite king, Mosiah, may have had this same passage in mind when he replaced the monarchy with a system of higher and lesser judges (Mosiah 29:11-13, 28-29) who would be chosen by the people (Mosiah 29:39-42; Alma 62:47; Helaman 1:13; 2:2; 6:15).

Some critics of the Book of Mormon, believing that Joseph Smith was its author, have protested that the Nephite judges presided at trials, while the biblical judges governed the people. It is true that some Book of Mormon references to the judges mention judicial proceedings and sentencing of criminals (Alma 10:13-14; 11:1-5; 3 Nephi 6:23), and that judges and lawyers are sometimes mentioned together (Alma 10:27, 29; Alma 14:2, 5, 18, 23-27). But we saw earlier that the biblical judges also heard legal cases. Moreover, the Nephite judges, like those of the Bible, also had administrative responsibilities.

In Alma 30:29, we find a man being brought for trial before "the chief judge who was governor over all the land." Alma 50:39 speaks of a man who "was appointed chief judge and governor over the people." We also read that "Pacumeni was appointed, according to the voice of the people, to be a chief judge and a governor over the people" (Helaman 1:13). From this, it appears that the Nephite judges were also governors, as were the judges of the Bible. For this reason, the Book of Mormon frequently speaks of "the *reign* of the judges." Moreover, one of their responsibilities, like that of the biblical judges, was to direct the wars against their enemies.

The chief Nephite military leaders were "appointed by the chief judges and the voice of the people" (Alma 46:34; 3 Nephi 3:17). From Alma 60:1, it is clear that "the chief judge and the governor over the land" was one of "those who have been chosen by this people to govern and manage the affairs of this war." Indeed, of Alma, the first Nephite judge, we read that "being the chief judge and the governor of the people of Nephi, therefore he went up with his people, yea, with his captains, and chief captains, yea, at the head of his armies, against the Amlicites to battle" (Alma 2:16). The actions of the Nephite chief judge Lachoneus in 3 Nephi 3 suggest that he provided leadership in both military and civil affairs.

CONCLUSION

The Nephite judges were probably patterned after the judges of the Bible, fulfilling the same functions as their predecessors. The only difference between then is chronological. The earlier judges preceded the establishment of the Israelite monarchy, while the Nephite monarch, having seen the bad results of the wicked king Noah (Mosiah 29:18) decided to abolish the hereditary office in favor of the earlier position of judge, allowing the people to select their own leaders.

Chapter 27

THE CAPTIVITY OF THE FATHERS

Now I say unto thee: Go, and remember the captivity of thy fathers in the land of Helam, and in the land of Nephi; and remember how great things he has done for them; for they were in bondage, and he has delivered them. (Mosiah 27:16)

The admonition of Mosiah 27:16 was delivered by an angel to Alma the younger when he appeared to chastise the young man and his friends for their wrongdoing. Alma heeded the warning, and fourteen years later, while recalling his experience with the angel,[1] he wrote,

> Yea, and I also remember the captivity of my fathers; for I surely do know that the Lord did deliver them out of bondage, and by this did establish his church; yea, the Lord God, the God of Abraham, the God of Isaac, and the God of Jacob, did deliver them out of bondage. Yea, I have always remembered the captivity of my fathers; and that same God who delivered them out of the hands of the Egyptians did deliver them out of bondage. (Alma 29:11-12)

THE BONDAGE OF ALMA AND HIS PEOPLE

Alma's people had twice been delivered from bondage. The Nephites who had resettled the land of Nephi suffered

---

[1] For a discussion of Alma's later reflections on the appearance of the angel, see John A. Tvedtnes, "The Voice of an Angel," in Noel B. Reynolds, *Book of Mormon Authorship Revisited: The Evidence for Ancient Origins* (Provo: FARMS, 1997).

The Bondage of Alma and His People

oppression under their wicked king Noah (Mosiah 11:1-14). The king and his priests had slain Abinadi, a prophet sent to warn them (Mosiah 17:5-20). But Alma's father, Alma the elder, believed the prophet and fled to the waters of Mormon, where he taught and baptized (Mosiah 17:2-4; 18:1-31). When the king discovered their location, he sent an army to destroy them, but Alma and his people fled (Mosiah 18:32-35). They settled in a land they named Helam, where they prospered for a time (Mosiah 23:1-20).

Abinadi had prophesied that the people would be brought into bondage to their enemies, meaning the Lamanites (Mosiah 11:21-25). The Lamanites took the land of Nephi and made Limhi king in the place of his father Noah. Limhi's people were rescued and led to the land of Zarahemla by a group from that city, led by Ammon. A Lamanite army tried to prevent their escape but became lost in the wilderness and stumbled across the Amulonites, former priests to king Noah who had fled during the earlier war.

While seeking the way back to the land of Nephi, these Lamanites and Amulonites encountered Alma's people at Helam. They placed them under bondage until the Lord miraculously delivered them and brought them safely to the land of Zarahemla (Mosiah 23:21-24:25).

Some years later, in a discourse delivered in the city of Zarahemla, Alma the younger related the story of the dual deliverance of his people from bondage in the cities of Nephi and Helam (Alma 5:1-5). He added:

> And now behold, I say unto you, my brethren, you that belong to this church, have you sufficiently retained in remembrance the captivity of your fathers? Yea, and have you sufficiently retained in remembrance his mercy and long-suffering towards them? And moreover, have ye sufficiently retained in remembrance that he has delivered their souls from hell? (Alma 5:6)

THE CAPTIVITY OF THE FATHERS

DELIVERY FROM SPIRITUAL BONDAGE

What interests us here is the fact that Alma tied the deliverance from physical bondage to God's power to deliver his people from spiritual bondage as well. But the comparison seems to have been first made in the record kept by his father. This becomes clear as we examine the words uttered by Alma the elder at the waters of Mormon:

> Behold, here are the waters of Mormon (for thus were they called) and now, as ye are desirous to come into the fold of God, and to be called his people, and are willing to bear one another's burdens, that they may be light; Yea, and are willing to mourn with those that mourn; yea, and comfort those that stand in need of comfort, and to stand as witnesses of God at all times and in all things, and in all places that ye may be in, even until death, that ye may be redeemed of God, and be numbered with those of the first resurrection, that ye may have eternal life—Now I say unto you, if this be the desire of your hearts, what have you against being baptized in the name of the Lord, as a witness before him that ye have entered into a covenant with him, that ye will serve him and keep his commandments, that he may pour out his Spirit more abundantly upon you? (Mosiah 18:8-10)

Alma inquired after the "desire of [the] hearts" of his people, asking them to enter into a "covenant with [God]," "to be called his people" and "to stand as witnesses of [him]." They were also to "bear one another's burdens, that they may be light" and "comfort those that stand in need of comfort." If they remained faithful to this covenant, they would "be redeemed of God."

COMPARING PHYSICAL AND SPIRITUAL BONDAGE

These same elements are found in the story of their deliverance from Lamanite/Amulonite bondage. Forbidden to pray vocally, the people called upon God in their hearts, and the Lord "did know the thoughts of their hearts" (Mosiah 24:12). He responded by speaking to their souls. He reminded them "of the covenant which ye have made with me" (Mosiah 24:13) and called them "my people" (Mosiah 24:14). He promised to "deliver them out of bondage" (Mosiah 24:13, 16-17), that they might "stand as witnesses for me" (Mosiah 24:14).

To remind them of their covenant to "bear one another's burdens, that they may be light," and "to comfort those that stand in need of comfort," the Lord counseled them to "be of good comfort" (Mosiah 24:13, 16). He would "ease the burdens . . . that even you cannot feel them upon your backs" (Mosiah 24:14).

> And now it came to pass that the burdens which were laid upon Alma and his brethren were made light; yea, the Lord did strengthen them that they could bear up their burdens with ease, and they did submit cheerfully and with patience to all the will of the Lord. (Mosiah 24:15)

The people were miraculously delivered soon afterward (Mosiah 24:16-25). It is obvious that Alma's speech at the waters of Mormon influenced the wording of his account of the deliverance of the people from bondage in the land of Helam. But there is more to the story. We note, for example, that Alma tied the bearing of burdens to patience (Mosiah 24:15-16). The Hebrew root meaning "bear" or "carry" is *sbl*, whence the noun *sēbel*, "burden," and the modern Hebrew term *sablānút*, "patience, longsuffering." By telling the people to "bear one another's burdens" (Mosiah 18:8), Alma was instructing them not only to help one another, but to be tolerant of others and patient. Amulek, who served as a missionary companion to Alma's son, Alma the younger, expressed similar thoughts when addressing the Zoramites:

> I would exhort you to have patience, and that ye bear with all manner of afflictions; that ye do not revile against those who cast you out . . . But that ye have patience and bear with those afflictions, with a firm hope that ye shall one day rest from all your afflictions. (Alma 34:40-41)

CONCLUSION

Many years later, when the younger Alma instructed his son Helaman in the care of the sacred records and other matters, he told him to "do as I have done, in remembering the captivity of our fathers" (Alma 36:2, 28-29). Moroni used similar terminology in his letter to the Nephite governor Pahoran (Alma 60:20). Alma's diligence in obeying the angel's instructions influenced later generations.

Chapter 28

WATCH AND PRAY

But that ye would humble yourselves before the Lord, and call on his holy name, and watch and pray continually, that ye may not be tempted above that which ye can bear, and thus be led by the Holy Spirit, becoming humble, meek, submissive, patient, full of love and all long-suffering. (Alma 13:28)

Alma addressed the inhabitants of the city of Ammonihah with the words recorded in Alma 13:28, but they rejected his message. Leaving these wicked people to their fate, Alma then went to the land of Sidom, where he established the church and remained until he saw "that the people were checked as to the pride of their hearts, and began to humble themselves before God, and began to assemble themselves together at their sanctuaries to worship God before the altar, watching and praying continually, that they might be delivered from Satan, and from death, and from destruction" (Alma 15:17).

During a later missionary journey to the Zoramites, Alma's companion, Amulek, who had heard him preach in Ammonihah, delivered the same message:

> Yea, and I also exhort you, my brethren, that ye be watchful unto prayer continually, that ye may not be led away by the temptations of the devil, that he may not overpower you, that ye may not become his subjects at the last day; for behold, he rewardeth you no good thing. (Alma 34:39)

During his visit to the land of Bountiful, Christ also warned the Nephites: "Ye must watch and pray always, lest ye be tempted by the devil, and ye be led away captive by him" (3 Nephi

18:15). "Ye must watch and pray always lest ye enter into temptation; for Satan desireth to have you, that he may sift you as wheat" (3 Nephi 18:18).

This was undoubtedly one of the Savior's most important messages, for he had also told his Palestinian disciples to "watch and pray" (Mark 13:33; Luke 21:36). Indeed, it was the last message he gave to his apostles during his mortal ministry, in the garden of Gethsemane. Finding Peter, James, and John asleep, he awoke them and warned, "Watch and pray, that ye enter not into temptation: the spirit indeed is willing, but the flesh is weak" (Matthew 26:41; see also Mark 14:38).

Peter took the Lord's words to heart and later wrote to the saints, "Be ye therefore sober, and watch unto prayer" (1 Peter 4:7). Paul, after admonishing the Ephesians to gird themselves with the armor of God for protection against evil, added, "Praying always with all prayer and supplication in the Spirit, and watching thereunto with all perseverance and supplication for all saints" (Ephesians 6:18). He also advised the Colossians to "Continue in prayer, and watch in the same with thanksgiving" (Colossians 4:2).

Similarly, Christ's Nephite disciples passed the word to those who came after. Moroni wrote,

> And after they had been received unto baptism, and were wrought upon and cleansed by the power of the Holy Ghost, they were numbered among the people of the church of Christ; and their names were taken, that they might be remembered and nourished by the good word of God, to keep them in the right way, to keep them continually watchful unto prayer, relying alone upon the merits of Christ, who was the author and the finisher of their faith. (Moroni 6:4)

With the restoration of the Church in Joseph Smith's day, it became the duty of home teachers to "visit the house of each member, and exhort them to pray vocally and in secret and attend to all family duties (D&C 20:47; see also verse 51), thus following in the footsteps of the Nephites of Moroni's day. The same section of the Doctrine and Covenants explains,

> But there is a possibility that man may fall from grace and depart from the living God; Therefore let the church take heed and pray always, lest they fall into temptation; Yea, and even let those who are sanctified take heed also. (D&C 20:32-34)

CONCLUSION

The importance of the Lord's admonition to "watch and pray" is stressed by the fact that it appears in three volumes of scripture: the Bible, the Book of Mormon, and the Doctrine and Covenants. The commandment is both timeless and timely.

Chapter 29

THE EVIL SPIRIT

I beseech of you that ye do not procrastinate the day of your repentance until the end; for after this day of life, which is given us to prepare for eternity, behold, if we do not improve our time while in this life, then cometh the night of darkness wherein there can be no labor performed. Ye cannot say, when ye are brought to that awful crisis, that I will repent, that I will return to my God. Nay, ye cannot say this; for that same spirit which doth possess your bodies at the time that ye go out of this life, that same spirit will have power to possess your body in that eternal world. (Alma 34:33-34)

Latter-day Saints typically misread this passage, believing that the "same spirit" refers to a person's own spirit. Critics have even used the passage to suggest that the Book of Mormon precludes those who have died from accepting proxy temple ordinances in their behalf. But a careful reading indicates first that Amulek was addressing those who had already known the gospel, telling them,

> For behold, if ye have procrastinated the day of your repentance even until death, behold, ye have become subjected to the spirit of the devil, and he doth seal you his; therefore, the Spirit of the Lord hath withdrawn from you, and hath no place in you, and the devil hath all power over you; and this is the final state of the wicked. (Alma 34:35)

From this, it is clear that the "same spirit" that possesses the wicked person and will continue to possess him in the hereafter

The Evil Spirit

is the devil, not the individual's spirit. Those who do the devil's will and refuse to repent will come under his power both in this world and the world to come. King Benjamin spoke of this as well:

> But, O my people, beware lest there shall arise contentions among you, and ye list to obey the evil spirit, which was spoken of by my father Mosiah. For behold, there is a wo pronounced upon him who listeth to obey that spirit; for if he listeth to obey him, and remaineth and dieth in his sins, the same drinketh damnation to his own soul; for he receiveth for his wages an everlasting punishment, having transgressed the law of God contrary to his own knowledge. (Mosiah 2:32-33)

Furthermore, King Benjamin, like Amulek after him, made it clear that this fate was reserved for those who knowingly rebelled against God and followed the devil:

> And now, I say unto you, my brethren, that after ye have known and have been taught all these things, if ye should transgress and go contrary to that which has been spoken, that ye do withdraw yourselves from the Spirit of the Lord, that it may have no place in you to guide you in wisdom's paths that ye may be blessed, prospered, and preserved—I say unto you, that the man that doeth this, the same cometh out in open rebellion against God; therefore he listeth to obey the evil spirit, and becometh an enemy to all righteousness; therefore, the Lord has no place in him, for he dwelleth not in unholy temples. Therefore if that man repenteth not, and remaineth and dieth an enemy to God, the demands of divine justice do awaken his immortal soul to a lively sense of his own guilt, which doth cause him to shrink

The Evil Spirit

> from the presence of the Lord, and doth fill his breast with guilt, and pain, and anguish, which is like an unquenchable fire, whose flame ascendeth up forever and ever. And now I say unto you, that mercy hath no claim on that man; therefore his final doom is to endure a never-ending torment. (Mosiah 2:36-39)

Benjamin warned his people about allowing their children to "serve the devil, who is the master of sin, or who is the evil spirit which hath been spoken of by our fathers, he being an enemy to all righteousness" (Mosiah 4:14; see also Alma 3:26-27). Among the fathers who spoke of this evil spirit was Nephi (2 Nephi 32:8). But Nephi had been taught by his own father, Lehi, who contrasted the "Holy Spirit" of God with "the spirit of the devil":

> And now, my sons, I would that ye should look to the great Mediator, and hearken unto his great commandments; and be faithful unto his words, and choose eternal life, according to the will of his Holy Spirit; And not choose eternal death, according to the will of the flesh and the evil which is therein, which giveth the spirit of the devil power to captivate, to bring you down to hell, that he may reign over you in his own kingdom. (2 Nephi 2:28-29)

Alma also contrasted the "Spirit of the Lord" with the "spirit of the devil," noting, like Lehi, that the wicked are "led captive by the will of the devil" until the resurrection (Alma 40:11-14).

After King Benjamin's people heard his words about opposite spirits, "they all cried with one voice, saying: Yea, we believe all the words which thou hast spoken unto us; and also, we know of their surety and truth, because of the Spirit of the Lord Omnipotent, which has wrought a mighty change in us, or in our hearts, that we have no more disposition to do evil, but to do good continually" (Mosiah 5:2). This is what Alma called being "spiritually . . . born of God" (Alma 5:14).

CONCLUSION

The words of the Lamanite king converted by Alma sum up the matter, and provide the question we should still be asking:

> What shall I do that I may have this eternal life of which thou hast spoken? Yea, what shall I do that I may be born of God, having this wicked spirit rooted out of my breast, and receive his Spirit, that I may be filled with joy, that I may not be cast off at the last day? (Alma 22:15)

Chapter 30

THE TWO GREAT SINS

Know ye not, my son, that these things are an abomination in the sight of the Lord; yea, most abominable above all sins save it be the shedding of innocent blood or denying the Holy Ghost? For behold, if ye deny the Holy Ghost when it once has had place in you, and ye know that ye deny it, behold, this is a sin which is unpardonable; yea, and whosoever murdereth against the light and knowledge of God, it is not easy for him to obtain forgiveness; yea, I say unto you, my son, that it is not easy for him to obtain a forgiveness (Alma 39:5-6)

In Alma 39:5-6, Alma demonstrated the seriousness of the sin committed by his son Corianton, who left his missionary labors and "did go over into the land of Siron among the borders of the Lamanites, after the harlot Isabel" (Alma 39:3). Alma explained that sexual sin was the "most abominable above all sins save it be the shedding of innocent blood or denying the Holy Ghost" (Alma 39:5). These two sins, murder and unchastity, go hand-in-hand, for both of them involve abuse of the human body and they involve the giving and taking of life—processes for which the Lord alone can set standards.

THE PROBLEM OF RESTITUTION

There is also the question of recompense. Full repentance requires that we restore that which we have taken from another, whether it be wordly possessions taken through theft or a good name taken through false witness. President Spencer W. Kimball wrote:

> When one is humble in sorrow, has unconditionally abandoned the evil, and confesses

to those assigned by the Lord, he should next
restore insofar as possible that which was
damaged. If he burglarized, he should return to
the rightful owner that which was stolen. Perhaps
one reason murder is unforgivable is that having
taken a life, the murderer cannot restore it.
Restitution in full is not always possible. Virginity
is impossible to give back.[1]

Among the ten commandments, the first four deal with
our relationship with God, while the fifth deals with our
relationship with our parents. The rest of the commandments have
to do with how we treat others. The first two of these are, "Thou
shalt not kill. Thou shalt not commit adultery" (Exodus 20:13-14;
Deuteronomy 5:17-18). These describe the two sins classified by
Alma as the most serious.

MEANING OF THE TWO COMMANDMENTS

A look at the Hebrew behind these prohibitions is
instructive. For example, the wording "thou shalt not kill"
suggests, in English, that killing of any kind is wrong, though the
Bible itself authorizes killing in some cases. Hebrew has a number
of different verbs that mean "to kill." Significantly, the Hebrew of
Exodus 20:13 reads *lōʾ tirṣaḥ*, which really means "don't murder,"
thus excluding accidental death or killing in wartime or in defense
of self or others. Subsequent portions of the law of Moses explain
what is murder and what is not and discusses wounding in which
the individual is not killed (Exodus 21:12-15, 18-32;
Deuteronomy 19:1-21; 21:1-4).

Exodus 20:14 and Deuteronomy 5:18 read *lōʾ tinʾāp* in the
Hebrew, which is best rendered "don't engage in illicit sexual

---

[1] Spencer W. Kimball, *Faith Precedes the Miracle* (Salt Lake City: Deseret, 1973), 182.

activities." The verb is not restricted to "adultery" as most Bible translations read. As with the sixth commandment, the law of Moses explains sexual sins in detail, making it clear that the term covers a wide range of illicit relations (Exodus 22:16-19; Leviticus 19:22-23; 20:10-21; Numbers 5:12-31; Deuteronomy 22:13-30; 23:17-18). Among the prohibited activities are homosexuality (Leviticus 18:22; 20:13), which is also condemned in the New Testament (1 Corinthians 6:9; 1 Timothy 1:10), and bestiality (Leviticus 18:23; 20:15-16).

The New Testament, being written in Greek, has separate terms for illicit sex in general (usually translated "fornication" in the King James Bible) and "adultery," and condemns all such activities. Paul lists unrepentant adultery, fornication (any illicit sex), homosexuality, and murder among the sins that exclude one from the kingdom of God (Galatians 5:19-21; 1 Corinthians 6:9-10).

THE UNPARDONABLE SIN

Under the law of Moses, one could repent and make restitution for most sins, offering a sacrifice as a token of one's repentance. But the murderer or adulterer, because he could not make recompense, had to forfeit his life. The rationale for executing the murderer is explained in Genesis 9:6: "Whoso sheddeth man's blood, by man shall his blood be shed: for in the image of God made he man." Since man is the image of God, murder is tantamount to blasphemy. This is probably why both murder and blasphemy against the Holy Ghost are termed unpardonable sins (Matthew 12:31; see also JST Matthew 12:37 and JST Mark 3:22-24).

In a revelation to the prophet Joseph Smith, the Lord declared:

> The blasphemy against the Holy Ghost, which shall not be forgiven in the world nor out of the world, is in that ye commit murder wherein ye

shed innocent blood, and assent unto my death,
after ye have received my new and everlasting
covenant, saith the Lord God; and he that abideth
not this law can in nowise enter into my glory, but
shall be damned, saith the Lord. (D&C 132:27)

Joseph Smith declared that "the unpardonable sin is to shed innocent blood, or be accessory thereto. All other sins will be visited with judgment in the flesh, and the spirit being delivered to the buffetings of Satan until the day of the Lord Jesus (*History of the Church*, 5:391; see also 6:253; 7:152).

"FLEE FORNICATION"

The apostle Paul warned his readers to "flee fornication" (1 Corinthians 6:18) and to "flee also youthful lusts" (2 Timothy 2:22). The *Testaments of the Twelve Patriarchs*, attributed to the sons of the Old Testament patriarch Jacob, contain similar teachings. Thus, *Testament of Reuben* 5:5 has the patriarch admonishing, like Paul, "flee from sexual promiscuity."[2]

Several of the other testaments speak of the "spirit of promiscuity" in a way that equates it with Satan (*Testament of Reuben* 5:3; *Testament of Levi* 9:9; *Testament of Judah* 14:2). When Testament of Joseph 7:4-5 speaks about "the spirit of Beliar [the devil]" and being "blinded by sin," it is in the context of sexual sin. Judah declared, "the spirit of envy and promiscuity plotted against me" (*Testament of Judah* 13:3). "The spirits of sexual promiscuity and of arrogance" are tied to Satan in *Testament of Dan* 5:6. Levi advised, "Be on guard against the spirit of promiscuity, for it is constantly active" (*Testament of Levi* 9:9). Several of the Testaments explicitly declare that sexual promiscuity leads men to

---

[2] The brief quotes from the *Testaments of the Twelve Patriarchs* are drawn from the English translation by Howard Clark Kee in James H. Charlesworth, *The Old Testament Pseudepigrapha* (Garden City: Doubleday, 1983), 775-828.

the devil (*Testament of Reuben* 6:1-3; *Testament of Simeon* 5:3; T. 4:6-7).

CONCLUSION

From these statements, we can see that the devil has been termed "the spirit of fornication." In the New Testament, Christ calls him "a murderer from the beginning" (John 8:44). He is the author of the two great sins of which Alma spoke.

Chapter 31

RAISED BY A HANDCLASP

He put forth his hand and raised the king from the earth, and said unto him: Stand. And he stood upon his feet, receiving his strength." (Alma 22:22)

Twice in the Book of Mormon, when individuals fell as if dead under the influence of the Spirit of the Lord, someone raised them by grasping their hand. This happened to Lamoni and his wife (Alma 19:29-30) and later to Lamoni's father (Alma 22:18-22), each of whom came to know the Lord during the experience.[1] While there are no exact parallels in the Bible, in Revelation 1:17 the apostle John falls down as dead before the risen Christ, who then lays his right hand upon him and tells him not to fear. Closer parallels to the Book of Mormon stories are found in various pseudepigraphic texts unavailable to Joseph Smith.

SIMILARITY TO OTHER ANCIENT WRITINGS

Apocalypse of Abraham 10:1-5; 11:1 has Abraham reporting that when he heard the voice of God speaking to him, "my spirit was amazed, and my soul fled from me. And I became like a stone, and fell face down upon the earth, for there was no longer strength in me to stand up on the earth." Then God sent an angel who "took me by my right hand and stood me on my feet . . . And I stood up and saw him who had taken my right hand and set me on my feet."[2]

---

[1] The Lamanite king Lamoni actually fell in a state of ecstasy on two occasions, on the first of which he merely awoke after three days (Alma 19:8-12).

[2] James H. Charlesworth, *The Old Testament Pseudepigrapha* (Garden City: Doubleday, 1983), 1:693-94.

A similar story is told of Enoch, who is quoted as saying, "Then I fell upon my face before the Lord of the Spirits. And the angel Michael, one of the archangels, seizing me by my right hand and lifting me up, led me out into all the secrets of mercy; and he showed me all the secrets of righteousness" (*1 Enoch* 71:2-3).[3] On another occasion, Enoch reported that, during a heavenly visit, "fear covered me and trembling seized me. And as I shook and trembled, I fell upon my face and saw a vision . . . I was prostrate on my face covered and trembling. And the Lord called me with his own mouth . . . And he lifted me up and brought me near to the gate, but I (continued) to look down with my face. But he raised me up" (*1 Enoch* 14:14, 24-25; 15:1).[4]

The fourth-century Christian historian Eusebius, in his *Praeparatio Evangelica* 9, cited a passage from Artapanus, in which it was reported that when Moses came out of prison and appeared before the king of Egypt, the monarch "bade Moses say the name of the god who had sent him . . . he bent forward and pronounced it in his ear. When the king heard it, he fell down speechless but revived when taken hold of by Moses."[5] The story bears resemblances to that of Aaron and the king of the Lamanites found in Alma 22. Aaron had just been delivered from prison when he came before the king (Alma 22:2), and it was while learning about God that the king "was struck as if he were dead" (Alma 22:5-11, 15-18), after which Aaron "put forth his hand and raised the king from the earth, and said unto him: Stand. And he stood upon his feet, receiving his strength" (Alma 22:22).

---

[3] *Ibid.*, 1:49.

[4] *Ibid.*, 1:21.

[5] *Ibid.*, 2:901.

LOSS OF PHYSICAL STRENGTH

These stories may reflect the fact that, after an appearance or vision of God, a prophet sometimes loses strength and falls to the ground, as happened with Moses (Moses 1:10), Lehi (1 Nephi 1:6-7), and Joseph Smith (Joseph Smith-History 1:20). The apostle Paul fell to the ground and was blinded when Christ appeared to him (Acts 9:3-4, 8). Occasionally, this happens when an angel appears (Matthew 28:2-4; 2 Enoch 1:5-8), as in the case of Alma the younger, who, with his companions, "fell to the earth" when the angel stopped them (Mosiah 27:12).

"The astonishment of Alma was so great that he became dumb, that he could not open his mouth; yea, and he became weak, even that he could not move his hands" (Mosiah 27:19). He remained in this condition for two days and two nights, during which time he, like the two Lamanite kings, came to know God (Alma 27:22-24). There is no indication, however, that he was raised by a handclasp like the kings.

The Bible reports that the prophet Daniel twice fell to the earth and did not arise until the angel touched him (Daniel 8:15-18; 10:4-11; note that in the latter story, the text says he also became weak).[6] In *4 Ezra* 10:25-30, we find Ezra, in vision, being frightened by a woman (the heavenly Jerusalem) whose face shone like lightning (like the angel at the tomb in Matthew 28:2-4). "I was too frightened to approach her, and my heart was terrified . . . I lay there like a corpse and was deprived of my understanding." Then the angel Uriel came and "he grasped my right hand and strengthened me and set me on my feet."[7]

In verses 7-11 of the Greek Septuagint addition to Esther

---

[6] There may be a tie between the handclasp to raise an individual from a near-death experience and the laying on of hands to heal the sick, that is, to bring them back from the brink of death.

[7] James H. Charlesworth, *The Old Testament Pseudepigrapha*, 1:547.

5, we find that when Esther appeared before the Persian king, "he was very dreadful" in appearance and she saw him "as an angel of God," and "fainted, and bowed herself upon the head of the maid that went before her." But the king "leaped from his throne, and took her in his arms, till she came to herself again, and comforted her with loving words."[8]

A parallel story is found in an early Christian document from Ethiopia, which cites from The Prayer of the Virgin Mary on Behalf of the Apostle Matyas (Mathias) in Parthia (northern Iran). "At the sight of these [angels] our Lady Mary was seized with great fear, and she fell down upon the ground as one dead. Then our Lord and Saviour Jesus Christ stretched out His hand, and raising her up made her to stand before Him."[9] In the Ethiopic *Conflict of Adam and Eve with Satan*, there are several instances of Adam falling to the ground as though dead, whereupon the Word of God appears and raises him up.

CONCLUSION

In light of these and other accounts, the Book of Mormon stories of people falling into ecstasy and being raised by a handclasp fits quite well into the ancient world from which the Nephite record came.

---

[8] For the King James translation, see The Rest of the Chapters of the Book of Esther 15:6-15, in *The Apocrypha*, frequently published by and under commission of Cambridge University Press. In addition to the resemblance to the ritual embrace (which, in the eternal sense, is administered by the heavenly king), the story may have a bearing on the custom mentioned in Alma 47:22-23, in which people prostrate themselves before the king, who then puts forth his hand to raise them. During the initiation of a master mason—a ceremony traditionally based on biblical precedents—the candidate is placed on the floor atop a cloth with the image of a coffin on it, to commemorate the death of Hiram Abiff, chief architect of Solomon's temple. He is then symbolically raised from the dead on the five points of fellowship, which includes clasping of the right hands.

[9] Sir E. W. Wallis Budge, *The Bandlet of Righteousness: An Ethiopian Book of the Dead* (London: Luzac, 1929), 118

Chapter 32

"THAT THEY MAY BE KEPT BRIGHT"

And now behold, since it has been as much as we could do to get our stains taken away from us, and our swords are made bright, let us hide them away that they may be kept bright, as a testimony to our God at the last day, or at the day that we shall be brought to stand before him to be judged, that we have not stained our swords in the blood of our brethren since he imparted his word unto us and has made us clean thereby . . . we will hide away our swords, yea, even we will bury them deep in the earth, that they may be kept bright, as a testimony that we have never used them. (Alma 24:15-16)

One of the great acts of faith recorded in the Book of Mormon is the burying of weapons of war by the Lamanites converted by the sons of Mosiah. Their king had advised the action, noting that "since God hath taken away our stains, and our swords have become bright, then let us stain our swords no more with the blood of our brethren . . . let us retain our swords that they be not stained with the blood of our brethren; for perhaps, if we should stain our swords again they can no more be washed bright through the blood of the Son of our great God, which shall be shed for the atonement of our sins" (Alma 24:12-13).

The desire of these Lamanites to make their swords bright by ridding them of the blood of the slain may reflect an idiom used in their language. A few centuries earlier, Jacob, declaring that he had warned the people of their sins, noted that "the God of Israel did witness that I shook your iniquities from my soul, and that I stand with brightness before him, and am rid of your blood" (2 Nephi 9:44). In this case, it is Jacob who, being "rid of . . . blood" retains his "brightness."

Critics have maintained that this is illogical, since burying the weapons would only speed up the rusting process by exposing them to the more constant moisture of the soil. The best response is that the Lamanite swords were probably similar to Mesoamerican sword-like weapons, made of sharp obsidian blades embedded in wooden clubs. William J. Hamblin and A. Brent Merrill have suggested that it was because of their wooden parts that the swords could be "stained" with blood, while blood could be simply wiped from a metal blade.[1] An inscription of the Assyrian king Shalmaneser III (858-824 B.C.) notes that, following a battle, his army marched to the Mediterranean sea, where they washed their weapons in the water.[2]

If the Lamanites' swords were metal, it would make more sense to reshape the metal into agricultural implements, as the Bible suggests (Isaiah 2:4; Joel 3:10; Micah 4:3), rather than bury them in the ground. But it is also possible that the term "brightness" refers to the swords themselves. An early Jewish text, *Abot de Rabbi Nathan* 33, indicates that the "lightning" (Hebrew *bārāq*) that appears in parallel with "arrows" in Psalm 18:15 (and repeated in 2 Samuel 22:15) is the sword, noting that the word representing the brightness of the sword in Ezekiel 21:15 is also *bārāq*.

A belief held among a number of different societies may explain the rationale behind the converted Lamanites burying their weapons. It is the belief that an individual wounded by a weapon will heal only if the weapon itself is safeguarded by hiding it. For example, among the Lkuñgen Indians of British Columbia the

---

[1] William J. Hamblin and A. Brent Merrill, "Swords in the Book of Mormon," in Stephen D. Ricks and William J. Hamblin, *Warfare in the Book of Mormon* (Salt Lake City: Deseret and FARMS, 1990). See also Matthew Roper, "On Cynics and Swords," in Daniel C. Peterson, ed., *FARMS Review of Books* 9/1 (1997).

[2] See the English translation in James B. Pritchard, *Ancient Near Eastern Texts* (3rd ed., Princeton University, 1969), 277.

friends of a wounded man will hide the weapon that caused the injury. In other cultures, it was believed that, in order for the man to heal, the offending weapon must be anointed, evidently to prevent rusting and to keep it bright. The prevalence of this tradition in sixteenth-century England was attested by Roger Bacon. As late as the nineteenth century, farmers in Suffolk would oil or grease a wound-causing scythe or other implement (including nails and even thorns) to keep them bright.

In Suffolk, should a man be stabbed with a knife, the knife would be greased and laid across his sickbed. Inhabitants of the Harz mountains believed that if one were cut with a knife or scissors, it was necessary to smear the implement with fat and hide it away in a dry place; as the knife dried, the wound was believed to heal.[3]

CONCLUSION

We do not know if this practice prevailed among the Lamanites, though the anointing of accouterments of war by their Israelite ancestors is attested in the Bible (2 Samuel 1:21; Isaiah 21:5). But we cannot rule out the possibility that they held some such belief.

---

[3] The accounts given here are drawn from Sir James Frazer and reviser Theodor H. Gaster, *the New Golden Bough* (New York: Mentor, 1964), 65-66.

Chapter 33

OATHS IN THE BOOK OF MORMON

And because of their oath they had been kept from taking up arms against their brethren; for they had taken an oath that they never would shed blood more; and according to their oath they would have perished; yea, they would have suffered themselves to have fallen into the hands of their brethren. (Alma 53:11)

Oaths and covenants play a special role among both Nephites and Lamanites, whether righteous or wicked.[1] This is because of the special emphasis placed on oaths and covenants in the law of Moses. The Lord declared, "If a man vow a vow unto the Lord, or swear an oath to bind his soul with a bond; he shall not break his word, he shall do according to all that proceedeth out of his mouth" (Numbers 30:2). Oaths were made in the name of the Lord. "Thou shalt fear the Lord thy God, and serve him, and swear by his name" (Deuteronomy 6:13).

The first Book of Mormon example of an oath made in the name of the Lord is found in 1 Nephi 3:15, where Nephi vowed to fulfill the Lord's commandment to obtain the brass plates. He began with the words, "As the Lord liveth, and as we live."

Nephi fulfilled the oath by dressing in Laban's clothing and ordering Laban's servant Zoram to bring the plates outside the city with him. When Zoram discovered the deception, he was about to flee but was held back by Nephi, who did not want the

---

[1] The Nephites who heard king Benjamin's speech entered into an oath and a covenant to keep the Lord's commandments (Mosiah 5:5-8; 6:1-3). The covenant associated with baptism is mentioned in Mosiah 18:10, 13 (see Alma 7:15); 21:31-32; 24:13. For oaths among members of the Nephite secret combination known as the Gadianton Robbers, see Helaman 1:11; 2:3; 6:22; 3 Nephi 6:28-30; 7:11.

OATHS IN THE LAW OF MOSES

people of Jerusalem alerted to their departure. Nephi recorded:

> I spake with him, that if he would hearken unto my words, as the Lord liveth, and as I live, even so that if he would hearken unto our words, we would spare his life. And I spake unto him, even with an oath, that he need not fear; that he should be a free man like unto us if he would go down in the wilderness with us. And I also spake unto him, saying: Surely the Lord hath commanded us to do this thing; and shall we not be diligent in keeping the commandments of the Lord? Therefore, if thou wilt go down into the wilderness to my father thou shalt have place with us. And it came to pass that Zoram did take courage at the words which I spake . . . and he promised that he would go down into the wilderness unto our father. Yea, and he also made an oath unto us that he would tarry with us from that time forth . . . When Zoram had made an oath unto us, our fears did cease concerning him. (1 Nephi 4:32-37)

OATHS IN THE LAW OF MOSES

To modern readers, it seems strange that a simple oath or promise should allay the fears of both Zoram and of Lehi's sons. It makes sense only in the context of ancient Israelite practice. The Lord told Moses:

> When thou shalt vow a vow unto the Lord thy God, thou shalt not slack to pay it: for the Lord thy God will surely require it of thee; and it would be sin in thee. But if thou shalt forbear to vow it shall be no sin in thee. That which is gone out of thy lips thou shalt keep and perform; even a

freewill offering, according as thou hast vowed unto the Lord thy God, which thou hast promised with thy mouth. (Deuteronomy 23:21-23)[2]

The Lord also commanded Israel, "And ye shall not swear by my name falsely, neither shalt thou profane the name of thy God" (Leviticus 19:12). This is the meaning of the third of the Ten Commandments, "Thou shalt not take the name of the Lord thy God in vain; for the Lord will not hold him guiltless that taketh his name in vain" (Exodus 20:7). Taking the Lord's name in vain meant making a vow in the Lord's name and not keeping it.[3] Because it was part of the ten commandments, the breaking of an oath made in the Lord's name could lead anciently to the death penalty.

RASH OATHS

In an extreme case, the Old Testament judge Jephthah swore that if the Lord would help him win a certain battle, he would offer to him in sacrifice the first thing he met upon returning home. He undoubtedly expected to see one of his animals as he neared his house. But it was his daughter who came running to greet the returning warrior. Despite the serious nature of killing an innocent human being, Jephthah sacrificed his daughter to fulfill the oath (Judges 11:30-40). The New Testament also has an example of a rash oath made by a group of men who "bound

---

[2] Jesus, commenting on the law of Moses, taught his disciples to not swear by anything holy, "but let your communication be, Yea, yea; Nay, nay: for whatsoever is more than these cometh of evil" (Matthew 5:33-37).

[3] In our modern world, where profanity is so commonplace, we often think that this commandment referred to profane use of the Lord's name. We have even redefined the verb "to swear" to mean "to utter profanities." The Bible often forbids profaning the Lord's name, but that is not what was originally intended by the third commandment.

themselves under a curse, saying that they would neither eat nor drink till they had killed Paul" (Acts 23:12; see also verse 14). They did not succeed in slaying the apostle, but we are not told whether the men starved to death.

Rash oaths are known from the Book of Mormon as well. The leaders of a Lamanite army, angry that the Nephite general Moroni's new fortifications had foiled their plans to destroy the city of Ammonihah, swore to attack the city of Noah (Alma 49:17); they were repelled because Noah, too, had been fortified. Their leader, Amalickiah, angrily swore to drink Moroni's blood (Alma 49:27). Giddianhi, leader of the Gadianton band of robbers, swore to exterminate the Nephites but was unable to accomplish his purposes (3 Nephi 3:8).

LAMANITE OATHS

These examples of unfulfilled oaths are rare. We learn from the Book of Mormon that even the Lamanites, who didn't believe in the ancient prophets, were strict in keeping their oaths. The Lamanite converts who called themselves Anti-Nephi-Lehies (and were later named the children of Ammon) swore that they would never again take up arms against their brethren (Alma 27:28-29), and we learn that they never broke this oath (Alma 53:11, 14-18; 43:1).[4]

When the Lamanites defeated the Nephites living in the city of Nephi, the Lamanite king took an oath that his people would not slay the Nephites, while the Nephite king, Limhi, swore that his people would pay half of their produce in tribute (Mosiah 19:25-26). The Lamanites, believing that the Nephites had broken

---

[4] For a discussion of this topic, see John A. Tvedtnes, "Sons of Mosiah: Emissaries of Peace," in Stephen D. Ricks and William J. Hamblin, *Warfare in the Book of Mormon* (Salt Lake City: Deseret Book and Foundation for Ancient Research and Mormon Studies, 1990). The Ammonites' sons who were too young to take the oath were not bound by it and served with Helaman in defending Nephite lands against a Lamanite invasion (Alma 56:3-9).

the peace, attacked the Nephites and the Lamanite king was captured (Mosiah 20:14-15). The king discovered that the Nephites were not only innocent of the charges, but that they intended to keep their bargain (Mosiah 20:22). He swore that his people would not slay them—a promise that they were careful to keep, even though they mistreated them otherwise (Mosiah 20:24; 21:3).[5]

During one of the Nephite-Lamanite wars, the Nephites, led by Moroni, had gained the advantage over the Lamanites. Moroni called for a cease to the fighting and promised the Lamanites that they could go home if they would promise not to come again to war against them (Alma 44:6-7). Zarahemnah, the Lamanite leader, was willing to deliver up his weapons, "but we will not suffer ourselves to take an oath unto you, which we know that we shall break, and also our children" (Alma 44:8). Moroni insisted that without the oath there would be more bloodshed (Alma 44:11). Some of the Lamanites threw down their weapons of war "and entered into a covenant of peace. And as many as entered into a covenant they suffered to depart into the wilderness" (Alma 44:15). The battle then resumed until the Lamanites were so defeated that Zarahemnah and the rest of his men entered into the same covenant (Alma 44:19). "And after they had entered into a covenant with him of peace they were suffered to depart into the wilderness" (Alma 44:20).

This action set a precedent for Nephite treatment of their enemies. Soon afterward, Moroni placed himself and his soldiers under covenant to maintain the liberty of their country against another Lamanite invasion (Alma 46:20-22, 31). Moroni swore to defend his people, their rights, country, and religion "even to the loss of his blood" (Alma 48:13). He later wrote, "I, Moroni, am

---

[5] See the discussion in S. Kent Brown, "Marriage and Treaty in the Book of Mormon: The Case of the Abducted Lamanite Daughters," in his book *From Jerusalem to Zarahemla: Literary and Historical Studies of the Book of Mormon* (Provo: BYU Religious Studies Center, 1998), 99-112.

constrained, according to the covenant which I have made to keep the commandments of my God" (Alma 60:34). Moroni's planned campaign against the Lamanites was delayed by the fact that a group of Nephite dissenters, led by a man named Amalickiah, rose up in support of the Lamanites, and Moroni's army was forced to confront them first. The defeated Amalickiahites who covenanted to defend their country were freed. The rest were slain (Alma 46:35), while Amalickiah and a few of his men went over to the Lamanites.

At one point during the war that ensued, four thousand Lamanite prisoners covenanted with Moroni that they would not again make war against the Nephites and were allowed to go to live with the children of Ammon (Alma 62:15-17). A generation later, Moroni's son Moronihah also allowed Lamanite captives to leave in peace (Helaman 1:33). Still later, repentant Gadianton robbers captured during a war were freed upon taking an oath to no longer commit murder (3 Nephi 5:4-5; 6:3).

CONCLUSION

Even the vilest of people were trusted by the Nephites once they had taken an oath to keep the peace. Stories such as these from the Book of Mormon should encourage us, as members of the Lord's Church, to likewise keep our covenants.

Chapter 34

IN THE STRENGTH OF THE LORD

And in the strength of the Lord they did contend against their enemies, until they had slain many thousands of the Lamanites. And it came to pass that they did contend against the Lamanites until they had driven them out of all the lands of their inheritance. (Words Of Mormon 1:14)

The Book of Mormon frequently notes that the Nephites fought against their enemies "in the strength of the Lord" (Mosiah 9:17; 10:10-11; Alma 46:20; 60:16; 61:18; 3 Nephi 3:12; 4:10).[1] But when they were disobedient, the Lord withheld his strength from them and they could not withstand their enemies (Helaman 7:22; Mormon 2:26). According to Jarom 1:7, they were able to withstand their enemies because of the faith of their leaders. In later times, it was a practice among the Nephites, when they were righteous, to choose prophets to lead their armies (3 Nephi 3:19). Mormon was one of those leaders.

THE LORD STRENGTHENS THE NEPHITE ARMIES

During the Amlicite war, despite the "great strength" of the Amlicites, "the Lord did strengthen the hand of the Nephites, that they slew the Amlicites with great slaughter, that they began to flee before them" and lost nearly twice as many men as the Nephites (Alma 2:17-19). When the Amlicites joined with the

---

[1] Though his people fought "in the strength of the Lord," Zeniff nevertheless admired "the Lamanites [who] knew nothing concerning the Lord, nor the strength of the Lord, therefore they depended upon their own strength. Yet they were a strong people, as to the strength of men" (Mosiah 10:11).

The Lord Strengthens The Nephite Armies

Lamanites and became innumerable (Alma 2:27, 35), "nevertheless, the Nephites being strengthened by the hand of the Lord, having prayed mightily to him that he would deliver them out of the hands of their enemies, therefore the Lord did hear their cries, and did strengthen them, and the Lamanites and the Amlicites did fall before them" (Alma 2:28). When Amlici engaged Alma in personal combat, Alma prayed to the Lord to save him, and "he was strengthened" and slew Amlici (Alma 2:28-31).

The Lord's assistance to the Nephites was particularly evident in the great war that took place in the days of captain Moroni. Helaman reported to Moroni that his men prayed "to God, that he would strengthen us, and deliver us out of the hands of our enemies" (Alma 58:10) and wrote, "We trust God will deliver us, notwithstanding the weakness of our armies, yea, and deliver us out of the hands of our enemies (Alma 58:37). He further noted how they had miraculously regained their lands (Alma 59:3).

Moroni himself noted that those who trust in God will be delivered from their enemies (Alma 61:13) and that victory comes to those who go forth in the strength of the Lord (Alma 60:16). He noted that God had often delivered the Nephites from their enemies (Alma 60:20-21). When he had to leave his armies for a time to put down a rebellion in the land of Zarahemla, he proposed to leave the strength and blessing of God on his men, so "none other power can operate against them" because of their faith (Alma 60:25-26). So Moroni gave his subordinates, Lehi and Teancum, power to conduct the war "according to the Spirit of God" (Alma 61:15, 21), and went forth against the dissenters "in the strength of God" (Alma 61:17-18).

In a subsequent war, the Nephites repented and prayed God to deliver them from their enemies in battle (3 Nephi 3:25; 4:8). They met the Lamanites "in the strength of the Lord" (3 Nephi 4:10) and were rescued by God (3 Nephi 4:30-33).

The scriptures often declare that God helps his followers in

IN THE STRENGTH OF THE LORD

their battles.[2] In the Bible, he is often called "Lord of hosts/armies."[3] David, who had been given strength to defeat the giant (*Ben-Sirach* 47:5), approached Goliath with these words:

> Thou comest to me with a sword, and with a spear, and with a shield; but I come to thee in the name of the Lord of hosts, the God of the armies of Israel, whom thou hast defied. This day will the Lord deliver thee into mine hand; and I will smite thee . . . that all the earth may know that there is a God in Israel. And all this assembly shall know that the Lord saveth not with sword and spear: for the battle is the Lord's, and he will give you into our hands. (1 Samuel 17:45-47)

When ancient heroes failed to keep the Lord's commandments, they lost the divine assistance that made them powerful. Thus, when Samson forsook his Nazirite oath, he was left powerless (Judges 16:15-21). In the last days of the Nephites, when they had become wicked, Mormon recorded, "the strength of

---

[2] Deuteronomy 7:2, 23; 20:1; 31:3-8; Joshua 11:6; Judges 20:28; 1 Samuel 7:10; 14:23; 5:19; 2 Samuel 5:23-25; 1 Kings 5:3; 8:44-45; 1 Chronicles 14:10; 2 Chronicles 13:13-16; 18:31; 20:15-17; Psalms 18:16-19; 24:8; 105:10-15; 140:7; Haggai 2:22; Zechariah 14:3; Jarom 1:7; Omni 1:7; Mosiah 9:17; 10:10, 19; Alma 2:28; 19:27; 48:16; 49:28; 60:20-21; 61:21; 3 Nephi 3:21, 25; 4:8. In early days, Israelite priests went into battle with the people, sometimes taking the ark of the covenant with them (Joshua 6:4-21; 1 Samuel 4:3-8; 14:18-20; 2 Chronicles 13:13-16). The priests were to admonish the people before battle (Deuteronomy 20:1-4).

[3] In the Bible, God is often called "the Lord of hosts," referring to the armies of heaven (e.g., 1 Samuel 17:45). The Hebrew term is transliterated "Lord of Sabaoth" in Romans 9:29; James 5:4; D&C 87:7; 88:2; 95:7; 98:2. Compare *History of the Church* 2:381, 426-7; 3:119; 5:111, where Joseph Smith spoke of the "armies of heaven," and *History of the Church* 7:271, where Brigham Young spoke of the "God of the armies of Israel."

the Lord was not with us . . . therefore we had become weak like unto our brethren [the Lamanites]" (Mormon 2:26).

THE LORD STRENGTHENS INDIVIDUALS

The Lord is also said to have strengthened individuals. The feats of strength performed by Samson are perhaps more well-known than those of any other Israelite. Samson, endowed by God with great strength, twice broke the cords with which he had been bound (Judges 16:4-12). At a place he named Lehi, "the spirit of the Lord came mightily" on Samson and he broke his bonds and slew his captors (Judges 15:14-15). In the Book of Mormon, the Lord gave Nephi strength sufficient to break the bands with which his brothers had restrained him (1 Nephi 7:17-18).

A similar story is told of Alma and Amulek, who "had power given unto them, insomuch that they could not be confined in dungeons; neither was it possible that any man could slay them; nevertheless they did not exercise their power until they were bound in bonds and cast into prison. Now, this was done that the Lord might show forth his power in them" (Alma 8:31). Receiving strength from the Lord after prayer, they were able to break the cords binding them. An earthquake then precipitated the fall of the prison and the inhabitants of the city of Ammonihah fled in fear from the two missionaries (Alma 14:26-29; see 26:29).[4] This power over the elements is noted earlier in the same chapter, when Amulek suggested that he and Alma "stretch forth our hands, and exercise the power of God which is in us" to save the believers from the flames, but the Spirit constrained Alma (Alma 14:10-11).

Most scriptural and pseudepigraphic texts agree that the strength of Israelite heroes came from God. Nephi wrote that he was "a man large in stature" and had "received much strength of

---

[4] The sons of Mosiah had been stoned, bound with strong cords, cast into prison, "and through the power and wisdom of God we have been delivered again" (Alma 26:29).

IN THE STRENGTH OF THE LORD

the Lord" (1 Nephi 4:31). In the pseudepigraphic *Testaments of the Twelve Patriarchs,* Simeon declared, "And I became extraordinarily strong; I did not hold back from any exploit, nor did I fear anything. My heart was firm, my courage was high, and my feelings were dispassionate. For by the Most High, manly courage is given to men in soul and body" (*Testament of Simeon* 2:3-5). Simeon's brother Judah, whose reputed feats of strength outnumber those of others, introduced the account of his accomplishments by saying that the Lord had blessed him (*Testament of Judah* 2:1). Isaac had blessed Judah with the words, "May the Lord give you might and strength to tread upon all who hate you . . . May all the nations fear before your face, and all of the nations tremble" (*Jubilees* 31:18). *Testament Judah* 3:10 records that his father Jacob "saw in a vision concerning me that a powerful angel accompanied me everywhere so that no one might touch me."

Nephi, noting how the Lord saved his father from those who wanted to slay him, wrote that because of their faith, the Lord makes his chosen ones "mighty even to the power of deliverance" (1 Nephi 1:20). Two Book of Mormon prophets, Nephi (1 Nephi 17:48-55) and Abinadi (Mosiah 13:1-6), could not be touched by their enemies because they were filled with the power of God. The sons of the younger Helaman, Nephi and Lehi, could not be slain (Helaman 5:23-24). Nephi later was taken from the midst of a crowd by the Spirit of the Lord (Helaman 10:16). The Lord protected Samuel the Lamanite from the stones and arrows cast at him by the inhabitants of Zarahemla (Helaman 16:2). Wicked people tried several times to kill the three translated Nephite disciples of Christ, but they survived every attempt (3 Nephi 28:19-22; 4 Nephi 1:30-33). They, like the biblical Daniel (Daniel 6:16-23), were unmolested by the wild beasts into whose den they were cast.

Another notable miracle is the preservation of the two thousand and sixty stripling warriors who, led by the elder Helaman, "fought as if with the strength of God . . . miraculous

The Lord Strengthens Individuals

strength . . . with such power" against the Lamanites. While two hundred of them received many wounds, not one died (Alma 56:56).

When the sons of Mosiah went on a mission to the Lamanites, the Lord promised their father that he would protected them (Mosiah 28:7; Alma 17:35; 19:22-23). They received power from the Lord to accomplish things impossible for mortals. Ammon saw the attack of a band of Lamanite robbers at the waters of Sebus as an opportunity to demonstrate his power to gain the attention of his host, king Lamoni (Alma 17:29). He slew six with sling stones and cut off the arms of a number of the men as they attacked him, slaying their leader in the process (Alma 17:34-39).

The king's servants, who witnessed his feats of strength, were "astonished at his power" (Alma 17:36) and told Lamoni of Ammon's "expertness and great strength" and his "power," expressing their belief that he could not be slain (Alma 18:3, 20, 22; 19:4, 15, 22-23). Lamoni declared to the young missionary, "I know, in the strength of the Lord thou canst do all things" (Alma 20:4; cf. 18:35). The queen also told him, "thou hast power to do many mighty works" in the name of God (Alma 19:4).

Ammon later declared, "I know that I am nothing; as to my strength, I am weak; therefore I will not boast of myself, but I will boast of my God, for in his strength I can do all things" (Alma 26:12). It was a lesson lost on later Nephites who, when they boasted in their own strength,[5] were left in their own strength and lost to the Lamanites (Helaman 4:13), who became as strong as the Nephites (Helaman 4:26; see also Mosiah 11:19; Helaman 16:15; Mormon 3:8; 4:8; cf. D&C 4:13).

---

[5] Alma counseled his son Shiblon, "Do not boast in your own wisdom, nor of your much strength" (Alma 38:11; compare D&C 105:24).

CONCLUSION

From this brief survey, we can see that the Nephites followed the ancient Israelite principle of turning their defense over to God during wartime, trusting that he would deliver them if they were faithful.

Chapter 35

"THAT WHICH IS TO COME"

And again my brethren, I would call your attention, for I have somewhat more to speak unto you; for behold, I have things to tell you concerning that which is to come. (Mosiah 3:1)

With these words, King Benjamin introduced the expression that came to denote Jesus Christ among the Nephites. The words "that which is to come" refer specifically to Christ, and not to future events in general. This becomes clear as we read the rest of the chapter (Mosiah 3), which is devoted to a message delivered to Benjamin by an angel. The entire message concerns the coming of Jesus Christ.

The angel said that the good news of salvation had been declared in advance by prophets "that thereby whosoever should believe that Christ should come, the same might receive remission of their sins, and rejoice with exceedingly great joy, even as though he had already come among them" (Mosiah 3:13). He stressed that it was essential that the people "believe that salvation was, and is, and is to come, in and through the atoning blood of Christ, the Lord Omnipotent" (Mosiah 3:18).

The Nephites received the angelic message with joy "because of the exceeding faith which they had in Jesus Christ who should come, according to the words which King Benjamin had spoken unto them" (Mosiah 4:3). The king urged them to stand "steadfastly in the faith of that which is to come, which was spoken by the mouth of the angel" (Mosiah 4:11). The people replied that they had received "the manifestations of his Spirit, have great views of that which is to come; and were it expedient, we could prophesy of all things" (Mosiah 5:3).

King Benjamin's words set the tone for Nephite leaders in subsequent generations. Helaman II told his sons:

"That Which Is to Come"

> O remember, remember, my sons, the words which king Benjamin spake unto his people; yea, remember that there is no other way nor means whereby man can be saved, only through the atoning blood of Jesus Christ, who shall come, yea, remember that he cometh to redeem the world. And remember also the words which Amulek spake unto Zeezrom, in the city of Ammonihah; for he said unto him that the Lord surely should come to redeem his people. (Helaman 5:9-10)

King Benjamin was not the first Nephite prophet to teach the advent of Christ. Lehi had spoken of "the Messiah who should come" (1 Nephi 10:11, 17). Nephi, too, spoke of the "Messiah to come" (2 Nephi 25:18). Nephi's brother, Jacob, wrote, "we also had many revelations, and the spirit of much prophecy; wherefore, we knew of Christ and his kingdom, which should come" (Jacob 1:6).

From the beginning, the central religious theme among the Nephites was the coming of Christ to atone for the sins of mankind (Alma 46:15). Jarom noted that "the prophets, and the priests, and the teachers, did labor diligently, exhorting with all long-suffering the people to diligence; teaching the law of Moses, and the intent for which it was given; persuading them to look forward unto the Messiah, and believe in him to come as though he already was" (Jarom 1:11).

Throughout their history, the Nephite faithful looked forward to the coming of Christ. Alma spoke of "that which was to come," meaning the atonement of Christ (Mosiah 18:2). Indeed, the advent of Christ became his principal message whenever he preached (Alma 5:21, 27; 9:26; 33:22; 39:15-16). In his great discourse delivered in the city of Gideon, Alma spoke of the atonement "which is to come" (Alma 7:6) in terms that stressed the importance he placed on the coming of Christ:

"That Which Is to Come"

> For behold, I say unto you there be many things to come; and behold, there is one thing which is of more importance than they all—for behold, the time is not far distant that the Redeemer liveth and cometh among his people. (Alma 7:7)

Samuel the Lamanite followed the same pattern. He told the Nephites in the city of Zarahemla that nothing could save them "save it be repentance and faith on the Lord Jesus Christ, who surely shall come into the world" (Helaman 13:6). "Five years more cometh," he declared, "and behold, then cometh the Son of God" (Helaman 14:2). He then enumerated the signs of Christ's birth and death. Meanwhile, the prophet Nephi was "working miracles among the people, that they might know that the Christ must shortly come— Telling them of things which must shortly come, that they might know and remember at the time of their coming that they had been made known unto them beforehand" (Helaman 16:4-5).

The importance of looking forward to Christ's coming is further strengthened by the fact that the major problem with Nephite dissenters was that they did not believe that anyone could know in advance of "things to come," and they therefore rejected Christ.[1] Sherem disputed with Jacob the validity of believing in "a being which ye say shall come many hundred years hence, saying that no one can tell of things to come" (Jacob 7:7).

Zeezrom employed a similar tactic against Alma and Amulek (Alma 11:35) and was refuted by Amulek (Alma 11:40). Similarly, the anti-Christ Korihor accused Alma and his people being "bound down under a foolish and a vain hope, why do ye

---

[1] According to Helaman 8:22-23, Lehi had been driven from Jerusalem because he testified of the coming of Christ. It is ironic, then, that some of his posterity rejected these prophecies.

yoke yourselves with such foolish things? Why do ye look for a Christ? For no man can know of anything which is to come" (Alma 30:13).

Unbelievers slew the prophet Abinadi because he "prophesied of many things which are to come, yea, even the coming of Christ" (Mosiah 7:26-28). He had testified of "things to come" (Mosiah 13:31; 16:6, 14).

Some apostates from the Nephite faith, such as the Zoramites and the Amalekites, made it a point of doctrine that there would be no Christ. In their weekly prayers, the Zoramites thanked God "that he did not lead them away after the tradition of their brethren, and that their hearts were not stolen away to believe in things to come, which they knew nothing about" (Alma 31:22). An unbelieving Amalekite declared to Mosiah's missionary son Aaron:

> We do not believe that thou knowest any such thing. We do not believe in these foolish traditions. We do not believe that thou knowest of things to come, neither do we believe that thy fathers and also that our fathers did know concerning the things which they spake, of that which is to come. (Alma 21:8)

Even after the signs of Christ's imminent birth began to appear, some continued to doubt, believing that the fulfillment of prophecy was coincidental (Helaman 16:16). Satan sought to "harden the hearts of the people against that which was good and against that which should come" (Helaman 16:22).

The unbelievers considered the doctrine of Christ's coming to be,

> a wicked tradition, which has been handed down unto us by our fathers, to cause us that we should believe in some great and marvelous thing which should come to pass, but not among us, but in a

"That Which Is to Come"

land which is far distant, a land which we know not; therefore they can keep us in ignorance, for we cannot witness with our own eyes that they are true. (Helaman 16:20).

It was precisely this latter point that differentiated the Nephite believers from the unbelievers. The faithful went beyond blind faith in accepting the witness of their fathers and sought for personal testimony of "Christ . . . who should come according to the spirit of prophecy" (Mosiah 13:31; 16:6, 14). Thus Alma declared:

> I am commanded to stand and testify unto this people the things which have been spoken by our fathers concerning the things which are to come . . . I know of myself that whatsoever I shall say unto you, concerning that which is to come, is true . . . I know that Jesus Christ shall come, yea, the Son, the Only Begotten of the Father, full of grace, and mercy, and truth. And behold, it is he that cometh to take away the sins of the world, yea, the sins of every man who steadfastly believeth on his name. (Alma 5:44, 48)[2]

Of Alma's testimony to the people in Gideon, to which we referred above, we read that he spoke "according to the revelation of the truth of the word which had been spoken by his fathers, and according to the spirit of prophecy which was in him, according to the testimony of Jesus Christ, the Son of God, who should come to redeem his people from their sins" (Alma 6:8).

This passage reflects one of Joseph Smith's most frequent sayings (based on Revelation 19:10), that "the testimony of Jesus is

---

[2] Note the mention of the "spirit of revelation" and the "spirit of prophecy" in verses 46-47 and compare Christ's coming in verse 50. See also Alma 34:8.

"That Which Is to Come"

the spirit of prophecy."[3] It is a frequent theme in the Book of Mormon as well, where the "prophecies concerning that which was to come" (Helaman 6:14) refer primarily to Christ (see Helaman 8:20). Alma and Amulek "testified...of the things which were to come, according to the spirit of prophecy which was in them" (Alma 10:12). The sons of Mosiah "did not suppose that salvation came by the law of Moses; but the law of Moses did serve to strengthen their faith in Christ; and thus they did retain a hope through faith, unto eternal salvation, relying upon the spirit of prophecy, which spake of those things to come" (Alma 25:16). Similarly, the sons of their converts, who fought in the great war under the prophet Helaman, had strong faith "in the prophecies concerning that which is to come" (Alma 58:40).

What differentiated the righteous and the unrighteous in the Book of Mormon was faith in Christ to come. The same is true in our day. Those who look forward with an eye of faith to Christ's second coming and keep his commandments will be found worthy when he returns.

Mormon wrote that the coming forth of his abridgement of the Nephite records would be a sign that the prophecies concerning the last days were soon to be fulfilled and that "ye need not say that the Lord delays his coming" (3 Nephi 29:1-2). Indeed, the major purpose of the Book of Mormon is, according to its Title Page, to convince us "that Jesus is the Christ," and to prepare us to "be found spotless at the judgment-seat of Christ."

In his final exhortation to us, the future readers of his work, Mormon wrote, "Believe in Jesus Christ, that he is the Son of God . . . and [that] he bringeth to pass the resurrection of the dead, whereby man must be raised to stand before his judgement-seat" (Mormon 7:5-6).

---

[3] Joseph Fielding Smith, Teachings of the Prophet Joseph Smith (Salt Lake City: Deseret, 1979), pages 119, 160, 265, 269, 300, 312, 315.

CONCLUSION

Shall we, then, doubt the prophecies of the Bible and the Book of Mormon concerning Christ's return to raise us from the dead and to reign on earth? Should we not, rather, follow the pattern set by the righteous Book of Mormon prophets in seeking a personal, spiritual witness of Christ whereby we can be sure that he will come again? The words of Moroni, addressed to us, point the way:

> And now, I would commend you to seek this Jesus of whom the prophets and apostles have written, that the grace of God the Father, and also the Lord Jesus Christ, and the Holy Ghost, which beareth record of them, may be and abide in you forever. Amen. (Ether 12:41)

Chapter 36

ANGELS ANNOUNCE THE COMING OF CHRIST

And it shall be made known unto just and holy men, by the mouth of angels, at the time of his coming, that the words of our fathers may be fulfilled, according to that which they have spoken concerning him, which was according to the spirit of prophecy which was in them. (Alma 13:26)

The pending birth of Jesus Christ was of such importance that God sent angels to declare the good news, or "gospel." One such angel, Gabriel, came to the Savior's earthly mother (Luke 1:26-31). After Mary became pregnant, an angel—perhaps the same one—was sent to reassure Joseph that "that which is conceived in her is of the Holy Ghost. And she shall bring forth a son, and thou shalt call his name Jesus: for he shall save his people from their sins" (Matthew 1:20-21). When Christ was born in Bethlehem, the good news was delivered to shepherds by an angel, joined by "a multitude of the heavenly host praising God" (Luke 2:8-14).

THE "GOSPEL" ANNOUNCED IN THE BOOK OF MORMON

This same pattern was followed when God announced the coming of Christ to Lehi and his descendants, as recorded in the Book of Mormon. Lehi saw God in vision, "surrounded with numberless concourses of angels in the attitude of singing and praising their God," and Christ "descending out of the midst of heaven." Because of this experience, Lehi was able to prophesy of the Messiah to come (1 Nephi 10:4-11, 17).

Lehi's son, Nephi, had a similar vision of Christ and learned of him from an angel (1 Nephi 11:13-33). Another of

The "Gospel" Announced in The Book of Mormon

Lehi's sons, Jacob, also testified of Christ, noting that he had learned about him from an angel (2 Nephi 10:3-5). Similarly, King Benjamin spoke of an angel who told him of Christ to come (Mosiah 3:2-10.).

Alma the Younger was visited by an angel (Mosiah 27:11) and remained paralyzed for three days. When he at length was able to speak, he testified of Christ to come (Mosiah 27:30-31). Some years later, as he explained to his sons what had happened when the angel appeared (Alma 36:5-10), Alma declared that during the time he was incapacitated, he had been rescued from hell by calling on the name of Jesus (Alma 36:17-20; 38:7-9). He declared:

> Yea, methought I saw, even as our father Lehi saw, God sitting upon his throne, surrounded with numberless concourses of angels, in the attitude of singing and praising God" (Alma 36:22).

To his son Corianton, Alma said, "I would say somewhat unto you concerning the coming of Christ . . . to declare glad tidings of salvation unto his people" (Alma 39:15). Knowing that Corianton found it difficult to believe that the coming of a Savior could have been known so far in advance (Alma 39:17), Alma asked, "Is it not as easy at this time for the Lord to send his angel to declare these glad tidings unto us as unto our children, or as after the time of his coming?" (Alma 39:19).

During his mission to the city of Ammonihah, Alma told the people that angels had recently appeared to others to declare the message of salvation that would soon come through Christ (Alma 9:25-29; 13:21-25). Amulek, who accompanied him, testified that he had learned from an angel about God and the Savior to come (Alma 11:31-33). Alma subsequently recorded other instances of angels appearing to teach people during his lifetime (Alma 19:34-35; 32:23; 40:11).

Alma further stressed that the plan of redemption had been declared by angels shortly after the fall:

Angels Announce the Coming of Christ

> God . . . saw that it was expedient that man should know concerning the things whereof he had appointed unto them; Therefore he sent angels to converse with them, who caused men to behold of his glory. And they began from that time forth to call on his name; therefore God conversed with men, and made known unto them the plan of redemption, which had been prepared from the foundation of the world...God did call on men, in the name of his Son, (this being the plan of redemption which was laid) saying: If ye will repent, and harden not your hearts, then will I have mercy upon you, through mine Only Begotten Son; Therefore, whosoever repenteth, and hardeneth not his heart, he shall have claim on mercy through mine Only Begotten Son, unto a remission of his sins; and these shall enter into my rest. (Alma 12:28-30, 33-35; see also Moses 5:57-59; 7:25, 27; D&C 29:42)

About a century later, an angel appeared to the Lamanite prophet Samuel and taught him of Christ and of the signs of his coming (Helaman 13:5-7; 14:28.). Samuel's teachings to the Nephites were supplemented by those of Alma's great-grandson Nephi, who worked "miracles among the people, that they might know that the Christ must shortly come—Telling them of things which must shortly come, that they might know and remember at the time of their coming that they had been made known unto them beforehand, to the intent that they might believe" (Helaman 16:4-5).

The prophesied signs of Christ's coming began to be fulfilled "and angels did appear unto men, wise men, and did declare unto them glad tidings of great joy" (Helaman 16:13-14). Within five years, Christ was born in Bethlehem. Nearly thirty years later, he appeared to the Nephites, who, thanks to the angels,

The "Gospel" Announced in The Book of Mormon

had been expecting him.

> For behold, God knowing all things, being from everlasting to everlasting, behold, he sent angels to minister unto the children of men, to make manifest concerning the coming of Christ; and in Christ there should come every good thing. And God also declared unto prophets, by his own mouth, that Christ should come... Wherefore, by the ministering of angels, and by every word which proceeded forth out of the mouth of God, men began to exercise faith in Christ; and thus by faith, they did lay hold upon every good thing; and thus it was until the coming of Christ. (Moroni 7:22-23, 25)

ANGELS WILL ANNOUNCE CHRIST'S SECOND COMING

This pattern applies also to the second coming of Christ, for God has, in our day, again sent angels to declare the coming of his son to reign on earth (D&C 88:92; D&C 133:17). When Christ ascended to heaven from the mount of Olives after his resurrection, two angels appeared to tell the apostles that he would return to earth in the same manner (Acts 1:9-12). When he comes again, he will return to that same mount of Olives with all the saints (Zechariah 14:4-5; cf. D&C 133:20). D&C 45:44 interprets the Zechariah passage as referring to angels.

Chapter 37

EVENTS SURROUNDING CHRIST'S DEATH AND RESURRECTION

And it came to pass that it did last for the space of three days that there was no light seen; and there was great mourning and howling and weeping among all the people continually; yea, great were the groanings of the people, because of the darkness and the great destruction which had come upon them. (3 Nephi 8:23)

The story of Jesus' appearance to the Nephites after his resurrection, told in 3 Nephi, has parallels in a Coptic document thought to date to the second or third century A.D.[1] The document is known as the *Pistis Sophia* ("faith/assurance of wisdom"). Though the British Museum acquired a manuscript of the text in 1785, by the time the Book of Mormon appeared, it had not yet been translated. The earliest French translation was in 1856. Several pages were translated into English in 1887, but the full text, translated by G. R. S. Mead, did not appear in English until 1896.

GREAT EARTHQUAKES

According to the *Pistis Sophia*, there was, at the time of Jesus' ascension into heaven, a great earthquake that lasted for three hours (I.3). An alternate view given in the manuscript is that the quake lasted from the third hour on the fifteenth day of the month

---

[1] In this study, Mead's revised translation of 1921 is used as reprinted by John M. Watkins, London, 1955. References are in the format I.2, where the Roman numeral denotes the book and the Arabic numeral the chapter in the *Pistis Sophia*.

Tybi until the ninth hour the following day. This accords with the statement in 3 Nephi 8:19 that "the quakings of the earth . . . did last for about the space of three hours; and it was said by some that the time was greater."[2]

For three days after the earthquake and other agitations of nature, the Nephites were "howling and weeping" in the darkness and lamenting the destruction of the people in a number of cities (3 Nephi 8:23-25; 10:8).[3] In *Pistis Sophis* I.4, we read that "the disciples sat together in fear and were in exceedingly great agitation and were afraid because of the great earthquake which took place, and they wept together, saying 'What will then be? Peradventure the Saviour will destroy all regions?' Thus saying, they wept together."[4] During this time, the heavenly host "all sang praises . . . so that the whole world heard their voices" (I.3). Among the Nephites, after the quaking had stopped, "all the people of the land" heard the voice of Christ (1 Nephi 9:1-10:8).

---

[2] Matthew 27:45 reports that the darkness accompanying Christ's crucifixion lasted for three hours in Jerusalem. According to Exodus 10:22, the darkness at the time of Israel's exodus from Egypt lasted three days. The Matthew text also speaks of an earthquake, the rending of the rocks, and the resurrection of the dead from opened graves (Matthew 27:51-53)—features also found in 3 Nephi 8:18; 23:9-12.

[3] In Exodus 10:22-23, we read that, during the "thick darkness," among the Egyptians, "they saw not one another, neither rose any from his place for three days: but all the children of Israel had light in their dwellings."

[4] In *Book of the Rolls* f.101a, the preexistent Christ declares to a dying Adam that, at the time of his death on the cross, "I will thunder in the height . . . I will darken the sun . . . I will cleave the rocks . . . I will frighten the powers of heaven . . . I will cause heaven to rain on the desert . . . I will open the graves . . . I will cause all creation to tremble . . . I will make a new earth, and after three days, which I have spent in the grave, I will raise up the body which I took from thee." The same text declares that "when Adam died, the sun was darkened, and the moon for seven days and seven nights, with a gross darkness." Margaret Dunlop Gibson, *Apocrypha Arabica* (London: C. J. Clay and Sons, 1901), 16-17.

Events Surrounding Christ's Death and Resurrection

THE LIGHT-GLORY OF HEAVENLY BEINGS

On the day following the earthquake, according to the *Pistis Sophia*, as the disciples "wept together . . . the heavens opened, and they saw Jesus descend, shining most exceedingly . . . so that men in the world cannot describe the light which was on him" (I.4).[5] Joseph Smith used similar terminology to describe the brilliant light that surrounded the Father and the Son when they appeared to him in the sacred grove in the spring of 1820 (Joseph Smith-History 1:16-17). We are also reminded of Joseph Smith's description of Moroni on the night of his first appearance, September 21/22, 1823: "his whole person was glorious beyond description, and his countenance truly like lightning. The room was exceedingly light, but not so very bright as immediately around his person" (Joseph Smith-History 1:32). The gradients of light are features shared by both Jesus and Moroni. Of Moroni's departure, Joseph Smith wrote, "I saw the light in the room begin to gather immediately around the person of him who had been speaking to me, and it continued to do so until the room was again left dark, except just around him; when, instantly, I saw, as it were, a conduit open right up into heaven, and he ascended until he entirely disappeared, and the room was left as it had been before this heavenly light had made its appearance" (Joseph Smith-History 1:43). In *Pistis Sophis* I.6, the apostles, unable to withstand the brilliant light, asked Jesus, "withdraw thy light-glory into thyself that we may be able to stand . . . Then Jesus drew to himself the glory of his light." The opening of the heavens and the drawing of the light to the person of the heavenly visitor is a feature shared by both stories.

---

[5] According to the text, there were three types of light—also called glories—that surrounded Jesus, each more brilliant than the other (*Pistis Sophia* I.4). These remind us of the three degrees of glory, with the terrestrial being more glorious than the telestial and the celestial being more glorious still (D&C 76:70-71, 78, 81, 89-92, 96-98; see also 1 Corinthians 15:40-44).

THE LIGHT-GLORY OF HEAVENLY BEINGS

The Book of Mormon does not say that Jesus was surrounded by light when he descended from heaven to visit the Nephites after his resurrection, but it is significant that he introduced himself by saying "I am Jesus Christ . . . I am the *light* and the life of the world" (3 Nephi 11:10-11, emphasis added). The Book of Mormon text notes that Jesus appeared to the Nephites "after his ascension into heaven" (3 Nephi 11:12), while the *Pistis Sophia* (I.3-4) has the reappearance of Christ to his apostles occur the day following his ascension. The apostles were frightened, so Jesus reassured them by saying, "Take courage. It is I, be not afraid" (I.5). To the Nephites, who had fallen "to the earth" (3 Nephi 11:12), he said, "Arise and come forth unto me, that ye may thrust your hands into my side, and also that ye may feel the prints of the nails in my hands and in my feet . . . And it came to pass that the multitude went forth, and thrust their hands into his side, and did feel the prints of the nails in his hands and in his feet" (3 Nephi 11:14-15). In *Pistis Sophia* I.6, "all the disciples took courage, stepped forward to Jesus, fell down all together, adored him, rejoicing in great joy."

TEACHINGS OF CHRIST

In both stories, Jesus then teaches the people, though the contents of his teachings are not identical. To the Nephites, he delivered the sermon he had previously given to his disciples in the Old World. To his Jewish apostles, who had already heard the sermon, he told of the premortal world from which they had come and of his return to his Father after the resurrection to receive his heavenly garment (*Pistis Sophia* I.6-7).

One passage is of particular importance because it, too, has a parallel in the Book of Mormon. Jesus told the twelve apostles, "when I set out for the world [from premortality], I brought from the beginning with me twelve powers, as I have told you from the beginning, which I have taken from the twelve saviours of the Treasury of the Light, according to the command of the First

Mystery [i.e., God]. These I then cast into the womb of your mothers, when I came into the world, that is those which are in your bodies today" (*Pistis Sophia* I.7).

This scene is like one from Lehi's vision, in which "he saw the heavens open, and . . . God sitting upon his throne," then "he saw One descending out of the midst of heaven, and he beheld that his luster was above that of the sun at noon-day. And he also saw twelve others following him, and their brightness did exceed that of the stars in the firmament. And they came down and went forth upon the face of the earth" (1 Nephi 1:8-11). The brilliance of Christ and his twelve apostles, as described by Lehi, reminds us that, in the *Pistis Sophia*, they are said to have come forth from "the Treasury of light."

Nephi, having asked to see what his father had seen in vision, was also shown Christ and his twelve apostles (1 Nephi 11:27-29). Like Lehi, he "saw the heavens open" and was shown Jesus' mother, Mary "a virgin, most beautiful and fair above all other virgins" who became "the mother of the Son of God, after the manner of the flesh" (1 Nephi 11:14-21). Similarly, in *Pistis Sophia* I.7, Jesus, speaking of his premortal life, says, "I looked down on the world of mankind and found Mary, who is called 'my mother' according to the body of matter," into whom his spirit was then placed when the spirits of the apostles were placed inside their mothers.

CONCLUSION

The similarities noted above do not suggest a dependent relationship between the Book of Mormon and the *Pistis Sophia*. But it is interesting to see two ancient documents give similar descriptions to post-resurrection appearances of Christ.

Chapter 38

THE TIMING OF CHRIST'S APPEARANCE TO THE NEPHITES[1]

For it was by faith that Christ showed himself unto our fathers, after he had risen from the dead; and he showed not himself unto them until after they had faith in him; wherefore, it must needs be that some had faith in him, for he showed himself not unto the world. (Ether 12:7)

Most casual readers of the Book of Mormon probably conclude that Jesus Christ appeared to the Nephites immediately after the great cataclysm accompanying the crucifixion, when the thick vapor dissipated. This is understandable in view of the fact that the appearance of Christ is discussed right after the description of the great destruction. In 1 Nephi 12:4-8 and 2 Nephi 26:1-9 one also has the impression that Christ would appear right after the vapor of darkness dispersed from off the land.

This traditional view has been questioned by LDS scholars Sidney B. Sperry,[2] S. Kent Brown[3] and Jerome Horowitz.[4] Two

---

[1] This was presented as a paper at the annual Symposium on the Archaeology of the Scriptures & Allied Fields, October 1988, sponsored by the Society for Early Historic Archaeology, and was circulated as a preliminary report, with a reprint of S. Kent Brown's article (see below), in John W. Welch (ed.), "When Did Jesus Appear to the Nephites in Bountiful?" (Provo: FARMS Paper BTW-89, 1989).

[2] Sidney B. Sperry, *The Book of Mormon Testifies* (2nd ed., Salt Lake City: Bookcraft, 1952), 294, note 4; repeated in his *Book of Mormon Compendium* (Salt Lake City, Utah: Bookcraft, 1968), 401, note 4.

[3] "Jesus among the Nephites: When Did It Happen?" in the C.E.S. *Religious Educators' Symposium on the New Testament* (15-17 August, 1984, BYU), which was republished as "When Did Jesus Visit the Americans?" in Brown's book, *From Jerusalem to Zarahemla: Literary and Historical Studies of the Book of Mormon* (Provo:

alternatives have been proposed by them. The first is that Christ appeared soon after his ascension, following a forty-day ministry among his original twelve apostles in the Old World. The other is that he came to the Nephites at the end of the thirty-fourth year of the new Nephite calendar.[5]

The passage on which these theories are based reads, in part:

> And it came to pass that in the ending of the thirty and fourth year, behold, I will show unto you that . . . soon after the ascension of Christ into heaven he did truly manifest himself unto them. (3 Nephi 10:18)

Both Brown and Horowitz make a case for Jesus appearing to the Nephites toward the end of the thirty-fourth year of the Nephite calendar. Since the great destruction that accompanied the death of Christ took place "in the thirty and fourth year, in the first month, on the fourth day of the month" (3 Nephi 8:5), this theory suggests that his appearance did not occur until almost one year later.

A reexamination of the evidence these scholars provide suggests an alternative view much closer to the traditional one. In hopes of arriving at a correct understanding, each point of evidence

---

BYU Religious Studies Center, 1998). Whenever Brown's position is mentioned hereafter, the reference is to the views expressed in that article.

[4] "Some Thoughts on 3 Nephi 10:18 Concerning the Time of Christ's Visit to the Nephites," a paper submitted to the Foundation for Ancient Research & Mormon Studies (FARMS). Whenever Horowitz's position on this issue is mentioned hereafter, the reference is to the views expressed in that paper.

[5] The Nephites employed three different calendars during their history. The first counted years from Lehi's departure from Jerusalem. After the judgeship was instituted by King Mosiah, they reckoned time from that date. A new calendric system was instituted a few years after the signs of Christ's birth were seen in the heavens and was based on when those signs were manifest. Hence, the crucifixion took place in the thirty-fourth year of the new calendar (3 Nephi 8:2, 5).

that has been raised by the scholars who have looked at the question is discussed below.

THE "ASCENSION"

Ascension Day has long been a Christian holy day, celebrating Christ's return to his Father after a forty-day post-resurrection ministry among his twelve apostles. However, it plays a very minor, almost non-existent role in the New Testament. One is led to wonder how much Christ's "ascension" in the Old World could have meant to Mormon (or to Nephi the disciple whose record he abridged).

Luke is our principal source for the "ascension" of Christ. In Luke 24:50-52, he tells how Jesus led the eleven to Bethany, on the eastern spur of the Mount of Olives, and rose to heaven. There can be no doubt from this account that the event took place on the day of Christ's resurrection (see verses 1, 13, 33, 36). Yet in Acts 1:3-12, also attributed to Luke, Christ is said to have risen from the Mount of Olives after spending some forty days with his disciples. Are there, then, two "ascensions" from the Mount of Olives?

Mark, after recounting the same basic story told in Luke 24 about the appearances of Jesus on the day of resurrection (Mark 16:9-14), recited Jesus' formal commission to the apostles (verses 15-18), then noted that he was received into heaven (verse 19). Consequently, his story supports the account in Luke 24, which has Christ ascending to heaven on the day of resurrection.

Matthew complicates matters by reciting the same commission noted in Mark, but saying that it was given atop a mountain in Galilee (Matthew 28:16-20). This event, of course, could not have taken place on the day of resurrection, when the apostles were in Jerusalem, not Galilee. Matthew makes no mention of an "ascension." Nor does John, whose account, being designed to show the divinity of Jesus, could have profited from the inclusion of the account of Jesus ascending to his Father.

The Timing of Christ's Appearance to the Nephites

Luke, our source for the formal "ascension" of Jesus, is probably the least trustworthy of the gospel writers.[6] He is also our only biblical source for the so-called "forty-day post-resurrection ministry." Mark implies (as did Luke in his earlier account) that Jesus rose to heaven from near Jerusalem on the day of resurrection. Matthew has him later appearing to his disciples in Galilee, finding agreement in his fellow-disciple John.[7]

Returning to the original question, we must concern ourselves with what "ascension" meant to Nephi the disciple or to Mormon. The "ascension" of Christ was, in fact, an essential doctrine of the pre-Christian Nephites, as we note in Mosiah 15:9; 18:2 and Alma 40:20. All three of these passages refer to Christ's saving power (for example, his role as intercessor before the throne of God), while two of them relate the ascension to his resurrection. This might imply that the event was to take place on the day of resurrection, as noted above.

Four centuries after Christ's visit to the New World, Moroni referred to the "ascension" of Christ (Moro 7:27). And, of course, we have several such references in the "Nephite Gospel," some of them dealing with his ascension from the city of Bountiful

---

[6] Though we cannot discuss the issue fully here, there is evidence that Mark's gospel became one of the primary sources of information for both Luke and Matthew. Luke generally accepted Mark's version without question, though in some cases he added details not found in Mark. Matthew, on the other hand, frequently corrected Mark, implying that he felt that Mark was in error. If we assume that the gospel of Matthew was really written by the apostle of that name, then we must accept his version as more authentic, for he was an eyewitness of most of the events he recorded. Mark and Luke are, at best, second- or third-generation Christians (despite Christian traditions that attempt to identify Mark with the young man in Gethsemane who ran away naked, and Luke with one of the two disciples who met the resurrected Christ on the road to Emmaus). When the gospels disagree, most Bible readers try to "wrest the scriptures" to bring them into "harmony" one with another. Others, noting that Mark and Luke generally agree in their mutual accounts, while Matthew differs, opt in favor of the majority—two-to-one—so Matthew (the only one to have known Jesus!) loses. The author prefers to treat Matthew as a first-hand account and Mark and Luke as secondary sources.

[7] This assumes that the gospel of John was written by the apostle of that name.

THE "ASCENSION"

(3 Nephi 11:21; 18:39; 19:1; 26:15). Of particular interest is the note that it had been prophesied that Christ would show himself to the Nephites after his ascension into heaven (3 Nephi 11:12).

Following his delivery of the "sermon on the mount," Christ said that the Nephites had heard the things that he had taught before he ascended to his Father (3 Nephi 15:1). At no point did he mention anything about a 40-day ministry in the Old World preceding that ascension.

Horowitz may be correct in stating that Christ's "ascension" was a process, not an event, referring to his return to the presence of the Father after his sojourn on earth. That is, he returned to the divine throne to become an intercessor and a mediator for mankind after having wrought the atonement, as a number of passages indicate. However, Mormon's reference to the appearance of the Savior to the Nephites "soon after the ascension of Christ" (3 Nephi 10:18-19) implies that this "ascension" was a specific, earlier event. In this case, it likely refers to his return to the Father on the day of his resurrection, and not after a "forty-day" period. This would accord with his instructions (given on the day of resurrection) to Mary Magdalene to inform the apostles that he was ascending to his Father (John 19:17), followed by his appearance to them later that same day.

THE "ENDING" OF THE YEAR

If Jesus appeared in the city Bountiful immediately after the three days of darkness, this would have occurred in the first month of the thirty-fourth year, not at the end of that year. Is Mormon then incorrect in 3 Nephi 10:18? This possibility has not been seriously considered, despite the fact that Mormon himself admitted that the records from which he made the abridgement may have been in error concerning their chronology:

> And now it came to pass that according to our record, and we know our record to be true, for behold, it was a just man who did keep the record

The Timing of Christ's Appearance to the Nephites

> ... And now it came to pass, if there was no mistake made by this man in the reckoning of our time, the thirty and third year had passed away. (3 Nephi 8:1-2)

While Mormon refused the possibility of error in the recording of events, he did imply that the "reckoning of our time" may be incorrect.

In citing the passage in 3 Nephi 10:18, some scholars fail to note all the words from Mormon (e.g., "I will show unto you") and do not quote verse 19, in which Mormon promised that he would give "an account" of the ministry of Christ "hereafter." The two verses should be read in context:

> And it came to pass that in the ending of the thirty and fourth year, behold, I will show unto you that . . . soon after the ascension of Christ into heaven he did truly manifest himself unto them—Showing his body unto them, and ministering unto them; and an account of his ministry shall be given hereafter. Therefore, for this time I make an end of my sayings. (3 Nephi 10:18-19)[8]

It is clear that Mormon was about to conclude his work for a time when he promised to show how Jesus appeared to the Nephites. Some have believed that this has a bearing on the promise to show "in the ending of the thirty and fourth year" the appearance of Christ. Horowitz has noted two ways in which people have read this passage; there are those who believe that Christ appeared in the New World "in the ending of the thirty and fourth year," while others see this timing as indicative of when the historical entry was made. Horowitz supports the first of these

---

[8] These verses are immediately followed by the preface to the Nephite "Gospel," which Mormon wrote when he took up the record again.

views. In response to the second, he wrote, "This part of the Book of Mormon is not the record written at the time or nearly a year later but is an abridgment written by Mormon centuries later."

But that is precisely the point. It is apparent from a study of Mormon's methodology that he took his material from *dated* Nephite annals. As evidence, note the following recitations of "years" for which he records no events:

> And it came to pass that the thirty and fourth year passed away, and also the thirty and fifth. (4 Nephi 1:1)

> And thus did the thirty and eighth year pass away, and also the thirty and ninth, and forty and first, and the forty and second, yea, even until forty and nine years had passed away, and also the fifty and first, and the fifty and second; yea, and even until fifty and nine years had passed away. (4 Nephi 1:6)

> And it came to pass that the seventy and first year passed away, and also the seventy and second year, yea, and in fine, till the seventy and ninth year had passed away; yea, even an hundred years had passed away. (4 Nephi 1:14; see also Helaman 3:2)

There is no logical reason for Mormon to have listed year-numbers without recording events for them unless he was keeping a running tally of the annals he consulted. Third Nephi 10:18-19 may be just such an entry, one in which Mormon tells his readers that he will be recording the events through the end of the thirty-fourth year.

There are only two other Book of Mormon passages in which the expression "in the ending of the year" occurs. One of these is Helaman 3:1:[9]

> And now it came to pass in the forty and third year of the reign of the judges . . . which affairs were settled in the ending of the forty and third year.

It is suggested that the meaning of this passage is that the "affairs" were settled "before the end" or "by the end" of the forty-third year. (The same meaning could be given to Alma 52:14.) If the Hebrew behind the passage reads b^e-$sôp$, literally, "in the ending" (preposition b + infinitive of the root swp, "to come to an end"), it would be akin to the passage found in 2 Kings 2:1, where we have b^e-$ha^{ca}lôt$ $YHWH$ $'et$ $'ēliyāhû$, literally, "in the Lord's bringing up Elijah.

Obviously, the events described after 2 Kings 2:1 did not take place "at the time" (or "when") Elijah was taken to heaven, but prior to that event. This led the KJV translators to render it "when the Lord *would* take up Elijah." But the text does not contain the grammatical elements to justify that translation. In view of the fact that the text then goes on to recount events which took place *prior* to his ascension, it appears that 2 Kings 2:1 uses an idiom that could be more correctly translated to read, "by the time the Lord took Elijah up" or "before the time the Lord took Elijah up."

By the same token, 3 Nephi 10:18, where it reads "in the ending of the thirty and fourth year," may have been using the same Hebrew idiom. In that case, Mormon would have meant "by the end of the thirty-fourth year" or "before the end of the thirty-fourth year" the events regarding Christ's appearance to the Nephites occurred.

---

[9] The other is in Alma 52:14.

THE "SETTLED CONDITION" OF THE NEPHITES

Those who assert that Christ's appearance to the Nephites was much later than his resurrection make certain basic assumptions about the "settled condition" of the Nephites that are not wholly supported by the textual evidence. These are:

1. The extent of the destruction was such that the people would have spent many months cleaning up and burying the dead.

2. The necessity of rescuing people from the rubble of destroyed buildings would have made it unlikely that the survivors could have been visited by Christ immediately after the destruction.

3. After the destruction, bread and wine, used in the sacrament when Jesus appeared, would not have been available.

4. Ether 12:7 clearly states "that Christ showed himself" unto the people only "after they had faith in him." This requires a lapse of time after the destruction for faith to be established in the hearts of the people.

EXTENT OF THE DESTRUCTION

The great destruction in 3 Nephi 8:12-18 occurred only in the "land northward," while the events in verses 8-11 were in the "land southward." Hence, it would be incorrect to assume that the following items relate to *all* of the land occupied by the Nephites (and Lamanites):

> There were some cities which remained; but the damage thereof was exceedingly great, and there were many of them who were slain. (3 Nephi 8:15)

And thus the face of the whole earth became

deformed. (3 Nephi 8:17; this is the same statement made in verse 12 in reference to the "land northward": "the whole face of the land was changed.")

The highways were broken up (3 Nephi 8:13).

Samuel the Lamanite specifically named Zarahemla and Gideon as cities that would be destroyed unless the people repented (Helaman 13:12-15), adding, "Yea, and wo be unto all the cities which are in the land round about, which are possessed by the *Nephites*, because of the wickedness and abominations which are in them" (Helaman 13:16).

At the time of the crucifixion, the voice announced the destruction of the cities of Zarahemla, Moroni, Moronihah, Gilgal, Onihah, Mocum, Jerusalem, Gadiandi, Gadiomnah, Jacob, Gimgimno, Jacobugath, Laman, Josh, Gad, and Kishkumen (3 Nephi 9:1-12). Note that several of the destroyed cities have Jaredite-sounding names and are hence probably to be associated with the robbers of the Gadianton band (compare Gadiandi, Gadiomnah),[10] whose first leader was, significantly, Kishkumen.[11] Verse 9 specifically states that the city of Jacobugath had been settled by the secret combination headed by Jacob, who had sought to become king.[12] Any tie to a Jaredite site implies that it was in the "land northward."

The voice from heaven declared to the survivors that they were being spared because they were "more righteous than" the people in the cities which were destroyed (3 Nephi 8:13). This is confirmed in other Book of Mormon passages. For example, the

---

[10] There is evidence that the secret combinations may have continued from Jaredite times via the Mulekites, but the details are too lengthy to discuss here.

[11] The names Kishkumen, Gadianton, etc., are clearly Jaredite in form, as unpublished studies of Jaredite names have demonstrated.

[12] Robert F. Smith has, in private discourse with the author, suggested that the name of the city is a combination of "Jacob" and the Jaredite place-name "Ogath."

EXTENT OF THE DESTRUCTION

Lord had told Nephi that he would not destroy those who believed in him, while the unbelievers would be destroyed by fire, tempest, earthquakes, and such, which are the very means by which the people died at the time of Christ's crucifixion (2 Nephi 6:14-15).

In 2 Nephi 26:1-9, Nephi tied the appearance of Christ to the destructions which, from their description, are the very ones that later took place at the time of the crucifixion. He stressed that it was the wicked who would perish in these cataclysms (verses 4-6) because they will have cast out the prophets and stoned and slain them (verses 3), which is precisely the reason Christ gave for the destruction of the wicked at the time of the crucifixion (3 Nephi 9:5, 7-11). The righteous, on the other hand, would obey the prophets and look for the signs; Christ would appear to them and heal them (2 Nephi 6:8-9).

> And it was the more righteous part of the people who were saved . . . And they were spared and were not sunk and buried up in the earth; and they were not drowned in the depths of the sea; and they were not burned by fire, neither were they fallen upon and crushed to death; and they were not carried away in the whirlwind; neither were they overpowered by the vapor of smoke and of darkness. (3 Nephi 10:12-13)

Since the destruction did not occur throughout all of the Nephite lands, there would be no necessity of rebuilding the temple and houses, or of rescuing people from the rubble. Indeed, the idea of such rescue efforts may be a modern concept related to earthquakes in which four- and five-story buildings (and taller) collapse and trap people beneath tons of rubble. It is much more likely that the Nephites lived in small houses, built with materials convenient to the geographical location of the city. Rescue efforts would probably have been minimal.

Brown notes that the Nephites from Bountiful knew to which cities they should go to bring others back to see the risen

Savior on the second day of his visit. This, he suggests, is evidence that enough time had passed for them to learn which cities were destroyed and which survived. We need not so presume, however. The text makes it clear that the heavenly voice told them which cities had been destroyed and in what manner (3 Nephi 19:1-3). Moreover, in the short time remaining before the visit of the next day, the people of Bountiful could only have gone to *nearby* towns or villages, where there was more likelihood that they had relatives and friends.

In connection with the messengers sent from Bountiful to other towns, Brown notes that "the roads must have been repaired." Assuming that there was extensive damage to the earth in the area of Bountiful, the roads could have been destroyed. But since automobiles were not in use by the Nephites and there is no evidence that they used carts, we can assume that their principal mode of travel was on foot, which wouldn't have been severely affected by damaged roads.[13]

BURYING THE DEAD

To assume that there was mourning for the loss of "loved ones" after the disaster presumes that some of the inhabitants of Bountiful were killed, which is, of course, possible. But there is evidence that the Book of Mormon peoples had clan and tribal structures.[14] Hence, people from Bountiful would not have had relatives scattered throughout the various Nephite/Lamanite settlements. Moreover, the Book of Mormon specifically states that the people stopped mourning soon after the destruction.

---

[13] Only once in the Book of Mormon do we encounter a "chariot," in the story of Ammon and Lamoni. There is no evidence in the text or in archaeology to indicate that there was widespread use of such vehicles. Kings may have been the only ones to possess them.

[14] See the author's article, "Book of Mormon Tribal Affiliation and Military Caste," in Stephen D. Ricks and William J. Hamblin (eds.), *Warfare in the Book of Mormon* (Salt Lake City: Deseret and FARMS, 1990).

BURYING THE DEAD

Upon hearing the voice of Jesus speaking through the thick darkness, "so great was the astonishment of the people that they did cease lamenting and howling for the loss of their kindred which had been slain" (3 Nephi 10:2). After three days, the darkness and trembling and noises disappeared (3 Nephi 10:9), and "the mourning, and the weeping, and the wailing of the people who were spared alive did cease; and their mourning was turned into joy" (3 Nephi 10:10).

Horowitz suggests that the people could not have assembled at the temple until after a long period of burying the dead and mourning. That view fails to take into account some very important facts. First, the cities destroyed in the great cataclysm are mentioned by name (3 Nephi 8:10, 24-25; 9:3-10), but Bountiful, where Jesus appeared, is not among them. Significantly, its temple was spared. When Mormon tells us that the "more righteous" were saved, he specifically notes that these were the people who were not buried in the earth, drowned in the sea or burned by fire (3 Nephi 10:12-13). Since these fates are precisely what happened to the destroyed cities, the implication is that those cities were wicked, while the city of Bountiful and perhaps other places were righteous. It may therefore be presumed that it was only the people living in Bountiful who were gathered on the day of Jesus' first visit, while others from nearby towns were invited to come the next day.

With this scenario in mind, it is unlikely that the people in Bountiful went out burying the dead of other cities. If clan or family members lived within close geographical proximity, the Nephites and Lamanites did not, as we moderns, have dead relatives to bury in various parts of the country. Moreover, if the cities listed were really swallowed up by the sea or the earth or destroyed by fire, it is unlikely that there were any remains to be buried. Even so, there are other examples in the Book of Mormon where the Nephites did not take time to bury their dead because of the vast numbers slain in war (Al 16:11; 28:11). It seems unreasonable, therefore, to expect that they would do so in the face of an even greater catastrophe.

The Timing of Christ's Appearance to the Nephites

AVAILABILITY OF BREAD AND WINE.

Horowitz and Brown argue that bread and wine could not have been available for the sacrament immediately after the destruction. Wine containers, they surmise, would have been destroyed in the cataclysm, and no one would have had time to make bread which, in most cultures, is made daily. But there are several reasons to think otherwise.

It has been assumed that their "kilns and ovens" were destroyed by the earthquakes, making it impossible to have fresh bread immediately after the crucifixion. This, however, presumes that the Nephites made bread in loaves as we do. The evidence is quite to the contrary. The bread of the ancient Near East (as among the Bedouin today) is a flat round bread, often unleavened, which is not baked, but cooked atop a flat piece of metal placed on rocks over an open fire. Its Mesoamerican equivalent is the tortilla. No ovens are needed for such bread. Even if they were used, the bread need not have been fresh; it could have been three days old and used out of necessity.

Furthermore, since there appears to have been less destruction in the city of Bountiful, we have no reason to believe that ovens and wine containers were destroyed.

APPEARANCE AFTER THE PEOPLE HAD FAITH

Citing Ether 12:7 as evidence that sufficient time to develop faith had passed between the crucifixion and Christ's appearance in Bountiful is also unwarranted. The passage in question is part of a discussion of faith:

> For it was by faith that Christ showed himself unto our fathers, after he had risen from the dead; and he showed not himself unto them until after they had faith in him; wherefore, *it must needs be that some had faith in him*, for he showed himself not unto the world. (Ether 12:7, emphasis added.)

APPEARANCE AFTER THE PEOPLE HAD FAITH

Read in its entirety, this passage can be seen as evidence that some, indeed, had faith in Christ. The Lord had told Nephi that he would not destroy those who believed in him, in a passage clearly referring to the destruction that would occur at the time of the crucifixion (2 Nephi 6:14-15). In another revelation, he noted that while the wicked would perish in the cataclysm, the righteous who obeyed the prophets would look for the signs and Christ would appear to them and heal them (1 Nephi 26:1-9). From these, it is evident that the survivors in Bountiful already had faith in Christ and had no necessity to wait until the end of the year for it to develop.

This is further demonstrated by events leading up to the time of Christ's coming. In year sixteen of the new (Christian) era, the Gadianton leader demanded the surrender of the government. The Nephites assembled to Zarahemla and Bountiful to defend themselves (3 Nephi 3). They defeated the Gadianton band (3 Nephi 1:4) and acknowledged that their victory resulted from their *repentance and humility* (3 Nephi 4:30-33). In the twenty-second year, *all* of the people came to have *faith in Christ* and the prophets (3 Nephi 5:1-3, 7). Four years later, all of the Nephites returned to their own lands with their families (3 Nephi 6:1).

In the twenty-ninth year, divisions began among the people because of riches (3 Nephi 6:10-13f). The next year, the Church was broken up in all the land except among a few Lamanites (3 Nephi 6:14). Prophets were sent to testify of several things, including the resurrection of Christ (3 Nephi 6:20). The judges secretly slew many of the prophets who testified of Christ (3 Nephi 6:23) (Christ mentions this as a reason for destroying the people caught in the cataclysm.) The wicked judges' friends and kindred gathered themselves together (3 Nephi 6:27) and entered into the covenants of the secret combinations (3 Nephi 6:28), wanting to establish a king over the land (3 Nephi 6:30). The chief judge was murdered (3 Nephi 7:1) and the people were divided into tribes by family, kindred and friends (3 Nephi 7:2), each tribe appointing its own leaders (3 Nephi 7:3, 14). Even the "more righteous part of the people had nearly all become wicked; yea, there were *but few righteous* among them" (3 Nephi 7:7). The secret combination named one Jacob as king, he having spoken against the prophets who testified of Jesus (3 Nephi 7:9-10). They fled to "the northernmost part of the land" (3 Nephi 7:12), which is the area most affected by the destruction at the time of the crucifixion.

In the thirty-first year, Nephi preached repentance and *faith on Jesus Christ* (3 Nephi 7:16). *A few converted and believed in Jesus* (3 Nephi 7:21). In the beginning of the thirty-third year (verse 23), *many were baptized* (3 Nephi 7:26). It would appear, then, that by the time of the crucifixion, there was a new core of believers in Christ.

We can conclude, therefore, that the "high spirituality" of the people (noted by Horowitz) does not necessarily imply that a lengthy time for repentance had passed since the great cataclysm. After all, we read that only the more righteous were spared (3 Nephi 10:12-13). Moreover, it is generally accepted that in times of crisis people turn to God.[15]

GATHERING AT THE TEMPLE

All twelve of those chosen as disciples were present in Bountiful at the time Jesus first appeared. Some see this as evidence that the people had gathered at the temple (such as for Passover) a year after the crucifixion. Indeed, the fact that the multitude is said to have "gathered" in the land of Bountiful (3 Nephi 11:1; preface to 3 Nephi) implies that they had, in fact, assembled from nearby towns. But they could just as well have been celebrating the Passover at the time of Jesus' death when they were caught by the cataclysms of nature and were, after three days, visited by the Savior.

---

[15] During the 1973 Yom Kippur War, virtually all Israeli soldiers became "religious" overnight and there was a severe shortage of religious paraphernalia such as the *tallith, tefillin,* and prayer books.

It is likely that the Nephites were, indeed, assembled for Passover, but the gathering of the people at the temple is not evidence that it was festival-time. The temple could have been a place of refuge from the storm. On the other hand, it is likely that only the truly righteous would be at the temple anyway. It is important to note that there were only 2,500 people at the temple on the first day of Jesus' visit (3 Nephi 17:25). It was not until these people had spread the word to other towns that the larger "multitude" is said to have assembled (3 Nephi 19:1-5). On the second day, they were so numerous that they had to divide into twelve groups.

SAMUEL'S PROPHECY

Jerome Horowitz notes that Nephi forgot to add the fulfillment of the prophecy of Samuel the Lamanite to the Nephite record.[16] He reasons, with Brown, that Christ would not have chided him for his failure to "remember that this thing had not been written" (3 Nephi 23:12) if the event were only a day old.

A different interpretation, however, appears from the text of 3 Nephi. It was the day after his first appearance to the Nephites that Christ asked Nephi to bring their records to him for review (3 Nephi 23:7-8; see 3 Nephi 19:1-2). Third Nephi 19:2-3 indicates that, after Christ's first appearance, the events of the day were "noised abroad among the people immediately, before it was yet dark" and "even all the night it was noised abroad concerning Jesus." As a competent scribe, Nephi most likely made a complete record of all that transpired that day while it was yet fresh in his

---

[16] 3 Nephi 23:7-13 states that it was the *fulfillment* of Samuel's prophecy about the resurrection of others at the time Christ rose from the dead that had not been recorded. The modern summary of chapter 23 indicates that it was "the words of Samuel the Lamanite concerning the resurrection" that were added to the record. This implies that the words in Helaman 14:25 reflect the portion Nephi added to the record at that time. This implication is not consistent with 3 Nephi 23:11, which specifically identifies the words that were not recorded.

memory and was being widely "noised abroad." That record would have been part of what Christ reviewed the next day. Finding that Nephi had missed one important point, namely the fulfillment of Samuel's prophecy, the record was corrected. Given all that happened, it is not surprising that, in recording the events culminating in the first appearance of Christ to the Nephites, Nephi forgot this one thing. Had it been a longer period of time, as Brown and Horowitz suggest, it is likely that Nephi would have forgotten a greater number of things.[17]

ARGUMENTS FOR AN EARLY APPEARANCE

Among the evidence sometimes elicited to indicate an appearance immediately after the three days of darkness the following statement should be included:

> They were marveling and wondering one with another, and were showing one to another the great and marvelous change which had taken place. And they were also conversing about this Jesus Christ, of whom the sign had been given concerning his death. (3 Nephi 11:2)

It seems likely that the people would not have been pointing out changes that had taken place if this event occurred nearly a year after the cataclysms following the crucifixion. The objection offered to this is that people had gathered from great distances for the first time in a year and hence the changes in the land of Bountiful were new to them. This is refuted by the fact that only 2,500 people were in Bountiful on the first day of Christ's appearance among them. Nor were people gathered in from "great distances" the next day, for it would have been impossible for them to have traveled so far overnight.

---

[17] The author is indebted to Richard R. Hopkins for this insight.

Arguments for an Early Appearance

The "calm" that prevailed at the temple in Bountiful is more likely attributable to the fact that this city did not suffer the fate of other wicked cities. (The very existence of the temple implies that the people were more righteous.) Changes in the land had been noted, to be sure. But here the text supports the view that the cataclysmic events had only recently taken place. Otherwise, why would the people be discussing a year-old event as though it were fresh and new?

After Christ's appearances in Bountiful, he appeared once more to the disciples as they were traveling (3 Nephi 27:1-28:17). They then went about preaching, during which time there were various attempts to imprison and slay them. Notwithstanding, they were successful in establishing the Church. It is only *after* telling of these events that Mormon notes, "And it came to pass that the thirty and fourth year passed away, and also the thirty and fifth" (4 Nephi 1:1). Hence, Christ's appearance would seem to have been much earlier than the "ending" of the thirty-fourth year, since there was time for the disciples to begin their travels and preaching.

CONCLUSION

The possibility remains that Jesus appeared to the people in Bountiful "soon" after his resurrection, possibly as early as the same or very next day. It is also possible that the appearance was as much as 40 to 50 days later, but there seems to be no basis for that argument and even less for the suggestion that it did not occur until as much as a year after his resurrection.

Chapter 39

CHRIST'S VISIT TO THE NEPHITES AS A TYPE OF HIS SECOND COMING

And it came to pass that the angel said unto me: Look, and behold thy seed, and also the seed of thy brethren. And I looked and beheld the land of promise; and I beheld multitudes of people, yea, even as it were in number as many as the sand of the sea. And it came to pass that I beheld multitudes gathered together to battle, one against the other; and I beheld wars, and rumors of wars, and great slaughters with the sword among my people. And it came to pass that I beheld many generations pass away, after the manner of wars and contentions in the land; and I beheld many cities, yea, even that I did not number them. And it came to pass that I saw a mist of darkness on the face of the land of promise; and I saw lightnings, and I heard thunderings, and earthquakes, and all manner of tumultuous noises; and I saw the earth and the rocks, that they rent; and I saw mountains tumbling into pieces; and I saw the plains of the earth, that they were broken up; and I saw many cities that they were sunk; and I saw many that they were burned with fire; and I saw many that did tumble to the earth, because of the quaking thereof. And it came to pass after I saw these things, I saw the vapor of darkness, that it passed from off the face of the earth; and behold, I saw multitudes who had not fallen because of the great and terrible judgments of the Lord. And I saw the heavens open, and the Lamb of God descending out of heaven; and he came down and showed himself unto them. (1 Nephi 12:1-6)

Though Nephi saw the great destructions that would accompany Christ's crucifixion before his resurrection and appearance to the Nephites, he was also aware that the prophet Zenos had written about these events (1 Nephi 19:10-12). Nephi also described the events that would precede Christ's coming to the New World in 2 Nephi 26:1-11. He noted that people would cast out and kill the prophets (2 Nephi 26:3, 5), that there would be fire, thunderings, lightnings, and earthquakes (2 Nephi 26:4, 6), that people would be swallowed up by the earth, covered by mountains, carried away in whirlwinds, and buried beneath buildings (2 Nephi 26:5).

But Nephi did not stop there. He went on to describe what would happen "in the last days," noting the "iniquity and all manner of abominations" among the people, who would "be visited of the Lord of Hosts, with thunder and with earthquake, and with a great noise, and with storm, and with tempest, and with the flame of devouring fire" (2 Nephi 27:1-2). From this description, it is clear that the wickedness and destructions found among the Nephites at the time of Christ's appearance in the land of Bountiful will also exist at the time of his second coming.

SIGNS PRECEDING CHRIST'S VISIT TO THE NEPHITES

Samuel the Lamanite also described the events that would precede the coming of Christ to the Nephites (Helaman 14:20-29). He spoke of earthquakes, tempests, thunderings, lightnings, and darkness, saying that "there shall be many mountains laid low, like unto a valley . . . [and] valleys which shall become mountains" (Helaman 14:21-27). He added that "the sun shall be darkened and refuse to give his light . . . and also the moon and stars" (Helaman 14:20) and prophesied that "many graves shall be opened, and shall yield up many of their dead; and many saints shall appear unto many" (Helaman 14:25).

All of the signs foreseen by Nephi and Samuel the Lamanite were manifest shortly before Christ came to the temple in

CHRIST'S VISIT TO THE NEPHITES AS A TYPE OF HIS SECOND COMING

Bountiful (3 Nephi 8-9). Great wickedness prevailed among many of the people and they cast out and stoned the prophets (3 Nephi 7:14; 8:25; 9:11). At the time of the crucifixion, there were earthquakes, tempests, whirlwinds, lightnings, thunder, and thick darkness. Some cities were burned with fire, others submerged beneath the waters, others covered over by mountains, and still others swallowed up in the earth. Moreover, graves were opened and some of the righteous dead arose and appeared to people (3 Nephi 23:9-11).

SIGNS PRECEDING CHRIST'S SECOND COMING

Mormon, who lived four centuries after Christ's post-resurrection appearance in the New World, wrote of the signs of his second coming, which would include the same elements witnessed by the Nephites: fires, tempests, vapors of smoke, and great wickedness (Mormon 8:26-31). He noted that these would "come in a day when the blood of saints shall cry unto the Lord, because of secret combinations and the works of darkness" (Mormon 8:27). This is reminiscent of Nephi's prophecy regarding the coming of Christ among his people: "wherefore the cry of the blood of the saints shall ascend up to God from the ground against them" (2 Nephi 26:3).

The darkening of the sun and moon, prophesied by Samuel as a sign of Christ's coming to the Nephites, is expected in the last days as well, as is indicated in the prophecy of Joel 2:28-32, which was cited by Moroni during his appearance to Joseph Smith in 1823 (Joseph Smith History 1:41).

The great upheavals that took place in the New World at the time of the crucifixion will be repeated in the last days, including earthquakes and great land upheavals (Zechariah 14:1-13). Christ will appear and the righteous dead will rise from the tomb (Isaiah 26:19-21; 1 Thessalonians 4:16). Just as his coming to the Nephites signaled an era of peace (4 Nephi 1:15-18), so, too, his second coming will usher in a millennium of peace.

LESSONS TO BE LEARNED

We live in circumstances very similar to those of the Nephites prior to Christ's appearing to them. While believers anticipate Christ's second coming, the more skeptical in our day reject the idea. The Nephites had their skeptics, who plotted to kill the believers if the signs prophesied by Samuel did not come to pass (3 Nephi 1:8-21). They said that the time had passed for the prophecies to be fulfilled (3 Nephi 1:5-6).

Even after the signs of his birth were given, there were those who tried to rationalize them away, being deceived by Satan and by their own fallible minds (3 Nephi 1:22; 2:1-3). So, too, we should expect that the signs of Christ's second coming will not convince everyone in our day. Joseph Smith spoke of the signs that will be given

> before the Son of Man will make His appearance, There will be wars and rumors of wars, signs in the heavens above and on the earth beneath, the sun turned into darkness and the moon to blood, earthquakes in divers places, the seas heaving beyond their bounds; then will appear one grand sign of the Son of Man in heaven. But what will the world do? They will say it is a planet, a comet, &c. But the Son of Man will come as the sign of the coming of the Son of Man, which will be as the light of the morning cometh out of the east. (*History of the Church* 5:337)

The more righteous among the Nephites gathered at the temple in Bountiful and became witnesses to the coming of Christ. If we wish to stand at Christ's second coming, we should do likewise. "Wherefore, stand ye in holy places, and be not moved, until the day of the Lord come; for behold, it cometh quickly, saith the Lord" (D&C 87:8).

CONCLUSION

What, then, can we learn from the parallels between the coming of Christ among the Nephites and his coming in glory to reign on the earth in the last days? First, we learn that some will say that he delays his coming, that the time is past for the fulfillment of the prophecies (3 Nephi 29:2; D&C 45:26). They will not believe the signs even when they see them, and Satan will deceive some. Many will ignore the prophets and even persecute the saints. If we do as the Lord has commanded, it will be said of us as Nephi wrote of his descendants,

> the righteous that hearken unto the words of the prophets, and destroy them not, but look forward unto Christ with steadfastness for the signs which are given, notwithstanding all persecution—behold, they are they which shall not perish. But the Son of righteousness shall appear unto them. (2 Nephi 26:8-9)

Chapter 40

PERFORMANCES AND ORDINANCES OF THE LAW

And now behold, I say unto you that the right way is to believe in Christ, and deny him not; and Christ is the Holy One of Israel; wherefore ye must bow down before him, and worship him with all your might, mind, and strength, and your whole soul; and if ye do this ye shall in nowise be cast out. And, inasmuch as it shall be expedient, ye must keep the performances and ordinances of God until the law shall be fulfilled which was given unto Moses. (2 Nephi 25:29)

In order to understand how Christ fulfilled the law of Moses, it is necessary to examine a bit of the history of that law and its constituent parts. From the prophet Joseph Smith, we learn that the Israelites of Moses' day rejected the higher law, in consequence of which the Lord gave them a lesser law, a law of carnal commandments (D&C 84:19-26; JST Exodus 34:1-2).

To the Galatians, the apostle Paul wrote, "Wherefore then serveth the law [of Moses]? It was added because of transgressions, till the seed [Christ] should come to whom the promise was made" (Galatians 3:19; cf. Mosiah 3:14). This suggests that the carnal law, with which the Israelites were cursed according to Joseph Smith, was superimposed atop something else they had received from God—presumably something that was part of the higher law. Because the ten commandments are authoritatively cited as the word of God in the Old and New Testaments, as well as the Book of Mormon and the Doctrine and Covenants, they must be part of the higher law that remained under the covenant made at Sinai. They would therefore not be part of the lesser "handwriting of ordinances" of which Paul said that Christ "took it out of the way, nailing it to his cross" (Colossians 2:14).

Christ told the Nephites, "in me is the law of Moses fulfilled" (3 Nephi 9:17; see also 3 Nephi 12:18-19, 46; 15:4-5, 8). But he seems to have suggested that only the lesser portion of that law was fulfilled when he said, "Behold, ye have the commandments before you, and the law is fulfilled" (3 Nephi 12:19).

The prophet Abinadi, while noting that salvation does not come by the law of Moses, indicated that it was, nonetheless, important to keep the commandments that were part of that law (Mosiah 12:31-33; 13:27-30; see also Alma 25:16).

In order to understand this subject, we must note that the law of Moses was comprised of three divisions, the commandments (sometimes called "law" or "testimonies"), the statutes (sometimes called "ordinances"), and the judgments.[1] These same three divisions of the law are listed in the Book of Mormon,[2] where the word "performances" sometimes replaces "judgments."[3] From some of the Book of Mormon passages (Alma 30:3; 2 Nephi 25:24-25, 30; 4 Nephi 1:12), we learn that it was the statutes and judgments (or ordinances and performances) that would be done away in Christ, while the commandments would remain as part of the higher law that Christ revealed during his ministry.

---

[1] Deuteronomy 4:1-2, 13-14; 5:28; 6:20; 26:17; 28:45; 2 Kings 17:34, 37; 2 Chronicles 19:10; 29:19; 33:8; 34:31; Nehemiah 9:13-14; 10:30; Jeremiah 32:11. There are many more passages in which just two of the three divisions are mentioned together.

[2] It was Avraham Gileadi who first noted this phenomenon and shared this information with the author in Jerusalem in 1972.

[3] 1 Nephi 17:22; 2 Nephi 5:10; 25:25, 30; Mosiah 6:6; Alma 8:17; 25:14-15; 31:9-10; 58:40; Helaman 3:20; 15:5; 4 Nephi 1:12. As in the Bible, there are several more passages in which just two of the three divisions are mentioned together (2 Nephi 1:16; Omni 1:2; Mosiah 13:30; Alma 30:3, 23; Helaman 6:34; 3 Nephi 25:4).

CONCLUSION

That portion of the law of Moses that was also part of the higher law rejected by the Israelites (including the ten commandments) was not abolished in Christ, while lesser elements of the law, such as animal sacrifice, were done away (3 Nephi 9:19). Christ explained to the Nephites, "Therefore those things which were of old time, which were under the law, in me are all fulfilled. Old things are done away, and all things have become new" (3 Nephi 12:46).

Chapter 41

BECOMING AS LITTLE CHILDREN

Therefore, whoso repenteth and cometh unto me as a little child, him will I receive, for of such is the kingdom of God. (3 Nephi 9:22)

The message of the resurrected Christ to the Nephites was a rephrasing of what he had declared among the Jews during his mortal ministry: "Except ye be converted, and become as little children, ye shall not enter into the kingdom of heaven" (Matthew 18:3 (see verses 1-14); cf. Luke 9:48 and see 1 Peter 2:1-2).

King Benjamin explained that little children "are blessed; for . . . the blood of Christ atoneth for their sins," while adults must "humble themselves and become as little children . . . none shall be found blameless before God, except it be little children, only through repentance and faith on the name of the Lord God Omnipotent" (Mosiah 3:16, 18, 21; cf. 15:22-25).

He also explained how we can become as little children:

> For the natural man is an enemy to God, and has been from the fall of Adam, and will be, forever and ever, unless he yields to the enticings of the Holy Spirit, and putteth off the natural man and becometh a saint through the atonement of Christ the Lord, and becometh as a child, submissive, meek, humble, patient, full of love, willing to submit to all things which the Lord seeth fit to inflict upon him, even as a child doth submit to his father. (Mosiah 3:19)

When his listeners covenanted to obey God, Benjamin declared that they should now "be called the children of Christ, his sons, and his daughters; for behold, this day he hath spiritually begotten you; for ye say that your hearts are changed through faith on his name; therefore, ye are born of him and have become his sons and his daughters" (Mosiah 5:7). From this, we learn that, to become as little children, we must be born again through a process that involves faith, repentance, and baptism.

When Christ first appeared to the Nephites in the city of Bountiful after his resurrection, he placed particular stress on the importance of becoming as little children, and tied it to repentance and baptism:

> And again I say unto you, ye must repent, and become as a little child, and be baptized in my name, or ye can in nowise receive these things. And again I say unto you, ye must repent, and be baptized in my name, and become as a little child, or ye can in nowise inherit the kingdom of God.
> (3 Nephi 11:37-38)

The Savior noted that the twelve disciples he had just chosen would have power to baptize, and promised the Nephites that "after that ye are baptized with water, behold, I will baptize you with fire and the Holy Ghost" (3 Nephi 12:1-2). He then recited the beatitudes (verses 3-12), which discuss the child-like qualities referred to in Mosiah 3:19, cited above. One of the beatitudes speaks of receiving the Holy Ghost and another of becoming children of God (3 Nephi 12:6, 9).

The promise to the twelve was fulfilled the following day, before Jesus' second visit. The disciples knelt and "did pray for that which they most desired; and they desired that the Holy Ghost should be given unto them" (3 Nephi 19:9). Nephi, the chief disciple, "went down into the water and was baptized...[then] he baptized all those whom Jesus had chosen" (3 Nephi 19:11-12).

> When they were all baptized and had come up out of the water, the Holy Ghost did fall upon

them, and they were filled with the Holy Ghost
and with fire. And behold, they were encircled
about as if it were by fire; and it came down from
heaven . . . and angels did come down out of
heaven and did minister unto them. And it came
to pass that while the angels were ministering
unto the disciples, behold, Jesus came and stood in
the midst and ministered unto them. (3 Nephi
19:13-15)

The scene is reminiscent of what had happened during Jesus' first visit to the Nephites, when he called for their little children and blessed them (3 Nephi 17:11-12, 21). Following this, angels descended "out of heaven as it were in the midst of fire; and they came down and encircled those little ones about, and they were encircled about with fire; and the angels did minister unto them" (3 Nephi 17:24; see 3 Nephi 26:14). It seems more than coincidental that this event took place the day before the baptism of the Nephite twelve. The juxtaposition of the two events seems to be teaching us that what the adults obtained through faith, repentance, and baptism was given to the children without prior conditions.

This was also Mormon's message to his son Moroni when he wrote against the abominable practice of child baptism. His message retains its value despite the passage of many centuries:

Behold I say unto you that this thing shall ye
teach—repentance and baptism unto those who
are accountable and capable of committing sin;
yea, teach parents that they must repent and be
baptized, and humble themselves as their little
children, and they shall all be saved with their little
children. (Moroni 8:10)

In our day, the Lord has reiterated that adults "must repent and be baptized," and explained that this included "children who have arrived at the years of accountability" (D&C 18:42). In another modern revelation, the minimum age of baptism is established as eight years (D&C 68:25, 27). The status of young children is stressed in the story of king Benjamin. All of his people, "except it were little children," "entered into a covenant with God to keep his commandments" (Mosiah 6:1-2).

CONCLUSION

The message remains today as it was when Christ spoke to the Nephites:

> Therefore, whoso repenteth and cometh unto me as a little child, him will I receive, for of such is the kingdom of God. Behold, for such I have laid down my life, and have taken it up again; therefore repent, and come unto me ye ends of the earth, and be saved. (3 Nephi 9:22)

Chapter 42

HUNGERING AND THIRSTING AFTER RIGHTEOUSNESS

And blessed are all they who do hunger and thirst after righteousness, for they shall be filled with the Holy Ghost. (3 Nephi 12:6)

Jesus uttered the words in 3 Nephi 12:6 to the Nephites assembled in the land of Bountiful when he appeared to them after his resurrection. One of the beatitudes from his sermon at the temple, they differ from the version of the sermon on the mount recorded in Matthew 5:6 by the addition of the words "for they shall be filled with the Holy Ghost."

One critic of the Book of Mormon noted that this addition of the Holy Ghost makes no sense because the Greek word used in Matthew 5:6 refers to being "filled" or "satisfied" as when one eats food. (Ironically, the critic didn't find it strange that Jesus should speak of eating "righteousness.") But the Greek term is only a translation equivalent, since Jesus would have addressed his Jewish disciples in Aramaic, a language closely related to Hebrew that had been adopted by the Jews in the fifth century B.C.

The Old Testament uses two different Hebrew verbs to denote being "filled" by eating. One of these is the root *śbʿ*, which means to be satiated.[1] But the normal Hebrew word meaning "to fill" (root *mlʾ*) is often used to denote being filled after eating.[2] Indeed, the two verbs are used in poetic parallelism in Ezekiel 7:19:

---

[1] Exodus 16:12; Leviticus 25:19; Deuteronomy 23:24; 26:12; 31:20; Nehemiah 9:25; Psalms 78:29; Proverbs 1:31; 25:16; 30:22; Lamentations 3:15; Ezekiel 39:20; Hosea 13:6; Haggai 1:6.

[2] Exodus 28:3; 31:3; 35:31; Job 15:21; 20:23; 38:39; Psalms 17:14; 81:10; 107:9; Ecclesiastes 6:7; Isaiah 56:12; Jeremiah 51:34; Ezekiel 3:3; 23:33-34.

282

"they shall not satisfy their souls, neither fill their bowels."

Explaining the emblems of the sacrament to the Nephites, Jesus said, "He that eateth this bread eateth of my body to his soul; and he that drinketh of this wine drinketh of my blood to his soul; and his soul shall never hunger nor thirst, but shall be filled" (3 Nephi 20:8). But "when the multitude had all eaten and drunk, behold, they were filled with the Spirit," not with bread and wine (3 Nephi 20:9). This seems appropriate, since the promise to those who worthily partake of the sacrament is that they will "have his Spirit to be with them" (Moroni 4:3; 5:2).

On the first occasion when Jesus had blessed bread for the Nephites in the land of Bountiful, we read that "when the multitude had eaten and were filled, he said unto the disciples: Behold there shall one be ordained among you, and to him will I give power that he shall break bread and bless it and give it unto the people of my church, unto all those who shall believe and be baptized in my name" (3 Nephi 18:5). He then specified that those who partook "shall have my Spirit" (3 Nephi 18:7). He blessed the wine "and [the disciples] did drink of it and were filled; and they gave unto the multitude, and they did drink, and they were filled" (3 Nephi 18:9). Jesus again stressed that the emblem of his blood was reserved for "those who repent and are baptized in my name," who, by partaking, shall have my Spirit" (3 Nephi 18:11).

From this, we can see not only that the people were "filled" when partaking of the sacrament, but that Christ promised them his Spirit. The fact that he specified that the sacrament was to be administered to those who had been baptized stresses the fact that the ordinance is a renewal of the baptismal covenant by which we also have access to the Spirit (3 Nephi 19:13; 26:17). Alma the elder explained this in terms very reminiscent of the sacramental prayers when he asked his people,

> Now I say unto you, if this be the desire of your hearts, what have you against being baptized in the name of the Lord, as a witness before him

that ye have entered into a covenant with him, that ye will serve him and keep his commandments, that he may pour out his Spirit more abundantly upon you? (Mosiah 18:10)

Jesus told his Nephite disciples "that whoso repenteth and is baptized in my name shall be filled" (3 Nephi 27:16). He later specified what he meant by the word "filled": "come unto me, and be baptized in my name, that ye may receive a remission of your sins, and be filled with the Holy Ghost" (3 Nephi 30:2).

CONCLUSION

From this, we can see that there is a high degree of consistency in the Book of Mormon accounts of baptism and partaking of the sacrament. Hungering after righteousness, one must repent and participate in the covenantal rite, whereupon one can be "filled with the Holy Ghost."

Chapter 43

THE JAREDITE OCEAN VOYAGE

For behold, ye shall be as a whale in the midst of the sea; for the mountain waves shall dash upon you. Nevertheless, I will bring you up again out of the depths of the sea; for the winds have gone forth out of my mouth, and also the rains and the floods have I sent forth. And behold, I prepare you against these things; for ye cannot cross this great deep save I prepare you against the waves of the sea, and the winds which have gone forth, and the floods which shall come. Therefore what will ye that I should prepare for you that ye may have light when ye are swallowed up in the depths of the sea? (Ether 2:24-25)

In Ether 2:24-25, it is evident that the Jaredite crossing of the ocean to the New World was accompanied by rains, winds, and heavy wave action. This is reiterated in Ether 6:5-8:

> And it came to pass that the Lord God caused that there should be a furious wind blow upon the face of the waters, towards the promised land; and thus they were tossed upon the waves of the sea before the wind. And it came to pass that they were many times buried in the depths of the sea, because of the mountain waves which broke upon them, and also the great and terrible tempests which were caused by the fierceness of the wind. And it came to pass that when they were buried in the deep there was no water that could hurt them, their vessels being tight like unto a dish, and also they were tight like unto the ark of Noah;

therefore when they were encompassed about by many waters they did cry unto the Lord, and he did bring them forth again upon the top of the waters. And it came to pass that the wind did never cease to blow towards the promised land while they were upon the waters; and thus they were driven forth before the wind.

The comparison with Noah's ark is significant because traditions about both stories associate the ocean voyage with mountainous waves and glowing stones to provide light within the ark.

A COMPARISON TO ACCOUNTS OF THE FLOOD

Speaking of the flood of Noah's time, an Ethiopic Christian text says,

> But when the windows opened wide, all stores [of water] and depths were opened, and all the stores of the winds, and the whirlwind, thick mist, gloom and darkness spread abroad. The sun and moon and stars, withheld their light. It was a day of terror, such as had never been. Then the sea all round, began to raise its waves on high like mountains; and it covered the whole face of the earth.[1]

While the Bible says the flood waters covered the mountains (Genesis 7:18-19), the story in this Ethiopic document makes the waves high like mountains, which closely parallels the wording in Ether 6:6.

The Jaredite account makes it clear that the high waves

---

[1] *Conflict of Adam and Eve* III, 9:6-7, in S. C. Malan, *The Book of Adam and Eve, also called The Conflict of Adam and Eve with Satan* (London: Williams & Norgate, 1882), 155.

resulted from intense winds that came from the Lord. A number of early traditions indicate that the tower of Babel—from which the Jaredites fled (Ether 1:33)—was destroyed by strong winds sent by God.[2] Some texts speak of the "flood of wind" that followed the flood of water.[3] Hugh Nibley has suggested that this time of great wind is what produced the stormy seas crossed by the Jaredites.[4]

LIGHT FOR THE VOYAGE

The book of Mormon describes how the brother of Jared prepared sixteen crystalline stones that the Lord touched, making them glow so that they could provide light to each of the vessels that would carry them across the ocean (Ether 2:22-3:4; 6:2-3). This story, too, is reminiscent of stories about the ark of Noah. Several early Jewish sources indicate that God told Noah to suspend precious stones or pearls inside of the ark to lighten it; in some traditions, it is a jewel-encrusted heavenly book. The gems would glow during the night and dim during the day so Noah, shut up in the ark, could tell the time of day and how many days

---

[2] For example, the story is found in the *Chronography* of Bar Hebraeus, *Jubilees* 10:26, and in *Sibylline Oracles* 3:101-107.

[3] In a story paralleling Abraham 1:15-20, *Conflict of Adam and Eve* III, 24:8 tells how God sent a wind, whirlwind, and earthquake to destroy the idols at the time Nimrod attempted to slay Abraham (cf. 25:1-2). The same story is told in *Book of the Rolls* folio 120a, *Book of the Cave of Treasures* folios 23b.2-24a.1, and *Book of the Bee* 23, where the blast is termed a "wind-flood" and is compared to the flood of water sent in the days of Noah. Significantly, early Jewish, Christian, and Muslim tradition attributes to Nimrod the construction of the tower of Babel.

[4] Hugh Nibley, *Lehi in the Desert, The World of the Jaredites, There Were Jaredites* (Salt Lake City: FARMS and Deseret, 1988), 359-79; *An Approach to the Book of Mormon* (3rd ed., Salt Lake City: FARMS and Deseret, 1988), 329-34; *Since Cumorah* (2nd ed., Salt Lake City: FARMS and Deseret, 1988), 208-10; *The Prophetic Book of Mormon* (Salt Lake City: FARMS and Deseret, 1989), 331-332; *The Ancient State* (Salt Lake City: FARMS and Deseret, 1991), 33-34; *Teachings of the Book of Mormon, Semester 4* (Provo: FARMS, 1993), 244-245, 269.

had passed.⁵ This was the explanation given by the rabbis for the *ṣôhar* that the Lord told Noah to construct in the ark. The word is rendered "window" in the King James version of Genesis 6:16 but "light" in some other translations.⁶

A similar tradition is found among the Arabs, who may have borrowed it from the Jews. Al-Kisā'ī reported that when Noah made the ark, he put the name of one of the prophets (including those yet to be born) on each of the pegs, "and they shone like the stars, except for the one with the name of Muhammad, which shone as brightly as the sun and the moon together."⁷

Rabbi Eliezer tells a similar story about the "great fish" that "the Lord had prepared" to swallow Jonah (Jonah 1:17). He notes that Rabbi Meir spoke of a pearl being suspended inside the fish to give light to Jonah like the noonday sun, and by which he was able to see all that was in the sea (*Pirqe de Rabbi Eliezer* 10).

---

⁵ TB *Sanhedrin* 108b; TY *Pesahim* 1.1; *Targum Pseudo-Jonathan* on Genesis 6:16; *Midrash Bereshit Rabbah* 31.11; *Pirqe de Rabbi Eliezer* 23; Rashi on Genesis 6:16. For a recap of the story, see Louis Ginzberg, ed., *The Legends of the Jews* (Philadelphia: Jewish Publication Society, 1937) 1.162-163. The first person to bring the Jewish tradition to the attention of Latter-day Saints was Janne M. Sjodahl, in his *An Introduction to the Study of the Book of Mormon*, (Salt Lake City, 1927), 248. The tradition was discussed at length by Hugh Nibley, "There Were Jaredites: The Shining Stones, *Improvement Era* 59 (September 1956):630-32, 672-75; *Lehi in the Desert, The World of the Jaredites, There Were Jaredites* (Salt Lake City: Deseret and FARMS, 1988), 366-379; *An Approach to the Book of Mormon* (3rd ed., Salt Lake City: Deseret and FARMS, 1988), 337-358; *Since Cumorah* (2nd ed., Salt Lake City: Deseret and FARMS, 1988), 209-10; *The Prophetic Book of Mormon* (Salt Lake City: Deseret and FARMS, 1989), 243-4, 329. For a study of this and other glowing stones stories, see John A. Tvedtnes, "Glowing Stones in Ancient and Medieval Lore," *Journal of Book of Mormon Studies* 6/2, Fall 1997.

⁶ The idea of a "window" came from the Latin Vulgate translation and is also found in the Greek translation by Aquila. The Aramaic *Targum Onkelos* renders it "light."

⁷ W. M. Thackston, Jr., transl., *The Tales of the Prophets of al-Kisā'ī* (Boston: Twayne, 1978), 2:98.

POSSIBLE ROUTES

According to Ether 2:25, the Jaredite barges were driven by the wind. Some critics have noted that strong winds would have enabled them to sail to the New World in less than the 344 days indicated for the voyage in Ether 6:11. But the Jaredite vessels were not sailing vessels and hence would have depended on ocean currents to cross the ocean, most likely the North Pacific.

In 1964 two prominent non-Mormon scholars, Clifford Evans and Betty J. Meggers noted that a boat caught off the coast of Japan would be carried by the North Pacific reaching land in about 11 months (330 days), which corresponds closely with the timeframe given in the book of Ether. They wrote:

> If a boatload of Early Middle Jomon fishermen left the sheltering bays of Kyushu and went out into the sea off the southeastern coast in October or November, they would have entered a zone with some of the strongest currents in the Northern Pacific, running northeastward at 24-43 miles per day. Records for the 40-year period between 1901-1940 tabulate 802 typhoons, of which 130 were in October and 67 in November. A canoe caught too far from shore by one of these storms might easily be swept by the combined northeasterly pressure of wind and current far out to sea before control was regained. Even if the occupants retained possession of their paddles, they might have been unable to turn back. During the month of November, westerly and northerly winds predominate in the northern hemisphere, and are steadiest and of greatest force between about the 40th and 55th parallels. In addition, the percentage of gales increases during November in high latitudes, occurring at an average frequency of one every 8-10 days over the

greater part of the northern Pacific except near coasts. A combination of these forces would have borne a canoe eastward along the great circle route, which on a flattened map curves far north of Hawaii. Records during the past century demonstrate the feasibility of such a drift vessel reaching land with living passengers after a voyage of 11 months.[8]

Another study produced the same year suggests that this current would bring a vessel to land somewhere off the coast of northern or central Mexico, depending on the time of year.[9]

CONCLUSION

Several aspects of the story of the Jaredite voyage across the ocean to the New World can be confirmed by ancient traditions that were generally unknown in Joseph Smith's day and by modern research. This information lends authenticity and credibility to the story told in the Book of Ether.

---

[8] Clifford Evans and Betty J. Meggers, "Transpacific origin of Valdivia Pottery on Coastal Ecuador," *XXXVI Congreso Internacional de Americanistas, Espana, 1964* (Sevilla, 1966), 66. The presentation was based on the discovery of Jomon period Japanese pottery in Ecuador, suggesting that the Japanese had, in fact, crossed the Pacific to South America in the late third millennium B.C. The author thanks Matthew Roper for bringing this study to his attention.

[9] Carl L. Hubbs and Gunnar I. Roden, "Oceanography and Marine Life along the Pacific Coast of Middle America," in Robert Wauchope, gen. ed., *Handbook of Middle American Indians* (Austin: University of Texas, 1964-1976), 1:148, 154-55, 160. Again, thanks for this information are due to Matthew Roper.

Chapter 44

THE ROLE OF THE BOOK OF MORMON IN THE RESTORATION OF THE CHURCH[1]

I told the brethren that the Book of Mormon was the most correct of any book on earth, and the keystone of our religion, and a man would get nearer to God by abiding by its precepts, than by any other book."
(Joseph Smith in *History of the Church* 4.461)

Latter-day Saints are generally aware of this declaration, though its full implications are not as apparent as they were when the prophet uttered these words. The declaration that the Book of Mormon can help us "get nearer to God" reflects the purpose of the book as stated in its Preface or Title page, where Moroni declared that the record was for "the convincing of the Jew and Gentile that Jesus is the Christ, the Eternal God, manifesting himself unto all nations." The idea originated with Nephi, the first of the Nephite prophet-scribes (2 Nephi 26:12) and was shared by Moroni's father Mormon (Mormon 5:14).

Amaleki, an early Nephite scribe, invited his future readers to "come unto Christ, who is the Holy One of Israel, and partake of his salvation, and the power of his redemption" (Omni 1:26). Moroni, the last of the Book of Mormon writers, addressing our generation, declared, "I would commend you to seek this Jesus of whom the prophets and apostles have written" (Ether 12:41).

The Book of Mormon is an important tool in helping the Church to fulfill its mission of bringing souls to Christ (D&C

---

[1] This chapter was circulated as a FARMS preliminary paper in 1997 and is published here for the first time.

3:20; 18:41; 20:59; 68:6, 25; 107:23, 35). For this reason, in 1982 it was retitled, "The Book of Mormon: Another Testament of Jesus Christ." The earliest converts to the Church were attracted not by stories of Joseph Smith's first vision or by impressive new and restored doctrines, but by the witness of the Spirit borne to them as they read the Book of Mormon.

There are several ways in which the Book of Mormon helps bring people to Christ: 1) It testifies of Christ, affirming his divinity and the truth of his teachings; 2) it provides a comprehensive explanation of the atonement by which salvation comes to mankind; 3) it explains how we can take full advantage of Christ's atonement, enabling us to return to the presence of both the Father and the Son. While the Book of Mormon is the keystone, Christ is the cornerstone of the Church, he on whom the Church is founded (Matthew 21:42; Acts 4:11; Ephesians 2:20; 1 Peter 2:6-7; Jacob 4:17).

THE FULNESS OF THE GOSPEL

The Lord declared to Joseph Smith that the Book of Mormon contained the "fulness of the gospel" (JS-H 1:34; D&C 20:9; 27:5; 42:12; see 135:3). Some have objected that, since the Book of Mormon does not discuss such key LDS beliefs as premortal existence, eternal progression, God as an exalted man, the plurality of gods, the three degrees of glory, baptism for the dead, eternal marriage, or the word of wisdom, it cannot contain the fulness of the gospel. This reasoning results from the misconception that the term "gospel" refers to all truth from God, and it is unfortunate that Latter-day Saints have come to use it in that sense.

Both the Book of Mormon and other scriptures define the gospel more narrowly, as the good news of Christ's atonement, with its first principles being faith, repentance, baptism, and receiving the Holy Ghost (1 Nephi 10:14; 15:13-14; 3 Nephi 27:13-21; Ether 4:18; D&C 3:20; 13:1; 20:9; 27:5; 33:11-12;

39:5-6; 42:12; 76:40-42; 84:26-27; 107:20; 135:3; 138:2-4, 57; JS-H 1:34; Articles of Faith 3-4). D&C 93:51 uses the term "the gospel of salvation," while Abraham 2:11 speaks of "the blessings of the Gospel, which are the blessings of salvation, even of life eternal" (see D&C 128:5, 17). In Jacob 7:6, the gospel is defined as "the doctrine of Christ," referring to the doctrine concerning Christ, rather than the totality of Christ's teachings, since he had not yet been born when these words were uttered (see Mormon 3:21; D&C 76:82). Elsewhere, the Book of Mormon equates the "fulness of the gospel" with coming "to the knowledge of the true Messiah" (1 Nephi 10:14; 15:13-14; see 3 Nephi 20:30-31; D&C 19:27).

The Book of Mormon contains the most lucid, complete explanation of the atonement of Christ found in any of the scriptures (see especially 2 Nephi 2, 9; Mosiah 15; Alma 34, 42), and therefore clearly qualifies as containing the fulness of the gospel. It also teaches that the plan of salvation was not introduced at the time of Christ's mortal ministry, but that it has always been with us. Christ was chosen before the world began to be our sacrifice for sin and to bring us back to God. Knowing that "all things have been done in the wisdom of him who knoweth all things" from the beginning (2 Nephi 2:24) reassures us that God is in control and that the power of salvation is not diminished by the bad things we see happening around us.

THE BOOK OF MORMON AND JOSEPH SMITH'S MISSION

The translation of the Book of Mormon was one of the principal tasks assigned to Joseph Smith as the prophet of a new dispensation (D&C 1:29; 24:1), a task that began even before the restoration of the priesthood and the reestablishment of the Church. Indeed, D&C 21:1, reflects the order in which Joseph's callings were received: "Behold, there shall be a record kept among you; and in it thou shalt be called a seer, a translator, a prophet, an apostle of Jesus Christ, an elder of the church." Joseph became a *seer* (from the verb *to see*) when he *saw* the Father and the Son in the sacred grove in the spring of 1820 (JS-H 1:14-20). He became a *translator* when Moroni delivered to him both the plates of the Book of Mormon and the interpreters (JS-H 1:30-54, 59-66). During the course of the translation, Joseph received a series of revelations, which established his role as a prophet (D&C 3-18). In 1829, he was ordained an apostle by Peter, James, and John (D&C 27:12; 128:20). Finally, at the organizational meeting of the Church, held April 6, 1830, Joseph became its "first elder" (D&C 20:2-5; 21:11; JS 1:72).

Mormon foresaw the coming forth of the Book of Mormon and recorded a prophecy concerning the event in 3 Nephi 29. A comparison of that chapter with statements made by Moroni to Joseph Smith on the night he revealed the existence of the plates bears such a striking resemblance to elements in Mormon's prophecy that it is likely that the resurrected Moroni had in mind the passage written by his father (Table 1).

Table 1. A Comparison of 3 Nephi 29 and Joseph Smith-History

3 Nephi 29	*JS-H*
The Book of Mormon is to come forth (verse 1).	Moroni revealed the existence of the Book of Mormon (verses 34, 42).
"These sayings [the Book of Mormon] shall come unto *the Gentiles*" (verse 1).	Moroni "stated that the fulness of *the Gentiles* was soon to come in" (verse 41).
The coming forth of the book would be a sign to Israel "concerning their restoration to the lands of their inheritance" (verses 1-3, 8-9; see Ether 4:17).	Moroni recited Isaiah 11, one of the major themes of which is the gathering of Israel in the last days (verse 40).

The Book of Mormon and Joseph Smith's Mission

3 Nephi 29	*JS-H*
Of "the house of Israel," Mormon declared "the Lord remembereth his covenant unto them, and he will do unto them according to that which he hath sworn" and would "execute judgment until the fulfilling of the covenant which he hath made unto the house of Israel" (verses 8-9).	Moroni quoted Malachi 3:5-6, in which there is a promise that the Lord "shall plant in the hearts of the children the promises made to the fathers, and the hearts of the children shall turn to their fathers" (verse 39).
Mormon mentions the "coming" of the Lord (verse 2) and "the *sword* of [the Lord's] justice" that will "soon overtake" the unbelievers (verse 4).	Moroni cited a variant of Malachi 4:1, 5-6, on the destruction of the wicked and the earth being wasted at "the coming of the great and dreadful day of the Lord" unless Elijah comes first (verses 36-39). Later, he spoke of "great desolations by famine, *sword*, and pestilence" (verse 45).
"The sword of his justice in his right hand; and behold, at that day, if he shall spurn at his doings he will cause that it shall soon overtake you. Wo unto him that shall deny the Christ and his works!" He also spoke of those who "shall become like unto the son of perdition, for whom there was no mercy" (verses 5-7).	Moroni cited the passage from Acts 3:22-23, stating that it referred to Christ and that "the day had not yet come when 'they who would not hear his voice should be cut off from among the people,' but soon would come (verse 40).
"Yea, wo unto him that shall deny the revelations of the Lord, and that shall say the Lord no longer worketh by revelation, or by prophecy, or by gifts, or by tongues, or by healings, or by the power of the Holy Ghost!" (verses 6-7).	Revelation is the theme of Moroni's appearance (verses 29-32, 43-44), with a discussion of the urim & thummim (verses 35, 42) and the vision of the hill (verse 46). Moroni also cited Joel 2:28-32, which speaks about the Lord pouring out his spirit in the last days (verse 41).

THE ROLE OF THE BOOK OF MORMON IN THE RESTORATION

3 Nephi 29	JS-H
"Yea, and wo unto him that shall say at that day, to *get gain*, that there can be no miracle wrought by Jesus Christ" (verse 7).	Joseph Smith was told that Satan would tempt him "to get the plates for the purpose of *getting rich*," and warned him to "have no other object in view in getting the plates but to glorify God" (verse 46).
"Yea, and ye need not any longer hiss, nor spurn, nor make game of the Jews, nor any of the remnant of the house of Israel" (verse 8).	Moroni told Joseph Smith that his name "should be had for good and evil among all nations, kindreds, and tongues, or that it should be both good and evil spoken of among all people" (verse 33).

CHURCH PRACTICES DRAWN FROM THE BOOK OF MORMON

From the beginning, the Book of Mormon formed the basis for many of the practices of the restored Church. Some of these are reflected in D&C 20, the original of which was largely patterned on the operation of the ancient Nephite church.[2] This section, which comprised the earliest constitution of the LDS Church, begins by devoting twelve verses (5-16) to the importance of the Book of Mormon in the mission of Joseph Smith leading up to the establishment of the Church.

On the day the Church was organized, April 6, 1830, those in attendance accepted what we now know as D&C 20 as "The Articles and Covenants of the church of Christ," a set of

---

[2] For a detailed study of D&C 20 and its precursors, see the FARMS preliminary report by Scott Faulring, "The Articles and Covenants of the Church: D&C 20 and Its Antecedents."

regulations governing Church organization and practices.³ Many of the ideas found in D&C 20, especially beginning with verse 30, were taken from the book of Moroni, notably chapters 2-6. Those chapters outline practices followed in the Nephite church following the visit of Christ and are in many instances based on instructions given by Christ during his appearance in the land of Bountiful. Since Moroni was about to hide up the record, making it unavailable until the time of Joseph Smith, it seems evident that his sole intent was to provide the future prophet with basic information on how the restored Church should be governed.

PRIESTHOOD OFFICES

In the Book of Mormon, we read of elders, priests, and teachers (2 Nephi 5:26; Jacob 1:18; Jarom 1:11; Mosiah 23:17; 25:19, 21; 26:7; 27:5; Alma 1:3, 26; 4:7, 16; 6:1; 15:13; 23:4; 30:31; 35:5; 45:22-23; Helaman 3:25; Moroni 3:1, 3-4; 4:1; 6:1, 7). D&C 20 mentions these offices, along with those of deacon, high priest, high councilor, and bishop. The latter three were not in the original of that section, but were added later as these offices were introduced into the Church. The ordination and duties of the elders, priests, teachers, and deacons, found in D&C 20:38-60 are drawn from Moroni 2-3. (Alma 6:1 also notes that Alma$_2$ "ordained priests and elders, by laying on his hands.")

In June of 1831, the first high priests were ordained (*History of the Church* 1:175). Looking back on the event more than half a century later, David Whitmer, who had left the Church, declared that he had been opposed to this move, on the grounds that, unlike the offices of elder, priest, and teacher, the office of

---

³ This title was given to that section in its preface in the 1833 Book of Commandments. See references to the "articles and covenants," "commandments and covenants," "laws and covenants," or sometimes just "covenants" in D&C 28:12, 14; 33:14; 42:13, 78; 51:4; 68:13, 24; 107:12, 20, 63, 85-87, 89; *History of the Church* 1.386; 2.525. From these passages, it is clear that some subsequent revelations were considered to be appendages to D&C 20.

high priest is not mentioned in the Book of Mormon.[4]

But Whitmer was wrong. In addition to the discourse of Alma$_2$ on Melchizedek and other high priests of earlier days (Alma 13), we learn that he was "high priest over the church of God" (Mosiah 26:7; 29:42; preface to book of Alma; Alma 4:4, 18; 5:3; 8:11, 23; 16:5) and that his father before him had been a high priest (Mosiah 23:16). One passage speaks of other Nephite "high priests" (Helaman 3:25), and we learn from other passages that each city or land in Nephite territory seems to have had a presiding high priest (Alma 30:20-22, 29).

After the departure of Alma$_2$, his sons, who are called "high priests over the church" (Alma 46:6, 38), led the Nephite church, appointing priests and teachers in each congregation (Alma 45:22-23). The fact that these sons were three in number (Alma 31:6-7; 35:16; 36-42) suggests that they may have been comparable to the First Presidency in the LDS Church. Indeed, when that presidency was first organized in December 1832, it was termed "the presidency of the high priesthood" or "the presidency of the Melchizedek priesthood" (D&C 68:15, 19; 81:2; 107:9, 17; 107:78-79; *History of the Church* 1:333, 353, 359; 2:4) and consisted, as it remains today, of a president and two counselors, with the counselors also being termed "presidents" (D&C 102:3, 33; 207:24, 29; *History of the Church* 1:24, 333, 370). In D&C 107:22, the "three Presiding High Priests" are said to "form a quorum of the Presidency of the Church."

The responsibility of the elders "to conduct the meetings as they are led by the Holy Ghost" (D&C 20:45) is also found in Moroni 6:9 and was repeated in D&C 46:2. Nephi had written that "when a man speaketh by the power of the Holy Ghost the power of the Holy Ghost carrieth it unto the hearts of the children of men" (2 Nephi 33:1). This seems to be behind the latter-day commandment to teach by the power of the Spirit (D&C 42:14-

---

[4] David Whitmer, *An Address to All Believers in Christ* (Richmond, Missouri, 1887), 62-67.

16) and the declaration that if both speaker and listener are empowered by the Spirit, there is understanding between them (D&C 50:13-22).

The concept of an unpaid clergy, for which the LDS Church is noted, was also a feature of the Nephite church (Mosiah 27:5; Alma 1:26).[5]

Because of the number of people in the land of Zarahemla, it was impossible for all of them to meet together to be taught, so Alma$_1$ established different congregations or churches and "to ordain[ed] priests and teachers over every church" (Mosiah 25:19-23). In D&C 20:49, 56, we find that priests are "to take the lead of meetings when there is no elder present" and that teachers are "to take the lead of meetings in the absence of the elder or priest." Indeed, just as the Nephite teachers were local officers in individual churches, the teacher in the restored Church "is to watch over the church always, and be with and strengthen them" (D&C 20:53), for which reason teachers have never served as missionaries.

BAPTISM

The wording of D&C 20:25 (those who are "baptized . . . and endure in faith to the end, should be saved") was drawn from Jesus' words to the Nephite disciples in 3 Nephi 27:16. But the concept of being "saved in the kingdom of God" through baptism is found in earlier Book of Mormon passages (2 Nephi 9:23-24; 25:13). Of course, baptism alone is not sufficient. D&C 20:29 declares "that all men must repent and believe on the name of Jesus Christ, and worship the Father in his name, and endure in faith on his name to the end, or they cannot be saved in the kingdom of

---

[5] Some critics have objected that, since General Authorities receive compensation for their full-time service, the LDS Church cannot truly be said to have an "unpaid ministry." But the salaries paid to these few dozen men fades into insignificance when one considers the tens of thousands of stake and district presidencies, bishoprics and branch presidencies, that receive no compensation for their time.

God." This is a paraphrase of 2 Nephi 9:23-24:

> And he commandeth all men that they must repent, and be baptized in his name, having perfect faith in the Holy One of Israel, or they cannot be saved in the kingdom of God. And if they will not repent and believe in his name, and be baptized in his name, and endure to the end, they must be damned; for the Lord God, the Holy One of Israel, has spoken it.

Nephi, after speaking of baptism (2 Nephi 31:17), counseled his readers to "endure to the end" through Christ in order to "be saved in the kingdom of God" (2 Nephi 31:20-21), and several other Book of Mormon passages speak of being "saved in the kingdom" (1 Nephi 13:37; 2 Nephi 33:12; Jacob 6:4; Alma 11:37; Ether 15:34; Moroni 10:21, 26; see 3 Nephi 11:33; 12:20).

The conditions outlined for baptism in D&C 20:37 are drawn from Moroni 6:1-3, which is based on the earlier practice from the time of Alma$_2$, noted in Alma 6:2.[6] In both 3 Nephi 11:23 and D&C 20:72, we find instructions that baptism is to be administered to those who repent, confirmed in Moroni 6:2.[7] The

---

[6] The mention of the reception of the Spirit in connection with remission of sins in D&C 20:37 may have been prompted by the fact that the conditions for baptism in Moroni 6:1-3 are immediately followed by the statement that those who "had been received unto baptism . . . were wrought upon and cleansed by the power of the Holy Ghost" (Moroni 6:4).

[7] That baptism is unto repentance is affirmed in Matthew 3:11; Mark 1:4; Luke 3:3; Acts 13:24; 19:4; Mosiah 26:21-22; Alma 5:62; 6:2; 7:14-15; 8:10; 9:27; 48:19; 49:30; Helaman 3:24; 5:17, 19; 3 Nephi 1:23; 7:24-26; Moroni 8:10-11. See also Acts 2:38; 2 Nephi 9:23-24; 13:11, 13-14; 31:17; 62:45; Helaman 16:4-5; 3 Nephi 11:37-38; 18:11, 30; 21:6; 23:5; 27:16, 20; 30:2; 4 Nephi 1:1; Mormon 3:2; 7:8; Ether 4:18; Moroni 7:34; 8:25; D&C 13:1 (=JS-H 1:69); 18:22, 41-42; 19:31; 33:11; 35:5; 39:6; 42:7; 49:13; 55:2; 68:25; 84:27; 107:20.

procedure and wording for baptism found in D&C 20:72-74 is based on Jesus' instructions to the Nephites in 3 Nephi 11:21-26. Today, the only difference in wording of the baptismal prayer is that while the Book of Mormon uses "having authority given me of Jesus Christ" (3 Nephi 11:25), D&C 20:73 reads "having been commissioned of Jesus Christ." But the original of the latter passage, in the 1833 Book of Commandments, was the same as the Book of Mormon reading (BC 24:53), and was changed in the 1835 Doctrine and Covenants (2:22) to the current wording. The sense, of course, is the same in both versions.

The fourth Article of Faith specifies "baptism by immersion for the remission of sins." Immersion is the method described in the Book of Mormon, in both 3 Nephi 19:10-13 and Mosiah 18:13-16.

YOUNG CHILDREN NOT TO BE BAPTIZED

Moroni cited a letter in which his father, Mormon, condemns the practice of infant baptism (Moroni 8). Mormon wrote that "little children need no repentance, neither baptism. Behold, baptism is unto repentance to the fulfilling the commandments unto the remission of sins" (Moroni 8:11). The idea is repeated in D&C 20:71: "No one can be received into the church of Christ unless he has arrived unto the years of accountability before God, and is capable of repentance" (see also D&C 18:42). The age of accountability is established as eight years in D&C 68:25. King Benjamin had already made the distinction between "little children" and those who knew the Lord's plan (Mosiah 2:34; see 26:1-4), while Abinadi taught that "little children also have eternal life" through Christ.

While baptism is not to be administered to young children, D&C 20:70 specifically instructs that they are to be blessed. This verse is patterned after Christ's blessing of children, found in both the Bible (Mark 10:13-16) and in the Book of Mormon (3 Nephi 17:21).

CHURCH MEMBERSHIP AND DISCIPLINE

D&C 20:81-83 calls for the keeping of membership records in the Church. Similarly, the Nephites took care to record the names of those who had been baptized (Moroni 6:4). D&C 20:80 requires that "any member of the church of Christ transgressing, or being overtaken in a fault, shall be dealt with as the scriptures direct," while D&C 20:83 speaks of those who "have been expelled from the church, so that their names may be blotted out of the general church record of names" (see also D&C 109:34).

Among the Nephites, the names of those guilty of unrepentant sins were "blotted out, and they were not numbered among the people of Christ," while those who repented and confessed their sins were forgiven (Moroni 6:7-8). In the Book of Mormon, this practice is first attested in the time of $Alma_1$ (Mosiah 26:13-36) and his son (Alma 1:24; 6:3). The restored church followed the same rule, being told by the Lord, "And him that repenteth not of his sins, and confesseth them not, ye shall bring before the church, and do with him as the scripture saith unto you, either by commandment or by revelation" (D&C 64:12). The "scripture" referred to here is evidently the Book of Mormon.

Confession as a necessary step in the repentance process is also discussed in D&C 42:88-92 and in other modern revelations (D&C 19:20; 58:43, 60; 59:12; 61:2; 64:7). This, too, is a principle found in the Book of Mormon, where we read that the repentant $Alma_2$ and the sons of Mosiah went about seeking to repair the damage that they had done to the church and confessing their sins (Mosiah 27:32-36; Alma 17:4). The Lord told $Alma_1$, "whosoever transgresseth against me, him shall ye judge according to the sins which he has committed; and if he confess his sins before thee and me, and repenteth in the sincerity of his heart, him shall ye forgive, and I will forgive him also" (Mosiah 26:29; see 26:35-36). Similarly, in D&C 82:1, the Lord said, "that inasmuch as you have forgiven one another your trespasses, even so I, the Lord, forgive you."

Among the Nephites, conviction of sins could be achieved only if "three witnesses of the church did condemn them before the elders" (Moroni 6:7). D&C 42:80-81 requires that such testimony come from "two witnesses of the church," but notes that "if there are more than two witnesses it is better."[8] That same revelation distinguishes between the kinds of wrongdoing that are judged by the Church and those that must be turned over to civil authorities (D&C 42:74-87). This same principle is found in Mosiah 26:1-12, where we read that king Mosiah left to the high priest Alma $_1$ the right to judge those found in sin; nevertheless, the king continued to punish those who committed specific crimes such as strife, theft, and murder (Mosiah 29:14-15). The distinction between civil and religious wrongs continued into the period of the judges (Alma 1:17-18; 30:7-11).

HOME TEACHING

Moroni 6:4 makes it clear that recording the names of members of the Church was to make it possible to nourish them "by the good word of God, to keep them in the right way, to keep them continually watchful unto prayer" (Moroni 6:4). This reminds us of D&C 20:47, 51, 53-54, which establishes the duties of teachers to "visit the house of every member, and exhort them to pray vocally and in secret and attend to all family duties." The Nephites "were strict to observe that there should be no iniquity among them" (Moroni 6:7), and modern home teachers are to "see that there is no iniquity in the church" (D&C 20:54). They are also to "see that the church meet together often, and also see that all the members do their duty" (D&C 20:55; see verse 75). Among the Nephites, "the church did meet together oft, to fast and to pray, and to speak one with another concerning the welfare of their souls" (Moroni 6:5; see verse 6). Jesus also commanded the

---

[8] Compare D&C 6:28; 128:3, where we read that "in the mouth of two or three witnesses shall every word be established."

Nephites to "pray in your families unto the Father" and to "meet together oft" (3 Nephi 18:21-22).

SACRAMENT OF THE LORD'S SUPPER

D&C 20:75 notes that "it is expedient that the church meet together often to partake of bread and wine in the remembrance of the Lord Jesus." Again, the idea is paralleled in the Book of Mormon, where we read, "And the church did meet together oft, to fast and to pray, and to speak one with another concerning the welfare of their souls. And they did meet together oft to partake of bread and wine, in remembrance of the Lord Jesus" (Moroni 6:5). This practice was based on Jesus' commandment in 3 Nephi 18:22, but it is also attested in Alma 6:6.

Moroni gives the sacramental prayers in Moroni 4, as they are found in D&C 20:76-79, noting that "the elder or priest did minister it--And they did kneel down with the church, and pray to the Father in the name of Christ, saying . . ." (Moroni 4:1-2). D&C 20:76 also specifies that "the elder or priest shall administer it; and after this manner shall he administer it—he shall kneel with the church, and call upon the Father in solemn prayer, saying . . ." (see verses 40, 46, 58).[9]

Christ commanded his Nephite disciples to administer the sacrament to those who had been baptized (3 Nephi 18:11, 30). He further instructed that they should not allow any to partake of the sacrament unworthily,[10] but added that the unbaptized must not be expelled from meetings of the Church (3 Nephi 18:22-23,

---

[9] For a study of the development of the sacrament prayers as used by the Nephites, see John W. Welch, "Our Nephite Sacrament Prayers," in Welch, ed., *Reexploring the Book of Mormon* (Salt Lake City: Deseret and FARMS, 1992), 286-289, and the 1986 FARMS paper by the same author, "The Nephite Sacrament Prayers: From King Benjamin's Speech to Moroni 4-5."

[10] See Mormon 9:29; 1 Corinthians 11:27-29.

28-32)—a concept already established in the days of Alma₂ (Alma 6:5). Likewise, in a modern revelation, he declared,

> Ye are commanded never to cast any one out from your public meetings, which are held before the world. Ye are also commanded not to cast any one who belongeth to the church out of your sacrament meetings; nevertheless, if any have trespassed, let him not partake until he make reconciliation. And again I say unto you, ye shall not cast any out of your sacrament meetings who are earnestly seeking the kingdom—I speak this concerning those who are not of the church. And again I say unto you, concerning your confirmation meetings, that if there be any that are not of the church, that are earnestly seeking after the kingdom, ye shall not cast them out (D&C 46:3-6).

This revelation came as a result of a dispute that arose in the early days of the restored Church regarding whether non-members should be allowed to attend such meetings. Those who opposed exclusion of the unbaptized pointed to the Book of Mormon teachings on the subject as evidence for their view, and this was confirmed by the Lord in his words to the prophet Joseph Smith.[11]

Jesus' instructions to the Nephites regarding the unbaptized were, "ye shall not cast him out from among you, but ye shall minister unto him and shall pray for him unto the Father, in my name; and if it so be that he repenteth and is baptized in my name, then shall ye receive him, and shall minister unto him of my flesh and blood" (3 Nephi 18:30). It is interesting that, in D&C 46:4-6, the instruction to "not cast any out" of the meetings is also

---

[11] See John Whitmer's *History of the Church*, chapter 4, cited in a footnote to D&C 46 in *History of the Church* 1:163-4.

followed by the instruction to pray. In this case, however, the Saints are to pray "that ye may not be seduced by evil spirits, or doctrines of devils" (D&C 46:7)—a concept that is related to Nephi's instructions in 2 Nephi 32:8.

PUBLIC AND PRIVATE PRAYER

We have noted the duty of home teachers to instruct the Saints to pray. Some early revelations instructed specific individuals to "pray vocally before the world as well as in secret, in your family, and among your friends, and in all places" (D&C 23:6; D&C 19:28). This same principle was taught by Amulek during his missionary service among the Zoramites. After listing the various places and circumstances in which one should pray (Alma 34:17-26), he added, "Yea, and when you do not cry unto the Lord, let your hearts be full drawn out in prayer unto him continually for your welfare, and also for the welfare of those who are around you" (Alma 34:27), then noted that prayer avails nothing unless one is charitable and assists the needy and the sick (Alma 34:28-29). Christ also instructed the Nephites to "pray in my church, among my people who do repent and are baptized in my name" (3 Nephi 18:16).

LAW OF CONSECRATION

The book of Mormon recounts that, following Christ's visit to the Nephites and his selection of twelve disciples, "they taught, and did minister one to another; and they had all things common among them, every man dealing justly, one with another" (3 Nephi 26:19). Within two years,

> the people were all converted unto the Lord, upon all the face of the land, both Nephites and Lamanites, and there were no contentions and disputations among them, and every man did deal justly one with another. And they had all things

common among them; therefore there were not rich and poor, bond and free, but they were all made free, and partakers of the heavenly gift (4 Nephi 1:2-3).[12]

This era of peace lasted for two centuries. It came to an end when some began to flaunt their wealth and would no longer help the poor. These actions led to class divisions that resulted in the establishment of apostate churches (4 Nephi 1:24-26).

But the basis of the Nephite law requiring that the rich share with the poor goes back to the time of Alma$_1$:

> Alma commanded that the people of the church should impart of their substance, every one according to that which he had; if he have more abundantly he should impart more abundantly; and of him that had but little, but little should be required; and to him that had not should be given. And thus they should impart of their substance of their own free will and good desires towards God, and to those priests that stood in need, yea, and to every needy, naked soul . . . imparting to one another both temporally and spiritually according to their needs and their wants. (Mosiah 18:27-29)

The practice continued in the days of Alma$_2$, of which we read, that the Nephites "did impart of their substance, every man according to that which he had, to the poor, and the needy, and the sick, and the afflicted" (Alma 1:27).

In Joseph Smith's day, the Lord commanded "that certain men . . . shall be appointed by the voice of the church; and they shall look to the poor and the needy, and administer to their relief

---

[12] Joseph Smith learned by revelation that Enoch's people also practiced the law of consecration (Moses 7:18-21).

that they should not suffer" (D&C 38:34-35). This imparting of goods "unto the poor and the needy" through the consecration of surplus property is also commanded in subsequent revelations (D&C 51:1-14; 72:9-12; 104:18; see D&C 70:7-11; 72:15-16). As in the case of the Nephites, stewardships were appointed to make "every man equal according to his family, according to his circumstances and his wants and needs" (D&C 51:3).

THE BOOK OF MORMON AS A SOURCE OF CHURCH DOCTRINE

The importance of the Book of Mormon in establishing Church doctrine cannot be overemphasized. The Lord has commanded that "the elders, priests and teachers of this church shall teach the principles of my gospel, which are in the Bible and the Book of Mormon, in the which is the fulness of the gospel" (D&C 42:12). The earliest missionaries of the Church went forth with the message of the restoration and of the translation of the Book of Mormon, which became the tool by which many early members came to accept Joseph Smith's prophetic calling.

The Lord declared that "the Book of Mormon and the holy scriptures are given of me for your instruction" (D&C 33:16) and later castigated Church members because they did not "remember the new covenant, even the Book of Mormon and the former commandments which I have given them, not only to say, but to do according to that which I have written" (D&C 84:55-57).

In a letter addressed to the bishop and the Saints in Zion, Missouri, dated January 14, 1833, the conference of high priests at Kirtland recommended that the bishop read the revelation and "tell them to read the Book of Mormon, and obey it; read the commandments that are printed, and obey them" (*History of the Church* 1:320). The importance of the Book of Mormon for Church doctrine was stressed by Joseph Smith at a conference held April 21, 1834, when he declared, "Take away the Book of

The Book of Mormon as a Source of Church Doctrine

Mormon and the revelations, and where is our religion We have none" (*History of the Church* 2:52).

An official declaration by the leaders of the Church in Missouri, issued in July 1834, declares that "the faith and religion of the Latter-day Saints are founded upon the old Scriptures, the Book of Mormon, and direct revelation from God" (*History of the Church* 2:133). The importance of these three sources of scripture—known today as the "standard works"—is also stressed in the minutes of the high council meeting held in Kirtland on September 24, 1834, under the presidency of Joseph Smith, which speak of the appointment of "a committee to arrange the items of the doctrine of Jesus Christ, for the government of the Church of Latter-day Saints, which Church was organized and commenced its rise on the 6th of April, 1830. These items are to be taken from the Bible, Book of Mormon, and the revelations which have been given to the Church up to this date, or that shall be given until such arrangements are made" (*History of the Church* 2:165).[13]

So important was the Book of Mormon to the restored Church that one of its early members, Almon W. Babbitt, was brought up "before a council of the Presidency . . . for not keeping the Word of Wisdom; *for stating the Book of Mormon was not essential to our salvation*, and that we have no articles of faith except the Bible" (*History of the Church* 2:252).

The Lord informed the Saints that one of the purposes of the Book of Mormon was to "bring to light the true points of my doctrine," to "establish my gospel, that there may not be so much contention . . . concerning the points of my doctrine" (D&C 10:62-63). Here, we shall discuss some of the doctrines of the

---

[13] The result was the "doctrine" portion of the 1835 Doctrine and Covenants, which comprised the Lectures on Faith, a series of lessons used in the school of the prophets. The "covenants" portion comprised the revelations given to Joseph Smith, some of which had been previously published in 1833 in the Book of Commandments, forerunner to the Doctrine and Covenants. The first section in our Doctrine and Covenants was originally intended as the "preface" to the Book of Commandments (D&C 1:6).

Church that are based on teachings found in the Book of Mormon. As with early Church practices, we shall see that some of these are found in D&C 20.

Unity of the Godhead. D&C 20:28 declares that the "Father, Son, and Holy Ghost are one God, infinite and eternal, without end." The wording is taken directly from the Book of Mormon (2 Nephi 31:21; Mosiah 15:5; Alma 11:44; 3 Nephi 11:27; Mormon 7:7). The role of the Holy Ghost as one who bears record of the Father and the Son (D&C 20:27) also derives from the Book of Mormon (1 Nephi 12:18; 3 Nephi 11:32, 35-36; 28:11; Ether 12:41).

Salvation & Judgment. The essential message of the plan of salvation, as noted earlier, is that Christ's atonement brought salvation and that he expects certain things of us. The idea of justification and sanctification through Christ and loving god with one's might, mind, and strength, found in D&C 20:30-34, also appears in Moroni 10:32-33.

The laws by which we shall be judged are found in the revelations of God. In D&C 20:20, we read that "by the transgression of these holy laws man became sensual and devilish, and became fallen man." Similar wording is found in Mosiah 16:3, Alma 42:10, Helaman 12:4, and Ether 3:2.

Speaking of "the holy scriptures" (D&C 20:11), we read that "by them shall the world be judged." Christ had told the Nephites that "out of the books which have been written, and which shall be written, shall this people be judged" (3 Nephi 27:25-26).

Preaching Repentance. The concept of repentance as an essential principle of the gospel is found throughout the Book of Mormon and the Doctrine and Covenants and has always been emphasized by the leadership of the Church. Earlier, we saw that baptism was administered by the Nephites only to those who were repentant, and that the Lord has established the same pattern in the restored Church.

Alma$_1$ instructed his people "that they should teach

nothing save it were the things which he had taught, and which had been spoken by the mouth of the holy prophets. Yea, even he commanded them that they should preach nothing save it were repentance and faith on the Lord, who had redeemed his people" (Mosiah 18:19-20). The concept of teaching only the revealed word of God and of emphasizing faith and repentance is one of the most frequently quoted instructions in the Doctrine & Covenants (D&C 6:9; 11:9; 14:8; 15:6; 16:6; 19:31; 34:6; 36:6).

The New Jerusalem. From the Book of Mormon, the early Latter-day Saints learned that there would be a "new Jerusalem" built on the American continent (3 Nephi 20:22; 21:23-24; Ether 13:2-6). The promise of a future Zion or New Jerusalem was also contained in the prophecy of Enoch, revealed to Joseph Smith in December, 1830 (Moses 7:62). Two months later, the Lord promised Joseph that he would reveal its location to him (D&C 42:9, 35, 62, 67; 45:64-68). At length the site of Zion or the New Jerusalem was designated as Independence, Missouri (D&C 84:2-4; *History of the Church* 1:188f, 359; see Articles of Faith 10). On several occasions, Joseph Smith and other early Church leaders tied the establishment of this new city with the Book of Mormon prophecies (*History of the Church* 2.52, 128, 261-2).

The Lord's Law of Warfare. In August, 1833, Joseph Smith received a revelation in which the Lord outlined his law of warfare for the benefit of members of the Church being persecuted by the Missouri mobs. He declared that the Saints would be blessed if they took no action after the first, second, and third attacks on their settlements, but that they would be justified in retaliating after that (D&C 98:23-31). He further declared he had commanded "Nephi, and thy fathers, Joseph, and Jacob, and Isaac, and Abraham, and all mine ancient prophets and apostles . . . that they should not go out unto battle" unless commanded, and that they should thrice "lift up a standard of peace" to aggressors before they would be justified in taking action (D&C 98:32-44).

That this was the law among the Nephites is confirmed in Alma 43:46, where we read that "the Lord had said unto them, and also unto their fathers, that: Inasmuch as ye are not guilty of the first offense, neither the second, ye shall not suffer yourselves to be slain by the hands of your enemies." In Mormon's day, the Lord declared, "thrice have I delivered them out of the hands of their enemies," but instead of repenting, the Nephites swore to avenge themselves against the Lamanites, in consequence of which Mormon relinquished his position as commander of the Nephite armies (Mormon 3:13-16).

The effect of following the Lord's law of warfare was that Moroni, "knowing that it was the only desire of the Nephites to preserve their lands, and their liberty, and their church, therefore he thought it no sin that he should defend them by stratagem" (Alma 43:30; see verse 23). A later Nephite general, Gidgiddoni, rejected suggestions that he launch an attack on the Gadianton robbers, saying that "if we should go up against them the Lord would deliver us into their hands" (3 Nephi 3:20-21).[14] Though the robbers planned to attack the Nephites, they had not yet come against them. The basic law was that neither the Latter-day Saints nor the Nephites should be the aggressors, though they were allowed to defend their families (D&C 98:31-33; Alma 43:23; 48:10, 14-16).

Religious Tolerance. The eleventh Article of Faith declares, "We claim the privilege of worshiping Almighty God according to the dictates of our own conscience, and allow all men the same privilege, let them worship how, where, or what they may." The Lord instructed Joseph Smith, "contend against no church, save it be the church of the devil" (D&C 18:20). This concept of religious tolerance is also found in the early Nephite church: "Now there was a strict law among the people of the church, that there should not any man, belonging to the church, arise and persecute those that did not belong to the church, and

---

[14] Centuries later, Mormon noted that the Lord would not sustain the Nephites when they launched an offensive against the Lamanites rather than fighting a defensive war (Mormon 4:1-5).

The Book of Mormon as a Source of Church Doctrine

that there should be no persecution among themselves" (Alma 1:21; see also Mosiah 27:2-4). As a result, there were Nephites who did not belong to the church that God had established among them (Mosiah 27:1, 8; Alma 4:11; 5:62).

Their belief and practice of religious liberty was one of the things that set the Nephites apart from many ancient peoples. The principle is explained in Alma 30:7-11:

> Now there was no law against a man's belief; for it was strictly contrary to the commands of God that there should be a law which should bring men on to unequal grounds. For thus saith the scripture: Choose ye this day, whom ye will serve. Now if a man desired to serve God, it was his privilege; or rather, if he believed in God it was his privilege to serve him; but if he did not believe in him there was no law to punish him. But if he murdered he was punished unto death; and if he robbed he was also punished; and if he stole he was also punished; and if he committed adultery he was also punished; yea, for all this wickedness they were punished. For there was a law that men should be judged according to their crimes. Nevertheless, there was no law against a man's belief; therefore, a man was punished only for the crimes which he had done; therefore all men were on equal grounds.

The same principle is held in the restored Church, as explained in D&C 134:4-5:

> We believe that religion is instituted of God; and that men are amenable to him, and to him only, for the exercise of it, unless their religious opinions prompt them to infringe upon the rights and liberties of others; but we do not believe that

> human law has a right to interfere in prescribing rules of worship to bind the consciences of men, nor dictate forms for public or private devotion; that the civil magistrate should restrain crime, but never control conscience; should punish guilt, but never suppress the freedom of the soul. We believe that all men are bound to sustain and uphold the respective governments in which they reside, while protected in their inherent and inalienable rights by the laws of such governments; and that sedition and rebellion are unbecoming every citizen thus protected, and should be punished accordingly; and that all governments have a right to enact such laws as in their own judgments are best calculated to secure the public interest; at the same time, however, holding sacred the freedom of conscience.

Because their system of government was the source of their religious liberty, the Nephites felt it their duty to defend both. Thus, we read that they "had sworn or covenanted to maintain their rights and the privileges of their religion by a free government" (Alma 51:6). Alma 43:47 declares that "the Lord has said that: Ye shall defend your families even unto bloodshed. Therefore for this cause were the Nephites contending with the Lamanites, to defend themselves, and their families, and their lands, their country, and their rights, and their religion."

The Nephite chief captain, Moroni, tied "faith . . . religion . . . rites of worship . . . church" and family to "that liberty which binds us to our lands and our country" (Alma 44:5). For this reason, when a crisis arose in his nation, he prepared a banner and wrote on it, "In memory of our God, our religion, and freedom, and our peace, our wives, and our children" (Alma 46:12). Nephite soldiers rallied around the banner to "enter into a covenant that they will maintain their rights, and their religion, that the Lord

God may bless them" (Alma 46:20; see also Alma 48:13; 54:10).

CONCLUSION

It seems obvious that God expects his people to follow the same basic practices and beliefs in different dispensations. From this point-of-view, we are not surprised to find modern revelations finding agreement with both the Bible and the Book of Mormon. But while both of these ancient volumes of scripture give much information about the plan of salvation, the Bible is mostly silent on how the early Christian church operated. Such is not the case with the Book of Mormon, where we have a fair amount of detail about many Church practices.

Church leaders have emphasized time and again that the Book of Mormon was not written for the Nephites, from whose records it was drawn, but for our day. Moroni hid the plates containing the book in a deliberate attempt to preserve them for a future generation. He wrote of Joseph Smith, who would bring the record to light (Mormon 8:16) and declared to his latter-day audience, "Behold, I speak unto you as if ye were present, and yet ye are not. But behold, Jesus Christ hath shown you unto me" (Mormon 8:35). His words in Ether 5:1-4 were addressed specifically to Joseph Smith:

> And now I, Moroni, have written the words which were commanded me, according to my memory; and I have told you the things which I have sealed up; therefore touch them not in order that ye may translate; for that thing is forbidden you, except by and by it shall be wisdom in God. And behold, ye may be privileged that ye may show the plates unto those who shall assist to bring forth this work; And unto three shall they be shown by the power of God; wherefore they shall know of a surety that these things are true. And in the mouth of three witnesses shall these

things be established; and the testimony of three, and this work, in the which shall be shown forth the power of God and also his word, of which the Father, and the Son, and the Holy Ghost bear record—and all this shall stand as a testimony against the world at the last day.

Immediately before recording the information that details such things as ordination to the priesthood, the blessing of the sacrament, the conditions for baptism, procedures for Church membership and discipline, and the conducting of Church meetings (Moroni 2-6), Moroni expressed the desire that these "few more things . . . may be of worth unto my brethren, the Lamanites, in some future day" (Moroni 1:4). In order for his desire to be fulfilled, it was necessary that the Church be restored to the earth.

It is clear that Moroni and his father Mormon deliberately included in the abridged record information that they knew would be helpful to Joseph Smith in reorganizing the Church on the earth in the last days. Once he had translated the Nephite record into English, Joseph had all of the essentials necessary to establish a fully-functioning Church, once the priesthood was restored.

Chapter 45

UNANSWERED QUESTIONS IN THE BOOK OF MORMON

Now these mysteries are not yet fully made known unto me; therefore I shall forbear. (Alma 37:11)

The author once had a student who, whenever she didn't know the answer to an exam question, would write, "See Alma 37:11." Even after many years of study, none of us has all the answers regarding the scriptures. Some of the questions we pose may not even have answers. Some of the chapters in this book seek to provide additional information on a few of these questions. In this chapter, we shall discuss a few of the remaining "unanswered questions" regarding the Book of Mormon.

DID LEHI'S FAMILY ENCOUNTER OTHER PEOPLE IN THE NEW WORLD BESIDES THE MULEKITES?

According to anthropologist John L. Sorenson, it is quite likely that Lehi's family encountered native peoples when they arrived in the promised land.[1] Unfortunately, the abridged account in 1-2 Nephi doesn't provide that information. But such encounters might explain a number of things, such as:

- How the Lamanites got a dark skin (2 Nephi 5:21) and how Lamanites who joined with the Nephites became white skinned (3 Nephi 2:14).

- Why the Lamanites so readily "became wild, and ferocious, and a blood-thirsty people, full of idolatry and filthiness" (Enos 1:20). Did they just "invent" idols, or were they introduced by other people? Where did the later Lamanites

---

[1] John L. Sorenson, "When Lehi's Party Arrived, Did They Find Others in the Land?" *Journal of Book of Mormon Studies* 1/1 (Fall 1992).

get the idea of human sacrifice (Mormon 4:15, 21)?

- Why the Lamanites were so much more numerous than the Nephites even in the first generations (Jarom 1:6). By the time of Mosiah II, the Nephites and Mulekites together "were not half so numerous" as the Lamanites (Mosiah 25:3).

HOW DID MOSIAH GET THE INTERPRETERS?

Latter-day Saints have become accustomed to referring to the two stones that came with the plates translated by Joseph Smith as the "Urim and Thummim." This is because this is the term that the Lord used in some early revelations to the Joseph Smith (D&C 10:1:17:1), and it is the term the prophet used in his 1838 account of the visit of the angel Moroni (Joseph Smith History 1:35, 52). But the Book of Mormon uses the term "interpreters," while the modern scriptural accounts employ the term found in the Bible.

The Lord gave the two stones to the brother of Jared and told him to "seal them up also with the things which ye shall write" (Ether 3:22-24, 27-28). The record kept by the brother of Jared at some point came into the hands of the Jaredite prophet Ether, who included it in the account he recorded on twenty-four plates of gold. When Ether had "finished his record . . . he hid them [the plates] in a manner that the people of Limhi did find them" (Ether 15:33).

The discovery of Ether's twenty-four plates by a group of men sent out by the Nephite king Limhi is recounted in Mosiah 8:6-12. Because none of his people could read the record, Limhi inquired of Ammon if he knew of anyone who could read the ancient language. Ammon replied,

> I can assuredly tell thee, O king, of a man that can translate the records; for he has wherewith that he can look, and translate all records that are of ancient date; and it is a gift from God. And the

How Did Mosiah Get the Interpreters?

things are called interpreters, and no man can look in them except he be commanded, lest he should look for that he ought not and he should perish. And whosoever is commanded to look in them, the same is called seer. And behold, the king of the people who are in the land of Zarahemla is the man that is commanded to do these things, and who has this high gift from God. (Mosiah 8:13-14)

Limhi was pleased to hear that king Mosiah, who then reigned in Zarahemla, would be able to translate the plates, and declared, "Doubtless a great mystery is contained within these plates, and these interpreters were doubtless prepared for the purpose of unfolding all such mysteries to the children of men" (Mosiah 8:19). Mosiah subsequently translated the record "by the means of those two stones which were fastened into the two rims of a bow" and the mystery of the Jaredites was solved (Mosiah 28:11-17).

What remains unanswered in all this is how Mosiah got the interpreters. They seem not to have been found by Limhi's men, for the expedition brought back only the plates, some breastplates, and some swords (Mosiah 8:9-11). Moreover, Mosiah already had the interpreters in his possession at the time that his subject, Ammon, learned of the plates of Ether. Were they the same interpreters given to the brother of Jared, or were they a different set of stones?

The evidence suggests that Mosiah probably possessed the same interpreters previously hidden by the brother of Jared. Mosiah transferred the plates of brass and "all the records" (which would include the account of Ether) to the custody of the younger Alma, "and also the interpreters" (Mosiah 28:20). Alma subsequently passed the twenty-four plates to his son Helaman, instructing him to "preserve these interpreters" (Alma 37:21). He then spoke about the future translator of the records, saying,

UNANSWERED QUESTIONS IN THE BOOK OF MORMON

> And the Lord said: I will prepare unto my servant Gazelem, a stone, which shall shine forth in darkness unto light, that I may discover unto my people who serve me, that I may discover unto them the works of their brethren, yea, their secret works, their works of darkness, and their wickedness and abominations. And now, my son, these interpreters were prepared that the word of God might be fulfilled, which he spake, saying: I will bring forth out of darkness unto light all their secret works and their abominations; and except they repent I will destroy them from off the face of the earth; and I will bring to light all their secrets and abominations, unto every nation that shall hereafter possess the land. And now, my son, we see that they did not repent; therefore they have been destroyed, and thus far the word of God has been fulfilled; yea, their secret abominations have been brought out of darkness and made known unto us. (Alma 37:23-26)

The twenty-four plates found by Limhi's people ultimately came into the hands of Moroni, who abridged the account to produce the book of Ether we know in the Book of Mormon (Ether Preface; 1:1-2). That he possessed the plates themselves, and not merely Mosiah's translation thereof, is suggested by the fact that just after recording the Lord's commandment to the brother of Jared to "seal up" (hide) both his record and the interpreters (Ether 3:22-24, 27-28), Moroni noted that the Lord had commanded him to write "the very words" of the brother of Jared "and he commanded me that I should seal them up; and he also hath commanded that I should seal up the interpretation thereof; wherefore I have sealed up the interpreters, according to the

How Did Mosiah Get the Interpreters?

commandment of the Lord" (Ether 4:4-5).[2]

When Moroni appeared to Joseph Smith in September of 1823, he told him of the plates he had hidden and noted "Also, that there were two stones in silver bows—and these stones, fastened to a breastplate, constituted what is called the Urim and Thummim—deposited with the plates; and the possession and use of these stones were what constituted 'seers' in ancient or former times; and that God had prepared them for the purpose of translating the book" (Joseph Smith History 1:35; see also 1:42, 52, 59).

The use of the term "seers" ties the two stones to Mosiah, whose role as seer was established by the fact that he possessed and used the interpreters. But the fact that "God had prepared them" reflects verbiage from the story of the brother of Jared, to whom the Lord had given the interpreters. In a revelation addressed to the three witnesses, the Lord spoke of the "the Urim and Thummim, which were given to the brother of Jared upon the mount, when he talked with the Lord face to face" (D&C 17:1). Clearly, the stones given to Joseph Smith were the very ones that had been sealed and prepared to translate the Jaredite record. But were they the same interpreters possessed by Mosiah? Based on the description of how Mosiah translated the Jaredite record, we must respond in the affirmative.

> And now he translated them by the means of those two stones which were fastened into the two rims of a bow. Now these things were prepared

---

[2] Though passages like this make one think of the "sealed portion" of the Book of Mormon (Joseph Smith History 1:65), the term "sealed" as used here by Moroni and elsewhere in the Book of Mormon and other ancient texts often means simply "hidden." Both the plates and the interpreters were hidden. It may be, of course, that Limhi's plates of gold were physically sealed shut and thus were that portion of the Book of Mormon that Joseph Smith did not translate. This issue will be dealt with by the author in a forthcoming book on the Book of Mormon and other hidden books.

from the beginning, and were handed down from generation to generation, for the purpose of interpreting languages; And they have been kept and preserved by the hand of the Lord, that he should discover to every creature who should possess the land the iniquities and abominations of his people; And whosoever has these things is called seer, after the manner of old times. (Mosiah 28:13-16)

The description of the interpreters as "fastened into the two rims of a bow" parallel's Joseph Smith's use of "two stones in silver bows."

We are still left with the question of how Mosiah got the interpreters. They were obviously not found with the plates by Limhi's people, since Mosiah already had them with him in the city of Zarahemla when the plates were brought to Limhi in the city of Nephi.

Some possible answers come to mind. The Lord could have retrieved the interpreters from their hiding place and given them to Mosiah. The Nephites of Zarahemla may have found the hiding place of the stones. They may have come into the possession of the Mulekites, who founded the city of Zarahemla, and then passed to Mosiah's grandfather when he became king of that land.

Some of these possibilities prompt other questions, such as why the interpreters were not with the plates Ether had hidden. For that matter, did Ether even possess the stones? His record never indicates that he had more than the plates. But if he possessed the account of the brother of his ancestor Jared, which Moroni translated from Ether's record, why did he not also have the interpreters? Did he retrieve the record that the brother of Jared had hidden (presumably with the interpreters), or did he possess a different version of the Jaredite history that gave some of the same information? The questions may, in fact, outnumber the answers when it comes to this issue.

WHERE DID ALMA GET HIS PRIESTHOOD AUTHORITY?

From the story of Alma baptizing people at the waters of Mormon, it is clear that Alma had "authority from God" (Mosiah 18:13, 17-18; see also 23:16-17). He was, in fact, the high priest over the Nephite church (Mosiah 23:16; 26:7). The younger Alma declared that he had "been consecrated by my father, Alma, to be a high priest over the church of God, he having power and authority from God to do these things" (Alma 5:3; see also Mosiah 29:42; Alma 4:4).

We know that the elder Alma was convinced by the preaching of the prophet Abinadi (Mosiah 17:2; Alma 5:11), but the account in Mosiah 17 suggests that Abinadi, then a prisoner in the palace of King Noah, was killed shortly thereafter. This seems to allow no time for him to ordain Alma. Could he have performed such an ordination before he was arrested and brought to trial before the king? If this be true, then Alma must have been converted by Abinadi's earlier preaching, not by his appearance in court. We simply do not have the answers, though the questions continue to intrigue us.

WAS ABINADI ONE OF ZENIFF'S PRIESTS?

When Noah replaced his father Zeniff as king of the Nephites living in the land of Nephi, "he put down all the priests that had been consecrated by his father, and consecrated new ones in their stead, such as were lifted up in the pride of their hearts" (Mosiah 11:5). The new priests professed to keep the law of Moses even while they disobeyed some of its more important principles (Mosiah 12:27-37; 13:27-28; 16:14-15). Later, when they became assimilated into Lamanite society, they even abandoned the pretense of following the law of Moses (Mosiah 24:4-5).

We know that Abinadi "spake with power and authority from God" (Mosiah 13:6). Amid the political and religious corruption in the land of Nephi, how did he receive this divine authority? It is possible that he was one of the deposed priests who had served under the righteous king Zeniff, but, alas, the record is silent on this matter.

WHO WERE THE AMALEKITES?

The Amalekites are first mentioned in Alma 21, where we learn that they were associated with the Lamanites and Amulonites and that they had built synagogues after the order of the Nehors (Alma 21:2-5, 16; 22:7). So hardened were these people that the sons of Mosiah managed to convert only one Amalekite and none of the Amulonites (Alma 23:14). Indeed, it was these two groups who stirred up others to fight against the Lamanites who had been converted by the sons of Mosiah (Alma 24:1-2; 27:2, 12, 29), and we read that "the greatest number of those of the Lamanites who slew so many of their brethren were Amalekites and Amulonites, the greatest number of whom were after the order of the Nehors" (Alma 24:28; see also verse 29).

The religion of Nehor was founded by a Nephite of that name who was subsequently executed for murder (Alma 1:2-15). He had gained followers in the Nephite city of Ammonihah (Alma 14:16, 18; 15:15), which the Nephites renamed "desolation of Nehors" after its destruction by a Lamanite army (Alma 16:11). The Book of Mormon never informs us how the religion of Nehor came to be accepted by both the Amalekites and the Amulonites, though we do learn that both of these people built synagogues to practice that religion (Alma 21:4).

Alma 43:13 lists the "Amalekites and Zoramites, and the descendants of the priests of Noah" among "those who had dissented from the Nephites," and we note that the Amalekites and Zoramites "were of a more wicked and murderous disposition than the Lamanites were, in and of themselves, therefore, Zerahemnah appointed chief captains over the Lamanites" (Alma 43:6; see also verse 44). The fact that most of the Lamanites at the time were nearly naked when they went into battle, while the Zoramites and Amalekites were clothed (Alma 43:20) suggests that both groups

WHO WERE THE AMALEKITES?

had their origin in the Nephite culture.

The Zoramites apostatized from the Nephite religion (Alma 30:59), then defected to the Lamanites (Alma 35:10-13; 43:4). The Amulonites were descendants of the priests of the wicked Nephite king Noah who had taken Lamanite wives and later were given positions of leadership in lands under Lamanite domination (Mosiah 23:31-35, 39; 24:1-11). We later find them living in the land of Amulon with the Amalekites (Alma 24:1).

But who were the Amalekites? Were they the same as the Amlicites, a Nephite apostate group who had joined the Lamanites in the time of Alma the elder (Alma 2:24)? If so, why the change in spelling 19 chapters later? We simply cannot be sure.

JUST HOW DID NEHOR DIE?

Nehor, the founder of the apostate religion that bore his name, was brought to justice, not because of his beliefs, but because he had slain an innocent man, the beloved soldier and teacher in the church, Gideon (Alma 1:2-14). "And it came to pass that they took him; and his name was Nehor; and they carried him upon the top of the hill Manti, and there he was caused, or rather did acknowledge, between the heavens and the earth, that what he had taught to the people was contrary to the word of God; and there he suffered an ignominious death" (Alma 1:15).

We are never told how Nehor was executed. The term "ignominious" merely suggests that he did not die honorably. Was he stoned, as was the most common punishment for murders under the law of Moses? Based on the fact that he made confession "between the heavens and the earth," some have suggested that he may have been hanged. But the expression may simply reflect the place of execution, atop a hill. Again, the Book of Mormon is silent on this subject.

Unanswered Questions in the Book of Mormon

HOW DID AN ISHMAELITE BECOME KING OF THE LAMANITES?

When the sons of Mosiah went to perform missionary labors among the Lamanites, "Ammon went to the land of Ishmael, the land being called after the sons of Ishmael, who also became Lamanites" (Alma 17:19). "Ammon was carried before the king [Lamoni] who was over the land of Ishmael; and his name was Lamoni; and he was a descendant of Ishmael" (Alma 17:21).

We are not surprised by the fact that Lamoni, a descendant of Ishmael, was king over the land named after his ancestor. But it seems curious that Lamoni's father was king over all the Lamanite territory (Alma 18:9; 22:1). To be sure, "the Lamanites . . . were a compound of Laman and Lemuel, and the sons of Ishmael, and all those who had dissented from the Nephites" (Alma 43:13, 35), so the Ishmaelites were part of the Lamanite nation. But the very name "Lamanite" suggests that descendants of Laman would have typically enjoyed royal privileges.[3]

It is possible, of course, that an Ishmaelite usurper had taken the throne, just as the Zoramite usurper Amalickiah later did (Alma 47:20-35; see Alma 52:3; Alma 54:16, 23-24). But the Book of Mormon is silent on the matter.

CONCLUSION

The only conclusion we can reach for the moment on the questions considered here is that we can come to no conclusion. Had the Book of Mormon been a full account of the history of the Nephites and Lamanites, rather than an abridgment, we might have the answers to these and other questions. But if past experience has taught us anything, it is that constant study of the scriptures, bringing to bear the latest scholarly tools and facts, often sheds

---

[3] There is an argument that the father-son relationship between Lamoni and the Lamanite king was one of lord and vassal, but that explanation seems too façile and not in accord with the record.

light on things that were previously obscure. It is therefore possible that subsequent research by someone will shed light on the questions we have discussed in this chapter. In any case, it is not unusual to find such unanswered questions in genuine ancient historical documents. It would be much more likely that the Book of Mormon was a clever fiction if it contained no unanswered questions.

Chapter 46

THE MESSIAH, THE BOOK OF MORMON, AND THE DEAD SEA SCROLLS

For behold, did not Moses prophesy unto them concerning the coming of the Messiah, and that God should redeem his people? Yea, and even all the prophets who have prophesied ever since the world began—have they not spoken more or less concerning these things? (Mosiah 13:33)

Jews and Christians have long disagreed on the concept of the Messiah. The Hebrew term means "anointed one," which is what *Christ* means in Greek. In the Old Testament, the term is most often applied to the kings of Israel and Judah.[1] To the Jews, therefore, the Messiah is the king who will restore the kingdom to Israel in the last days. To the Christians, the Messiah is the Son of God, a divine being who came to die to atone for the sins of the world and to bring salvation from death and hell.

The Nephite belief in a Messiah who would bring salvation through his death and resurrection dates from the early sixth century B.C. The plan of redemption was revealed to the prophet Lehi even before he left the Old World (1 Nephi 1:19; 10:4-11). Non-believers have sometimes criticized the Book of Mormon for placing New Testament beliefs in an Old Testament timeframe. The concept of resurrection through the atonement of the Messiah was one of the most prominent teachings of the pre-Christian Nephites (see 1 Nephi 19:7-10; Jarom 1:11; Mosiah 26:2; Alma

---

[1] 1 Samuel 2:35; 24:6, 10; 26:9, 11, 16, 23; 2 Samuel 1:14, 16; 19:21; 22:51; 23:1; 1 Chronicles 16:22; 2 Chronicles 6:42; Psalm 2:2; 18:50; 20:6; 45:7; 84:9; 89:20, 38, 51; 105:15; Lamentations 4:20; Habakkuk 3:13.

16:19; 21:9; 26:7; 27:28; Helaman 14:15-17).

Typical of Book of Mormon teachings about Christ is the following statement by Jacob:

> Wherefore, beloved brethren, be reconciled unto him through the atonement of Christ, his Only Begotten Son, and ye may obtain a resurrection, according to the power of the resurrection which is in Christ, and be presented as the first-fruits of Christ unto God, having faith, and obtained a good hope of glory in him before he manifesteth himself in the flesh. And now, beloved, marvel not that I tell you these things; for why not speak of the atonement of Christ, and attain to a perfect knowledge of him, as to attain to the knowledge of a resurrection and the world to come? (Jacob 4:11-12)

Modern Christians, following the example of the New Testament, refer to many Old Testament "proof texts" to support their belief that Jesus was and is the Messiah. Most of these are quickly dismissed by Jews and by many Christian Bible scholars on the grounds that the original context of the passages is unrelated to their later use. Only Isaiah 53 has strong support as a prophecy of a savior-messiah to come.[2] Other Old Testament messianic prophecies cannot be clearly shown to foresee Christ's atonement.

Some pre-Christian pseudepigrapha suggest a belief in a savior-messiah. But the relevant passages have typically been dismissed as later Christian interpolations. Early Jews and Christians exchanged recriminations about the scriptures. The Jews accused the Christians of adding verbiage to support their belief in Jesus, while some Christians accused the Jews of removing passages favorable to Jesus. The Book of Mormon, while prophetically

---

[2] See Abinadi's use of Isaiah 53 in Mosiah 14-15.

chastising Christians for their ingratitude toward the Jews for the scriptures (2 Nephi 29:4-6), notes that many "plain and precious parts of the gospel of the Lamb" would be removed from biblical books (1 Nephi 13:32; read verses 29-40).

SOME MESSIAH TEXTS FROM THE DEAD SEA SCROLLS

The discovery of the Dead Sea Scrolls near Qumran in the mid-twentieth century brought to light the oldest known copies of Old Testament books[3] and unfolded an array of other works, most of them previously unknown.

A messianic scroll from Cave 11, called 11QMelch or 11Q13 by scholars, casts Melchizedek in a divine saving role similar to that given to Jesus in the New Testament. Jesus is compared to Melchizedek in Hebrews 5:6, 10; 6:20; 7:1, 10-11, 15, 17, 21. Melchizedek, whose name can mean "legitimate king," is the archetypical king in the Old Testament and is therefore a fitting symbol of the Messiah.[4]

The Qumran scroll says that Melchizedek "will restore them, and proclaim liberty to them, relieving them [of the burden] of all their iniquities" (see Leviticus 25:10; Isaiah 61:1). It further speaks of the "expiation" (see Leviticus 29:9) and says that Melchizedek "will raise up the holy ones of El (God) for deeds of judgment." The text identifies him with the God standing in the congregation of God in Psalm 82:1-2 and says that "Melchizedek will exact the ven[geance] of E[l's] judgments" (see Isaiah 61:2).

The "time for Melchiz[edek]'s year of favor" (see Isaiah 61:2) is termed "the day [of salvation about w]hich [God] spoke

---

[3] Some of the Dead Sea Scrolls were written in the mid-second century B.C., the latest just before A.D. 70.

[4] In addition to his role as priest-king of Salem in Genesis 14:18-20, Melchizedek is mentioned in one of the "royal" psalms, Psalms 110:4. In the *Doctrine and Covenants*, we learn that Melchizedek's priesthood is after "the order of the Only Begotten Son" (D&C 76:57; 107:2-4; 124:123).

[through the mouth of Is]aiah the prophet, who said, ['How] beautiful on (the) mountains are the feet of the hera[ld of good who proclaims salvatio]n, saying to Zion, "Your God [is king.'"]." The mountains in this passage from Isaiah 52:7 are said to be the prophets, while "the herald i[s the one an]ointed of the spir[it about] whom Dan[iel] said: [`Until an anointed, a prince, (there will be) seven weeks']" (from Daniel 9:25), while the herald "is the one about whom it is w[ritte]n, when [it says . . .] to comfo[rt the] m[ourners of Zion] to [in]struct them in all the ages of the wo[rld] in truth."[5]

The latter reference is to Isaiah 61:2-3, the passage that Jesus cited when he proclaimed that he was the Messiah (Luke 4:16-21). It is significant that several references to it appear in the Melchizedek scroll. That scroll also appeals frequently to Leviticus 25 (which refers to the Jubilee) and to Isaiah 52. The interpretation of the mountains of Isaiah 52:7 as the prophets and the herald of good tidings as a Messiah figure is paralleled by Abinadi's explanation of the same passage in Mosiah 12:20-21; 15:13-24, to which we shall return below.[6]

Other portions of the Dead Sea Scrolls are even stronger in their support of the view that a knowledge of a savior-messiah was had in ancient Israel. An Aramaic scroll, 4Q246, is of particular interest because it contains concepts found in the angel Gabriel's announcement of Christ's birth in Luke 1 and even parallels some of the language of that chapter (see Table 2).[7]

---

[5] For an in-depth study of this and related texts from Qumran, see Paul J. Kobelski, *Melchizedek and Melchireša‘*, The Catholic Biblical Quarterly Monograph Series 10 (Washington: Catholic Biblical Association of America, 1981). The translation used here is from pages 7-10 of Kobelski's monograph.

[6] See also the discussion in Chapter 21, "How Beautiful Upon the Mountains."

[7] The translation is from Florentino García Martínez, *The Dead Sea Scrolls Translated* (2nd ed., Leiden: Brill, 1996), 138.

Table 2. A Comparison of 4Q246 Column 2 and Luke 1.

4Q246 Column 2	Luke 1
1. He will be called son of God, and they will call him son of the Most High . . .	32. He . . . shall be called the Son of the Highest: and the Lord God shall give unto him the throne of his father David:
5. His kingdom will be an eternal kingdom, and all his paths in truth and uprigh[tness].	33 And he shall reign over the house of Jacob for ever; and of his kingdom there shall be no end . . .
6. The earth (will be) in truth and all will make peace. The sword will cease in the earth,	
7. And all the cities will pay him homage. He is a great God among the gods (?).	34 . . . that holy thing which shall be born of thee shall be called the Son of God.
8. . . . His kingdom will be an eternal kingdom.	

Another messianic text that is of particular significance to Book of Mormon studies is 4Q521, also called 4QMessianic Apocalypse. The first portion of the text (which is the most complete) is shown in Table 3 (the column/line numbers have been added for reference).

Some Messiah Texts From The Dead Sea Scrolls

Table 3. The Messianic Apocalypse.

2.1 [for the hea]vens and the earth will listen to his Messiah,
2.2 [and all] that is in them will not turn away from the holy precepts.
2.3 Be encouraged, you who are seeking the Lord in his service! *Blank*
2.4 Will you not, perhaps, encounter the Lord in it all those who hope in their heart?
2.5 For the Lord will observe the devout, and call the just by name,
2.6 and upon the poor he will place his spirit, and the faithful he will renew with his strength.
2.7 For he will honour the devout upon the throne of eternal royalty,
2.8 freeing prisoners, giving sight to the blind, straightening out the twisted.
2.9 Ever shall I cling to those who hope. In his mercy he will jud[ge,]
2.10 and from no-one shall the fruit [of] good [deeds] be delayed,
2.11 and the Lord will perform marvelous acts such as have not existed, just as he sa[id][8]
2.12 for he will heal the badly wounded and will make the dead live, he will proclaim good news to the meek
2.13 give lavishly [to the need]y, lead the exiled and enrich the hungry.[9]

Most of the elements found in this text are found in the messianic passage in Isaiah 61:1-3, where we read of the Spirit,

---

[8] The allusion is to Isaiah 48:7.

[9] Florentino García Martínez, *The Dead Sea Scrolls Translated*, 394.

anointing (becoming a messiah or "anointed one"), good tidings, broken heart, liberty for the captives and opening of the prison (all in verse 1), and joy (verse 3). Jesus quoted most of this passage in the synagogue at Nazareth and declared that it was fulfilled in him (Luke 4:16-21).

All of the elements found in the Dead Sea text are also found in the Book of Mormon. For example, the concept of the heavens and the earth listening to (obeying) the Messiah (Messianic Apocalypse 2.1) is reflected in the Book of Mormon title for Christ, "the Father of heaven and of earth" (see, for example, Helaman 14:12; 16:18).[10]

The idea of seeking the Lord (Messianic Apocalypse 2.3-4) is found in a number of Bible passages (see Deuteronomy 4:29; Isaiah 55:6; Acts 17:27). Note especially Isaiah 11:10 (cited in 2 Nephi 21:10) and Malachi 3:1 (cited in 3 Nephi 24:1), which seem to refer to the Messiah. Note also Jesus' statement about seeking and finding (Matthew 7:7-8), which he repeated to the Nephites (3 Nephi 14:7-8). Of particular importance is the admonition of Moroni, "And now, I would commend you to seek this Jesus of whom the prophets and apostles have written" (Ether 12:41). Messianic Apocalypse 2.3-4 ties those who seek the Lord with those "who hope in their heart". Three passages (3 Nephi 9:20; Moroni 7:43-44; 8:26) promise the Holy Ghost to those who approach God with a broken heart, reminding us of a similar promise in Messianic Apocalypse 2.6. In the latter, we read that the Lord will renew the faithful by his strength. This idea is found in Alma 44:3-4 and Alma 48:15 (see also Alma 50:22).

The freeing of the prisoners (Messianic Apocalypse 2.8) is found in Isaiah 11:9 (cited in 1 Nephi 21:9) and Isaiah 61:1, as noted above. The latter was probably alluded to in Helaman 5:11, where we read of "the tidings of redemption" through the

---

[10] Other examples are discussed below. Compare the words addressed by Jesus to the Father, "Thy will be done on earth as it is in heaven" (3 Nephi 13:10; Matthew 5:10).

Redeemer.

More important, however, is that the Book of Mormon contains a series of discourses and essays in which clusters of these same elements appear. We shall examine each of these, referring to the line in the Qumran text where the same concepts are found.

LEHI'S ADMONITIONS

In his old age, the Book of Mormon prophet Lehi gathered his family to give advice and blessings (2 Nephi 1-4). In 2 Nephi 2, speaking of the "redemption [that] cometh in and through the Holy Messiah" (2 Nephi 2:6), he declared that "the Holy Messiah . . . layeth down his life according to the flesh, and taketh it again by the power of the Spirit, that he may bring to pass the resurrection of the dead, being the first that should rise" (2 Nephi 2:8). Messianic Apocalypse 2.12 says the Messiah will resurrect the dead, while 2.6 speaks of his Spirit.

Lehi noted that the Messiah's "sacrifice for sin" was for "all those who have a broken heart and a contrite spirit" (2 Nephi 2:7), reminding us of those who "are seeking the Lord" and "hope in their heart" in Messianic Apocalypse 2.4. A short while later, Lehi seems to have classified himself as one of these when he said, "my heart is broken and my spirit is contrite" (2 Nephi 4:32). Also significant is Lehi's use of the term "holy messiah," which, while it is found nowhere in the Bible, is found in one of the Dead Sea Scrolls, 1Q30.

NEPHI'S TEACHINGS

Nephi wrote of "the things which [his father Lehi] spake by the power of the Holy Ghost, which power he received by faith on the Son of God—and the Son of God was the Messiah who should come—I, Nephi, was desirous also that I might see, and hear, and know of these things, by the power of the Holy Ghost, which is the gift of God unto all those who diligently seek him, as well in times of old as in the time that he should manifest himself unto the children of men" (1 Nephi 10:17).

Consequently, Nephi experienced the same vision as his father and wrote of Christ to come in terms similar to those of his father. In the passage just quoted, we note the reference to the Spirit (see 1 Nephi 12:18), as in Messianic Apocalypse 2.6, and to those who "seek him." This latter is expressed in Messianic Apocalypse 2.3-4 in terms of those who "hope in their heart," who seek and find the Lord. This idea is found in 1 Nephi 2:19, "Thou hast sought me diligently, with lowliness of heart."[11] The concept is based on Deuteronomy 4:29. As we saw above, the theme of seeking and finding the Lord is of frequent occurrence in the scriptures. In 1 Nephi 10:19, Nephi combined it with mention of the Spirit. In another place (2 Nephi 27:30), Nephi wrote of the meek, the poor, and of rejoicing, all concepts found in the Messianic Apocalypse 2.4, 6, 13.

Nephi wrote that the faithful "shall be lifted up at the last day, and shall be saved in the everlasting kingdom of the Lamb; and whoso shall publish peace, yea, tidings of great joy, how beautiful upon the mountains shall they be" (1 Nephi 13:37). Being "lifted up" typically refers to resurrection, which is found in Messianic Apocalypse 2.12, as here, in connection with glad tidings. There is an allusion to the kingdom in Messianic Apocalypse 2.7.

Other concepts common to Nephi's writings and the Messianic Apocalypse are the Lord's strengthening of the obedient (1 Nephi 17:3; Messianic Apocalypse 2.6) and the Messiah's healing power (2 Nephi 26:9; Messianic Apocalypse 2.8, 12). Nephi is the first Book of Mormon writer to call Christ "the Father of heaven and of earth" (2 Nephi 25:12), a title reminding us that Messianic Apocalypse 2.1 indicates that the Messiah is obeyed in heaven and on earth.

---

[11] Compare "the meek and the poor in heart" in 2 Nephi 28:13.

JACOB'S TEACHINGS

Jacob frequently referred to his father's teachings in his discourses and writings.[12] One of these discourses is found in 2 Nephi 6-10, another in Jacob 2-3.

In his first discourse, Jacob noted that Christ would "die for all men, that all men might become subject unto him" (2 Nephi 9:5). This reminds us of Messianic Apocalypse 2.1, which says that "the heavens and the earth will listen to [obey] his Messiah." Jacob then goes on to speak of the resurrection and the "infinite atonement" (2 Nephi 9:6-7, 12).

> Wherefore, how great the importance to make these things known unto the inhabitants of the earth, that they may know that there is no flesh that can dwell in the presence of God, save it be through the merits, and mercy, and grace of the Holy Messiah, who layeth down his life according to the flesh, and taketh it again by the power of the Spirit, that he may bring to pass the resurrection of the dead, being the first that should rise. (2 Nephi 9:8)

Like his father Lehi, Jacob made specific mention of the Spirit. At the conclusion of the discourse, he said, "Wherefore, may God raise you from death by the power of the resurrection, and also from everlasting death by the power of the atonement, that ye may be received into the eternal kingdom of God, that ye may praise him through grace divine. Amen" (2 Nephi 10:25). As noted above, an allusion to the kingdom is found in Messianic Apocalypse 2.7.

---

[12] See the author's article, "The Influence of Lehi's Admonitions on the Teachings of his son Jacob," *Journal of Book of Mormon Studies* 3/2 (Fall 1994) :34-48.

In his second discourse, Jacob likewise followed his father's example, speaking of "the pure in heart, and the broken heart" (Jacob 2:10), and dwelling on the resurrection to be brought about by the atonement of Christ (Jacob 4:11-12). After recording that discourse, he wrote more about the resurrection (Jacob 6:9) and, again following his father's lead, spoke of Christ as having "power, both in heaven and in earth; and also, that Christ shall come" (Jacob 7:14).

KING BENJAMIN'S DISCOURSE

One of the most famous discourses in the Book of Mormon is the one delivered by king Benjamin at the temple in Zarahemla (Mosiah 2-6). He announced,

> For behold, the time cometh, and is not far distant, that with power, the Lord Omnipotent who reigneth, who was, and is from all eternity to all eternity, shall come down from heaven among the children of men, and shall dwell in a tabernacle of clay, and shall go forth amongst men, working mighty miracles, such as healing the sick, raising the dead, causing the lame to walk, the blind to receive their sight, and the deaf to hear, and curing all manner of diseases. (Mosiah 3:5)

The miracles enumerated by king Benjamin are essentially the same as those found in Messianic Apocalypse 2.8, 12. Also of significance is the fact that the Messiah "reigneth," evidently in heaven, as in Messianic Apocalypse 2.1 (compare the "throne of eternal royalty" in 2.7). But the parallel becomes even stronger in Mosiah 3:8, where king Benjamin said, "And he shall be called Jesus Christ, the Son of God, the Father of heaven and earth, the Creator of all things from the beginning; and his mother shall be called Mary" (Mosiah 3:8; cf. 5:15). This message, he said, brought "great joy" to all those who believed (Mosiah 3:13).

Some of these concepts were repeated by the people's liturgical words when they asked to receive a forgiveness of sins through "the atoning blood of Christ . . . who created heaven and earth, and all things; who shall come down among the children of men" (Mosiah 4:2).

These parallels alone suggest that the ideas common to the Messianic Apocalypse and king Benjamin's discourse are more than coincidental. The case becomes stonger as we read that king Benjamin asked his people to "take upon you the name of Christ" (Mosiah 5:8). "Whosoever doeth this shall be found at the right hand of God, for he shall know the name by which he is called; for he shall be called by the name of Christ" (Mosiah 5:9). He exhorted his listeners to "hear and know the voice by which ye shall be called, and also, the name by which he shall call you" (Mosiah 5:12). The parallel with Messianic Apocalypse 2.5, in which the Lord calls the just "by name" is striking.

This new name was to be taken into the hearts of Benjamin's audience (Mosiah 5:11-12), which had been "changed through faith on his name" (Mosiah 15:7, 13-14). Here we have a parallel with those "who hope in their heart" and who "encounter the Lord" (Messianic Apocalypse 2.4). Significantly, the concept of the change of heart and of being "called by name" are found in close proximity in both texts.

ABINADI'S MESSAGE

At about the same time that king Benjamin was delivering his message to a very receptive audience in the city of Zarahemla, the Nephites in the land of Nephi were rejecting a similar message from a prophet named Abinadi. After quoting the "suffering servant" messianic prophecy from Isaiah 53 (Mosiah 14), Abinadi spoke of Christ to come (Mosiah 15).[13]

Like Nephi and king Benjamin, Abinadi termed the Messiah "the very Eternal Father of heaven and of earth" (Mosiah 15:4). Coming to earth, he would suffer himself "to be mocked, and scourged, and cast out, and disowned by his people," and would work "many mighty miracles" (Mosiah 15:5-6).

Nevertheless, "he shall be led, yea, even as Isaiah said, as a sheep before the shearer is dumb, so he opened not his mouth. Yea, even so he shall be led, crucified, and slain" (Mosiah 15:6-7). This would break "the bands of death" and provide a resurrection for mankind (Mosiah 15:8-9, 20-22, 24-26; 16:7-8).

Abinadi also mentioned the "kingdom of God" (Mosiah 15:11; see Messianic Apocalypse 2.7) and spoke of the "good tidings" mentioned in Isaiah 52:7 and in Messianic Apocalypse 2.12 (Mosiah 15:18).[14]

After his death, Abinadi's message was echoed by Alma the Elder at the Waters of Mormon, where he taught "concerning that which was to come,[15] and also concerning the resurrection of the dead, and the redemption of the people, which was to be brought to pass through the power, and sufferings, and death of Christ, and his resurrection and ascension into heaven" (Mosiah 18:2).

THE TEACHINGS OF ALMA THE YOUNGER

Alma the younger, though rebellious for a time, was greatly influenced by the teachings of his father. In his first

---

[13] One of the Dead Sea Scrolls, 4Q183, a small fragmentary text, may have relied on Isaiah 53:5 when it speaks of somone who "atoned for their sins through their sufferings." See Florentino García Martínez, *The Dead Sea Scrolls Translated*, 213.

[14] Abinadi's use of Isaiah 52 in connection with the messianic prophecy in Isaiah 53 teaches us that there is a direct tie between the two.

[15] See Chapter 35, "That Which is to Come," in this volume, which explains how this term is used of Christ in the Book of Mormon.

recorded major address, he said,

> Yea, thus saith the Spirit: Repent, all ye ends of the earth, for the kingdom of heaven is soon at hand; yea, the Son of God cometh in his glory, in his might, majesty, power, and dominion. Yea, my beloved brethren, I say unto you, that the Spirit saith: Behold the glory of the King of all the earth; and also the King of heaven shall very soon shine forth among all the children of men. (Alma 5:50; see also 7:9)

The idea of the Messiah as king of heaven and earth (compare Messianic Apocalypse 2.1) was later reflected in the teachings of Alma's missionary companion Amulek, who called him "the very Eternal Father of heaven and of earth, and all things which in them are; he is the beginning and the end," who should "come into the world to redeem his people" and to bring about redemption, that they might "rise from the dead" (Alma 11:38-42). Alma had spoken of the joy that comes from knowing of the resurrection to be provided by Christ (Alma 4:14), thus reflecting the ideas in Messianic Apocalypse 2.12. His teachings also parallel the calling of the just by name in Messianic Apocalypse 2.5:

> Behold, I say unto you, that the good shepherd doth call you; yea, and in his own name he doth call you, which is the name of Christ; and if ye will not hearken unto the voice of the good shepherd, to the name by which ye are called, behold, ye are not the sheep of the good shepherd. (Alma 5:38)[16]

In words similar to Messianic Apocalypse 2.4, Alma spoke to the Zoramites of the "poor in heart" and the "lowly in heart,"

---

[16] Compare Alma 12:30, 33, which includes an admonishment to "not harden your hearts."

indicating that they are blessed (Alma 32:3-4, 8, 12). He also taught them about the redemption and resurrection to be brought by the Messiah (Alma 33:22).

Some of Alma's choicest comments were reserved for the admonitions delivered to his three sons. He spoke of the resurrection brought by the atonement of Christ (Alma 40:2-3; 41:2) and tied it to the Lord's deliverance of Israel from Egypt and other instances of "bondage and captivity" (Alma 36:28). In this, we are reminded that the primary meaning of *redemption* in Old Testament passages is to deliver from slavery or prison, as in Messianic Apocalypse 2.8 (see Mormon 9:13).[17]

Alma also stressed the importance of being "lowly in heart":

> Preach unto them repentance, and faith on the Lord Jesus Christ; teach them to humble themselves and to be meek and lowly in heart; teach them to withstand every temptation of the devil, with their faith on the Lord Jesus Christ. Teach them to never be weary of good works, but to be meek and lowly in heart; for such shall find rest to their souls. (Alma 37:33-34)

Like Messianic Apocalypse 2.12, Alma spoke of the "glad tidings of salvation" associated with the coming of the Messiah (Alma 39:15-16, 19).

CONCLUSION

It seems unlikely that Jesus would have been so well received by his Jewish disciples had he not conformed to their concept of the Messiah. Some of the recently-released Dead Sea

---

[17] Book of Mormon prophets, beginning with Lehi, taught that Christ redeems from the chains and captivity of the devil. See 2 Nephi 1:13, 18, 21, 23, 27-29; 3:5; 9:8-10, 12, 19, 26, 45-46.

Conclusion

Scrolls show that at least some Jews of that time expected a Messiah who would be a divine savior, performing many miracles and bringing the resurrection. In this context, the pre-Christian teachings of a Messiah found in the Book of Mormon are perfectly reasonable. We can agree with Alma's words addressed to his son Corianton, whose faith was weakening: "Is it not as easy at this time for the Lord to send his angel to declare these glad tidings unto us as unto our children, or as after the time of his coming?" (Alma 39:19).

Chapter 47

UNTRANSLATED WORDS IN THE BOOK OF MORMON

And after having received the record of the Nephites, yea, even my servant Joseph Smith, Jun., might have power to translate through the mercy of God, by the power of God, the Book of Mormon. (D&C 1:29)

Anyone who knows a foreign language knows that it is not always possible to accurately translate a word into one's own tongue. A good example is the French word *chez*. If one uses the expression *chez Paul*, it might be rendered in English "with Paul," "at Paul's house," "at Paul's place" (including a place of business), or even "pertaining to Paul." Yet the word *chez* means neither "with" nor "house" nor "place" nor "pertaining." It is not really translatable into English.

The Book of Mormon includes several words that were not translated into English, probably because no English equivalent was known to the prophet Joseph Smith. In this chapter, we shall examine those words.

ZIFF

The word "*ziff*" denotes something that was taxed by wicked King Noah, along with gold, silver, copper, brass, iron, and agricultural produce (Mosiah 11:3). Because *ziff* and the other metals were used to ornament the king's buildings (Mosiah 11:8-11), it is likely that it was some type of metal. The word may derive from the Hebrew *ziw*, meaning "splendor, brightness."[1] In a 1964

---

[1] This suggestion was first made by Robert F. Smith, in a private communication to the author.

paper, Read H. Putnam speculated that ziff may have been zinc or tumbaga, which is an alloy of copper and gold.[2] Because tumbaga is particularly beautiful and has a definite redness, Robert F. Smith compared the word *ziff* with the Arabic roots *zhw* and *zyy*, meaning "adorn, cause to shine, redden."[3] These roots are cognate to the Hebrew *ziw*, Arabic and Hebrew being related languages.

It may be that *ziff* denotes a metal found in nature, such as electrum, which is a mixture of gold and silver. Another naturally occurring alloy may be what the medieval chemists called *kharsini*, which may have been a combination of arsenic and antimony.[4]

Plato wrote of a metal called *orichalkos* (Greek for "mountain copper") that was formerly mined in Atlantis and that was the most valuable of metals after gold (*Critias* 114). He indicated that the metal gleamed and that it was used, along with bronze, tin, silver, and gold, to decorate buildings (*Critias* 116). He also noted that the first ten kings of Atlantis wrote their laws in *orichalkos* on a sacrificial pillar in the temple of Poseidon (*Critias* 119-20). Strabo also spoke of *orichalkos*, indicating that it was a mixture of zinc and copper (*Geography* 13.1.56). Consequently, though associated by Plato with myths about Atlantis, the metal

---

[2] "Were the Plates of Mormon of Tumbaga?" *The Fifteenth Annual Symposium on the Archaeology of the Scriptures* (Provo: University Archaeological Society, BYU, 16 May 1964), 106, citing Sperry, *Problems of the Book of Mormon* (Salt Lake City: Bookcraft, 1964), 147, and Mosiah 11:8.

[3] Private communication to the author.

[4] L. G. Alieva and A. M.Gasanova wrote an article (in Russian) on the "Problem of the unknown metal kharsini in medieval written sources," in *Doklady Akademii Nauk Azerbaidzhanskoi SSR* 37/4 (1981), 84-87. An English abstract of the article appeared in *Art and Archaeology Technical Abstracts* 19/1 (1982):111, and reads as follows: "References in the writings of medieval chemists to kharsini are not clear in identifying the materials. According to modern chemists, kharsini is brass or antimony. Evidence is presented, however, that kharsini is a native metal which contains both arsenic and antimony."

actually existed and was known to the ancient Greeks. Because it was mined, it was evidently not an artificial alloy.

SHEUM AND NEAS

The terms *sheum* and *neas* are included in a list of food crops that includes corn, wheat, barley, and other seeds (Mosiah 9:9). Consequently, they probably denote cereal grains.

Sheum is a common Akkadian word referring to cereal grains, often used to denote either wheat or barley. *Neas* is harder to explain, but we may compare it with the Late Babylonian term *nešu*, the name of an unidentified plant. Or the ending may be related to the Sumerian word *aš*, again denoting either wheat or cereal grains in general. The initial element may be from Sumerian *ni*, which is known in the word *ni-gig*, denoting something of grain.[5] Sumerian and Akkadian were languages spoken in ancient Mesopotamia, where the tower of Babel was built. It may be that the words *sheum* and *neas* were used by the Jaredites, who came from that region, and that they were later borrowed by the Nephites.

Though we can guess at their meanings, we cannot know what plants were designated by the terms *sheum* and *neas*. There are several possibilities, including what we now call *amaranth*, a cereal grain from the New World that was unknown in Lehi's homeland.

CURELOMS AND CUMOMS

Perhaps the most mysterious of the untranslated terms in the Book of Mormon are the *cureloms* and *cumoms* of Ether 9:19. They are included in a list of animals said to have been "useful" to the Jaredites, including horses, asses and elephants. The preceding verse (Ether 9:18), on the other hand, lists animals that the

---

[5] Some of these etymological suggestions came from Robert F. Smith, while others originated with the author.

Jaredites ate, such as cattle, oxen, cows, sheep, swine, goats and "other kinds of animals." From this context, it is clear that the *cureloms* and *cumoms* were non-food animals, perhaps used as pack animals.

There are many animals in the New World that were not known in the world from which the Jaredites and Lehi's family came, and some of these could well have served as pack animals. One thinks of the various camelids, such as the llama, the alpaca, and the vicuña, or the tapir. Unfortunately, the languages of Mesopotamia, where the Jaredites originated, are not helpful in identifying the *cureloms* and *cumoms*. It is possible that the terms were borrowed from other people the Jaredites encountered during their travels. It is likely that Moroni did not know to what animals these terms referred and hence merely used the words he found in the Jaredite record.

CONCLUSION

While we cannot clearly identify the untranslated words in the Book of Mormon, the context in which they are used allows us to determine that *ziff* refers to a metal, that *sheum* and *neas* refer to plants (probably cereal grains), and that *cureloms* and *cumoms* refer to animals. In the case of three of these words—*ziff*, *sheum*, and *neas*—we have precedents in the languages spoken in the homelands of the Book of Mormon peoples that confirm these identifications.

Their very existence is strong evidence that the Book of Mormon is a translation. If it had been written by Joseph Smith, such untranslated words, especially ones that correlate closely with ancient Old World languages wholly unknown to Joseph Smith, would almost certainly have been absent.

Appendix

OTHER BOOK OF MORMON ARTICLES BY THE AUTHOR

BOOK OF MORMON LANGUAGE

"Hebraisms in the Book of Mormon: A Preliminary Survey," *BYU Studies* 11/2 (Autumn 1970); also available in FARMS reprint C&T-82

"The Language of my Father," *The New Era*, May 1971

"Linguistic Implications of the Tel Arad Ostraca," *Newsletter and Proceedings of the Society for Early Historic Archaeology* No. 127 (October 1971)

"A Phonemic Analysis of Nephite & Jaredite Proper Names," *Newsletter and Proceedings of the Society for Early Historic Archaeology* No. 141 (December 1977); also available as FARMS reprint TVE-77

I Have a Question: "Since the Book of Mormon is largely the record of a Hebrew people, is the writing characteristic of the Hebrew language?" *The Ensign*, October 1986 ; also available in FARMS reprint C&T-82

I Have a Question: "Since the Book of Mormon is largely the record of a Hebrew people, is the writing characteristic of the Hebrew language?" in *A Sure Foundation: Answers to Difficult Gospel Questions* (Salt Lake City: Deseret Book, 1988)

"The Hebrew Background of the Book of Mormon," in John L. Sorenson and Melvin J. Thorne (eds.), *Rediscovering the Book of Mormon* (Salt Lake City: Deseret and FARMS, 1991)

"The Hebrew Background of the Book of Mormon," *Witness* 77 (Independence: Foundation for Research in Ancient America, Summer 1992)

APPENDIX: OTHER BOOK OF MORMON ARTICLES BY THE AUTHOR

"Hebraisms in the Book of Mormon" (Provo: FARMS, 1993), videotape with transcript
"Vineyard or Olive Orchard?" in Stephen D. Ricks and John W. Welch (eds.), *The Allegory of the Olive Tree: The Olive, the Bible, and Jacob 5* (Salt Lake City: Deseret and FARMS, 1994)
"Faith and Truth," *Journal of Book of Mormon Studies* 3/2 (Fall 1994)
"Jewish and Other Semitic Texts Written in Egyptian Characters" (co-authored with Stephen D. Ricks), *Journal of Book of Mormon Studies* 5/2 (Fall 1996)
"Word Groups in the Book of Mormon," *Journal of Book of Mormon Studies* 6/2 (Fall 1997)
"The Hebrew Origin of Some Book of Mormon Place-Names" (co-authored with Stephen D. Ricks), *Journal of Book of Mormon Studies* 6/2 (Fall 1997)
"A Visionary Man," *Journal of Book of Mormon Studies* 6/2 (Fall 1997)
"Ancient Manuscripts Fit Book of Mormon Pattern" (co-authored with John Gee), *Insights*, February 1999

COMPOSITION AND AUTHORSHIP OF THE BOOK OF MORMON

"Composition & History of the Book of Mormon," *The New Era*, September 1974
"Isaiah Variants in the Book of Mormon," a book-length preliminary report (Provo, UT: FARMS TV-81, 1983)
"Isaiah Variants in the Book of Mormon," in Monte S. Nyman (ed.), *Isaiah and the Prophets* (Provo: BYU Religious Studies Center and Bookcraft, 1984)
"Colophons in the Book of Mormon," *Insights: An Ancient Window* (Provo: FARMS, 1990), No. 3
"Mormon's Editorial Promises," *Insights: An Ancient Window* (Provo: FARMS, 1990), No. 3

APPENDIX: OTHER BOOK OF MORMON ARTICLES BY THE AUTHOR

"Mormon's Editorial Promises," in John L. Sorenson and Melvin J. Thorne (eds.), *Rediscovering the Book of Mormon* (Salt Lake City: Deseret and FARMS, 1991)

"Colophons in the Book of Mormon," in John L. Sorenson and Melvin J. Thorne (eds.), *Rediscovering the Book of Mormon* (Salt Lake City: Deseret and FARMS, 1991)

"Colophons in the Book of Mormon," in John W. Welch, *Reexploring the Book of Mormon* (Salt Lake City: Deseret and FARMS, 1992)

"Variantes de Isaias en el Libro de Mormon," in Josue Sanchez (translator & ed.), *El Libro de Mormon Ante la Critica* (Salt Lake City: Publishers Press, 1992).

"The Voice of an Angel," in Noel B. Reynolds, *Book of Mormon Authorship Revisited: The Evidence for Ancient Origins* (Provo: FARMS, 1997)

ANCIENT NEAR EAST TIES

"The Nephite Feast of Tabernacles," in John W. Welch (ed.), *Tinkling Cymbals: Essays in Honor of Hugh Nibley* (privately published by John W. Welch, 1978); also available as FARMS reprint TVE-78

"King Benjamin and the Feast of Tabernacles," in John M. Lundquist and Stephen D. Ricks (eds.), *By Study and Also by Faith, Essays in Honor of Hugh Nibley*, Vol. 2 (Salt Lake City: Deseret and FARMS, 1990)

"The Nephite Purification Ceremony," presented at the 6th annual Spend a Day with the Book of Mormon symposium, sponsored by the Foundation for Research on Ancient America, Independence, MO, October 6, 1990 (videotape)

"Borrowings from the Parable of Zenos," in Stephen D. Ricks and John W. Welch (eds.), *The Allegory of the Olive Tree: The Olive, the Bible, and Jacob 5* (Salt Lake City: Deseret and FARMS, 1994)

"More on the Hanging of Zemnarihah," FARMS Update No. 111,

APPENDIX: OTHER BOOK OF MORMON ARTICLES BY THE AUTHOR

Insights: An Ancient Window (April 1997), 2
"The Workmanship Thereof Was Exceedingly Fine," *Journal of Book of Mormon Studies* 6/1 (Spring 1997)
"Glowing Stones in Ancient and Medieval Lore," *Journal of Book of Mormon Studies* 6/2 (Fall 1997)
"The Nephite and Jewish Practice of Blessing God After Eating One's Fill" (co-authored with Angela M. Crowell), *Journal of Book of Mormon Studies* 6/2 (Fall 1997)

NEPHITE CULTURE

"Was Mormon a Member of a Military Class?" *Newsletter and Proceedings of the Society for Early Historic Archaeology* No. 163 (April, 1988)
"Book of Mormon Tribal Affiliation & Military Castes" (Provo, UT: FARMS Paper TVE-89, 1989)
"The Sons of Mosiah: Emissaries of Peace," in Stephen D. Ricks and William J. Hamblin (eds.), *Warfare in the Book of Mormon* (Salt Lake City: Deseret and FARMS, 1990)
"Book of Mormon Tribal Affiliation and Military Caste," in Stephen D. Ricks and William J. Hamblin (eds.), *Warfare in the Book of Mormon* (Salt Lake City: Deseret and FARMS, 1990)
"Seven Tribes: An Aspect of Lehi's Legacy" (co-authored with John L. Sorenson and John W. Welch), in John W. Welch, ed., *Reexploring the Book of Mormon* (Salt Lake City: Deseret and FARMS, 1992)
I Have a Question: "What were the ages of Helaman's 'stripling warriors'?" *The Ensign*, September 1992

DOCTRINAL AND HISTORICAL ESSAYS

"Olive Oil: Symbol of the Holy Ghost," in Stephen D. Ricks and John W. Welch (eds.), *The Allegory of the Olive Tree: The Olive, the Bible, and Jacob 5* (Salt Lake City: Deseret and

APPENDIX: OTHER BOOK OF MORMON ARTICLES BY THE AUTHOR

FARMS, 1994)
"Historical Parallels to the Destruction at the Time of the Crucifixion," *Journal of Book of Mormon Studies* 3/1 (Spring 1994)
"My First-Born in the Wilderness," *Journal of Book of Mormon Studies* 3/1 (Spring 1994)
"The Influence of Lehi's Admonitions on the Teachings of His Son Jacob," *Journal of Book of Mormon Studies* 3/2 (Fall 1994)
"Cities and Lands in the Book of Mormon," *Journal of Book of Mormon Studies* 4/2 (Fall 1995)
"The *Iliad* and the Book of Mormon," *Journal of Book of Mormon Studies* 5/1 (Spring 1996)
"Knowledge of Christ to Come," *Journal of Book of Mormon Studies* 5/1 (Spring 1996)
"*Rod* and *Sword* as the Word of God," *Journal of Book of Mormon Studies* 5/2 (Fall 1996)
"His Stewardship Was Fulfilled," *Journal of Book of Mormon Studies* 5/2 (Fall 1996)
"The Land of Nephi," *Ancient America Foundation Newsletter*, new series No. 10 (March 1997)
"Drought and Serpents," *Journal of Book of Mormon Studies* 6/1 (Spring 1997)
"As a Garment in a Hot Furnace," *Journal of Book of Mormon Studies* 6/1 (Spring 1997)
"Another Parallel to King Benjamin's Tower," *Journal of Book of Mormon Studies* 6/2 (Fall 1997)
"El Libro de Mormón: Otro testamento de Jesucristo," *Antorcha* (March 1998)
"Book of Mormon References to Isaiah 52," *Provo Sun*, October 25, 1998
"A Modern Example of a Night without Darkness," *Insights*, October 1998
"Earth Sees Nights Without Darkness in Modern Times," *Orem Daily Journal*, December 6, 1998

APPENDIX: OTHER BOOK OF MORMON ARTICLES BY THE AUTHOR

"Book of Mormon Answers: 'Fulness of the gospel' and 'familiar spirit'," *Journal of Book of Mormon Studies* 7/1 (1998), uncredited

REVIEWS

Review of David A. Palmer, *In Search of Cumorah: New Evidences for the Book of Mormon from Ancient Mexico*, in *Newsletter and Proceedings of the Society for Early Historic Archaeology* No. 149 (June 1982)

Review of Hugh Nibley, *Since Cumorah*, in Daniel C. Peterson (ed.), *Review of Books on The Book of Mormon*, 2 (Provo: FARMS, 1990)

Review of Brenton G. Yorgason, *Little Known Evidences of the Book of Mormon*, in Daniel C. Peterson (ed.), *Review of Books on The Book of Mormon,* 2 (Provo: FARMS, 1990)

"A Response to Some Criticisms of the Book of Mormon," presented at the 6th annual Spend a Day with the Book of Mormon symposium, sponsored by the Foundation for Research on Ancient America, Independence, MO, October 6, 1990 (videotape)

Review of Jerald and Sandra Tanner, *Covering Up the Black Hole in the Book of Mormon*, in Daniel C. Peterson (ed.), *Review of Books on The Book of Mormon*, 3 (Provo: FARMS, 1991)

Review of Wesley P. Walters, *The Use of the Old Testament in the Book of Mormon*, in Daniel C. Peterson (ed.), *Review of Books on The Book of Mormon*, 4 (Provo: FARMS, 1992)

Review of Brent Lee Metcalfe, ed., *New Approaches to the Book of Mormon: Explorations in Critical Methodology*, in Daniel C. Peterson (ed.), *Review of Books on The Book of Mormon*, 6/1 (Provo: FARMS, 1994)

Review of Jerald and Sandra Tanner, *Answering Mormon Scholars: A Response to Criticism of the Book "Covering Up the Black Hole in the Book of Mormon, Volume 1,"* in Daniel C. Peterson (ed.), *Review of Books on The Book of Mormon*, 6/2 (Provo:

APPENDIX: OTHER BOOK OF MORMON ARTICLES BY THE AUTHOR

FARMS, 1994)

"'Joseph Smith's Use of the Apocrypha': Shadow or Reality?" (co-authored with Matthew Roper), in Daniel C. Peterson (ed.), *Review of Books on The Book of Mormon* 8/2 (Provo: FARMS, 1996)

"What's in a Name? A Look at the Book of Mormon Onomasticon," in Daniel C. Peterson (ed.), *Review of Books on The Book of Mormon* 8/2 (Provo: FARMS, 1996)

Contributor to Donald W. Parry, Jeanette W. Miller, Sandra A. Thorne, eds., *A Comprehensive Annotated Book of Mormon Bibliography* (Provo: Research Press, 1996)

Contributor to Donald W. Parry, Jeanette W. Miller, Sandra A. Thorne, eds., *A Guide to Publications on the Book of Mormon: A Selected Annotated Bibliography* (Provo: FARMS, 1996)

"Not Your Everyday Wordprint Study: Variations on a Theme," *FARMS Review of Books* 9/2 (Provo: FARMS, 1997)

"Jewish Seafaring and the Book of Mormon," *FARMS Review of Books* 10/2 (Provo: FARMS, 1998)

Bibliography

ANCIENT AND MEDIEVAL SOURCES

1 Enoch, also known as the *Ethiopic Apocalypse of Enoch*. An amplification of the story of the biblical patriarch Enoch. It is actually a collection of several earlier books, including a *Book of Noah*. The only complete version is in the Ethiopic Ge'ez language, though fragments are also known in Greek and Latin. Until the discovery of Aramaic fragments of the text from the first century B.C. among the Dead Sea Scrolls, the oldest known copies had been from the eighth century A.D. For an English translation, see James H. Charlesworth, *The Old Testament Pseudepigrapha* (Garden City, NY: Doubleday, 1983), 1:5-90; and Robert Henry Charles, *The Apocrypha and Pseudepigrapha of the Old Testament* (Oxford: Clarendon, 1913), 2:162-281.

2 Enoch, also known as the *Slavonic Apocalypse of Enoch*. An amplification of the story of the biblical patriarch Enoch, thought to have been written in the first century A.D. Two recensions are known in Old Church Slavonic, one of which (A) is shorter than the other (J). For an English translation, see James H. Charlesworth, *The Old Testament Pseudepigrapha* (Garden City, NY: Doubleday, 1983), 1:91-222; and Robert Henry Charles, *The Apocrypha and Pseudepigrapha of the Old Testament* (Oxford: Clarendon, 1913), 2:425-69.

3 Baruch. A book attributed to Baruch, the scribe of the prophet Jeremiah, but actually written in the first to third century A.D. For an English translation, see James H. Charlesworth, *The Old Testament Pseudepigrapha* (Garden City, NY: Doubleday, 1983), 1:653-680.

3 Enoch. Misnomer for a book usually known as *Sepher Hekalot* ("the book of the palaces"), *Pirqe Rabbi Yishmael* (chapters of Rabbi Ishmael), or *The Book of Rabbi Ishmael the High Priest.* Originally written in Hebrew, it is attributed to Rabbi Ishmael, a Palestinian Jewish leader who died ca. A.D. 132. It recounts what he saw during his heavenly ascent, including his encounter with Enoch, who, in Jewish tradition, became the heavenly scribe. For English translations, see James H. Charlesworth, *The Old Testament Pseudepigrapha* (Garden City, NY: Doubleday, 1983), 1:223-316.

4 Baruch. A text attributed to Baruch, scribe of the prophet Jeremiah, but thought to have been composed in the first or second century A.D. (Medieval manuscripts give it the subtitle "The Things Omitted from Jeremiah the Prophet.") For an English translation, see James H. Charlesworth, *The Old Testament Pseudepigrapha* (Garden City, NY: Doubleday, 1983), 2:413-26.

4 Ezra. An apocryphal work attributed to the Old Testament priest-scribe Ezra. Though the original text was written in Greek, it did not form part of the Apocrypha in the Greek Septuagint version of the Bible. It is known principally from its inclusion in the Apocrypha section of the Latin Vulgate Bible and in the Syriac Peshitta. It is also known from Ethiopic, and Armenian documents. For an English translation, see James H. Charlesworth, *The Old Testament Pseudepigrapha* (Garden City, NY: Doubleday, 1983), 1:517-560; and Robert Henry Charles, *The Apocrypha and Pseudepigrapha of the Old Testament* (Oxford: Clarendon, 1913), 2:542-624.

4 Maccabees. A first-century A.D. Jewish philosophical text that illustrates the principles it intends to teach by drawing on historical events. For an English translation, see James H.

BIBLIOGRAPHY: ANCIENT AND MEDIEVAL SOURCES

Charlesworth, *The Old Testament Pseudepigrapha* (Garden City, NY: Doubleday, 1983), 2:531-64.

Abot de Rabbi Nathan ("the fathers of/according to Rabbi Nathan"). A commentary on the Mishnaic tractate *Pirqe Aboth,* attributed to Rabbi Nathan, though its Hebrew style has suggested to some that it may date from before the Mishnah, which was written in the second century A.D., with some later additions. Different manuscript represent different versions. For an English translation of Version A, see Judah Goldin, *The Fathers According to Rabbi Nathan* (New York: Schocken, 1974). For an English translation of Version B, see Anthony J. Saldarini, *The Fathers According to Rabbi Nathan, Version B* (*Studies in Judaism in Late Antiquity*; Leiden: Brill, 1975).

Against Heresies. Several books of this title were prepared by early Christian Fathers. One was written by the second-century Irenaeus, bishop of Lyon, of which an English translation was published in Alexander Roberts and James Donaldson, eds., *Ante-Nicene Fathers* (orig. 1885; reprint Peabody, MA: Hendrickson, 1994), 1:309-567. A similarly-titled book was written by Epiphanius, bishop of Cyprus, who died in A.D. 403.

Antiquities of the Jews. A book written by the first-century Jewish historian Flavius Josephus. The most well-known English version is the oft-reprinted translation made by William Whiston in the sixteenth century. A more recent translation is the one published by Harvard University in the Loeb Classical Library series.

Apocalypse of Abraham. Though attributed to Abraham and known only from Old Slavonic examples, this work is thought to be a Palestinian text composed in Hebrew in the first or second century A.D. For an English translation, see James

BIBLIOGRAPHY: ANCIENT AND MEDIEVAL SOURCES

H. Charlesworth, *The Old Testament Pseudepigrapha* (Garden City, NY: Doubleday, 1983), 1:681-706.

Apocalypse of Elijah. A text attributed to the Old Testament prophet Elijah but composed sometime between the first and fourth century A.D. For an English translation, see James H. Charlesworth, *The Old Testament Pseudepigrapha* (Garden City, NY: Doubleday, 1983), 1:721-54.

Apocalypse of Zephaniah. A text ascribed to the biblical prophet Zephaniah, but thought to have been written in the first century B.C. or the first century A.D. For an English translation, see James H. Charlesworth, *The Old Testament Pseudepigrapha* (Garden City, NY: Doubleday, 1983), 1:497-516.

Apocrypha. A set of twelve books that were included in many Bibles and are still found in Bibles used by the Roman Catholic Church. The original King James translation of the Bible included them, but because doubt was cast on their authenticity, most Protestant Bibles of today exclude them. Cambridge University in England, the major publisher of the King James Bible, continues to publish the Apocrypha, but under separate cover.

Bandlet of Righteousness. An Ethiopic Christian magical text that derives from earlier Egyptian magical texts via Coptic Christian intermediaries. For an English translation, see Sir Ernest W. Wallis Budge, *The Bandlet of Righteousness: An Ethiopian Book of the Dead* (London: Luzac, 1929).

Ben-Sirach. This is the name by which most scholars denote the book called Ecclesiasticus in the King James version of the Apocrypha. Along with the other books of the Apocrypha, it was excluded from most Bibles because no Hebrew version was known. But copies of the Hebrew text have since turned up among the Dead Sea Scrolls and in the first-century A.D. synagogue at Massada. The book was written by one Jesus (Joshua) Ben-Sirach, probably in the second century B.C.

Book of the Angels. A sacred text of the Falasha or Bani Israel, an Ethiopian people who claim to be of Israelite origin. For an English translation, see Wolf Leslau, *Falasha Anthology* (New Haven: Yale, 1951), 55-56.

Book of the Bee. Written in the early thirteenth century A.D. in Syriac by the Armenian-born bishop Shelemon (Solomon) of Basra, using the Bible and early commentaries on the Bible. It is closely related to the *Book of the Cave of Treasures*, the *Book of the Rolls*, and the *Conflict of Adam and Eve with Satan*. An Arabic translation of the text is on a manuscript at Oxford University. For an English translation, see Sir Ernest A. Wallis Budge, *The Book of the Bee* (Oxford: Clarendon, 1886).

Book of the Mysteries of the Heavens and the Earth. An Ethiopic Christian text written in the thirteenth century by Bakhayla Mîkâ'êl, also known as Zôsîmâs. For an English translation, see Sir Ernest A. Wallis Budge, *The Book of the Mysteries of the Heavens and the Earth and Other Works of Bakhayla Mîkâ'êl (Zôsîmás)* (Oxford, 1935).

Book of the Rolls. An Arabic version of a book attributed to the first-century A.D. writer Clement of Rome. For an English translation, see Margaret Dunlop Wilson, *Apocrypha Arabica* (London: C. J. Clay, 1901), in the chapter entitled "*Kitab al-Magall*, or The Book of the Rolls."

Chronicles of Jerahmeel. A history of the Jews, written in the twelfth century by Jerahmeel ben Solomon, who gathered traditions found in a number of other books, some of which have survived. For an English translation, see Moses Gaster, *The Chronicles of Jerahmeel; or, The Hebrew Bible*

BIBLIOGRAPHY: ANCIENT AND MEDIEVAL SOURCES

Historiale (reprint, New York: Ktav 1971).

Chronicon ("chronicle"). A book written by Eusebius, bishop of Caesarea (ca. 260-339). No English translation exists for the Greek original.

Concerning Adam, Eve and the Incarnation. A Christian Armenian document of unknown date. For an English translation, see Michael E. Stone, *Armenian Apocrypha Relating to Adam and Eve* (Leiden: Brill, 1996), 8-79.

Conflict of Adam and Eve with Satan. An Ethiopic Christian document bearing affinities to the *Book of the Bee*, the *Book of the Rolls*, and the *Cave of Treasures*. For an English translation, see Rev. S. C. Malan *The Book of Adam and Eve, also called The Conflict of Adam and Eve with Satan* (London: Williams and Norgate, 1882).

Critias. One of a trilogy written by the Greek philosopher Plato (ca. 428-347 B.C.), in which he speaks of the lost continent of Atlantis. Numerous English translations exist.

Damascus Document. A document first discovered in the genizah of the old Karaite synagogue in Cairo, Egypt in the latter part of the 19th century. Half a century later, other copies were found among the Dead Sea Scrolls. The document is generally dated to about the 2nd century B.C. For an English translation, see Florentino García Martínez, *The Dead Sea Scrolls Translated* (2nd. ed., Leiden: Brill, 1996), 33-73.

Dialogue with Trypho. An apologetic work written by the early Christian writer Justin Martyr (died ca. A.D. 163). For an English translation, see Alexander Roberts and James Donaldson, eds., *Ante-Nicene Fathers* (orig. 1885; reprint Peabody, MA: Hendrickson, 1994), 1:194-270.

Discourse on Abbaton by Timothy Archbishop of Alexandria folio 16b, in Ernest A. Wallis Budge, *Coptic Martyrdoms in the Dialect*

BIBLIOGRAPHY: ANCIENT AND MEDIEVAL SOURCES

of Upper Egypt (London: Oxford University, 1914) and also in Budge's *Egyptian Tales and Romances* (London:Thornton Butterworth, 1935), 195-203.

Epistle of Barnabas. A letter attributed to the apostle Barnabas, missionary companion of Paul, who is frequently mentioned in the New Testament. The document was highly regarded by early Christians, but later rejected. For an English translation, see Roberts and James Donaldson, *Ante-Nicene Fathers* (original 1885; reprint Peabody, MA: Hendrickson, 1994), 1:133-150.

Epistle to the Philadelphians. A letter written by Ignatius, bishop of Antioch, Syria, who died in the year A.D. 107. For an English translation, see Alexander Roberts and James Donaldson, *Ante-Nicene Fathers* (original 1885; reprint Peabody, MA: Hendrickson, 1994), 1:79-85.

Ezekiel the Tragedian. A work written by one Ezekiel in the second century B.C. For an English translation, see James H. Charlesworth, *The Old Testament Pseudepigrapha* (Garden City, NY: Doubleday, 1983), 803-20.

Geography. A geographical work written by the Roman traveler and writer Strabo (ca. 63 B.C.-A.D. 24). Several English translations are available.

Gospel of Bartholomew. An early Christian document attributed to the apostle Bartholomew. For an English translation, see Montague Rhodes James, *The Apocryphal New Testament* (Oxford, Clarendon Press, 1924), 166-80; Edger Hennecke and Wilhelm Schneemelcher, *New Testament Apocrypha* (Philadelphia, Westminster Press, 1962), 484-507.

Habakkuk Commentary. One of the Dead Sea Scrolls discovered in 1947, comprising a commentary on the biblical book of the prophet Habakkuk. The text was probably composed in the second or first century B.C. For an English translation, see Florentino García Martínez, *The Dead Sea Scrolls Translated* (2nd. ed., Leiden: Brill, 1996), 197-201.

Jasher. Though the title of the book is the same as that of the book of Jasher mentioned in the Bible, it is not the ancient book, but a product of thirteenth-century A.D. Spain, a collection of older Jewish traditions assembled by Rabbi Moses de Leon. The most readily-available English translation is the much-reprinted *The Book of Jasher* (reprint from Salt Lake City: J. H. Parry & Co., 1887).

Jubilees. A reworking of the account of the biblical book of Genesis, including stories of the patriarchs not found in the Bible. Though originally a Jewish work, it was preserved through the centuries mostly in its Ethiopic translation by the Christians of Abyssinia (Ethiopia), though there also exist fragments in Greek, Syriac, and Latin. Fragments of the Hebrew version were found among the Dead Sea Scrolls in the mid-twentieth century. For an English translation, see James H. Charlesworth, *The Old Testament Pseudepigrapha* (Garden City, NY: Doubleday, 1983), 2:35-142; and Robert Henry Charles, *The Apocrypha and Pseudepigrapha of the Old Testament* (Oxford: Clarendon, 1913), 2:2-82.

Life of Adam and Eve. A pseudepigraphic account of the first human couple, written in the first century A.D. For an English translation, see James H. Charlesworth, *The Old Testament Pseudepigrapha* (Garden City, NY: Doubleday, 1983), 2:249-296; and Robert Henry Charles, *The Apocrypha and Pseudepigrapha of the Old Testament* (Oxford: Clarendon, 1913), 2:123-54.

Lives of the Prophets. A text that a number of scholars have suggested was originally written in Hebrew by Egyptian Jews during the lifetime of Jesus himself. For an English translation of the Jeremiah passage, see James H. Charlesworth, *The Old Testament Pseudepigrapha* (Garden City: Doubleday, 1985), 2:379-400.

Martyrdom and Ascension of Isaiah. A pseudepigraphic account of the death and heavenly ascension of the Old Testament prophet Isaiah, written sometime between the second and fourth centuries A.D. For an English translation, see James H. Charlesworth, *The Old Testament Pseudepigrapha* (Garden City, NY: Doubleday, 1983), 2:143-176; and Robert Henry Charles, *The Apocrypha and Pseudepigrapha of the Old Testament* (Oxford: Clarendon, 1913), 2:155-62.

Midrash Rabbah. An early rabbinic commentary on the stories found in the Old Testament books of Genesis through Deuteronomy and a few others. Though much of the material is older, the composition itself dates to the end of the fourth or the beginning of the fifth century A.D. For an English translation, see H. Freedman and Maurice Simon, *Midrash Rabbah* (London: Socino Press, 1961 [orig. 1939]), 5 volumes.

Midrash Tehillim. An early rabbinic commentary on the biblical book of Psalms (called *tehillim* in Hebrew), for which there is no English translation.

Pesiqta Rabbati. a ninth-century Hebrew document that includes discourses from rabbis of the third to fourth centuries A.D., the majority of which were from Palestine. For an English translation, see William G. Braude, introduction to *Pesikta Rabbati,* Yale Judaica Series, vol. 18 (New Haven: Yale University Press, 1968).

Pirqe de Rabbi Eliezer ("paragraphs of Rabbi Eliezer"). A work attributed to Rabbi Eliezer, son of Hyrqanos, who lived in the latter half of the first century through the first decades of the second century A.D. While the work may have originated at an early date, its present Hebrew composition is from the twelfth or thirteenth century. Some fragments also came from the Old Cairo Genizah, where the earliest copy of the Zadokite or Damascus Document, later discovered among the Dead Sea Scrolls, was found. For an English translation, see Gerald Friedlander, translator, *Pirkê de Rabbi Eliezer* (London, 1916; reprint, New York: Hermon Press, 1965).

Pistis Sophia. A fifth-century Coptic Gnostic Christian text found in Egypt, recounting post-resurrection teachings of Jesus to his disciples. For an English translation, see Carl Schmidt and Violet MacDermot, *Pistis Sophia* (Leiden: Brill, 1978); and G. R. S. Mead, *Pistis Sophia* (London: Theosophical Publishing Society, 1896).

Praeparatio Evangelica ("preparation for the gospel"). A treatise written by Eusebius, bishop of Caesarea (ca. 260-339) that often refers to earlier texts available to him. The English translation of the extract from the writings of Artapanus, cited in this work, is from James H. Charlesworth, *The Old Testament Pseudepigrapha* (Garden City: Doubleday, 1983), 2:901.

Psalms of Solomon. A set of Psalms attributed to Solomon that were included in the Old testament book of that name in some early Bibles, despite the fact that they apparently date from long after Solomon's time. For an English translation, see James H. Charlesworth, *The Old Testament Pseudepigrapha* (Garden City: Doubleday, 1983), 2:639-70.

Qur'an. The sacred book of the Muslims, said to have been delivered to the prophet Muhammad (ca. A. D. 570-632) by the angel Gabriel. It is a collection of revelations to the prophet, written in Arabic. Many English translations are available.

Talmud. Though there is a Jerusalem Talmud (*Yerushalmi*), the term is most frequently applied to the Babylonian Talmud, a work on Jewish law began in the third century A.D. and completed in the fifth century. The *Talmud* is made up of a series of tractates, each of which centers around specific aspects of the law. For an English translation, see I. Epstein, gen. ed., *The Babylonian Talmud,* 18 vols., (original 1896; reprint, London: Soncino Press, 1961).

Targum Neofiti. A second-century Palestinian Jewish translation of portions of the Old Testament into Aramaic. For an English translation see Martin McNamara, *Targum Neofiti* (*The Aramaic Bible*, Collegeville, MN: The Liturgical Press, a multi-volume work begun in 1992).

Targum Pseudo-Jonathan. A Palestiniah Jewish translation of portions of the Old Testament into Aramaic, attributed to Jonathan Ben-Uzziel, who lived in the late first to the early second century A.D. For an English translation, see Michael Maher, *Targum Pseudo-Jonathan* (*The Aramaic Bible*, Collegeville, MN: The Liturgical Press, a multi-volume work begun in 1992).

Targum Tosefta. Meaning "addition to the translation," this is a collection of early rabbinic additions to the Aramaic translation of the Pentateuch or five books of Moses. It is unavailable in English translation.

Temple Scroll. One of the Dead Sea Scrolls discovered in 1947, it was probably written in the second or first century B.C. For an English translation, see García Martínez, *The Dead Sea Scrolls Translated* (2nd. ed., Leiden: Brill, 1996), 154-84.

BIBLIOGRAPHY: ANCIENT AND MEDIEVAL SOURCES

Testament of Abraham. A book attributed to the biblical patriarch Abraham, but thought to have been written in the first or second century A.D. For an English translation, see James H. Charlesworth, *The Old Testament Pseudepigrapha* (Garden City, NY: Doubleday, 1983), 1:871-902. The Falasha also have a version of the *Testament of Abraham*, an English translation of which appears in Wolf Leslau, *Falasha Anthology* (New Haven: Yale, 1951).

Testament of Amran. A work attributed to Amram, father of Moses, but probably composed in the second or first century B.C. It is one of the Dead Sea Scrolls. For an English translation, see García Martínez, *The Dead Sea Scrolls Translated* (2nd. ed., Leiden: Brill, 1996), 272-75.

Testament of Asher. See *Testaments of the Twelve Patriarchs*.

Testament of Dan. See *Testaments of the Twelve Patriarchs*.

Testament of Benjamin. See *Testaments of the Twelve Patriarchs*.

Testament of Gad. See *Testaments of the Twelve Patriarchs*.

Testament of Isaac. A book attributed to the biblical patriarch Isaac, but thought to have been written in the second century A.D. For an English translation, see James H. Charlesworth, *The Old Testament Pseudepigrapha* (Garden City, NY: Doubleday, 1983), 1:903-12.

Testament of Issachar. See *Testaments of the Twelve Patriarchs*.

Testament of Judah. See *Testaments of the Twelve Patriarchs*.

Testament of Levi. See *Testaments of the Twelve Patriarchs*.

Testament of Naphtali. See *Testaments of the Twelve Patriarchs*.

Testament of Simeon. See *Testaments of the Twelve Patriarchs*.

Testament of Reuben. See *Testaments of the Twelve Patriarchs*.

BIBLIOGRAPHY: ANCIENT AND MEDIEVAL SOURCES

Testaments of the Twelve Patriarchs. A collection of pseudepigraphic texts anciently held to be the deathbed testaments of the twelve sons of Jacob or Israel. Long known in Greek, Amhairic (Ethiopic), and Old Church Slavonic, fragments of individual testaments have been discovered in the Old Cairo Synagogue and among the Dead Sea Scrolls. The latter suggest that the texts were composed by the second century B.C. For an English translation, see James H. Charlesworth, *The Old Testament Pseudepigrapha* (Garden City: Doubleday, 1983), 775-828; and Robert Henry Charles, *The Apocrypha and Pseudepigrapha of the Old Testament* (Oxford: Clarendon, 1913), 2:282-367.

Thanksgiving Hymns. A collection of hymns or psalms of thanksgiving, found among the Dead Sea Scrolls in 1947. For an English translation, see García Martínez, *The Dead Sea Scrolls Translated* (2nd ed., Leiden: Brill, 1996), 317-70.

The Histories. A book written by the sixth-century B.C. historian, geographer, and traveler, Herodotus. Many English translations exist.

Wisdom of Solomon. One of the books of the Apocrypha, of which many English translations exist, most notably the King James version published by Cambridge University in England.

Zohar ("illumination"). A Hebrew kabbalistic text thought to have been compiled in Spain in the thirteenth century A.D., but including numerous older traditions. Most of the text has been translated into English and is available in Harry Sperling, Maurice Simon, and Paul P. Levertoff, *The Zohar* (New York: The Rebecca Bennett Publications Inc., 1958), 5 volumes.